The Confessions of St. Augu... more languages than any Lat... quent, deeply felt, and beau... praised throughout the centuries by men of many different faiths and walks of life as the greatest spiritual autobiography of all time. Now this great classic appears in a distinguished new translation for the modern reader by John K. Ryan, whose translation of St. Francis de Sales's *Introduction to the Devout Life* was widely praised by reviewers of all faiths as the finest modern translation of that book.

St. Augustine is a master of a Latin style that ranges from bare simplicity to most elaborate rhetoric and from the utmost compression to very full and detailed expression. But whether he is writing in one way or another, and no matter what is his immediate subject, his great concern in making his confession to God and before men is complete and exact truth. Every page that he writes is charged with such emotions as he alone could give to them. Yet feeling and art are everywhere subject to depth and precision of thought.

Monsignor Ryan's main purpose in the present translation is to give a clear and accurate rendering of the *Confessions*. His method in translating this work has been first to try to determine what St. Augustine thought, and then to state those thoughts in clearly understandable English for the modern reader. He has resisted temptations "to paraphrase and to substitute current expressions that correspond, more or less, to those that St. Augustine set down."

How successful Monsignor Ryan has been in capturing the thought and flavor of St. Augustine's writing will be immediately apparent to the reader of the present translation.

THE CONFESSIONS
OF ST. AUGUSTINE

Translated, with an Introduction
and Notes, by JOHN K. RYAN

IMAGE BOOKS

A DIVISION OF DOUBLEDAY & COMPANY, INC.
GARDEN CITY, NEW YORK

PRINTING HISTORY

Image Books edition published September 1960

Nihil Obstat: Marius G. Schneider, O.F.M.
                Censor Deputatus
Imprimatur: ✠ Patrick A. O'Boyle
               Archbishop of Washington
               April 19, 1960

The nihil obstat and imprimatur are official declarations that a book or pamphlet is free of doctrinal or moral error. No implication is contained therein that those who have granted the nihil obstat and the imprimatur agree with the content, opinions, or statements expressed.

Cover by Herbert Marcelin
Typography by Joseph P. Ascherl

Library of Congress Catalog Card Number 60–13725
Copyright © 1960 by Doubleday & Company, Inc.
Printed in the United States of America

Piae Memoriae
THOMAE FRANCISCI *et* MARIAE KELLY RYAN
"parentum meorum in hac luce transitoria, et fratrum meorum sub te patre in matre catholica, et civium meorum in aeterna Hierusalem, cui suspirat peregrinatio populi tui ab exitu usque ad reditum,"
dicatum

CONTENTS

TRANSLATOR'S INTRODUCTION	17
PRINCIPAL DATES IN ST. AUGUSTINE'S LIFE	39
THE CONFESSIONS OF ST. AUGUSTINE	41

BOOK 1. CHILDHOOD

CHAPTER
1.	*God and the Soul*	43
2.	*God Omnipresent*	43
3.	*God's Immensity*	44
4.	*Divine Attributes*	45
5.	*Augustine's Prayer*	45
6.	*The Infant Augustine*	46
7.	*The Psychology of Infancy*	49
8.	*The Growth of Speech*	50
9.	*Adult Cruelty and Folly*	51
10.	*The Attraction of Shows*	53
11.	*Baptism Deferred*	53
12.	*Good out of Evil*	55
13.	*Studies in Greek and Latin*	55
14.	*A Dislike for Greek*	57
15.	*A Prayer for God's Help*	58
16.	*The Influence of Immoral Literature*	58
17.	*A Twofold Prize*	60
18.	*Errors of Speech and Acts of Malice*	60
19.	*A Passion to Shine*	62
20.	*A Prayer of Thanks*	63

BOOK 2.
AUGUSTINE'S SIXTEENTH YEAR

CHAPTER
1.	*The Depths of Vice*	65
2.	*Love and Lust*	65
3.	*A Year of Idleness*	67
4.	*The Stolen Fruit*	69

5.	*Why Men Sin*	70
6.	*The Anatomy of Evil*	71
7.	*Grace That Keeps and Heals*	73
8.	*Comrades in Crime*	74
9.	*Evil Communications*	75
10.	*A Soul in Waste*	75

BOOK 3. LATER YOUTH

CHAPTER

1.	*A Student at Carthage*	77
2.	*A Lover of Shows*	78
3.	*The Wreckers*	79
4.	*Cicero's Influence*	81
5.	*Introduction to Sacred Scripture*	82
6.	*The Manichees*	82
7.	*Problems and Answers*	85
8.	*The Natural and the Positive Laws*	87
9.	*God's Judgments and Ours*	89
10.	*The Superstition of the Manichees*	90
11.	*Monica's Dream*	90
12.	*A Bishop's Prophecy*	92

BOOK 4. AUGUSTINE THE MANICHEAN

CHAPTER

1.	*The Teacher as Seducer*	93
2.	*A Sacrifice to Devils*	94
3.	*The Astrologers*	95
4.	*The Death of a Friend*	97
5.	*A Sweet Sorrow*	98
6.	*His Love for the Lost Friend*	99
7.	*Departure from Thagaste*	100
8.	*The Healing Powers of Time and Change*	101
9.	*A Higher Love*	102
10.	*A Changing Universe*	102
11.	*Whole and Part*	103
12.	*Life and Death*	104

Contents

13.	*First Authorship*	106
14.	*Problems of Reputation*	106
15.	*Pursuit of Truth*	108
16.	*False Conceptions of God*	110

BOOK 5. AT ROME AND MILAN

CHAPTER

1.	*A Prayer*	113
2.	*The Rugged Ways*	113
3.	*Faustus the Manichean and the Astronomers*	114
4.	*Knowledge and Happiness*	117
5.	*The Character and Doctrine of Mani*	117
6.	*Faustus in Person*	119
7.	*Faustus as Teacher*	120
8.	*A Road to Rome*	122
9.	*Sickness at Rome*	124
10.	*False Philosophy and False Theology*	126
11.	*Scriptural Problems*	128
12.	*Dishonest Students at Rome*	129
13.	*A New Career at Milan*	129
14.	*The Influence of St. Ambrose's Preaching*	130

BOOK 6. YEARS OF STRUGGLE

CHAPTER

1.	*The Widow's Son*	133
2.	*Outworn Customs*	134
3.	*The Example and Words of St. Ambrose*	135
4.	*Errors Refuted; Truth not yet Found*	137
5.	*The Authority of the Scriptures*	138
6.	*False Happiness and Empty Joys*	140
7.	*Alypius of Thagaste*	142
8.	*Alypius and the Gladiators*	144
9.	*Alypius and the Thief*	145
10.	*Alypius as a Public Official*	147
11.	*An Examination of Conscience*	148
12.	*A Discussion on Marriage*	150

Contents

13.	Arrangements for Marriage	152
14.	Proposals for Community Life	152
15.	The Mother of Adeodatus	153
16.	In the Garden of Epicurus	154

BOOK 7.
PROBLEMS OF THOUGHT AND BELIEF

CHAPTER
1.	New Knowledge of God's True Nature	157
2.	A Refutation of the Manichees	159
3.	Free Will and the Problem of Evil	160
4.	God the Absolute Good	161
5.	God's Omnipotence and the Fact of Evil	162
6.	Astrologers and Horoscopes	163
7.	A Soul Still Tormented	166
8.	God's Healing Hand	168
9.	Sacred Scripture and Pagan Philosophy	168
10.	The Infinite Light	170
11.	Finite and Infinite	171
12.	Every Being Is Good	172
13.	Universal Good	172
14.	A Return to Idolatry	173
15.	The Temporal and the Eternal	174
16.	The Relative and the Absolute	174
17.	A Momentary Vision	175
18.	The Way of Humility	176
19.	The Divinity of Jesus Christ	177
20.	The Soul's True Country	178
21.	The Pilgrim Way	179

BOOK 8. THE GRACE OF FAITH

CHAPTER
1.	Truth Seen but not Followed	181
2.	The Conversion of Victorinus	183
3.	The Law of Contrasts	185
4.	Mutual Joy	187

5.	*The Inner Conflict*	188
6.	*The Story of Ponticianus*	190
7.	*The Naked Self*	193
8.	*In the Garden*	195
9.	*The Two Wills*	196
10.	*Man's Single Nature*	197
11.	*The Voice of Continence*	199
12.	*The Voice as of a Child*	201

BOOK 9. THE NEW CATHOLIC

CHAPTER
1.	*A Soul Set Free*	205
2.	*End of a Worldly Career*	206
3.	*Conversion and Death of Verecundus and Nebridius*	207
4.	*At Cassiciacum*	209
5.	*Resignation of a Professorship*	213
6.	*Baptism, Easter 387*	214
7.	*Saints Gervase and Protase*	215
8.	*Monica's Youth*	216
9.	*Monica, Wife of Patricius*	218
10.	*The Vision at Ostia*	221
11.	*The Death of St. Monica*	223
12.	*Monica's Burial; Augustine's Grief*	224
13.	*Remembrance in Prayer*	227

BOOK 10. A PHILOSOPHY OF MEMORY

CHAPTER
1.	*Joy and Hope*	229
2.	*The Soul Seen Plain*	229
3.	*The Ears of Men*	230
4.	*Help Men to Hear Me Aright*	231
5.	*God's Knowledge and Man's Ignorance*	232
6.	*The Life of Life*	233
7.	*The Power of Sensation*	235
8.	*The Fields of Memory*	236

9.	*A Higher Memory*	238
10.	*Learning as Remembrance*	239
11.	*Thought and Memory*	240
12.	*Mathematics and Memory*	241
13.	*Memory of Memories*	241
14.	*Problems of Memory*	242
15.	*Image and Reality*	244
16.	*The Problem of Forgetting*	244
17.	*Beyond Memory*	246
18.	*Lost Things Found Again*	247
19.	*The Forgotten Name*	247
20.	*What All Men Seek*	248
21.	*The Longed-for Life*	249
22.	*The Only Happiness*	251
23.	*Truth and Happiness*	251
24.	*God, Truth Itself*	253
25.	*Lord of Mind and Memory*	253
26.	*The First Petition*	254
27.	*The Everlasting Love*	254
28.	*Life Is a Warfare*	255
29.	*Command What You Will*	255
30.	*Persistence of Temptation*	256
31.	*Problems of Food and Drink*	257
32.	*Inner Doubt and Darkness*	260
33.	*Music as Means and End*	261
34.	*Custody of the Eyes*	262
35.	*Empty Curiosity and Frivolous Interests*	264
36.	*The Pride of Life*	266
37.	*Problems of Praise*	268
38.	*False Humility*	270
39.	*Presumption and Selfishness*	271
40.	*Light and Love*	271
41.	*Truth and the Lie*	272
42.	*A False Mediator*	273
43.	*The One Mediator*	273

BOOK 11. TIME AND ETERNITY

CHAPTER

1. *For Love of Love* — 277
2. *The Treasures of Scripture* — 277
3. *The Language of Truth* — 279
4. *Evidence of Creation* — 280
5. *Creator of All Things* — 281
6. *God's Voice* — 282
7. *The Word of God* — 282
8. *Christ Our Teacher* — 283
9. *Wisdom Itself* — 284
10. *A Skeptical Objection* — 284
11. *Past, Present, and Future* — 285
12. *A Frivolous Answer* — 286
13. *Before All Time* — 286
14. *What Is Time?* — 287
15. *Can Time Be Long or Short?* — 288
16. *Time and Measurement* — 290
17. *Prophecy and History* — 290
18. *Induction and Prediction* — 291
19. *A Prayer for Light* — 292
20. *Three Kinds of Time* — 292
21. *Measures of Time* — 293
22. *A New Task* — 294
23. *Bodily Motion as Time* — 295
24. *Measures of Movement* — 296
25. *The Deepening Problem* — 297
26. *The Definition of Time* — 297
27. *Where Time Is Measured* — 298
28. *The Mental Synthesis* — 301
29. *The One and the Many* — 302
30. *God Alone Is Eternal* — 302
31. *Unchanging Thought, Unchanging Act* — 303

BOOK 12. FORM AND MATTER

CHAPTER

1. A Creature of Needs — 305
2. The Two Heavens — 305
3. Matter and Form — 306
4. A Proper Name — 306
5. The Problem of Matter — 307
6. An Appeal to Reason — 307
7. Heights and Depths — 308
8. Darkness over the Deep — 309
9. The Highest Heaven — 310
10. The Fountain of Life — 310
11. The Soul a Pilgrim — 311
12. Things Immune to Time — 312
13. In a Glass, Darkly — 313
14. The Two-edged Sword — 314
15. Answers to Objectors — 314
16. The City of God — 317
17. Other Theories — 318
18. Interpretation of Scripture — 319
19. A Recapitulation — 320
20. Exegesis of Genesis 1:1 — 321
21. Interpretations of Genesis 1:2 — 321
22. Objections and Answers — 322
23. Meaning and Reality — 324
24. Truths Seen and Stated — 324
25. A Reduction to First Principles — 325
26. Had I Been Moses — 327
27. Two Analogies — 328
28. Various Valid Interpretations — 329
29. Four Kinds of Priority — 330
30. A Test of Truth — 332
31. Levels of Truth — 332
32. What God Wants Us to Know — 333

BOOK 13.
THE CREATION OF THE WORLD

CHAPTER		
1.	*Without You I Am Nothing*	335
2.	*The Source of Being and Value*	336
3.	*Let There Be Light*	337
4.	*Diffusive Good*	337
5.	*The Trinity*	338
6.	*The Spirit over the Waters*	338
7.	*Lift up Your Hearts*	339
8.	*Fall and Rise*	340
9.	*The Upward Steps*	340
10.	*The Happiness of Pure Spirits*	341
11.	*The Greatest Mystery*	342
12.	*The Body of Christ*	343
13.	*Thirst for the Living God*	343
14.	*Vessels of Honor*	344
15.	*A Firm Foundation*	345
16.	*Light and the Enlightened*	347
17.	*The Embittered and the Compassionate*	347
18.	*Signs and Times*	348
19.	*The Rich Young Man*	350
20.	*What the Sea Brings Forth*	351
21.	*The Living Soul*	352
22.	*In His Image*	355
23.	*Two Kinds of Dominion*	356
24.	*Increase and Multiply*	358
25.	*An Obligation Prefigured*	360
26.	*The Gift and the Fruit*	361
27.	*True Works of Mercy*	363
28.	*The Good and the Very Good*	363
29.	*Time and God's Vision*	364
30.	*Manichean Dualism*	364
31.	*Knowledge of the Good*	365
32.	*A Summation of Praise*	366
33.	*Praise and Love*	367

34.	*The Structure of the Church*	367
35.	*The Peace of God*	369
36.	*The Everlasting Sabbath*	369
37.	*Eternal Act, Eternal Rest*	369
38.	*The Only Gateway*	369

NOTES 371
BIBLIOGRAPHY 425
INDEX 427

INTRODUCTION

By common consent the work known as the *Confessions* of St. Augustine has a special place among the world's great books. Autobiographical in character, it is not an attempt to tell the story of all the years of the writer's life, least of all of the outward events of those years. But no writer ever went deeper into his own character and deeds, passed keener judgments upon himself, or revealed himself more fully and more humbly to others. It may be asserted also that no writer of his own life's story had such wealth of thought and feeling to draw upon as had St. Augustine. For this reason, his book is not only a most penetrating psychological study and a unique document for understanding the spiritual and ascetical life, but it is also a storehouse of thought for the philosopher and the theologian, and for others as well. Because it was written by a man who, like Plato, combined immense creative abilities as an artist with immense critical and constructive abilities as a thinker, it is a book apart in form as well as in content. In brief, the thirteen books of St. Augustine's *Confessions* were written by a man who had great emotional powers along with great powers of intellect and will, who had lived a life of conscious depravity as a quasi-pagan and had turned to a life of austerity as a Catholic, who had genius in philosophy, theology, and psychology, who was a pioneer in scriptural studies, who was extraordinary as a master of language, and who had strong personal attraction to others and marked qualities of leadership.

Because of such things it is not to be wondered that this unique book should immediately have found many readers and that more than fifteen hundred years after its publication it still attracts countless readers and affects them deeply. It is assuredly a great book, one of the greatest indeed, great in its authorship, great in its diverse but unified subject matter, great in the form into which that subject matter has been cast, great in the end for which it was written, and great in the good effects that it has unfailingly produced. That this is true even a casual reader of the *Confessions* will perceive in part. For it to become more and more apparent, it is necessary for him to read slowly and carefully, and to obey the injunction of the prayer "to read, mark, learn, and inwardly digest." It is evident that the more the reader knows about the efficient cause of the *Confessions*, that is, the more he knows about the character, life, and times of St. Augustine of Hippo, the more he will get out of the book itself. So also, it is obviously to the reader's advantage to have knowledge concerning what may be called the intellectual content of the work, as well as its moral and emotional content. The more he brings to his reading of the *Confessions* the more he will take from it, for the work contains some of the deepest findings of the *philosophia perennis*, as stated by Plato, and Aristotle, and Plotinus, and the great Stoic thinkers, as well as St. Augustine's own development of earlier doctrines and his additions to them. St. Augustine's purpose, the final cause towards which he worked, and the means that he took to achieve his end must likewise be subjects of careful study on the part of the reader. If he tries for such things, according to his abilities, he will gain a rich reward. To become familiar with St. Augustine's *Confessions* is to make one's own, to some extent at least, an inexhaustible source of intellectual stimulation, of esthetic delight, of moral help, and of spiritual enlightenment.

Augustine's Life

St. Augustine,[1] bishop, confessor, and doctor of the Church, was born on November 13, 354, in the town of Thagaste, in Numidia Proconsularis, where today stands the Arab village of Souk-Ahras, near the eastern border of Algeria. In the middle of the fourth century Thagaste was a prosperous town in the rich agricultural district that the Romans had developed in northern Africa. The native inhabitants of the region belonged to a race that was perhaps European in origin. Typically, its members were fair-skinned, with brown or yellow hair, and blue eyes. Called Afri (Africans) by the Romans, or more restrictedly, from geographical and other considerations, Mauri (Moors), Libyans, and Getulians, some of them at least were also called *barbari*, or near barbarians, by the

Romans. It is from this fact that their descendants, the modern Berbers of northern Africa, derive their name. At various times they were brought into contact with other races, such as the Phoenicians, Greeks, Romans, and Jews, sometimes by conquest, sometimes by trade. Despite the inevitable intermingling with conquerors, traders, and others, they remained the abiding native stock. The Afri had their own language, which was related to that of the ancient Egyptians, and their own religion. In it the powers of nature were held in awe, spirits, especially those of the dead, were placated, and in time two chief divinities, Baal Hammon and Tanit, his consort, were honored. Magical rites, human sacrifice, and certain abominable practices had a place in their religion. The weight of the evidence is that Augustine belonged to this native north African stock. However, his family was certainly associated with the Roman ruling class and the Christian community in Thagaste.

Augustine's father was Patricius, a pagan, an owner of some property, and a minor official, a decurion, or town councillor. Neither his Latin name nor his official position is proof that he was racially a Roman in whole or even in part. Augustine's mother was Monica, or Monnica,[2] as the name was spelled. Born about the year 323, she was perhaps somewhat younger than her husband; unlike him, she was a faithful Catholic from her childhood. At least two other children were born to Patricius and Monica, both of them probably after Augustine's birth: Navigius, his brother, who appears briefly in the *Confessions*, and a sister, traditionally known as Perpetua, who entered the religious life.

In keeping with an unfortunate custom of his time, Augustine was not baptized in infancy, although he was enrolled as a catechumen. His devout mother gave him some instruction in Christianity and he learned to revere the name of Christ, to have devotion to the martyrs, and to have a great desire for immortality. Seriously sick at one time as a child, he begged to be baptized, but he recovered and his baptism was again delayed. He must have given evidence of intellectual and literary powers from his earliest years, and the hopes and ambitions not only of Patricius but of Monica as well were high in his regard. His languages from childhood were Punic and Latin, and as a child he was sent to school in Thagaste to acquire the fundamentals of the education necessary for a successful public career. He was taught badly by a brutal master, and as a consequence he never acquired a mastery of Greek, although before the end of his life he came to have considerable knowledge of the language. Probably at the age of eleven, he was sent to Madauros, the modern Mdaourouch, twenty miles to the south of Thagaste, for further studies. There he studied pagan literature and perhaps made some acquaintance with the works of Plato. Madauros was a stronghold of paganism and the two or three years that he spent there must have had a bad effect upon his moral formation.

As his father's finances did not permit him to keep Augustine at Madauros, the boy returned home and spent his sixteenth year in idleness. Then, in the autumn of 370, because of financial assistance provided by Romanianus, a wealthy citizen of Thagaste, he was able to enroll in the rhetoric schools of Carthage. In the same year Patricius died, a convert to the Catholic Church. As he describes in the *Confessions,* Augustine's moral corruption was made complete as a student at Carthage. He took as concubine an unnamed woman, apparently his social inferior, and in 371/2 their son Adeodatus was born. It was a Punic custom to include the name of Baal in a child's name, and Adeodatus, "given by God," is the Latin form of Iatanbaal, "gift of Baal." Augustine retained this unnamed mother of Adeodatus for many years, before he finally dismissed her and sent her back to Africa from Milan.

During his years in Carthage, Augustine became a member of the pseudo-Christian sect known as the Manicheans. The Manichean religion took its name from Mani, its founder, a Babylonian who lived from 215 to 277. Mani claimed to have had various revelations, including one in which he learned that he was the Holy Spirit, the third person of the Holy Trinity. His religion derived from many sources, but its chief characteristics may be summed up as follows. It was gnostic, that is, it claimed to have a special knowledge that led to salvation; it was a form of extreme metaphysical and moral dualism, in that it held for the reality and power of evil as well as of good;

it had its sacred literature, which it stressed rather than ritual; it rejected the Old Testament and subjected it to detailed attack; it likewise attacked the New Testament, although not rejecting it completely; it looked upon the body as evil and advocated a spurious asceticism; it claimed to appeal to reason and to offer a rational solution to the problems of life; it was a missionary religion and held that it was universal, not only in providing salvation for all men, but also in having spread over the whole civilized world. Certainly, when Augustine fell victim to it, Manicheism had become a powerful force in the world. Whether any remnants of Manicheism as a formal religion still survive is debatable, but various Manichean beliefs and practices[3] have their modern advocates.

Augustine's abilities and personality, the deficiencies of his religious and moral formation, and the problems, both moral and intellectual, that beset him all contributed to turning him into Mani's most notable conquest. In keeping with his own character as well as to the spirit of Manicheism, he became a missionary in its behalf and prevailed upon various friends to join the sect. Yet it was inevitable that Augustine would come to see the absurdities that made up Manichean doctrine and the degradation that resulted from its acceptance. In time, by divine grace, he was able to break loose from the sect and to become its greatest opponent and a principal source of knowledge with regard to its teachings and practices.

As a student in Madauros and Carthage, and later as a teacher, Augustine learned many things of great value. His knowledge of grammar, rhetoric, and literature grew, as did that of mathematics, music, and natural science. He made his first acquaintance with Roman and Greek philosophy, and he must have made some early ventures in the way of philosophical speculation. His *Confessions* give a clear if not always detailed account of his intellectual development. In the year 373 he became acquainted with Cicero's *Hortensius,* an exhortation to the philosophical life, based upon Aristotle's *Protrepticus,*[4] and it had a profound effect upon him. During his years as a teacher, first in Thagaste, next in Carthage, later in Rome, and finally in Milan, his knowledge of philosophy grew in depth and extent. He became acquainted with the work of

Plotinus (ca. A.D. 205–270), the last of the great Greek thinkers, and of other Neoplatonists, and their thought became a most important part in his personal *praeparatio evangelica*, the formation of his mind so that on the natural level it would be ready for acceptance of the gospel of Christ.

In his *Enneads*[5] Plotinus presents a compact but complete body of thought, a system of ontic emanation, irradiation, or process. All forms of existence flow necessarily from the divinity and all strive to return to it. The divinity is a graded triad or trinity, of which the first hypostasis is the one, the first, the good, the simple, the absolute, the unconditioned, the transcendent, the infinite, the father. Its act, or superact, is most perfect, and is therefore thought. This thought, which the one, i.e., the first, the absolute, or the father, thinks, is the divine mind, which contains the divine ideas and is identified with them. Moreover, the divine mind contains, and even is, all particular minds, which are shadows of it. Being good, this second hypostasis in the divine triad produces good; it is creative. The third hypostasis is the all-soul, the eternal emanation from and image of the divine mind. The divine mind has two acts, one of upward contemplation, directed to the one, the other, the act of generation, directed downwards to lower things. So also the all-soul has two acts, one whereby it contemplates the divine mind, and the other whereby it generates lower possible existents. Here again, as is evident, Plotinus makes application of the principle that what is good does good: the good is diffusive of itself. This divine triad is a unity. The all-soul is the manifestation of the outgoing energy of the divinity, and generates the sense-perceived universe about us, even lowly matter, the principle of limitation. Obviously, the Plotinian system is essentially pantheistic in character, but its tendency is away from pantheism and towards such a lofty theism as Augustine taught.

Plotinus had his doctrine as to the nature, powers, and destiny of man, and here too he influenced Augustine. By reveling in its own free will, by rebellious pride, the soul fell away from the divine, and spends itself on the manifold lower things that exist. It is the aim of Plotinus in his moral philosophy first to show to the soul the ignoble, shameful character of the things it now honors, and then to teach it, or to recall to it, its true dignity and destiny, to turn it away from the many and back to the one. In ethics, Augustine also learned from Seneca (ca. 4 B.C.–A.D. 65) and other Stoic thinkers, as have many other thinkers since his time. He learned much from Plato, and much too from Aristotle, although far less from Aristotle than from Plato. This knowledge was gained partly from Aristotle's own works and partly from other sources. The account of this intellectual progress, much of which consisted, of course, in increasing knowledge of Sacred Scripture and of the Church's teachings, must be read in the *Confessions*, along with the account of his moral development.

The two great intellectual influences upon Augustine prior to his conversion were Manicheism and Greek philosophy, especially as this latter found expression in the works of Plotinus and other Neoplatonists. The influence of Manicheism was for evil; that of Neoplatonism was for good. Intellectually, and also morally, his conversion involved a complete break with Manichean influences and an advance in and beyond Neoplatonism. Although this process of conversion had its beginnings in Africa, its full development took place in Italy.

From 376 to 383 Augustine taught in Carthage and then set out for Rome. He tells how his mother followed him down to the seashore, and how he tricked her and set off without her. Apparently, he left behind his mistress and their son Adeodatus, and this is an indication of his desire to break with his evil past. However, like Monica, they later joined him in Milan. In Rome, Augustine again set up as a teacher, and as in Carthage, met with difficulties from his students. Whereas some students in Carthage were undisciplined and destructive in their conduct, some of them in Rome were dishonest and defrauded him of their fees. In Rome he continued his Manichean associations and resided in a Manichean household, where he suffered a very severe illness which almost proved fatal. After about a year he had the great good fortune to receive an official appointment as professor of rhetoric in the imperial city of Milan. For two years he successfully taught the arts of speech there, but while doing so grew more and more dissatisfied with his moral, intellectual, and spiritual state.

He desired to live a good life, but was too weak to do so. The mother of Adeodatus was sent back to Africa, and the break was a hard one for Augustine as well as for her. Arrangements were made for a future marriage, but in the meantime he took up with another woman. It was during this period that he became acquainted with the works of the Neoplatonists. More important still, he came under the influence of St. Ambrose, the great man who was then bishop of Milan, although the two men never came to know one another closely. His knowledge of true Catholic teaching slowly grew. Finally, going through the great crisis that he describes with such consummate art in the *Confessions*, Augustine was converted to the faith. At the height of his soul's turmoil he heard a voice, like that of a child, chanting, "Take and read! Take and read!" He seized a copy of the New Testament, and the words that first met his eyes were those of St. Paul: "Not in chambering and drunkenness, not in debauchery and wantonness, not in strife and jealousy. But put on the Lord Jesus Christ, and as for the flesh, take no thought for its lusts." This was late in the summer of 386.

Quietly resigning his chair of rhetoric, Augustine, together with certain relatives and friends, retired in October to a villa at Cassiciacum, north of Milan. There they discussed philosophical problems, especially those concerning truth and certitude and what constitutes the happy life. Early in March 387, the group returned to Milan and Augustine, Adeodatus, and his friend Alypius gave in their names at the cathedral as candidates for baptism. Lent was spent in preparation for receiving the sacrament, and during the night of Holy Saturday and Easter Sunday, April 24 and 25, 387, Augustine was baptized a Christian by St. Ambrose.

Monica's long prayers and sacrifices had now been answered. Her son had become a Catholic. He had broken with his evil past and abandoned his career in the world. With her and his son and other friends, he would now return to Africa to begin a new career of service to God and his Church. The party must have made immediate plans for the return journey, as in the summer of 387 they were in lodgings at Ostia, the port of Rome. There, as is described in some of the most wonderful and moving passages in the *Confessions*, Monica died and was buried. After a second residence in Rome of about a year, Augustine returned to Africa late in 388. He stayed briefly in Carthage and then returned to Thagaste, where he sold his small patrimony and established a religious community. Among its first members was Adeodatus, but this brilliant youth, to whose character and intellectual powers his father pays high tribute, died in 389 or 390. Within the community Augustine fulfilled his religious duties, thought, studied, and wrote. His reputation spread rapidly, as is evident from subsequent events. Early in 391 he went to the nearby seaport of Hippo Regius, where the bishop was Valerius, an old man, Greek by birth, and unskilled in Latin and Punic. As Bishop Valerius needed an auxiliary, his people brought the very unwilling Augustine before him, demanding that he be given the place. Ordained a priest by Valerius, Augustine began a new and arduous career as an administrator. The task confronting him was great because of the mixture of nationalities and religions at Hippo, and especially because of the strength of the Donatist heresy. As at Thagaste, Augustine established a monastery, and under his direction it became a center of Catholic sanctity and learning. In it were trained a number of the notable bishops who contributed to the greatness of the Church in northern Africa in the fifth century. Augustine himself was consecrated coadjutor Bishop of Hippo in 395 or early 396. It is probable that Valerius died shortly thereafter, so that from 396 to his death in 430 Augustine was Bishop of Hippo.

The four decades spent by Augustine as a priest and bishop were a time of intense activity as a thinker, writer, and spiritual leader. The Church was menaced by various heresies and anti-Christian forces, against which he exerted all his great powers. To combat the Manicheans, he wrote some of his most important works, and in 392 engaged in a notable public debate with Fortunatus, one of their ablest representatives. The Donatists offered even more serious opposition. Taking its name from Donatus, a fourth-century claimant to the see of Carthage, the sect was nationalistic in character and had as a chief tenet the rebaptism of those baptized by ministers whom the Donatists held to be unworthy. Augustine attempted to conciliate the Donatists, met them in public debate, and wrote against them. He found that he had to protect the faithful in his diocese not only from the trickery and doctrinal hostility of the Donatists, but in some instances from physical attacks. Although the law was now on the side of the Church, Catholics still had to suffer from violence at the hands of pagans, with whom the Donatists sometimes allied themselves. A further danger to the Church arose in Africa early in the fifth century with the appearance and spread of the Pelagian heresy. Against the Pelagian exaggeration of man's natural powers to do good and its errors with regard to the necessity of divine grace, Augustine provided the leadership and learning that were necessary. Along with related works, his writings in refutation of Pelagianism have earned for him the title of doctor of grace and constitute one of his greatest contributions to theology.

During these years when Augustine was combatting the Manicheans, Donatists, Pelagians, and others, in addition to carrying out all the manifold duties of his office, catastrophic events were taking place in Italy. Led by Alaric, barbarian armies swept down from the north and besieged and captured Rome itself. The fall of the city sent a deep and terrible shock throughout the ancient world. One of its indirect results was Augustine's masterpiece, *The City of God*. Begun in 413, this massive work was not completed until 426. In its twenty-two books he describes two cities, the city of this world and the city of God, and in this way offers his interpretation of human history.

The succession of great books that Augustine produced was accompanied by many lesser writings: letters, like those to his friend Nebridius, to St. Jerome, with regard to his translation of the Bible, and to Count Boniface, a general at the head of troops in north Africa; detailed answers to inquiries put to him on such diverse matters as the interpretation of Cicero's philosophy and the right to self-defense among others; and short treatises on a variety of subjects. In the closing years of his life he made a review of his writings and corrected them where he thought it was necessary. He was beset not only by practical problems arising from his duties and from the demands, sometimes unreasonable, made upon him from every side, but also by ill health. When one reviews Augustine's labors as a bishop and writer, the magnitude and variety of his labors are revealed as almost incredible. Under increasingly difficult conditions, he continued his work up to the end. Death came to him on August 28, 430, while a victorious Vandal army lay siege to Hippo.

Throughout his life Augustine had a great reputation and exerted untold influence. Since his death his reputation has never ceased to grow and his influence has spread from the borders of the Mediterranean into every part of the world. Today the words of the inscription on his earliest known portrait are even more valid than when they were first written. They read: "Various fathers have said many things, but this man has said everything with Roman eloquence, thundering forth mystical meanings."[6]

Augustine's Writings

So prolific was St. Augustine as a writer that in the course of time it came to be said, *"Mentitur qui se totum legisse fatetur:* He lies who says that he has read all of his works." Certain works were inevitably lost in the course of centuries; the surviving works have been printed by the Abbé Migne in sixteen large volumes, each volume containing approximately twelve hundred double-columned pages. Only a few of them will be named here: his great masterpiece on the philosophy of history, *The City of God;* works against the Manicheans, such as *Against Adeimantus the Manichean, On the Book of Genesis against the Manicheans, On the Morals of the Catholic Church and the Morals of the Manicheans,* and *Against Faustus the Manichean;* treatises against the Pelagian and Donatist heresies, commentaries on Sacred Scripture; theological tractates; works on ethics and moral theology; and philosophical works, such as *On the Teacher, Against the Academics, On the Happy Life, On Lying, The Immortality of the Soul,* and the *Soliloquies.*

The Confessions: *Purpose and Character*

The title of St. Augustine's autobiographical work indicates its chief purpose and character: it is a statement of what he has done and of what he is that he addresses directly to almighty God. When he attaches this term to his work, we immediately think of it as being a confession of sins. So it is, and so its author meant it to be. St. Augustine reveals with complete candor the sins that he has committed against God. These are not merely offenses against the sixth commandment; such sins are only the most gross and obvious of the wrongs that he has done. They include his long years of concubinage with the mother of Adeodatus, a shorter such association with another unnamed woman, and whatever other offenses he was guilty of due to the concupiscence of the flesh. In addition to such things, he confesses sins of pride and ambition, of frivolity and vanity, of ingratitude and damage to others, of conceit and deceit, of lying and dishonesty. So too, under the heading of wrong deeds, he lists his intellectual errors, his addiction to falsity both in theology and in philosophy. For Augustine was not only a Manichee in religion and one who gave his assent to other false doctrines, but he was guilty of skepticism and other grave errors in philosophy.

Along with his sins and errors, Augustine confesses temptations that assail him. If he is able to resist them, it is because of God's grace and not of any strength of his own. If he has not been the victim of certain vices and errors, it is not due to his own virtue or merit. Thus with regard to the misuse of liquor: it is just as truly God's work that he has been kept safe from alcoholism as it is God's work that others have been rescued from it. So too he sees that there is danger of attributing something to himself even in the confession of his sins. Is he truly and sincerely repentant for them? Does he perhaps take a secret pride in his reformation? There is nothing here that escapes his great powers of psychological analysis and the complete honesty that dictates both the analysis and his statement of it.

Yet if the confession of sins is a principal thing in Augustine's work, it is not the only principal thing. His work is rightly called *Confessions*, in the plural. He does not merely make confession of sin in general; he makes confessions of particular, separate sins. Again, he makes not only confessions of sins, but confessions of other kinds as well. Augustine's book, in fact, is a threefold confession. It is a confession of sins, a confession of faith, and a confession of praise. Everything he sees about him and everything that he finds within him provide evidence for God's existence and nature. Everything that he has done, even his sinful deeds, and everything that has been done to him proclaim to him the existence and power of God, "maker and ruler of all things, but of sins only the ruler." By God's grace he finds God, and by God's grace he is united to God. Hence Augustine rightly confesses not only his evil deeds, exceedingly great in thought, word, and deed, but also his belief and trust in God, his gratitude to God, and his praise of God.

Because it is such a threefold confession, St. Augustine's book is a unique description of the threefold way that makes up the spiritual life. It is a case history, without parallel in the library of psychology, of a soul as it travels the purgative way, the illuminative way, and the unitive way. On the first stage of this lifelong journey, Augustine is engaged in the process of cleansing his soul, or better, of submitting it to God's cleansing hands, so that it will be rid of actual sins, although not of temptations to them. Even when sunk deepest into moral and spiritual filth, he has some perception of his state of degradation and some desire to rise out of it. This light grows stronger and he is cleansed of his philosophical and theological errors. In time he can give wish to be rid of his sins of the flesh: "Give me continence and chastity," he prays, "but not yet." But at length grace prevails even over such things, and Augustine's conversion is in one sense a twofold conversion: it is a conversion of the intellect and it is a conversion of the will. In another sense it is a threefold conversion: philosophical, moral, and religious. It is a purgation of sins against supernatural truth, the truth revealed by God in his Church, a purgation of sins against natural truths, as found in valid philosophy, and a purgation of sins in the moral order.

As Augustine follows this purgative way, the natural light of intellect grows stronger. When his conversion is completed and he is received into the Church, the supernatural light of sanctifying grace is added to this natural light of reason and intellect. The stronger this twofold light becomes, the closer becomes his union with its source. He is united to God by confession of his sins and by sincere, total, and abiding repentance for them, by belief in all that God has revealed, by the testimony of all that his own powerful mind could discover, by his gratitude for God's goodness, and by his acts of praise for what God is and does. He is united to God by sanctifying grace and by such mystical experiences as he describes or hints at in the *Confessions*. These three ways, the purgative, the illuminative, and the unitive, are not to be thought of as completely separate in time, so to speak, as if the second succeeded entirely to the first, and the third displaced the second. St. Augustine illustrates the fact that purgation is a lifelong process. For him, the light flooding his soul constantly grows stronger and his union with God constantly grows closer and deeper.

All the particular episodes in the lives of Augustine and his friends as related in the *Confessions*, and all the reflections that he makes on them and on the varied subjects that rise up in his thought and memory, may be described as documentation of this threefold conversion and the three-staged way that he travels. Nothing is irrelevant, and the principle of economy that may be discerned in the way Augustine writes may likewise be seen in his selection of things to write about. The subject matter of the book may be roughly classified as follows: Augustine's character and motives, and events in his own experience; the character and deeds of others who are closely related to him and affect his conversion; philosophical, psychological, and theological problems, including those of scriptural exegesis. In the first class are all such episodes as his school days in Thagaste, Madauros, and Carthage, his own career as a teacher, his two serious illnesses, the death of his friend at Thagaste, and his successive moves to Carthage, Rome, and Milan. Illustrative of the second class are his relations with his mother, St. Monica, the incidents of Alypius

Introduction 31

and the thief and of Alypius at the gladiatorial spectacles in Rome, the impression that St. Ambrose made upon him, the conversion of Simplicianus, and the story of Ponticianus.

Among the philosophical problems that confront Augustine are some that he touches upon very briefly and others that he discusses at length. He offers a theory of time that is both deep and thorough and that has been very influential in subsequent thought. His natural theology is extended and important. From every order of reality he is able to show that God exists and that he is self-existent; that he is infinite; that he is one and only one; that he is supremely good; that he is truth itself; that being one, good, and true, he is likewise supremely beautiful. Herein he offers a profound and convincing statement of the metaphysics of being, both infinite and finite, and of the transcendental attributes of unity, truth, and goodness. He puts to work Aristotle's doctrine of the ten categories, namely, the category of substance and the nine categories of accidents. Great and effective use is made of the Aristotelian doctrine of matter and form for the solution of difficult problems with regard to the creation of things. A further passage in Aristotle's system that is referred to in passing is that of the basic questions that must be asked and answered in any scientific investigation. No philosopher has written better upon the problem of evil than Augustine, and some of his thought on this most difficult subject is found in the *Confessions*. Here too is found his analysis of a moral act into its elements of objective deed, end or purpose, and circumstances. Finally, Augustine gives an object lesson on the importance of sound philosophy, the relation that it bears to theology and the other sciences, the service that it can render in answering objections, and its ability to detect and state analogies between different orders of thought and reality.

Augustine's elaborate discussion of the nature of memory is the most extended piece of psychology in the book, but his doctrines as to the relation between sense and intellect, the way that sense operates, the freedom of the will, and the successive stages of the voluntary act are also important. In theology, in addition to the basic doctrines of God's existence, nature, and activity, and the mystery of the Trinity, Augustine has important passages on the divinity and humanity of Christ, the Church as Christ's mystical body, the sacraments, divine grace, and prayer, including prayer for the dead. In Books 11–13 he shows his mastery of scriptural exegesis and lays down important principles for the interpretation of Scripture. All of these subjects, whether those based on human experience, or those found in metaphysics, ethics, and psychology, or those taken from theology and scriptural studies, are interrelated and show the unity of truth and being.

The structure of the *Confessions* is simple. In Books 1–9 Augustine tells the story of his life from infancy up to his conversion and the death of his mother on their return journey to Africa, the period covering the first thirty-three years of his life. Book 10 describes his state of mind at the time he was writing these reminiscences of events that had ended ten years previously. It is a further examination of conscience, but with emphasis upon present difficulties rather than upon past failures. Because he has completed the prodigious feat of memory that finds expression in Books 1–9, Augustine is naturally concerned with the character and operation of this power within him. He takes up also the psychological problem of man's desire for happiness.

Books 11, 12, and 13 are an elaborate exegesis of the opening verses in the book of Genesis. Being concerned with his own existence, nature, and destiny as a finite being, and wishing above all to know himself and to know God, it is inevitable that St. Augustine should take up the subjects of time and eternity and of God's creation of all things. Objections are sometimes made to the effect that because of these last three books the work lacks unity and organization, but they are not well founded. Augustine intended neither to give a complete account of his life nor to give only an account of his life. He did not intend even to give a detailed account of the years leading up to his conversion. What he provides by way of autobiography in Books 1–9 is essentially spiritual biography; it is primarily an account of his interior life rather than of his outward deeds. This spiritual account is brought up to date, so to speak, in Book 10. Moreover, he wishes to complete his picture by stating his actual theological position, to use a

Introduction

phrase offered by Gibb and Montgomery, and this he gives in Books 11–13. Finally, Augustine has certain subsidiary ends in view in writing his *Confessions*. Current controversy within the Church as to the character and interpretation of Sacred Scripture and attacks made by heretics upon the Church provided to some extent an occasion for the *Confessions*, and more particularly for these latter books. But in Books 11, 12, and 13, as in Book 10 and in Books 1–9, Augustine continually keeps in view his threefold confession, of sins, of faith, and of praise, and his threefold way, of purgation, of light, and of union with God.

Style

For his *Confessions* Augustine adopted the form of a prolonged meditation, or prayer addressed directly to God. Obviously, this is a most difficult kind of writing to sustain at length, but Augustine never departs from it, beginning with the memorable invocation at the start and continuing to the words with which it closes. Between these two there are interspersed many formal prayers of petition, praise, and thanksgiving. In addition to the prayers and meditations there are many different types of writing, each one adapted to the particular subject matter at hand, and yet each kept by Augustine's art within the basic style of earnest personal approach to God.

The reader cannot help noting the many subsidiary styles within the *Confessions*. Augustine is engaged in an effort to recall events long past and to make a detailed examination of conscience. Hence in a large part of his work he shows his marvelous powers of psychological analysis and his equally marvelous powers of presenting psychological states by means of vivid and appropriate images. A notable instance of this is his description of his last interior struggles before accepting the evangelical counsel of chastity; another is his comparison of himself to a man half asleep and drowsily saying that he will get up in a moment. Where he is confronted with problems in metaphysics or theology and engaged in scriptural interpretation, he has other ways of writing. There are narrative passages and striking descriptions, as in the incidents of Alypius and the thief and Alypius and the gladiators, the profession of faith of Simplicianus in Rome, and the account given by Ponticianus of the conversion of the two special agents.

Augustine shows himself to be a master at presenting living men and women. Character studies abound, and he gives not only full-bodied portraits, such as those of himself and of St. Monica, but also less elaborate pictures and quick sketches. Among these latter are the brief but effective passages in which he presents Patricius, his father, Adeodatus, Alypius, St. Ambrose, Faustus the Manichean, and Vindicianus.

There are passages of splendid rhetoric, lofty and sonorous but never indulged in merely for its own sake and always filled with the deepest thought. Without ceasing to be prose, at such times his writing can take on the character and value of great poetry. His disturbance of thought and torment of conscience before his conversion are reflected in the excitement and restlessness of his writing, whereas his peace of heart after the great turmoil in the garden is repeated in serene passages that convey rest and quiet by their very sound and movement.

This great variety of styles is all the more remarkable because of the speed with which the work was written. That its books and chapters were composed with haste is everywhere apparent. No doubt many of the prayers and shorter passages were jotted down as they arose in Augustine's mind or after he spoke them to God. Other passages were doubtless written out by his own hand, but there is ample evidence that much of the work was dictated to an amanuensis. Yet if it is clear that the thirteen books of the *Confessions* were written or dictated with haste, it is also clear that they were composed with great care. By its very nature the work involved an unparalleled exercise of memory. Augustine recalled countless persons, things, and deeds with great clearness and exactness. But marvelous as his memory must have been, he had no illusions as to its perfection. Hence he will put in many qualifying phrases, such as, "as it were," "as if," "a kind of," and "I know not what." He is scrupulously exact both in displaying the past as he sees it and in telling the reader that he makes no claim to a total recall that is without gaps or perhaps minor errors. So also he reveals his scrupulous care when he writes of the most abstruse and abstract theological and philosophical subjects. As the translator pursues his task, he finds that there are few if any of Augustine's words that he can ignore or discount. Adverbs, prepositions, and conjunctions that do not at first seem important soon reveal the fact that they have been chosen with care and that it will be well to keep them in translation, for they express some close shade of meaning or fine but needed distinction. While Augustine did not possess the same mastery over the long and involved sentence that he had over the short and compact statement, yet even when most involved he practises economy in the use of words. He kept in mind the Stoic norms of good writing, especially those concerned with clarity and economy of statement.

The Confessions *in English*

The first translation into English of the *Confessions* was made by a Catholic priest and convert to the Church, Sir Tobie Matthew (1577–1655), son of the Protestant archbishop of York, friend of Lord Bacon and translator of his *Essays* into Italian. His translation may be looked upon as a contribution to the counterreformation. First published, with copious apologetic and controversial notes, in London in 1620, it was republished without the notes in Paris in 1628. It is free and not always accurate. Dom Roger Hudleston, O.S.B. has published a revision of the Matthew translation (London, 1923), which has proved popular and gone through several printings. In 1631 William Watts, an Anglican clergyman, published a new version which is partly based on Sir Tobie Matthew's work and partly a new translation. A revision of Watts was done in 1912 by W. H. D. Rouse for the Loeb Classical Library. Abraham Woodhead, a convert to the Church, published a new translation in London in 1676.

As one of the activities of the Tractarian movement, John Henry Newman, John Keble, and Edward Bouverie Pusey planned and began a great Library of the Fathers, to be made up of English translations of certain of the chief classics of the early Church. To this library Pusey contributed a translation of the *Confessions*, based on the seventeenth-century Benedictine edition of the original text[7] and on Matthew and Watts in the English. First published in London in 1838, it has gone through many editions. It is an able work and has been very influential upon subsequent translators. Newman was concerned that Pusey should not be rigorously literal in his translation, but whether he had a more direct hand in Pusey's English rendering of the *Confessions* the present writer does not know. Other translations have been by J. G. Pilkington (London, 1876), Frank J. Sheed (London and New York, 1944), Vernon J. Bourke (New York, 1953), a very literal translation done with the "special editorial work of Dr. Bernard M. Peebles," of the Catholic University of America, and Albert C. Outler (Philadelphia, 1955). A version of Books 1–9 made by Charles Bigg (London, 1897) has been popular, but is so free that it is difficult to classify it as a translation.

The Present Translation

In making this new English version of the *Confessions* I have profited greatly from the work of various editors of the Latin text and from the work of certain earlier translators, particularly Pusey's thorough reworking of Matthew-Watts. For the original text I have used Skutella's revision of Pius Knöll's edition, first published as a part of the *Corpus Scriptorum Ecclesiasticorum Latinorum*. I have also found the Gibb-Montgomery edition very helpful, have profited from the Campbell-McGuire edition of selections from Books 1–9, and have made some use of Labriolle and Capello. Because of the labors of various editors, translators, and other Augustinian scholars, translating and editing the *Confessions* have become something of a co-operative task. Few textual problems remain, the countless references that St. Augustine makes to Scripture have been verified, and his various references to profane authors have long since been traced out.

It has been my main purpose to give a clear and accurate rendering of the *Confessions*. As has already been pointed out, St. Augustine is a master of a Latin style that ranges from bare simplicity to most elaborate rhetoric and from the utmost compression to very full and detailed expression. But whether he is writing in one way or another, and no matter what is his immediate subject, his great concern in making his confession to God and before men is complete and exact truth. His natural genius and his training as a rhetorician enable him to do things with words that are beyond our abilities, foreign to our training, and perhaps in some instances without appeal to our tastes. Every page that he writes is charged with such emotions as he alone could give to it. Yet feeling and art are everywhere subject to depth and precision of thought. Hence the first and great commandment for a translator of this work is to determine, as far as he can, what St. Augustine thought, and to state it, as far as he can, in our alien tongue. In striving for this end, I have resisted, *pace* the late Msgr. Knox,[8] almost every temptation to paraphrase and to substitute current expressions that correspond, more or less, to those that St. Augustine set down.

To no small degree, the emotion that Augustine put into his Latin words will almost necessarily show through their English parallels. If a translator could go beyond this and give an English approximation of the noble eloquence, the beautiful cadences, the subtle turns of phrase, and the elaborate plays upon words that are found, along with countless other feats of language, in these thirteen books, he would himself have something of greatness as a writer. The present translator wishes only that he had greater skill for his task and greater time to devote to it. Repeated revisions of a work such as this are needed even to approach this ideal of joining something like Augustine's command over words to that *primum necessarium* of truth and accuracy.

Because of the special character and purposes of the series in which this translation appears, it has been necessary to keep the notes at a minimum. I would have liked to add many more of them, especially upon the philosophical subjects that St. Augustine so profoundly and fruitfully discusses. Particular reference must be made to the scriptural texts that are found on almost every page. Augustine uses the Old Latin version of the Bible which antedated St. Jerome's Vulgate. In many places it differs in detail from the Vulgate and from still later Latin texts. Also, St. Augustine often, or even usually, quotes from memory. Again, he often adapts a scriptural passage to the general form of the *Confessions* as a direct address to God or to some immediate purpose. Thus he will say, "You are great, O Lord," whereas the psalm says "Great is the Lord," and instead of St. Paul's "of him, and by him, and in him are all things," he writes, "of whom, and by whom, and in whom are all things." Hence, when St. Augustine quotes directly, and in certain other instances, I have used quotation marks along with the scriptural reference; otherwise, only the reference to the proper place in the Bible has been given. Since Augustine's thought and way of speech are highly scriptural, it has not been thought necessary to document every minor phrase that derives from his vast knowledge of both the Old and the New Testament, or has passed from Scripture into common speech. Biblical quotations in English are adaptations of the traditional Rheims-Douai version, as I have found it closer to the text used by St. Augustine than are later English editions. In accordance with biblical scholarship, the best contemporary as well as the best older usage, consistency of style, and my own strong preferences, I have reduced the use of capital letters to a minimum, whether in reference to God or in other instances.

I have assigned titles of my own to each of the thirteen books and to the several chapters in each of the books.

JOHN K. RYAN

The School of Philosophy,
The Catholic University of America,
Feast of St. Augustine, Bishop, Confessor,
   and Doctor of the Church,
August 28, 1959

PRINCIPAL DATES
IN ST. AUGUSTINE'S LIFE

354	Born on November 13, in Thagaste, Numidia Proconsularis, the son of Patricius and Monica.
354–365	Infancy and first studies.
ca. 365–369	Studies in Madauros.
369–370	A year of idleness at home.
370	Autumn, becomes a student of rhetoric in Carthage.
371–372	Birth of his son Adeodatus; death of Patricius.
373	Reads Cicero's *Hortensius* and is aroused to a love of philosophy.
373–375	Conducts a school at Thagaste.
ca. 373–384	An auditor in the Manichean sect.
376	Autumn, returns to Carthage and opens a school.
377	Wins a poetry prize.
ca. 380	Writes *De pulchro et apto*, his first published work.
383	Autumn, opens a school of rhetoric in Rome. Affected by skepticism in philosophy.
384	Becomes professor of rhetoric in Milan. Hears St. Ambrose preach; becomes a catechumen; studies Neoplatonic philosophy.
386	Resigns chair of rhetoric; is converted to the Catholic Church. Retires with friends to a retreat at Cassiciacum.
387	Easter, baptized, together with Adeodatus, at Milan. Autumn, death of Monica at Ostia.
388	Return to Africa.
389–390	Death of Adeodatus at Thagaste, where Augustine had established a religious community.
391	Ordained priest at Hippo.

Principal Dates in St. Augustine's Life

395	Consecrated bishop and made assistant to Valerius, Bishop of Hippo.
ca. 397–400	Writes his *Confessions*.
403–412	Controversy with the Donatists.
412–421	Controversy with the Pelagians.
413–426	Writes *The City of God*.
416	Publication of *On the Trinity*.
421	Writes the *Enchiridion*.
427	Writes his *Retractions*.
430	August 28, dies during the siege of Hippo by the Vandals.

THE CONFESSIONS
OF ST. AUGUSTINE

BOOK 1
CHILDHOOD

Chapter 1
God and the Soul

(1) You are great, O Lord, and greatly to be praised: great is your power and to your wisdom there is no limit.[1] And man, who is a part of your creation, wishes to praise you, man who bears about within himself his mortality, who bears about within himself testimony to his sin and testimony that you resist the proud.[2] Yet man, this part of your creation, wishes to praise you. You arouse him to take joy in praising you, for you have made us for yourself, and our heart is restless until it rests in you.[3] Lord, grant me to know and understand which is first, to call upon you or to praise you, and also which is first, to know you or to call upon you? But how does one who does not know you call upon you? For one who does not know you might call upon another instead of you. Or must you rather be called upon so that you may be known? Yet "how shall they call upon him in whom they have not believed? Or how shall they believe without a preacher?"[4] "And they shall praise the Lord that seek him,"[5] for they that seek him find him,[6] and finding him they shall praise him. Lord, let me seek you by calling upon you, and let me call upon you by believing in you, for you have been preached to us. Lord, my faith calls upon you, that faith which you have given to me, which you have breathed into me by the incarnation of your Son and through the ministry of your preacher.[7]

Chapter 2
God Omnipresent

(2) How shall I call upon my God, my God and my Lord, since, in truth, when I call upon him, I call him into myself?

What place is there within me where my God can come? How can God come into me, God who made heaven and earth?[1] O Lord my God, is there anything in me that can contain you? In truth, can heaven and earth, which you have made and in which you have made me, contain you? Or because without you whatever is would not be, does it hold that whatever exists contains you? Since I do indeed exist, and yet would not be unless you were in me, why do I beg that you come to me? I am not now in hell, yet you are even there. For "if I descend into hell, you are present."[2] Therefore, my God, I would not be, I would in no wise be, unless you were in me. Or rather, I would not be unless I were in you, "from whom, by whom, and in whom are all things."[3] Even so, O Lord, even so. To what place do I call you, since I am in you? Or from what place can you come to me? Where can I go beyond heaven and earth, so that there you may come to me, my God, who have said, "I fill heaven and earth?"[4]

Chapter 3
God's Immensity

(3) Do heaven and hell therefore contain you, since you fill them? Or do you fill them, and does there yet remain something further, since they do not contain you? Where then do you diffuse what remains of you after heaven and hell have been filled? Or do you who contain all things have no need to be contained by anything further, since you fill all the things you fill by containing them? The vessels that are filled by you do not restrict you, for even if they are shattered, you are not poured forth. When you are poured upon us,[1] you are not cast down, but you raise us up;[2] you are not scattered about, but you gather us up. You fill all things, and you fill them all with your entire self. But since all things cannot contain you in your entirety, do they then contain a part of you, and do all things simultaneously contain the same part? Or do single things contain single parts, greater things containing greater parts and smaller things smaller parts? Is one part of you greater, therefore, and another smaller? Or are you entire in all places, and does no one thing contain you in your entirety?

Chapter 4
Divine Attributes

(4) What, then, is my God? What, I ask, unless the Lord God? Who is Lord but the Lord? Or who is God but our God?[1]

Most high, most good, most mighty, most almighty; most merciful and most just; most hidden and most present; most beautiful and most strong; stable and incomprehensible; unchangeable, yet changing all things; never new, and never old, yet renewing all things;[2] leading proud men into senility, although they know it not;[3] ever active, and ever at rest; gathering in, yet needing nothing; supporting, fulfilling, and protecting things; creating, nourishing, and perfecting them; searching them out, although nothing is lacking in you.

You love, but are not inflamed with passion; you are jealous, yet free from care; you repent, but do not sorrow; you grow angry, but remain tranquil. You change your works, but do not change your plan; you take back what you find, although you never lost it; you are never in want, but you rejoice in gain; you are never covetous, yet you exact usury. Excessive payments are made to you, so that you may be our debtor—yet who has anything that is not yours? You pay debts, although you owe no man anything; you cancel debts, and lose nothing. What have we said, my God, my life, my holy delight? Or what does any man say when he speaks of you? Yet woe to those who keep silent concerning you, since even those who speak much are as the dumb.

Chapter 5
Augustine's Prayer

(5) Who will give me help, so that I may rest in you? Who will help me, so that you will come into my heart and inebriate it, to the end that I may forget my evils and embrace you, my one good? What are you to me? Have pity on me, so that I may speak! What am I myself to you, that you command me to love you, and grow angry and threaten me with mighty woes unless I do? Is it but a small affliction if I do not love

you? Unhappy man that I am, in your mercy, O Lord my God, tell me what you are to me. "Say to my soul: I am your salvation."[1] Say this, so that I may hear you. Behold, my heart's ears are turned to you, O Lord: open them, and "say to my soul: I am your salvation." I will run after that voice, and I will catch hold of you. Do not hide your face from me.[2] Lest I die, let me die, so that I may see it.

(6) Too narrow is the house of my soul for you to enter into it: let it be enlarged by you. It lies in ruins; build it up again. I confess and I know that it contains things that offend your eyes. Yet who will cleanse it? Or upon what other than you shall I call? "From my secret sins cleanse me, O Lord, and from those of others spare your servant."[3] I believe, and therefore I speak out.[4] Lord, all this you know. Have I not accused myself to you, my God, of my sins, and have you not forgiven the iniquity of my heart?[5] I do not contend in judgment with you[6] who are truth itself. I do not deceive myself, lest my iniquity lie to itself.[7] Therefore, I do not contend in judgment with you, for "if you, O Lord, will mark iniquities: Lord, who shall stand it?"[8]

Chapter 6
The Infant Augustine

(7) Yet grant me to plead before your mercy, grant me who am dust and ashes[1] to speak, for behold, it is not a man who makes mock of me but your mercy that I address. Perhaps even you deride me, but when you have turned towards me, you will have mercy on me.[2] What do I want to say, Lord, except that I do not know whence I came into what I may call a mortal life or a living death. Whence I know not. Your consolation and your mercies[3] have raised me up, as I have heard from the parents of my flesh, for by one and in the other you fashioned me in time. I myself do not remember this. Therefore, the comfort of human milk nourished me, but neither my mother nor my nurses filled their own breasts. Rather, through them you gave me an infant's food in accordance with your law and out of the riches that you have distributed even down to the lowest level of things. You gave me to want no more

Book 1. Childhood

than you gave, and you gave to those who nursed me the will to give what you gave to them. By an orderly affection they willingly gave me what they possessed so abundantly from you. It was good for them that my good should come from them; yet it was not from them but through them. For from you, O God, come all good things, and from you, my God, comes all my salvation. This I afterwards observed when you cried out to me by means of those things which you bestow both inwardly and outwardly. For at that time I knew how to seek the breast, to be satisfied with pleasant things, and to cry at my bodily hurts, but nothing more.

(8) Later on, I began to laugh, at first when asleep and then when awake. This has been told to me concerning myself, and I believe it, since we see other infants acting thus, although I do not remember such acts of my own. Then little by little I perceived where I was, and I wished to make my wants known to those who could satisfy them. Yet I could not do so, because the wants were within me, while those outside could by no sensible means penetrate into my soul. So I tossed my limbs about and uttered sounds, thus making such few signs similar to my wishes as I could, and in such fashion as I could, although they were not like the truth. When they would not obey me, either because they did not understand or because it would be harmful, I grew angry at older ones who were not subject to me and at children for not waiting on me, and took it out on them by crying.[4] That infants are of this sort I have since learned from those whom I have been able to observe. That I was such a one they have unwittingly taught me better than my nurses who knew me.

(9) But see, my infancy is dead long ago, and I still live. Lord, you who live forever and in whom nothing dies—since before the beginning of the ages, and before anything that can even be called "before," you are, and you are God and Lord of all that you have created, and with you stand the causes of all impermanent things and with you abide the unchanging sources of all changing things, and in you live the sempiternal reasons of all unreasoning and temporal things—tell to me, your suppliant, O God, in your mercy, tell to me, your wretched servant, whether my infancy followed another

age of mine that was already dead. Or was it that time which I passed within my mother's womb? Of that time something has been told to me, and I have seen pregnant women. What was there even before this, my joy, my God? Was I anywhere, or anyone? I have no one to tell me this, neither father nor mother could do so, nor the experience of others, nor my own memory. Do you laugh at me for questioning you of such things? Do you command me to praise you and confess to you only for what I know?

(10) I confess to you, O Lord of heaven and earth,[5] and I utter praise to you for my first being and my infancy, which I do not remember. You have endowed man so that he can gather these things concerning himself from others, and even on the words of weak women believe much about himself. For even then I had being and lived, and already at the close of my infancy I looked for signs by which I could make known my meanings to others. Where except from you, O Lord, could come such a living being? Who has the art and power to make himself? Is there any channel, through which being and life flow into us, that comes from any source but you, Lord, who have made us? In you being and life are not different things, because supreme being and supreme life are one and the same. You are supreme and you are not changed.[6] Nor is this present day spent in you—and yet it is spent in you, for in you are all these times. Unless you contained them, they would have no way of passing on. And because your years do not fail,[7] your years are this every day. No matter how many have already been our days and the days of our fathers, they have all passed through this single present day of yours, and from it they have taken their measures and their manner of being. And others still shall also pass away and receive their measures and their manner of being. "But you are the Selfsame,"[8] and all things of tomorrow and all beyond, and all things of yesterday and all things before, you shall make into today, and you have already made them into today.

What matters it to me if someone does not understand this? Let him too rejoice and say, "What is this?"[9] Let him rejoice even at this, and let him love to find you while not finding it out, rather than, while finding it out, not to find you.

Chapter 7
The Psychology of Infancy

(11) Graciously hear me, O God. Woe to the sins of men! Yet a man says this, and you have mercy upon him, for you have made him, but the sin that is in him you have not made. Who will bring to my mind the sins of my infancy? For in your sight no man is clean of sin,[1] not even the infant who has lived but a day upon earth. Who will bring this to my mind? Does not each little child now do this, for in him I now perceive what I do not remember about myself? How then did I sin at that age? Was it because I cried out as I tried to mouth the breast? Indeed if I did so now—not of course as one gaping for the breast, but for food fitting to my years—I would be laughed at and most justly blamed. Hence at that time I did reprehensible things, but because I could not understand why anyone should blame me, neither custom nor reason allowed me to be blamed. As we grow up, we root out such things and throw them aside. Yet I have never seen anyone knowingly throw aside the good when he purges away the bad.

But even then were these things good: to try to get by crying even what would be harmful if it were given to me, to be bitterly resentful at freemen, elders, my parents, and many other prudent people who would not indulge my whims, when I struck at them and tried to hurt them as far as I could because they did not obey orders that would be obeyed only to my harm? Thus it is not the infant's will that is harmless, but the weakness of infant limbs. I myself have seen and have had experience with a jealous little one; it was not yet able to speak, but it was pale and bitter in face as it looked at another child nursing at the same breast.

Who is unaware of such things? Mothers and nurses claim to make up for them by some sort of correctives. Yet is it really innocence not to allow another child to share in that richly flowing fountain of milk, although it is in great need of help and derives life from that sole source of food? These things are easily put up with, not because they are of little or no account, but because they will disappear with increase in age.

This you can prove from the fact that the same things cannot be borne with patience when detected in an older person.

(12) Therefore, O Lord my God, you have given to the infant life and a body, which, as we see, you have thus furnished with senses, equipped with limbs, beautified with a shapely form, and, for its complete good and protection, have endowed with all the powers of a living being. For all such things you command me to praise you and to confess you, and to "sing to your name, O Most High."[2] For you are God, all-powerful and good, even if you made only such things. For no other can do this but you, the One, from whom is every measure, you, the absolute Form,[3] who give form to all things and govern all things by your law.

Therefore, O Lord, this age which I do not remember to have lived, which I have taken on trust from others, which I conclude myself to have passed from observing other infants, although such testimonies are most probable, this age I hesitate to join to this life of mine which I have lived in this world. In so far as it belongs to the dark regions of forgetfulness, it is like that which I lived in my mother's womb. But "if I was conceived in iniquity," and if my mother nourished me within her womb in sins,[4] where, I beseech you, O Lord my God, where or when was your servant innocent? But, see, I now set aside that period. What matters that now to me of which I recall no trace?

Chapter 8
The Growth of Speech

(13) Did I not advance from infancy and come into boyhood? Or rather, did it not come upon me and succeed to my infancy? Yet infancy did not depart: for where did it go? Still, it was no more, for I was no longer an infant, one who could not speak, but now I was a chattering boy. I remembered this, and afterwards I reflected on how I learned to talk. Grown up men did not teach me by presenting me with words in any orderly form of instruction, as they did my letters a little later. But I myself, with that mind which you, my God, gave me, wished by means of various cries and sounds and movements

of my limbs to express my heart's feelings, so that my will would be obeyed. However, I was unable to express all that I wished or to all to whom I wished. I pondered over this in memory: when they named a certain thing and, at that name, made a gesture towards the object, I observed that object and inferred that it was called by the name they uttered when they wished to show it to me. That they meant this was apparent by their bodily gestures, as it were by words natural to all men, which are made by change of countenance, nods, movements of the eyes and other bodily members, and sounds of the voice, which indicate the affections of the mind in seeking, possessing, rejecting, or avoiding things. So little by little I inferred that the words set in their proper places in different sentences, that I heard frequently, were signs of things. When my mouth had become accustomed to these signs, I expressed by means of them my own wishes. Thus to those among whom I was I communicated the signs of what I wished to express. I entered more deeply into the stormy society of human life, although still dependent on my parents' authority and the will of my elders.

Chapter 9
Adult Cruelty and Folly

(14) O God, my God, great was the misery and great the deception that I met with when it was impressed upon me that, to behave properly as a boy, I must obey my teachers. This was all that I might succeed in this world and excel in those arts of speech which would serve to bring honor among men and to gain deceitful riches. Hence I was sent to school to acquire learning, the utility of which, wretched child that I was, I did not know. Yet if I was slow at learning, I was beaten. This method was praised by our forebears, many of whom had passed through this life before us and had laid out the hard paths that we were forced to follow. Thus were both toil and sorrow multiplied for the sons of Adam.

We discovered, Lord, that certain men prayed to you and we learned from them, and imagined you, as far as we could, as some sort of mighty one who could hear us and help us, even though not appearing before our senses. While still a boy, I began to pray to you, my help and my refuge,[1] and in praying to you I broke the knots that tied my tongue. A little one, but with no little feeling, I prayed to you that I would not be beaten at school. When you did not hear me—and it was "not to be reputed folly in me"[2]—my punishments, which were then a huge and heavy evil to me, were laughed at by older men, and even by my own parents who wished no harm to befall me.

(15) Lord, is there any man of so great a soul, who clings to you with so mighty love, is there anyone, I ask you—for indeed a certain type of stolidity is capable of this—is there anyone who so devoutly clings to you and is thus so deeply affected that he deems of little consequence the rack, the hook, and similar tools of torture—to be saved from which men throughout the whole world pray to you with great fear—although he loves those who dread such things most bitterly? If there is such a man, he acts in the way in which our parents laughed at the torments we boys suffered from our teachers.[3] In no less measure did we fear our punishments, and no less did we beseech you to let us escape.

Yet we sinned by writing, reading, and thinking over our lessons less than was required of us. Lord, there was in us no lack of memory or intelligence, for you willed that we should have them in sufficient measure for our years. Yet we loved to play, and this was punished in us by men who did the same things themselves. However, the trivial concerns of adults are called business, while such things in children are punished by adults.[4] Yet no one has pity on either children or grown-up men, or on both. Perhaps some fine judge of things approves my beatings. For I played ball as a child; by such play I was kept from quickly learning arts by which, as an adult, I would disport myself in a still more unseemly fashion. Did the very man who beat me act different from me? If he was outdone by a fellow teacher in some trifling discussion, he was more tormented by anger and envy than I was when beaten by my playmate in a ball game.

Book 1. Childhood

Chapter 10
The Attraction of Shows

(16) Yet I sinned, O Lord my God, ruler and creator of all natural things, but of sins only the ruler.[1] I sinned, O Lord my God, by going against the commands of my parents and of those teachers. Later on, indeed, I could put to good use the learning that they wanted me to acquire, no matter with what purpose in my regard. I was disobedient, not out of a desire for better things, but out of love for play. I loved to win proud victories in our contests, and to have my ears tickled by false stories, so that they would itch all the more intensely for them, with the same kind of curiosity glittering more and more in my eyes for shows, the games of grown-up men. For their producers are invested with such honor that almost all parents desire it for their children. Hence they gladly let them be beaten if, by attending just such shows, they are kept from studies by which their parents wish them to rise to putting on similar plays. Lord, in your mercy look down upon these things and deliver us who now call upon you. Deliver also those who do not yet call upon you, so that they may call upon you and you may deliver them.[2]

Chapter 11
Baptism Deferred

(17) While still a boy, I had heard of that eternal life promised to us through the humility of the Lord our God, who lowered himself to our pride. I was signed with the sign of his cross, and seasoned with his salt,[1] as soon as I issued from my mother's womb, for she trusted greatly in you. Lord, you saw how, one day when I was still a child, I suddenly burned with fever from a stomach affliction and was very close to death. You saw, my God, for you were already my keeper,[2] with what effort of mind and with what faith I entreated the mercy of my own mother and of the Church, the mother of us all, for the baptism of your Christ, my God and Lord. The mother of my flesh was distraught—for she most lovingly was

bringing forth[3] my eternal salvation in her chaste heart and in faith in thee—and would have at once hastened to arrange that I be initiated into the sacraments of salvation and be washed in them,[4] I first confessing you, Lord Jesus, for the remission of my sins. However, I immediately recovered from that illness. So my cleansing was delayed, as if it must needs be that I would become yet more defiled if I lived, for indeed the guilt and defilement of sins committed after that cleansing would be greater and more dangerous. Thus I already believed, as did also my mother and the whole household, except my father alone.[5] Still he did not overthrow in me the authority of my mother's devotion, so that I would not believe in Christ, even as he did not yet believe in him. For she strove in every way that you, my God, would be my father rather than he. In this you aided her, so that she overcame her husband, to whom she, the better partner, was subject. For in this she assuredly was serving you who ordered her to do so.

(18) I beseech you, my God, for I wish to know this, if you likewise wish me to know it, to what purpose was my baptism delayed at that time? Was it for my good that the reins of sin should be laid loose upon me, as it were, or were they not laid loose for my own good? How then is it that even now there rings in my ears from all sides, concerning one thing and another, the cry, "Let him be! Let him do it! He is not yet baptized!" Yet with regard to bodily health we do not say, "Let him be wounded still more! He is not yet healed!" How much better were it, then, if I had been quickly healed, and it had resulted, through my friends' diligence and my own, that my soul's health, which I had thus received, would be kept safe under the protection of you who gave it to me! Better in truth would this have been! But how many and how great seemed the waves of temptation that threatened me after my childhood! My mother already knew them well, and she wished to commit to them that clay of which I was later to be formed rather than the actual image itself.[6]

Book 1. Childhood

CHAPTER 12
Good out of Evil

(19) In boyhood itself, when there was less to be feared in my regard than from youth, I did not love study and hated to be driven to it. Yet I was driven to it, and good was thus done to me, but I myself did not do good. I would have learned nothing unless forced to it. No one does good against his will, even if what he does is good. Nor did those who drove me on do well: the good was done to me by you, my God. They did not see to what use I would put what they forced me to learn, beyond satisfying the insatiable desires of a rich beggary and a base glory. But you, before whom the hairs of our head are numbered,[1] turned to my advantage the error of all those who kept me at my studies. The error of myself, who did not want to study, you used for my chastisement. For I, so small a boy and yet so great a sinner, was not unworthy of punishment. Thus by means of men who did not do well you did well for me, and out of my sinning you justly imposed punishment on me. You have ordered it, and so it is, that every disordered mind should be its own punishment.

CHAPTER 13
Studies in Greek and Latin

(20) Why I detested the Greek language when I was taught it as a little boy I have not yet fully discovered. I liked Latin very much, not the parts given by our first teachers but what the men called grammarians teach us.[1] The first stages of our education, when we learn reading, writing, and arithmetic, I considered no less a burden and punishment than all the Greek courses. Since I was but "flesh, and a wind that goes and does not return,"[2] where could this come from except from sin and vanity of life? Better indeed, because more certain, were those first studies by which there was formed and is formed in me what I still possess, the ability to read what I find written down and to write what I want to, than the later studies wherein I was required to learn by heart I

know not how many of Aeneas's wanderings, although forgetful of my own, and to weep over Dido's death, because she killed herself for love, when all the while amid such things, dying to you, O God my life, I most wretchedly bore myself about with dry eyes.

(21) Who can be more wretched than the wretched one who takes no pity on himself, who weeps over Dido's death, which she brought to pass by love for Aeneas,[3] and who does not weep over his own death, brought to pass by not loving you, O God, light of my heart, bread for the inner mouth of my soul, power wedding together my mind and the bosom of my thoughts? I did not love you, and I committed fornication against you,[4] and amid my fornications from all sides there sounded the words, "Well done! Well done!"[5] Love of this world is fornication against you,[6] but "Well done! Well done!" is said, so that it will be shameful for a man to be otherwise. I did not weep over these facts, but I wept over the dead Dido "who sought her end by the sword."[7] I forsook you, and I followed after your lowest creatures, I who was earth, turning to earth. If I had been forbidden to read those tales, I would have grieved because I could not read what would cause me to grieve. Such folly is deemed a higher and more profitable study than that by which I learned to read and write.

(22) Now let my God cry out in my soul, and let your truth say to me, "It is not so. It is not so." Far better is that earlier teaching. See how I am readier to forget the wanderings of Aeneas and all such tales than to read and write. True it is that curtains hang before the doors of the grammar schools, but they do not symbolize some honored mystery but rather a cloak for error. Let not men whom I no longer fear inveigh against me when I confess to you, my God, what my soul desires, and when I acquiesce in a condemnation of my evil ways, so that I may love your ways, which are good.[8] Let not these buyers and sellers of literature inveigh against me if I put this question to them: "Did Aeneas ever come to Carthage, as the poet says?" For if I do, the more unlearned will answer that they do not know; the more learned will even deny that it is true. But if I ask them with what letters the name Aeneas is spelled, all who have learned this much will

Book 1. Childhood

assigned divine attributes to us."[1] But with more truth it is asserted that he did indeed make up these tales, but he attributed divine powers to vicious men so that debauchery might not be accounted debauchery, and so that whoever does such things would seem to imitate not profligate men but the gods of heaven.

(26) Nevertheless, O hellish flood, the sons of men are thrown into you with fees paid, so that they may learn these fables. A great thing is made of it when some of this is acted out publicly in the forum, supervised by laws decreeing salaries over and above the students' fees. You dash against your rocks, you roar and say: "Here is learned the use of words! Here eloquence is acquired, most necessary for winning cases and expressing thoughts!" But for this would we never have understood the words "golden shower," "lap," "deceit," "temples of heaven," and the others written in the same place, unless Terence had brought a depraved youth upon the stage who took Jove as his model in adultery? All the while he looks at a picture painted on the wall in which is shown the tale of how Jove rains a golden shower into Danaë's lap and thus tricks the girl.[2] See how he arouses himself to lust, as if by heavenly instruction, as he says

> "Ah, what a God!
> He shakes the highest heavens with his thunder!
> Shall I, poor mortal man, not do the same?
> I've done it, and with all my heart, I'm glad."[3]

In no way, in no way whatsoever, are these words used here learned more easily because of this filthy scene, but because of these words that vile deed is more boldly perpetrated. I do not condemn the words, which are as it were choice and precious vessels, but that wine of error which through them was proffered to us by drunken teachers. Unless we drank it, we were flogged, and we had no freedom of appeal to any sober judge. Yet, O my God, in whose sight I now safely recall this, in my wretchedness I willingly learned these things and took delight in them. For this I was called a boy of great promise.

Chapter 17
A Twofold Prize

(27) Grant me, my God, to speak a little about my own abilities, your gift to me, and of the foolish things on which they were squandered. A task was assigned to me that disturbed my mind, either by reason of the praise or disgrace to be awarded or for fear of a flogging. I was to speak Juno's words, as she expresses both anger and sorrow because she could not "turn back the Trojan king from going to Italy."[1] I had heard that Juno never spoke these words, yet we were compelled to wander off and follow in the steps of these poetic fictions, and to put into prose what the poet had spoken in verse. The boy spoke in the most praiseworthy way in whom, in keeping with the rank of the character he played, such emotions as anger and sorrow stood forth, clothed with appropriate language.

What did all this matter to me, my God, my true life? For what good was I, for my declamation, acclaimed above so many of my schoolmates and boys of the same age? What was all this but smoke and wind? Was there no other subject on which to exercise my talents and my tongue? Your praises, Lord, your praises, set forth in your Scriptures, would have held up my heart's young vine, so that it would not have been snatched away by empty trifles, the filthy prey of flying creatures. In more ways than one is sacrifice offered to the transgressor angels.[2]

Chapter 18
Errors of Speech and Acts of Malice

(28) What wonder was it that I was thus carried away into vain practices and went far from you, my God? For the men set up for my models were utterly dejected when caught in a barbarism or solecism while telling about some of their own acts, even though the acts themselves were not bad. But if they would describe some of their lustful deeds in detail and good order and with correct and well-placed words, did

they not glory in the praise they got? Lord, you who are long-suffering, most merciful, and most truthful, you see these things, and yet you remain silent.[1] But will you keep silent forever? Even now you will draw out of this most terrible pit the soul[2] that seeks you and thirsts for your delights, and whose heart says to you, "I have sought your face; your face, Lord, will I seek."[3] I was far from your face in the darkness of my passions. Not on foot, and not by distance of place do we depart from you or return to you. That younger son of yours did not look for horses or chariots or ships; he did not fly away on visible wings; he did not make a journey on foot, so that by living a prodigal's life in a far country he could waste the substance that you had given him as he started out.[4] For you were a loving father because you gave this to him, but still more loving when he came back in want. Therefore, he departed from you by lustful affections, that is, by darksome affections, and this is to be far from your face.

(29) Regard, O Lord my God, patiently regard, as is your wont, how carefully the sons of men observe the proprieties as to letters and syllables received from former speakers, and how they neglect everlasting covenants of eternal salvation which they have received from you. Thus if a man who accepts or teaches the ancient conventional forms of pronunciation violates the rules of grammar, and utters the word *homo* (man) without sounding the "h" in the first syllable,[5] he will offend men more than if, contrary to your laws, he who is a man himself would hate another man. It is as if he thought an enemy more pernicious to him than his own hatred by which he is aroused against the other. Or as if he thought that he could do more damage to another by persecuting him than he does to his own heart by this hostility. Certainly, no knowledge of letters is more interior to us than that written in conscience: that one does to another what he himself does not want to suffer.[6]

How hidden you are, you who dwell on high in silence, you the sole great God! By unwearying law you impose the penalty of blindness upon unlawful desires. When a man who seeks fame for eloquence stands before a human judge, with a throng of men standing about him, and inveighs against his opponent with most savage hatred, he guards most watchfully lest by a slip of the tongue he should say *inter 'omines*. But he takes no care lest by his furious spirit he cause a man to be taken away from among men.[7]

Chapter 19
A Passion to Shine

(30) On the threshold of such customs lay I, a wretched boy, and this was the stage and arena where I was more fearful of committing a barbarism than I was on guard, if I did commit one, against envying those who did not. I state these things and confess them to you, my God, because for such things I was praised by men, to please whom was for me at that time to live a life of honor. I did not see the whirlpool of filth into which I was "cast away from before your eyes."[1] For in your eyes what was then more vile than I? By my deeds I even displeased such men, by countless lies deceiving tutor and masters and parents out of love for play, desire to see frivolous shows, and restless hope of imitating the stage.

I also committed thefts from my parents' cellar and table, either under the sway of greediness or to have something to offer other boys who would sell me their playthings, in which, of course, they took equal delight. Often beaten at games, out of a vain desire for distinction I tried even there for dishonest victories. And what was I so loath to put up with, and what did I so fiercely denounce, if I caught others at it, as what I did to them? If I was caught and argued with, I chose to fight rather than to give in.

Is this boyish innocence? It is not, O Lord, it is not: I pray you, my God, that I may say it. For these are the practices that pass from tutors and teachers, and from nuts and balls and birds, to governors and kings, and to money and estates and slaves. These very things pass on, as older years come in their turn, just as heavier punishments succeed the birch rod. Therefore, it was the symbol of humility found in the child's estate that you, our King, approved when you said, "Of such is the kingdom of heaven."[2]

Chapter 20

A Prayer of Thanks

(31) But yet, Lord, thanks must be given to you, our God, the most excellent and best creator and ruler of the universe, even if you had willed only to bring me to childhood. Even then I existed, had life and feeling, had care for my own well-being, which is a trace of your own most mysterious unity from which I took my being. By my inner sense I guarded the integrity of my outer senses, and I delighted in truth, in such little things and in thoughts about such little things. I did not want to err; I was endowed with a strong memory; I was well instructed in speech; I was refined by friendship. I shunned sadness, dejection, and ignorance. What was there that was not wonderful and praiseworthy in such a living being?

All these things are the gifts of my God: I did not give them to myself. These things are good, and they all made up my being. Therefore, he who made me is good, and he is my good. Before him I rejoice for all these goods out of which I had my being even as a child. But in this was my sin, that not in him but in his creatures, in myself and others, did I seek pleasure, honors, and truths. So it was that I rushed into sorrow, conflict, and error. Let there be thanks to you, my sweetness, my honor, my trust, my God, let there be thanks to you for your gifts. Keep them for me. Thus you will keep me, and the things that you gave me will be both increased and perfected, and I will be with you, for you have also given it to me that I exist.

BOOK 2
AUGUSTINE'S SIXTEENTH YEAR

Chapter 1
The Depths of Vice

(1) I wish to bring back to mind my past foulness and the carnal corruptions of my soul. This is not because I love them, but that I may love you, my God. Out of love for your love I do this. In the bitterness of my remembrance, I tread again my most evil ways, so that you may grow sweet to me, O sweetness that never fails, O sweetness happy and enduring, which gathers me together again from that disordered state in which I lay in shattered pieces, wherein, turned away from you, the one, I spent myself upon the many.[1] For in my youth, I burned to get my fill of hellish things. I dared to run wild in different darksome ways of love. My comeliness wasted away.[2] I stank in your eyes, but I was pleasing to myself and I desired to be pleasing to the eyes of men.

Chapter 2
Love and Lust

(2) What was there to bring me delight except to love and be loved? But that due measure between soul and soul, wherein lie the bright boundaries of friendship, was not kept. Clouds arose from the slimy desires of the flesh and from youth's seething spring. They clouded over and darkened my soul, so that I could not distinguish the calm light of chaste love from the fog of lust. Both kinds of affection burned confusedly within me and swept my feeble youth over the crags of desire and plunged me into a whirlpool of shameful deeds. Your wrath was raised above me, but I knew it not. I had been deafened by the clanking chains of my mortality, the penalty of my pride of soul. I wandered farther away from

you, and you let me go. I was tossed about and spilt out in my fornications; I flowed out and boiled over in them, but you kept silent. Ah, my late-found joy! you kept silent at that time,[1] and farther and farther I went from you, into more and more fruitless seedings of sorrow, with a proud dejection and a weariness without rest.

(3) Who might have tempered my misery, turned to good use the fleeting beauties of those lowest things, and put limits to their delights, so that youth's flood might have spent itself on the shore of married life, if rest in such pleasures could not be gained by the end of begetting children, as your law, O Lord, prescribes? Even so do you fashion the offspring of our mortality, for you have power to stretch forth a gentle hand and soften those thorns that had no place in your paradise.[2] For your omnipotence is not far from us, even when we are far from you. Or I might have listened more heedfully to your voice as it sounded from the clouds: "Nevertheless, such shall have tribulation of the flesh. But I spare you."[3] "It is good for a man not to touch a woman."[4] And again: "He that is without a wife is solicitous for the things that belong to God, how he may please God. But he that is with a wife is solicitous for the things of this world, how he may please his wife."[5] I should have listened more heedfully to these words, and having thus been made a eunuch for the sake of the kingdom of heaven,[6] I would have looked with greater joy to your embraces.

(4) But I, poor wretch, foamed over: I followed after the sweeping tide of passions and I departed from you. I broke all your laws, but I did not escape your scourges. For what mortal man can do that? You were always present to aid me, merciful in your anger, and charging with the greatest bitterness and disgust all my unlawful pleasures, so that I might seek after pleasure that was free from disgust, to the end that, when I could find it, it would be in none but you, Lord, in none but you. For you fashion sorrow into a lesson to us.[7] You smite so that you may heal. You slay us, so that we may not die apart from you.[8]

Where was I in that sixteenth year of my body's age, and how long was I exiled from the joys of your house? Then it was that the madness of lust, licensed by human shamelessness but forbidden by your laws, took me completely under its scepter, and I clutched it with both hands. My parents took no care to save me by marriage from plunging into ruin. Their only care was that I should learn to make the finest orations and become a persuasive speaker.

Chapter 3
A Year of Idleness

(5) In that year my studies were interrupted, with my return from Madauros,[1] the nearby city in which I had already resided to take up the study of literature and oratory, while the money for the longer journey to Carthage was being raised, more by the determination than by the finances of my father, a moderately well-off burgess[2] of Thagaste. To whom do I tell these things? Not to you, my God, but before you I tell them to my own kind, to mankind, or to whatever small part of it may come upon these books of mine. Why do I tell these things? It is that I myself and whoever else reads them may realize from what great depths we must cry unto you.[3] And what is closer to your ears than a contrite heart and a life of faith?[4]

Who at that time did not praise and extol my father because, beyond the resources of his own estate, he furnished his son with everything needed for this long sojourn to be made for purposes of study? No such provision was made for their sons by many far richer citizens. But meanwhile this same father took no pains as to how I was growing up before you, or as to how chaste I was, as long as I was cultivated in speech, even though I was left a desert, uncultivated for you, O God, who are the one true and good Lord of that field which is my heart.[5]

(6) During the idleness of that sixteenth year, when, because of lack of money at home, I lived with my parents and did not attend school, the briars of unclean desires spread thick over my head, and there was no hand to root them out. Moreover, when my father saw me at the baths, he noted how I was growing into manhood and was clothed with stirring

youth. From this, as it were, he already took pride in his grandchildren, and found joy in telling it to my mother. He rejoiced over it in that intoxication, wherein this world, from the unseen wine of its own perverse will, tending down towards lower things, forgets you, its creator, and loves your creature more than yourself.[6] But you had already begun to build your temple within my mother's breast and to lay there the foundations of your holy dwelling place. My father, indeed, was still a catechumen, and that a recent one. But she was moved by a holy fear and trembling, and although I was not yet baptized she feared the crooked ways on which walk those who turn their back on you and not their face towards you.[7]

(7) Ah, woe to me! Do I dare to say that you, my God, remained silent when I departed still farther from you? Did you in truth remain silent to me at that time? Whose words but yours were those that you sang in my ears by means of my mother, your faithful servant? Yet none of them sank deep into my heart, so that I would fulfill them. It was her wish, and privately she reminded me and warned me with great solicitude, that I should keep from fornication, and most of all from adultery with any man's wife. Such words seemed to be only a woman's warnings, which I should be ashamed to bother with. But they were your warnings, and I knew it not. I thought that you kept silent and that only she was speaking, whereas through her you did not remain silent to me. In her person you were despised[8] by me, by me, her son, "the son of your handmaid,"[9] and your servant.

But I did not know this, and I ran headlong with such great blindness that I was ashamed to be remiss in vice in the midst of my comrades. For I heard them boast of their disgraceful acts, and glory in them all the more, the more debased they were. There was pleasure in doing this, not only for the pleasure of the act, but also for the praise it brought. What is worthy of censure if not vice? But lest I be put to scorn, I made myself more depraved than I was. Where there was no actual deed, by which I would be on equal footing with the most abandoned, I pretended that I had done what I had not done, lest I be considered more contemptible because I was actually more innocent, and lest I be held a baser thing because more chaste than the others.

(8) See with what companions I ran about the streets of Babylon, and how I wallowed in its mire as though in cinnamon and precious ointments![10] That I might cling even more firmly to its very navel, my invisible enemy crushed me under foot and seduced me, for I was easy to seduce. The mother of my flesh, who had fled from the center of Babylon,[11] but lingered in other parts of the city, just as she had warned me against unchastity, so also had some concern over what her husband had said about me, to restrain within the bounds of married love, if it could not be cut back to the quick, what she knew to be a present disease and a future danger. Yet she took no final care for this, because of fear that my prospects would be hindered by the impediment of a wife. These were not those hopes of the life to come which my mother herself had, but those hopes for learning, which, as I knew, both parents desired too much: he, because he almost never thought of you, and only of vain things for me; she, because she thought that the usual studies would be not only no obstacle but even of some help to me in attaining to you. Thus recalling things as far as I can, I conjecture that such were my parents' attitudes. Meanwhile, the lines of liberty at play were loosened over me beyond any just severity and the result was dissolution and various punishments. In all these things, my God, there was a mist that darkened for me the serene light of your truth, and my "iniquity came forth as it were from fatness."[12]

Chapter 4
The Stolen Fruit

(9) Surely, Lord, your law punishes theft, as does that law written on the hearts of men, which not even iniquity itself blots out. What thief puts up with another thief with a calm mind? Not even a rich thief will pardon one who steals from him because of want. But I willed to commit theft, and I did so, not because I was driven to it by any need, unless it were by poverty of justice, and dislike of it, and by a glut of evil-

doing. For I stole a thing of which I had plenty of my own and of much better quality. Nor did I wish to enjoy that thing which I desired to gain by theft, but rather to enjoy the actual theft and the sin of theft.

In a garden nearby to our vineyard there was a pear tree, loaded with fruit that was desirable neither in appearance nor in taste. Late one night—to which hour, according to our pestilential custom, we had kept up our street games—a group of very bad youngsters set out to shake down and rob this tree. We took great loads of fruit from it, not for our own eating, but rather to throw it to the pigs; even if we did eat a little of it, we did this to do what pleased us for the reason that it was forbidden.

Behold my heart, O Lord, behold my heart upon which you had mercy in the depths of the pit. Behold, now let my heart tell you what it looked for there, that I should be evil without purpose and that there should be no cause for my evil but evil itself. Foul was the evil, and I loved it. I loved to go down to death. I loved my fault, not that for which I did the fault, but I loved my fault itself. Base in soul was I, and I leaped down from your firm clasp even towards complete destruction, and I sought nothing from the shameful deed but shame itself!

Chapter 5
Why Men Sin

(10) There is a splendor in beautiful bodies, both in gold and silver and in all things. For the sense of touch, what is suitable to it affords great pleasure, and for each of the other senses there is a just adaptation of bodily things. Worldly honor, too, and the power to command and to rule over others have their own appeal, and from them issues greed for revenge. But even to gain all these objects, we must not depart from you, O Lord, or fall away from your law. This life which we live here has its own allurements, which come from its own particular mode of beauty and its agreement with all these lower beauties. The friendship of men, bound together by a loving tie, is sweet because of the unity that it fashions among

Book 2. *Augustine's Sixteenth Year*

many souls. With regard to all these things, and others of like nature, sins are committed when, out of an immoderate liking for them, since they are the least goods, we desert the best and highest goods, which are you, O Lord our God, and your truth and your law. These lower goods have their delights, but none such as my God, who has made all things, for in him the just man finds delight, and he is the joy of the upright of heart.[1]

(11) When there is discussion concerning a crime and why it was committed, it is usually held that there appeared possibility that the appetites would obtain some of these goods, which we have termed lower, or there was fear of losing them. These things are beautiful and fitting, but in comparison with the higher goods, which bring happiness, they are mean and base. A man commits murder: why did he do so? He coveted his victim's wife or his property; or he wanted to rob him to get money to live on; or he feared to be deprived of some such thing by the other; or he had been injured, and burned for revenge. Would anyone commit murder without reason and out of delight in murder itself? Who can believe such a thing? Of a certain senseless and utterly cruel man[2] it was said that he was evil and cruel without reason. Nevertheless, a reason has been given, for he himself said, "I don't want to let my hand or will get out of practice through disuse."[3] Why did he want that? Why so? It was to the end that after he had seized the city by the practice of crime, he would attain to honors, power, and wealth, and be free from fear of the law and from trouble due to lack of wealth or from a guilty conscience. Therefore, not even Catiline himself loved his crimes, but something else, for sake of which he committed them.

Chapter 6
The Anatomy of Evil

(12) What was it that I, a wretch, loved in you, my act of theft, my deed of crime done by night, done in the sixteenth year of my age? You were not beautiful, for you were but an act of thievery. In truth, are you anything at all, that I may speak to you? The fruit we stole was beautiful, for it

was your creation, O most beautiful of all beings, creator of all things, God the good, God the supreme good and my true good. Beautiful was the fruit, but it was not what my unhappy soul desired. I had an abundance of better pears, but those pears I gathered solely that I might steal. The fruit I gathered I threw away, devouring in it only iniquity, and that I rejoiced to enjoy. For if I put any of that fruit into my mouth, my sin was its seasoning. But now, O Lord my God, I seek out what was in that theft to give me delight, and lo, there is no loveliness in it. I do not say such loveliness as there is in justice and prudence, or in man's mind, and memory, and senses, and vigorous life, nor that with which the stars are beautiful and glorious in their courses, or the land and the sea filled with their living kinds, which by new births replace those that die, nor even that flawed and shadowy beauty found in the vices that deceive us.

(13) For pride imitates loftiness of mind, while you are the one God, highest above all things. What does ambition seek, except honor and glory, while you alone are to be honored above all else and are glorious forever? The cruelty of the mighty desires to be feared: but who is to be feared except the one God, and from his power what can be seized and stolen away, and when, or where, or how, or by whom? The caresses of the wanton call for love; but there is naught more caressing than your charity, nor is anything to be loved more wholesomely than your truth, which is beautiful and bright above all things. Curiosity pretends to be a desire for knowledge, while you know all things in the highest degree. Ignorance itself and folly are cloaked over with the names of simplicity and innocence, because nothing more simple than you can be found. What is more innocent than you, whereas to evil men their own works are hostile? Sloth seeks rest as it were, but what sure rest is there apart from the Lord? Luxury of life desires to be called plenty and abundance; you are the fullness and the unfailing plenty of incorruptible pleasure. Prodigality casts but the shadow of liberality, while you are the most affluent giver of all good things. Avarice desires to possess many things, and you possess all things. Envy contends for excellence: what is more excellent than you? Anger seeks venge-

Book 2. *Augustine's Sixteenth Year* 73

ance: who takes vengeance with more justice than you?[1] Fear shrinks back at sudden and unusual things threatening what it loves, and is on watch for its own safety. But for you what is unusual or what is sudden? Or who can separate you from what you love? Where, except with you, is there firm security? Sadness wastes away over things now lost in which desire once took delight. It did not want this to happen, whereas from you nothing can be taken away.

(14) Thus the soul commits fornication when it is turned away from you and, apart from you, seeks such pure, clean things as it does not find except when it returns to you. In a perverse way, all men imitate you who put themselves far from you, and rise up in rebellion against you. Even by such imitation of you they prove that you are the creator of all nature, and that therefore there is no place where they can depart entirely from you.

What, therefore, did I love in that theft of mine, in what manner did I perversely or viciously imitate my Lord? Did it please me to go against your law, at least by trickery, for I could not do so with might? Did it please me that as a captive I should imitate a deformed liberty, by doing with impunity things illicit bearing a shadowy likeness of your omnipotence? Behold, your servant flees from his Lord and follows after a shadow![2] O rottenness! O monstrous life and deepest death! Could a thing give pleasure which could not be done lawfully, and which was done for no other reason but because it was unlawful?

Chapter 7
Grace That Keeps and Heals

(15) "What shall I render to the Lord,"[1] for he recalls these things to my memory, but my soul is not made fearful by them? Lord, I will love you, and give thanks to you, and confess to your name,[2] since you have forgiven me so many evils and so many impious works. To your grace and to your mercy I ascribe it that you have dissolved my sins as if they were ice. To your grace I ascribe also whatsoever evils I have not done. For what evil is there that I, who even loved the crime

for its own sake, might not have done? I confess that you have forgiven me all my sins, both those which I have done by my own choice and those which, under your guidance, I have not committed.

Who is the man who will reflect on his weakness, and yet dare to credit his chastity and innocence to his own powers, so that he loves you the less, as if he had little need for that mercy by which you forgive sins to those who turn to you. There may be someone who has been called by you, and has heeded your voice, and has shunned those deeds which he now hears me recalling and confessing of myself. Let him not laugh to scorn a sick man who has been healed by that same physician who gave him such aid that he did not fall ill, or rather that he had only a lesser ill. Let him therefore love you just as much, nay even more. For he sees that I have been rescued from such depths of sinful disease by him who, as he also sees, has preserved him from the same maladies.

Chapter 8
Comrades in Crime

(16) What fruit had I,[1] so wretched a boy, from those deeds which I now blush to recall, especially from that theft in which I loved the theft itself and nothing else? For the theft itself was nothing, and by that very fact I was all the more miserable. Yet alone, by myself, I would not have done it—such, I remember, was my state of mind at that time—alone I would never have done it. Therefore, I also loved in it my association with the others with whom I did the deed. Then it was not only the theft that I loved? No, truly, nothing else, because my association with the others was itself nothing. But what is it, in all truth? Who is there to teach me, except him who enlightens my heart[2] and uncovers its darkness? What else is it that has aroused my mind to seek out, and to discuss, and to consider these things? If I had then merely liked the pears that I stole, and merely wished to eat them, I could have done so by myself, were doing that wrong deed enough to lead me to my pleasure. Nor would I have needed to arouse the itch of my desires by a rubbing together of guilty minds. But my

Book 2. Augustine's Sixteenth Year

pleasure lay not in the pears: it lay in the evil deed itself, which a group of us joined in sin to do.

CHAPTER 9
Evil Communications

(17) What was my state of mind? Truly and clearly, it was most base, and woe was it to me who had it. Yet, what was it? Who understands his sins?[1] It was like a thing for laughter, which reached down as it were into our hearts, that we were tricking those who did not know what we were doing and would most strenuously resent it. Why, then, did even the fact that I did not do it alone give me pleasure? Is it because no one can laugh readily when he is alone? No one indeed does laugh readily when alone. However, individual men, when alone and when no one else is about, are sometimes overcome by laughter if something very funny affects their senses or strikes their mind. But that deed I would not have done alone; alone I would never have done it.

Behold, the living record of my soul lies before you, my God. By myself I would not have committed that theft in which what pleased me was not what I stole but the fact that I stole. This would have pleased me not at all if I had done it alone; nor by myself would I have done it at all. O friendship too unfriendly! Unfathomable seducer of the mind, greed to do harm for fun and sport, desire for another's injury, arising not from desire for my own gain or for vengeance, but merely when someone says, "Let's go! Let's do it!" and it is shameful not to be shameless!

CHAPTER 10
A Soul in Waste

(18) Who can untie this most twisted and intricate mass of knots? It is a filthy thing: I do not wish to think about it; I do not wish to look upon it. I desire you, O justice and innocence, beautiful and comely to all virtuous eyes, and I desire this unto a satiety that can never be satiated. With you there

is true rest and life untroubled. He who enters into you enters into the joy of his Lord,[1] and he shall have no fear, and he shall possess his soul most happily in him who is the supreme good. I fell away from you, my God, and I went astray, too far astray from you, the support of my youth, and I became to myself a land of want.[2]

BOOK 3
LATER YOUTH

Chapter 1
A Student at Carthage

(1) I came to Carthage, where a caldron of shameful loves seethed and sounded about me on every side.[1] I was not yet in love, but I was in love with love, and by a more hidden want I hated myself for wanting little. I sought for something to love, for I was in love with love; I hated security, and a path free from snares.[2] For there was a hunger within me from a lack of that inner food, which is yourself, my God. Yet by that hunger I did not hunger, but was without desire for incorruptible food, not because I was already filled with it, but because the more empty I was, the more distaste I had for it. Therefore, my soul did not grow healthy, but it was ulcered over, and it cast outside itself and in its misery was avid to be scratched by the things of sense,[3] things that would not be loved if they lacked all soul. To love and to be loved was sweet to me, and all the more if I enjoyed my loved one's body.

Therefore, I defiled the very source of friendship by the filth of concupiscence, and its clear waters I befouled with the lust of hell. Yet foul and vicious as I was, with overflowing vanity, I took pride in being refined and cultured. I plunged headlong into love, whose captive I desired to be. But my God, my mercy, with how much gall did you sprinkle all that sweetness of mine, and how good you were to do it![4] For I was loved, and I had gained love's bond of joy. But in my joy I was bound about with painful chains of iron, so that I might be scourged by burning rods of jealousy, and suspicion, and fear, and anger, and quarreling.

Chapter 2
A Lover of Shows

(2) The theater enraptured me, for its shows were filled with pictures of my own miseries and with tinder for my fires. Why is it that a man likes to grieve over doleful and tragic events which he would not want to happen to himself? The spectator likes to experience grief at such scenes, and this very sorrow is a pleasure to him. What is this but a pitiable folly? For the more a man is moved by these things, the less free is he from such passions. However, when he himself experiences it, it is usually called misery; when he experiences it with regard to others, it is called mercy.[1] But what sort of mercy is to be shown to these unreal things upon the stage? The auditor is not aroused to go to the aid of the others; he is only asked to grieve over them. Moreover, he will show greater approval of the author of such representations, the greater the grief he feels. But if men's misfortunes, whether fictitious or of ancient times, are put on in such manner that the spectator does not feel sorrow, then he leaves in disgust and with disapproval. If grief is aroused in him, he remains in the theater, full of attention and enjoying himself.

(3) Tears and sorrow, therefore, are objects of love. Certainly, every man likes to enjoy himself. But while no man wants to be wretched, does he nevertheless want to be merciful? Now since mercy cannot exist apart from grief, is it for this sole reason that grief is loved? This also has friendship as its source and channel. But where does it go? Where does it flow? Why does it run down into a torrent of boiling pitch,[2] into those immense surges of loathsome lusts? For into these it is changed, and by its own choice it is turned from the purity of heaven into something distorted and base. Shall mercy, therefore, be cast aside? By no means. At certain times, therefore, sorrows may be loved. But shun uncleanness, O my soul! With God as my keeper, the God of our fathers, worthy to be praised and exalted above all forever,[3] shun uncleanness!

Today still I feel compassion, but in those days at the theater I felt joy together with the lovers when by shameful means they had joy in one another, although those things were only pretended in the show, and when they lost each other, I became sad like one who feels compassion. Both situations gave me delight. But now I have more pity for one who rejoices in a shameful deed than for one who has suffered, so to speak, damage to a pernicious pleasure or loss of some vile joy. This is surely the truer mercy, and sorrow finds no delight in it. Although any man who sorrows over a sinner is commended for his act of charity, yet one who shows fraternal mercy prefers rather that there be no occasion for his sorrow. If there is a good will that is at the same time bad-willed, which cannot be, then only a truly and sincerely merciful man can wish that there might be some unfortunates, so that he could show mercy to them. Hence, a certain kind of sorrow can be commended, but none can be loved. Such mercy is yours, O Lord God, for you love our souls with a purity of love more deep and wide than that we have for ourselves, and you are unalterably merciful, because you suffer no wound from sorrow. "And for these things who is sufficient."[4]

(4) But in my wretchedness at that time I loved to feel sorrow, and I sought out opportunities for sorrow. In the false misery of another man as it was mimicked on the stage, that actor's playing pleased me most and had the strongest attraction for me which struck tears from my eyes. What wonder was it that I, an unhappy sheep straying from your flock and impatient of your protection, should be infected with loathsome sores? Hence came my love for such sorrows, by which I was not pierced deep down—for I did not like to suffer such things, but only to look at them—and by which, when they were heard and performed, I was scratched lightly, as it were. As a result, as though from scratches made by fingernails, there followed a burning tumor and horrid pus and wasting away. Such was my life, but was it truly life, my God?

CHAPTER 3
The Wreckers

(5) Your faithful mercy hovered above me but from afar. Upon what great evils did I waste myself, and what a sacri-

legious desire for knowledge did I pursue, so that it might bring me, a deserter from you, down into the depths of apostasy and into the deceitful service of demons! To them I made a sacrifice of my evil deeds, by all of which you scourged me. Even during the celebration of your mysteries, within the walls of your church, I dared to desire and to arrange an affair for procuring the fruit of death. Hence you scourged me with heavy punishments, but nothing in proportion to my faults, O you my most mighty mercy, my God, my refuge from those terrible dangers amid which I wandered, too proud of neck, so that I might depart far from you, loving my own ways and not yours, loving a fugitive's freedom!

(6) Moreover, my studies, which were called honorable, were directed to the practice of law, so that I might excel at it and become so much the more distinguished because so much the more crafty. So great is the blindness of men, who even glory in their blindness! I was already the leading student in the school of rhetoric, and in my pride I rejoiced and I was swollen up with vanity. However, I was much more reserved than others, as you know, O Lord. I kept entirely apart from the acts of wreckage which were perpetrated by the wreckers[1]—this cruel and diabolical name is a sort of emblem of their sophistication—among whom I lived with a sort of shameless shame, since I was not one of them. I associated with them and sometimes took pleasure in their friendship. But I always abhorred their deeds, that is, their acts of wreckage, by which they wantonly mocked at the natural shyness of the new students. By their coarse tricks they overturned this modesty, and thus they provided for their own perverted fun. Nothing is more like the acts of demons than their conduct. How could they be better named than as wreckers? For they themselves had been altogether overturned and perverted in the first instance by devils who laugh at them and through trickery secretly seduce them in the very way in which they love to deride and trick others.

Chapter 4
Cicero's Influence

(7) Among such associates of my callow youth I studied the treatises on eloquence, in which I desired to shine, for a damnable and inflated purpose, directed towards empty human joys. In the ordinary course of study I came upon a book by a certain Cicero,[1] whose tongue almost all men admire but not his heart. This work contains his exhortation to philosophy and is called *Hortensius*. This book changed my affections. It turned my prayers to you, Lord, and caused me to have different purposes and desires. All my vain hopes forthwith became worthless to me, and with incredible ardor of heart I desired undying wisdom. I began to rise up,[2] so that I might return to you. I did not use that book to sharpen my tongue: that I seemed to purchase with the money my mother gave to me, since I was in my nineteenth year and my father had died two years before. I did not use it, then, to sharpen my tongue, nor did it impress me by its way of speaking but rather by what it spoke.

(8) How I burned, O my God, how I burned with desire to fly away from earthly things and upwards to you, and yet I did not know what you would do with me! For with you there is wisdom.[3] Love of wisdom has the name philosophy in Greek, and that book set me on fire for it. There are some who may lead others astray by means of philosophy, coloring and falsifying their errors with that great, and beauteous, and honest name. Almost all such men, both of Cicero's time and of earlier periods, are marked out and refuted in that book. There also he makes clear the salutary warning of your Spirit, given to us through your good and devout servant: "Beware lest any man deceive you through philosophy and vain deceit, according to the tradition of man, according to the elements of the world, and not according to Christ: For in him dwells all the fulness of the Godhead corporeally."[4] At that time, as you, the light of my heart, do know, these apostolic words were not yet known to me. But I was delighted with the exhortation only because by its argument I was stirred up and

enkindled and set aflame to love, and pursue, and attain and catch hold of, and strongly embrace not this or that sect, but wisdom itself, whatsoever it might be. In so great a blaze only this checked me, that Christ's name was not in it. For this name, O Lord, according to your mercy,[5] this name of my Savior, your Son, my tender heart had holily drunken in with my mother's milk and kept deep down within itself. Whatever lacked this name, no matter how learned and polished and veracious it was, could not wholly capture me.

Chapter 5
Introduction to Sacred Scripture

(9) I accordingly decided to turn my mind to the Holy Scriptures and to see what they were like. And behold, I see something within them that was neither revealed to the proud nor made plain to children, that was lowly on one's entrance but lofty on further advance, and that was veiled over in mysteries. None such as I was at that time could enter into it, nor could I bend my neck for its passageways. When I first turned to that Scripture, I did not feel towards it as I am speaking now, but it seemed to me unworthy of comparison with the nobility of Cicero's writings. My swelling pride turned away from its humble style, and my sharp gaze did not penetrate into its inner meaning. But in truth it was of its nature that its meaning would increase together with your little ones, whereas I disdained to be a little child and, puffed up with pride, I considered myself to be a great fellow.

Chapter 6
The Manichees

(10) And so I fell in with certain men,[1] doting in their pride, too carnal-minded and glib of speech, in whose mouth were the snares of the devil[2] and a very birdlime confected by mixing together the syllables of your name, and the name of our Lord Jesus Christ, and the name of the Paraclete, our comforter, the Holy Spirit.[3] These names were never absent from their mouths, but were only the tongue's sound and clat-

ter, while their hearts were empty of truth. Yet they were always saying, "Truth! Truth!" Many times they said it to me, but it was never inside them. They spoke falsehoods, not only of you, who are truly truth, but even of the elements of this world, your creation. With regard to such matters, for love of you, O my Father, supremely good, beauty of all things beautiful,[4] I should have given over even those philosophers who speak the truth. O Truth, Truth, how intimately did even the very marrow of my mind sigh for you, while these men boomed forth your name at me so many times and in so many ways, by the voice alone and by books many and huge! Such were the platters on which the sun and the moon, your beauteous works, but still only your works and not you yourself, and not even chief among your works, were brought to me while I hungered for you. For your spiritual works are above those corporeal things, bright and heavenly though these latter be.

But I hungered and thirsted not for those higher works, but for yourself, O Truth, "with whom there is no change or shadow of alteration."[5] But still they put before me on those platters splendid fantasies. Far better were it to love the sun itself, for the sun is at least true to our eyes, than those false images which deceive the mind by means of our eyes. Yet because I thought that they were you, I fed upon them, not avidly indeed, because you did not taste in my mouth as you are in truth—for you were not those empty figments—nor did I receive nourishment from them, but rather was I myself exhausted by them. Food in dreams is very like the food of waking men, but sleepers are not fed by it: they merely sleep. But those fantasies were in nowise similar to you, as you have now told me, because they were corporeal fantasies, false bodies, and real bodies, whether in the heavens or on earth, which we see by bodily sight, are more certain than they. These things we behold in common with beasts of the field and birds of the air, and they are more certain than those which we conjure up in imagination. Again, there is more certainty when we fashion mental images of these real things than when by means of them we picture other vaster and unlimited bodies that do not exist at all. On such empty phantoms was I fed—and yet I was not fed.

But you, my Love, for whom I faint so that I may be made strong, you are not these bodies which we look upon, even though they be in the heavens; nor are you such things as we do not see up there. For you have created all these things, but still you do not hold them among your greatest works. How far, therefore, are you removed from those fantasies of mine, fantasies of bodies that in no wise exist! Fantasies of bodies that exist are more certain than those others, and bodies are more certain than the images of them. Yet you are not those bodies. Nor are you the soul, which is the life of bodies, and therefore the life of bodies is better and more certain than the bodies. But you are the life of souls, the life of lives, living yourself, and you, O life of my soul, are never changed!

(11) Where, therefore, were you, and at what distance from me? I had wandered far from you, and I was held back even from the husks of the swine to whom I was feeding husks.[6] How much better were the fables of the grammarians and the poets than these booby traps! For a verse and a song and Medea flying aloft[7] were surely more useful than "the five elements,"[8] severally devised because of "the five dens of darkness," which are completely non-existent but yet can kill one who believes in them. For I can turn verse and song into good food. Again, although I sang of Medea flying aloft, I did not assert that it was a fact; although I heard it sung, I did not believe it. But I did believe in those fantasies. Woe! Woe! By what steps was I led down into the depths of hell, struggling and burning for want of the truth! For then I sought for you, my God—I confess it to you who had mercy on me, even when I was not yet contrite—then I sought for you, not according to intellectual understanding, by which you willed to raise me above brute beasts, but according to carnal sense. But you were more inward than my inmost self, and superior to my highest being.

I met with that bold woman, void of prudence, Solomon's riddle, seated on a stool at her doorway and saying to me, "Freely eat you of secret bread and drink of sweet stolen waters!"[9] She seduced me, for she found me dwelling outside myself in my fleshly eye, and chewing over within myself such things as I had devoured through it.

Chapter 7
Problems and Answers

(12) For I did not know that other being, that which truly is, and I was as it were subtly moved to agree with those dull deceivers when they put their questions to me: "Whence is evil?" "Is God confined within a corporeal form?" "Does he have hair and nails?" "Are those to be judged just men who had many wives, killed other men, and offered sacrifices of animals?" Ignorant in such matters, I was disturbed by these questions, and while actually receding from the truth, I thought I was moving towards it. The reason was that I did not know that evil is only the privation of a good, even to the point of complete nonenity. How could I see this, when with eyes I could see only bodies, and with my soul only phantasms? I did not know that God is a spirit, in whom there are no members having length and breadth and in whom there is no mass. For mass is less in each part than in its whole, and if it is unlimited, it is then less in any spatially definite part than in its unlimited extent. It is never everywhere whole and complete, as is a spirit, as is God. Further, I was absolutely ignorant as to what it is in ourselves that makes us be, or how in the Scriptures we are said to be made to the image of God.[1]

(13) I did not know that true interior justice, which judges not according to custom but by the most righteous law of almighty God. By this law the customs of various regions and times were adapted to times and places. But the law itself is everywhere and always the same; it is never one thing in one place and different in another. According to that law, Abraham and Isaac and Jacob and Moses and David, and all those others who found praise in God's mouth, were just men. But by ignorant men, who judged by man's day[2] and measured the ways of all mankind by their own particular customs, they were judged to be unrighteous. It is as if a man who knew nothing of armor, and could not tell what piece is made for what member, would try to cover his head with a greave or

put a helmet on his leg, and then would complain that it did not fit properly. Or it is as if on a certain day when business was forbidden in the afternoon, someone would grow angry because he was not allowed to sell goods as he had in the morning. Or as if one notes in a house how some vessel is handled by a certain slave while it is not allowed to the wine bearer to do so. Again, as if a certain thing is permitted out behind the stable which is forbidden at the table, and one became indignant, because while it is but one dwelling of one family, the same thing is not allowed to all the members and in all places.

Such are all those who complain when they hear that a certain thing was licit for the righteous in another age, whereas it is not permitted to them in our time, because God commanded one thing for some men and something else for others, for certain temporary reasons, although those of both ages were subject to the same justice. Indeed, they can see that in one man, and on one day, and within one house different things are proper to different members; that a thing is permitted up to now which an hour later will not be permitted, and that something is allowed or commanded in one part of the country while it is forbidden and punished in another near by. Is justice therefore at variance with itself and changeable? No, rather the times which it rules over are not identical, for the very reason that they are times. But men, whose life upon the earth is short, because their senses are not able to harmonize the causes prevailing in earlier times and among other peoples, with which they are unacquainted, with those with which they are acquainted, can easily observe in a single body, or on one day, or in a given house, what is proper to each member, at what moment, and for which parts or persons. They find difficulty with the former, but give approval to the latter.

(14) I did not know these things at that time, nor did I advert to them. They beat upon my eyes on every side, and yet I did not see them. I composed poems, and it was not permissible for me to place any foot wherever I wished, but different kinds in different meters and never in any given verse the same foot in all places alike. The very art by which I com-

posed poems did not have different laws in different places, but was always all the same. I did not perceive how justice, to which good and holy men submit, contains in a far more excellent and sublime manner at one and the same time all that it commands, and still is in no part at variance with itself, and how, at various times and not all at once, it distributes and commands what is proper. In my blindness I blamed the holy fathers not only for using present things, as God ordered and inspired them to do, but even for foretelling future things, as God had revealed to them.

Chapter 8
The Natural and the Positive Laws

(15) Can it be wrong for any of us at any time or in any place to love God with his whole heart, and with his whole soul, and with his whole mind, and to love his neighbor as himself?[1] Therefore, vicious deeds that are contrary to nature, are everywhere and always detested and punished, such as were those of the men of Sodom.[2] Even if all nations should do these deeds, they would all be held in equal guilt under the divine law, for it has not made men in such fashion that they should use one another in this way. For in truth society itself, which must obtain between God and us, is violated, when the nature of which he is author is polluted by a perverted lust. But those base deeds which are contrary to human customs must be avoided according to the diversity of customs, so that what has been agreed upon among men by the custom of a city or nation, or established by law, may not be violated at the will of a citizen or traveler. Every part that is not in harmony with its whole is a vile thing.

But when God commands something contrary to the customs or laws of a people, it must be done, even if it has never been done before; if it has been neglected, it must be restored; and if it has never been established, it must be established. If it is lawful for a king to command within the city over which he rules something that neither he nor any predecessor had ever ordered, and if it is not against social principles for him to be obeyed, or rather if it be against the principles of society for him not to be obeyed—for it is a general law of human society for men to obey their rulers—how much more must God, ruler of all creation, be obeyed without hesitation in whatever he imposes upon it! Just as among the authorities in human society the greater authority is set above the lesser in the order of obedience, so God stands above all others.

(16) This also holds among crimes where there is a lust to do injury, either by abusive language or by violence. Each of these can be for the sake of revenge, as in the case of enemy against enemy, or for the sake of gaining some external profit, as in the case of the bandit against the traveler; or for the sake of escaping evil, as with a man who is an object of fear; or out of envy, as when a less fortunate man envies another who is happier, or when a man who has prospered in some fashion fears he will be equaled by another, or regrets that the other is already such; or out of sheer pleasure at another's evil, as with those looking at gladiators or those who deride others or play jokes on them.

These are the chief kinds of iniquity, and they spring forth from lust for power, of the eyes, or of sensuality, whether from one of these, or two, or all three together.[3] Thus a man lives contrary to three and seven, the ten-stringed psaltery,[4] your ten commandments, O God most high and most sweet. But what shameful deeds can affect you who are incorruptible? Or what crimes can weigh against you, to whom injury can never be done? What you take vengeance on is what men inflict on themselves, for even when they sin against you, they do evil to their own souls. Man's iniquity lies to itself,[5] whether by corrupting and perverting their own nature, which you have made and set in order, or by an immoderate use of things permitted to men, or with regard to things not granted to them by a burning lust for that use which is contrary to nature.[6] Or they are held guilty for raging in mind and word against you and for kicking against the goad,[7] or when they break the limits of human society and boldly rejoice in their own private schemes and sects with regard to whatever pleases them or offends them. Such things are done, when you are forsaken,[8] O fountain of life, who are the sole and true creator and ruler of the universe, and when by personal pride a false unity is loved in the part.[9]

Therefore, by humble devotion return is made to you, and you cleanse us from our evil ways, and are merciful to the sins of those who confess to you, and graciously hear the groans of those shackled by sin, and you free them from the chains that we have made for ourselves. This you do, if we do not raise up against you the horns[10] of a false liberty, in avarice of having more and in danger of losing everything, and in putting more love upon our own personal good than upon you, the good of all that is.

Chapter 9
God's Judgments and Ours

(17) Along with base deeds and crimes and so many other iniquities there are the sins of those who are making progress. These sins are reprehended by good judges in the light of the rule of perfection, but they are praised out of a hope of fruit, as is the blade for the grain. There are certain things that seem like vice or crime, but are not sins, because they neither offend you, our Lord God, nor human society. Instances are when a man gathers for a time certain things suitable to his needs, and it is uncertain whether he does this out of greediness; or when certain acts are punished by proper authority with a view to correcting them, and it is uncertain whether this was done out of a desire to inflict harm. Hence many things which would seem fit to be disapproved by men have been approved by your testimony, and many things praised by men have been condemned by you as judge. For often the outward appearance of the deed is one thing, while the mind of the doer and unknown circumstances at the time are another. But when you suddenly command some unusual and unforeseen deed, even one you had once forbidden, and although you for a time keep secret the reason for your command, who can doubt that it must be done, although it may be against the law of some human society, since only that human society which serves you is just? Happy are they who know that it was you who gave the command. For by your servants all things are done

either to show what is needful at present or to foretell the future.

Chapter 10
The Superstition of the Manichees

(18) I was ignorant of such things, and I mocked at those holy men, your servants and prophets. But what did I accomplish when I derided them, except that I should become a thing of scorn to you? For slowly, little by little, I was led on to such follies as to believe that a fig weeps when it is plucked and that the mother tree sheds milky tears. And if some "saint"[1] ate this fig—providing, forsooth, that it was picked not by his but by another's sinful hand—then he would digest it in his stomach, and from it he would breathe forth angels! While he groaned and retched in prayer, he would even breathe forth bits of God! And those bits of the most high and true God would have remained bound up in that piece of fruit, unless they had been let loose by the teeth and belly of an elected saint! In my wretched state I believed that more mercy should be shown to the fruits of the earth than to men, for whose sake they were brought forth. If a non-Manichee who was sorely hungry begged a mouthful I would think it was like condemning it to capital punishment to give it to him.

Chapter 11
Monica's Dream

(19) "You put forth your hand from on high,"[1] and you drew my soul out[2] of that pit of darkness, when before you my mother, your faithful servant, wept more for me than mothers weep over their children's dead bodies. By that spirit of faith which she had from you, she saw my death, and you graciously heard her, O Lord. Graciously you heard her, and you did not despise her tears when they flowed down from her eyes and watered the earth beneath, in whatsoever place she prayed. Graciously you heard her. For whence was that dream by which you consoled her, so that she consented to live with me and to share the same table with me in my home?

Book 3. Later Youth

For this she had begun to be unwilling to do, turning her back on my errors and detesting them. She saw herself standing upon a certain wooden rule,[3] and coming towards her a young man, splendid, joyful, and smiling upon her, although she grieved and was crushed with grief. When he asked her the reasons for her sorrow and her daily tears—he asked, as is the custom, not for the sake of learning but of teaching[4]—she replied that she lamented for my perdition. Then he bade her rest secure, and instructed her that she should attend and see that where she was, there was I also. And when she looked there she saw me standing on the same rule. Whence was this, but that your ears were inclined towards her heart,[5] O you, the good omnipotent, who so care for each one of us as if you care for him alone, and who care for all as for each single person?

(20) Whence too was this, that when she had narrated the vision to me and I attempted to distort it to mean rather that she should not despair of becoming what I already was, she immediately replied without any hesitation: "No!" she said. "It was not said to me, 'Where he is, there also are you,' but 'Where you are, there also is he.'" I confess to you, Lord, that my memory of this, as best I can recall it, and I often spoke of it, is that I was more disturbed by your answer to me through my mother—for she was not disturbed by the likely-seeming falsity of my interpretation and quickly saw what was to be seen, which I certainly did not see before she spoke—than by the dream itself. By this dream the joy of that holy woman, to be fulfilled so long afterwards, was predicted much beforehand so as to bring consolation in her then present solicitude. For almost nine years passed, in which I wallowed "in the mire of the deep"[6] and in the darkness of error, and although I often strove to rise out of it, I was all the more grievously thrust down again. But all the while, that chaste, devout, and sober widow, one such as those you love, already livelier in hope, but no less assiduous in weeping and mourning, ceased not in all her hours of prayer to lament over me before you. Her prayers entered into your sight,[7] but you still abandoned me to turn and turn yet again in that darkness.

Chapter 12
A Bishop's Prophecy

(21) Meanwhile you gave my mother another answer that I recall, although I pass over many things because I hasten to those which most urge me to confess to you, and there are many things that I do not remember. You gave her another answer, then, through one of your priests, a certain bishop brought up in the Church and well trained in your books. When that woman besought him that he would deign to talk with me, refute my errors, correct my evil beliefs, and teach me good ones—for he was accustomed to do this for those whom he found to be properly disposed—he refused, very prudently indeed, as I later understood. He told her that I was as yet lacking in docility, that I was puffed up by the novelty of that heresy, and that I had already unsettled many unlearned men with numerous trifling questions, just as she had indicated to him. "But let him be," he said. "Only pray to the Lord in his behalf. He will find out by reading what is the character of that error and how great is its impiety."

At the same time also, he narrated how he himself as a little child had been handed over to the Manichees by his deluded mother, and how he had not only read through almost all their books but had even copied them out, and how it had appeared to him, although he had no one to argue with him and convince him, that he must flee from this sect, and so he had fled from it. When he had spoken these words, and she still would not keep quiet, but by her entreaties and flowing tears urged him all the more to see me and discuss matters with me, he became a little vexed and said: "Go away from me now. As you live, it is impossible that the son of such tears should perish." As she was often wont to recall in her conversations with me, she took this as if it had sounded forth from heaven.

BOOK 4
AUGUSTINE THE MANICHEAN

Chapter 1
The Teacher as Seducer

(1) For the same period of nine years, from the nineteenth year of my age to the twenty-eighth,[1] we were seduced and we seduced others, deceived and deceiving by various desires, both openly by the so-called liberal arts[2] and secretly[3] in the name of a false religion, proud in the one, superstitious in the other, and everywhere vain. On the one hand, we pursued an empty fame and popularity even down to the applause of the playhouse, poetical competitions, and contests for garlands of grass, foolish plays on the stage, and unbridled lusts. On the other hand, as we desired to be cleansed from all such defilements by the help of men who wanted to be styled "the elect" and "the saints," we brought them food from which, in the workshop of their own bellies, they would fabricate angels and gods through whom we would be set free.[4] Such things did I pursue and do in company with my friends who were deceived by me and with me.

Let proud men, who have not yet for their good been cast down and broken by you, my God, laugh me to scorn, but in your praise let me confess my shame to you. Permit me, I beseech you, and enable me to follow around in present recollection the windings of my past errors, and to offer them up to you as a sacrifice of jubilation. For without you, what am I to myself but the leader of my own destruction? What am I, when all is well with me, except one sucking your milk and feeding on you, the incorruptible food?[5] What manner of man is any man, since he is but a man? Let the strong and mighty laugh us to scorn, and let us, the weak and needy,[6] confess ourselves to you.

Chapter 2
A Sacrifice to Devils

(2) In those years I taught the art of rhetoric, and being vanquished by greed, I sold a skill at speech designed for victories in court. I preferred, as you, Lord, know, to have good students—such, that is, as are called good—and without deceit I taught them to be deceitful, not so that they would work against the life of an innocent man, but sometimes in behalf of a guilty client. From afar, O God, you saw me falling down on slippery ground, and you saw my faith shining amid much smoke, and this faith I who was their comrade showed forth in my teaching to men who loved vanity and sought for lies.[1]

In those years I had a woman companion, not one joined to me in what is named lawful wedlock, but one whom my wandering passion, empty of prudence, had picked up. But I had this one only, and moreover I was faithful to her bed. With her I learned at first hand how great a distance lies between the restraint of a conjugal covenant, mutually made for the sake of begetting offspring, and the bargain of a lustful love, where a child is born against our will, although once born he forces himself upon our love.[2]

(3) I remember also how I once decided to enter a theatrical poetry contest and how some sort of soothsayer asked what payment I would give him in order to win the prize. As I detested and abominated such filthy rites, I told him that not even if the crown were immortal and made of gold, would I let him slay a fly to secure my triumph. It was his plan to slay certain living creatures in his sacrifices, and apparently by such acts of honor to beseech the help of demons for my cause. Yet it was not out of a chaste devotion to you, O God of my heart, that I spurned this evil thing. I did not know how to love you, for I knew only how to think upon gleaming corporeal things. When the soul sighs for such figments, does it not commit fornication against you, and trust in error, and feed the winds?[3] In truth, I would not let sacrifice be made to demons in my behalf, but to those same demons by my superstition I sacri-

ficed myself. What else is it to feed the winds but to feed the demons, that is, by our errors to become objects of pleasure and derision to them?

Chapter 3
The Astrologers

(4) However, I did not refrain from openly consulting those impostors whom they call astrologers, because they offered, so to speak, no sacrifices and directed no prayers to spirits for the purpose of divination. Yet true Christian devotion rightly rejects and condemns their art. To you, Lord, it is good to confess and to say: "Have mercy on me! Heal my soul, for I have sinned against you!"[1] It is good not to abuse your mercy by seeking a freedom to sin, and to remember the words of the Lord, "Behold, you are made whole; sin no more, lest some worse thing happen to you."[2] All this sound health they strive to destroy when they say, "The cause of your sinning was fixed unchangeably by the heavens," and "The planet Venus (or Saturn or Mars) has done this," meaning that man, made up of flesh and blood and proud corruption, is free from fault and that the creator and ruler of the sky and the stars must bear the blame. Who is he unless you, our God, sweetness and source of justice, who render to every man according to his works[3] and do not despise a contrite and a humbled heart?[4]

(5) There was at that time a certain man,[5] wise, most highly skilled in the art of medicine, and most renowned for it, who as proconsul placed by his own hand upon my foolish head the crown won in a contest. He did not do this as a physician, for you alone are the healer of that disease, you who resist the proud and give grace to the humble.[6] But did you fail me, even in the person of that aged man, or did you refrain from healing my soul? For I became better acquainted with him and attended assiduously and earnestly to his discussions, which were without grace of language but both pleasant and solid because of his lively opinions. When he learned from my conversation that I was given to study of the books of the nativity calculators, he advised me in a kind and fatherly man-

ner to throw them away and not to waste the care and labor needed for useful pursuits on such a worthless study. He told me that in the early years of his life he had learned the art with a view to gaining a living by it, thinking that if he could understand Hippocrates,[7] he would surely be able to understand that sort of learning. However, he had later given it up and had devoted himself to medicine for the sole reason that he found such studies completely false, and as a serious man he did not want to seek a livelihood by deceiving people. "You," he said, "have the profession of rhetoric by which to maintain yourself in the world of men, and yet you pursue this delusion, not out of any need at home but of your own accord. Hence you ought to trust me all the more in this matter, since I labored to acquire a mastery over it because I wished to make my living by it alone."

When I inquired of him why it was that so many of the things they foretold turned out to be true, he answered, as far as he could, that the power of chance, which is diffused everywhere throughout the nature of things, brings this about. If a man consults at random the pages of some poet who sings and thinks of things far different, a verse often appears that is wonderfully appropriate to the business at hand.[8] It is not to be marvelled at, then, he said, if from the human soul, by a sort of higher instinct that knows nothing of what goes on within itself, there would be uttered, not by art but by chance, something relevant to the affairs and deeds of the questioner.

(6) All this, indeed, you brought about for me either by him or through him, and you drew outlines upon my memory of what I afterwards investigated for myself. But at that time neither he nor my most dear Nebridius,[9] a truly good and chaste youth, who laughed at the whole business of divination, was able to persuade me to cast aside such things, as the authority of the authors I read moved me more than they. Nor did I as yet find any sure proof, such as I looked for, from which it would appear to me without ambiguity that the true predictions made by the men consulted were spoken by fortune or chance and not by the stargazers' art.

Chapter 4
The Death of a Friend

(7) During those years, when I first began to teach—it was in the town in which I was born—I gained a friend, my equal in age, flowering like me with youth, and very dear to me because of community of interests. As a boy, he had grown up with me, we had gone to school together, and had played games together. But in childhood he was not such a friend as he became later on, and even later on ours was not a true friendship, for friendship cannot be true unless you solder it together among those who cleave to one another by the charity "poured forth in our hearts by the Holy Spirit, who is given to us."[1] Yet it was sweet to us, made fast as it was by our ardor in like pursuits. I had turned him away from the true faith, which he did not hold faithfully and fully as a youth, and towards those superstitious and pernicious fables because of which my mother wept over me. This man was now wandering with me in spirit, and my soul could not endure to be without him. But behold, you were close at the back of those fleeing from you, you who are at once the God of vengeance[2] and the fount of mercy, who in a marvelous manner convert us to yourself. Behold, you took the man from this life when he had scarce completed a year in my friendship, sweet to me above every sweetness of that life of mine.

(8) What one man can number all your praises which he has felt in himself alone?[3] What was it that you did at that time, my God, and how unsearchable are the depths of your judgments?[4] Tormented by fever, he lay for a long time senseless in a deadly sweat, and when his life was despaired of, he was baptized while unconscious. For this I cared nothing and I presumed that his soul would retain rather what it had taken from me and not what had been done to his unconscious body. But it turned out far different: he was revived and regained his strength. Immediately, upon my first chance to speak to him, and I could do this just as soon as he could talk, since I had not left him, as we relied so much upon one another, I tried to make jokes with him, just as though he would joke

with me about that baptism which he had received when he was far away in mind and sense. He had already learned that he had received it. But he was horrified at me as if I were an enemy, and he warned me with a swift and admirable freedom that if I wished to remain his friend, I must stop saying such things to him. I was struck dumb and was disturbed, but I concealed all my feelings until he would grow well again and would be fit in health and strength. Then I would deal with him as I wished. But he was snatched away from my madness, so that he might be kept with you for my consolation. After a few days, while I was absent, he was attacked again by the fever and died.

(9) My heart was made dark by sorrow, and whatever I looked upon was death.[5] My native place was a torment to me, and my father's house was a strange unhappiness. Whatsoever I had done together with him was, apart from him, turned into a cruel torture. My eyes sought for him on every side, and he was not given to them. I hated all things, because they no longer held him. Nor could they now say to me, "Here he comes," as they did in his absence from them when he lived. To myself I became a great riddle, and I questioned my soul as to why it was sad and why it afflicted me so grievously,[6] and it could answer me nothing. If I said to it, "Hope in God," it did right not to obey me, for the man, that most dear one whom she had lost, was more real and more good to her than the fantasy[7] in which she was bade to hope. Only weeping was sweet to me, and it succeeded to my friend in my soul's delights.

Chapter 5

A Sweet Sorrow

(10) Lord, these things have now passed away and time has eased my wound. Am I able to hearken to you, who are truth, and to turn my heart's ear to your mouth, that you may tell me why weeping is sweet to those in misery? Is it that you, although present in all places, have flung our misery far away from yourself, and do you abide unchanged in yourself, while we are spun about in our trials? Yet unless we could

weep into your ears, no trace of hope would remain for us. Whence is it, then, that sweet fruit is plucked from life's bitterness, from mourning and weeping, from sighing and lamenting? Does sweetness lie there because we hope that you will graciously hear us? This rightly holds for our prayers, since they contain our desire of attaining to you. But does it hold for that grief and mourning over what was lost, with which I was overwhelmed? I did not hope that he would come back to life, nor did I beg for that by my tears; I only sorrowed and wept, for I was wretched and I had lost my joy. Or is weeping itself a bitter thing, and does it give us pleasure because of distaste for things in which we once took joy, but only at such times as we shrink back from them?

Chapter 6
His Love for the Lost Friend

(11) Why do I speak of these things? For now is not the time for questioning, but for confessing to you. Wretched was I, and wretched is every soul that is bound fast by friendship for mortal things, that is torn asunder when it loses them, and then first feels the misery by which it is wretched even before it loses those things. Such was I at that time, and I wept most bitterly and I found rest in my bitterness. So wretched was I that I held that life of wretchedness to be more dear to me than my friend himself. For although I wished to change it, yet I was more unwilling to lose it than I was to lose my friend. I do not know whether I would have wished its loss, even for his sake, as is told of Orestes and Pylades, if it is not a fiction, who wished to die together for one another, since to them not to live together was worse than death. But in me there had arisen I know not what sort of affection, one far different from theirs, for most heavily there weighed upon me both weariness of life and fear of dying.[1] I believe that the more I loved him, the more did I hate and fear death, which had taken him away from me, as my cruelest enemy. I thought that it would speedily devour all men, since it had been able to devour him. All this I was, and I remember it.

Behold my heart, my God, behold what is within it! See

this, for I remember it, O you who are my hope, who cleanse me from the uncleanness of such affections, who direct my eyes to you and pluck my feet out of the snare.[2] I marveled that other men should live, because he, whom I had loved as if he would never die, was dead. I marveled more that I, his second self, could live when he was dead. Well has someone said of his friend that he is half of his soul.[3] For I thought that my soul and his soul were but one soul in two bodies.[4] Therefore, my life was a horror to me, because I would not live as but a half. Perhaps because of this I feared to die, lest he whom I had loved so much should wholly die.

Chapter 7
Departure from Thagaste

(12) O madness, which does not know how to love men, as men should be loved! O foolish man, who so rebelliously endures man's lot! Such was I at that time. Therefore I raged, and sighed, and wept, and became distraught, and there was for me neither rest nor reason. I carried about my pierced and bloodied soul, rebellious at being carried by me, but I could find no place where I might put it down. Not in pleasant groves, not in games and singing, not in sweet-scented spots, not in rich banquets, not in the pleasures of the bedchamber, not even in books and in poetry did it find rest. All things grew loathsome, even the very light itself; and whatsoever was not he was base and wearisome to me—all except groans and tears, for in them alone was found a little rest. But when my soul was withdrawn from these, a mighty burden of misery weighed me down. To you, O Lord, ought it to have been lifted up,[1] to be eased by you. I knew it, but I willed it not, nor was I able to will it, and this the more because for me, when I thought upon you, you were not something solid and firm. For to me then you were not what you are, but an empty phantom, and my error was my god. If I attempted to put my burden there, so that it might rest, it hurtled back upon me through the void, and I myself remained an unhappy place where I could not abide and from which I could depart. For where could my heart fly to, away from my heart? Where could I

fly to, apart from my own self?[2] Where would I not pursue myself? But still I fled from my native town. Less often would my eyes seek him where they were not used to seeing him, and from Thagaste I came to Carthage.[3]

CHAPTER 8
The Healing Powers of Time and Change

(13) Time does not take time off, nor does it turn without purpose through our senses: it works wondrous effects in our minds. See how it came and went from day to day, and by coming and going it planted in me other hopes and other memories, and little by little they filled me up again with my former sources of delight. My sorrow gave way to them, but to it succeeded not new sorrows, but yet causes of new sorrows. Why did that sorrow penetrate so easily into my deepest being, unless because I had poured out my soul upon the sand by loving a man soon to die as though he were one who would never die? Most of all, the solace of other friends restored and revived me, and together with them I loved what I loved in place of you. This was a huge fable and a long-drawn-out lie, and by its adulterous fondling, our soul, itching in its ears,[1] was corrupted.

But that fable did not die for me, even when one of my friends would die. There were other things done in their company which more completely seized my mind: to talk and to laugh with them; to do friendly acts of service for one another; to read well-written books together; sometimes to tell jokes and sometimes to be serious; to disagree at times, but without hard feelings, just as a man does with himself; and to keep our many discussions pleasant by the very rarity of such differences; to teach things to the others and to learn from them; to long impatiently for those who were absent, and to receive with joy those joining us. These and similar expressions, proceeding from the hearts of those who loved and repaid their comrades' love, by way of countenance, tongue, eyes, and a thousand pleasing gestures, were like fuel to set our minds ablaze and to make but one out of many.

Chapter 9
A Higher Love

(14) This is what we love in our friends, and love in such wise that a man's conscience condemns him if he does love one who returns his love, or if he does not return the love of one who loved him first, seeking nothing from that person but signs of good will. Hence the mourning, if anyone should die, the shadows cast by sorrow, the heart drenched in tears, the sweetness turned all bitter, and from the lost life of the dead, death for the living.

But blessed is the man who loves you,[1] and his friend in you, and his enemy for your sake. For he alone loses no dear one to whom all are dear in him who is not lost. But who is this unless our God, the God who made heaven and earth[2] and fills all things because by filling them he made them?[3] No man loses you except one who forsakes you, and if he forsakes you, where does he go or where does he flee, except from you well-pleased back to you all wrathful? Where does he find your law but in his own punishment? "And your law is the truth,"[4] and you are the truth.[5]

Chapter 10
A Changing Universe

(15) "Convert us and show us your face," O God of hosts, "and we shall be saved."[1] For whatever way the soul of man turns, it is fixed upon sorrows any place except in you, even though it is fixed upon beautiful things that are outside of you and outside itself. Yet these beauteous things would not be at all, unless they came from you. They rise and they set, and by rising, as it were, they begin to be. They increase, so as to become perfect, and when once made perfect, they grow old and die, and even though all things do not grow old, yet all die. Therefore, when they take their rise and strive to be, the more quickly they grow so that they may be, so much the faster do they hasten towards ceasing to be. This is the law of their being. So much have you given them, because they are parts of things that do not exist all at once, but all of them, by

successive departures and advents, make up the universe of which they are parts. See, too, how our speech is accomplished by significant sounds. There would be no complete speech unless each word departs, when all its parts have been uttered, so that it may be followed by another. For all these things let my soul praise you, O God, creator of all things,[2] but let it not be caught tight in them by the love that comes from the body's senses. These things go where they were going so that they may cease to be, and thus they rend the soul asunder with pestilent desires. For the soul wishes to be and it loves to find rest in things that it loves. But in such things there is no place where it may find rest, for they do not endure. They flee away, and who can follow them by fleshly sense? Or who can grasp them, even when they are close at hand?

Fleshly sense is slow, because it is a fleshly sense: that is its nature. It suffices for a certain thing, for which it was made. It does not suffice for something different, namely, to hold fast things running their course from their proper beginning to their proper end. In your Word, by which they are created, they hear these words: "From here, and unto there!"

Chapter 11
Whole and Part

(16) Do not be foolish, O my soul, and do not deafen your heart's ear with the tumult of your folly. Hear you: the Word himself cries out for you to return, and with him there is a place of quiet that can never be disturbed, where your love cannot be forsaken, if itself does not forsake that place. Behold, these present things give way so that other things may succeed to them, and that this lowest universe may be constituted out of all its parts. "But do I depart in any way?" asks the Word of God. Establish there your dwelling place. Entrust to it whatever you have, my soul, wearied at last by deceptions. Entrust to the truth whatever you have gained from the truth, and you will suffer no loss. All in you that has rotted away will flourish again; all your diseases will be healed;[1] all in you that flows and fades away will be restored, and made anew, and bound around you. They will not drag

you down to the place to which they descend, but they will stand fast with you and will abide before the God who stands fast and abides forever.[2]

(17) Why, then, are you perverted, and still following after your own flesh? Let it follow you who have been converted. Whatever you perceive by means of the flesh exists but in part; you do not know that whole of which these things are parts, but yet they give you delight. But if fleshly sense had been capable of comprehending the whole, and had not, for your punishment, been restricted to but a part of the universe, you would wish that whatever exists at present would pass away, so that all things might bring you the greater pleasure. For by that same fleshly sense you hear what we speak, and you do not want the syllables to stand steady; you want them to fly away, so that others may succeed to them and you may hear the whole statement. So it is always with all things out of which some one being is constituted, and the parts out of which it is fashioned do not all exist at once. All things together bring us more delight, if they can all be sensed at once, than do their single parts. But far better than such things is he who has made all things, and he is our God, and he does not depart, for there is none to succeed to him.

Chapter 12
Life and Death

(18) If you find pleasure in bodily things, praise God for them, and direct your love to their maker, lest because of things that please you, you may displease him. If you find pleasure in souls, let them be loved in God. In themselves they are but shifting things; in him they stand firm; else they would pass and perish. In him, therefore, let them be loved, and with you carry up to him as many as you can. Say to them:

"Let us love him, for he has made all things, and he is not far from us.[1] He did not make all things and then leave them, but they are from him and in him. Behold where he is: it is wherever truth is known. He is within our very hearts, but our hearts have strayed far from him. 'Return, you transgressors, to the heart,'[2] and cling to him who made you. Stand fast

Book 4. Augustine the Manichean

with him, and you will in truth stand fast. Rest in him, and you will in truth have rest. Whither, upon what rough ways, do you wander? Whither do you go? The good you love is from him, but only in so far as it is used for him is it good and sweet. But with justice will it become bitter, if you, as a deserter from him, unjustly love what comes from him. Whither do you walk, farther and farther along these hard and toilsome roads?[3] There is no rest to be found where you seek it: seek what you seek, but it lies not where you seek it. You seek a happy life in the land of death, but it is not there. How can you find a happy life where there is no life?

(19) "But our life came down to us,[4] and he took away our death, and he slew it out of the abundance of his own life. He thundered forth and cried out to us to return hence to him, into that secret place from which he came forth to us. For he came first into the Virgin's womb, wherein our human nature, our mortal flesh, was espoused to him, lest it remain forever mortal. And from there he came forth 'as a bridegroom coming out of his bridal chamber,' and he 'rejoiced as a giant to run the way.'[5] For he did not delay, but he ran forth and cried out by words and deeds, by death and life, by descent and ascension, crying out for us to return to him. And he departed from our eyes, so that we might return into our own hearts and find him there. He departed, but lo, he is here. He would not stay long with us, and yet he does not leave us. He departed from here, whence he has never departed, for 'the world was made by him' and 'he was in the world,'[6] and he 'came into this world to save sinners.'[7] My soul confesses to him, and he heals it, for it has sinned against him.[8] 'O you sons of men, how long will you be dull of heart?'[9] Even now, after the descent of life to you, do you not wish to ascend and to live? But how can you ascend when you have set yourselves up high and have placed your mouth against heaven?[10] Descend, so that you may ascend, so that you may ascend to God. For you have fallen by ascending against God."

Tell this to those souls, so that they may weep in the valley of tears,[11] and thus you will carry them along with you up to God. For it is of his spirit that you tell them this, if you speak while burning with the fire of charity.

Chapter 13
First Authorship

(20) I did not know all this at the time, but I loved lower beautiful creatures, and I was going down into the very depths. I said to my friends: "Do we love anything except what is beautiful? What then is a beautiful thing? What is beauty? What is it that attracts us and wins us to the things that we love? Unless there were a grace and beauty in them, they could in no wise move us." I observed with care and saw that in bodies themselves it is one thing to be a whole, as it were, and therefore beautiful, and another to be suitable, because well adapted to something else, just as a bodily part is adapted to the whole body, a shoe to the foot, and the like. This consideration welled up in my mind out of the depths of my heart, and I wrote the books called "On the Beautiful and the Fitting," two or three, I think, in number. You know it, O God, but it now escapes my memory. We do not have them now, for they have been lost by us, how I do not know.

Chapter 14
Problems of Reputation

(21) What was it, O Lord my God, that moved me to dedicate this treatise to Hierius, an orator in the city of Rome? I did not know him even by sight, but I loved the man because of his renown for that learning which was eminent in him, and I had heard and liked certain statements of his. But I was especially pleased with him because he pleased others who raised him up by their praises. They marveled that a Syrian, first educated in Greek eloquence, should later become so wonderful a master of Latin and so deeply learned in all matters that pertain to philosophy. A man is praised and loved even though absent. Does such love pass from the praiser's mouth into the hearer's heart? Far from it: it is rather that one lover is inflamed by another. Hence it is that a man who is praised comes to be loved, when he is believed to be portrayed

by someone who praises him with a sincere heart, that is, when someone both loves and praises him.

(22) Thus at that time I loved men upon the judgment of men, and not upon your judgments, my God, by which no one is deceived. Still, why was this not the same as in the case of a famous charioteer or hunter whose fame is made by popular acclaim? Why was it far different and more serious, and just such praise as I would like for myself? I did not want to be praised and loved as actors are, even though I myself would praise and love them. I preferred to live in obscurity rather than to be famous in that way, even to be held in hate rather than loved as they are. Where are the drives for such varied and diverse types of love distributed within a single soul? Why is it that I love in another man what I hate in myself, for unless I hated it, I would not detest and spurn it, although each of us is a man? It is not just as a fine horse is loved by a man who would not want to be a horse himself, even if he could be one, so the same thing must be asserted of an actor, for the actor holds fellowship with us in nature. Therefore, do I not love in a man what I would hate to be, precisely because I am a man? Man is a mighty deep, whose very hairs you have numbered,[1] O Lord, and they are not lessened before you. But man's hairs are easier to count than his affections and the movements of his heart.

(23) But that orator was of the sort which I loved so much that I wished myself to be such. In my pride, I wandered off and "was carried about with every wind,"[2] but still most secretly was I ruled by you. How can I know and how can I confess with certainty to you that I loved him out of love for those praising him rather than for the actual things for which he was praised? For if these men had not praised him but heaped abuse upon him, and in abusing and despising him had recounted the same things of him, I would not have been inflamed and aroused towards him. Certainly, the facts would not have been different, and the man himself would have been no different; only the feelings of the speakers would have been different.

See where a man's feeble soul lies stricken when it does not cling to the solid support of truth. Just as blasts raised by their tongues blow out of the breasts of men who think they know, so also the soul is borne about and turned around, bent this way and bent that. The light is clouded over from it, and it does not descry the truth. But look! it is before us! It was to be a great thing for me, if my style and my studies became known to that man. If he should approve of them, I would be all the more on fire. But if he disapproved of them, my heart, void and empty of your solidity, would have been deeply wounded. But yet I gladly turned over in my mind and in contemplation placed upon my lips that subject of the beautiful and the fitting upon which I wrote to him. Although there was no one to join with me in praising the book, I myself admired it.

Chapter 15
Pursuit of Truth

(24) As yet I could not perceive that the hinge of this great issue lies in the creative wisdom of you, the almighty one, "who alone do wonderful things."[1] My mind moved among bodily forms; I defined and distinguished the beautiful, as that which is such by itself alone, and the fitting, as that which is fair because it is adapted to some other thing. I supported this by examples drawn from bodies. I turned to the nature of the mind, but the false opinion that I held concerning spiritual things did not permit me to discern the truth. Yet the force of truth itself dazzled my eyes, and I turned my flickering mind from incorporeal things to lines, colors, and expanding quantities, and because I could not perceive them in the mind, I thought that I could not perceive my mind itself. Further, since in virtue I loved peace and in vice I hated discord, I noted that there was unity in the one and division in the other. It seemed to me that the rational mind, the nature of truth, and the nature of the highest good lay in that unity. On the other hand, in my folly I thought that in the division of irrational life there was some kind of substance and nature of the highest evil. This would be not only a substance but actual life, and yet it did not come from you, my God, from whom are all things. I called the first a monad, as if it were pure, sexless mind. The second I called a dyad, like anger in cruel

Book 4. Augustine the Manichean

deeds and lust in shameful acts. But I did not know whereof I spoke. I had not as yet known or learned that evil is not a substance and that our own mind is not the highest and the incommunicable good.

(25) Crimes are committed, if the mind's disposition for vigorous action becomes vicious and rises up in an insolent and disordered manner, and deeds of shame are done if that affection in the soul to drink in carnal pleasures is left unchecked. Just so do errors and false opinions corrupt our life if reason itself is vitiated. Such was it in me at that time. I did not know that it must be enlightened by another light in order to be a partaker in the truth, since it is not itself the essence of truth, for you will light my lamp, O Lord my God, you will enlighten my darkness,[2] and of your fullness we have all received.[3] For you are the true light, which enlightens every man coming into this world,[4] and in you there is no change or shadow of variation.[5]

(26) I strove towards you, but I was driven back from you, so that I might taste of death,[6] for you resist the proud.[7] What more proud, than for me to assert in my strange madness that I am by nature what you are? For while I was mutable, and this was manifest to me by the fact that I wished to be wise, so that I might pass from worse to better, I yet preferred to think that even you were mutable, than that I was not that which you are. Therefore, you rejected me and you resisted my bold but fickle neck. I imagined for myself bodily forms, and being flesh, I accused the flesh. Like a wind that goes, I did not return to you,[8] but I walked on and on into things that are not, neither in you, nor in me, nor in the body. And they were not created for me by your truth, but by my folly they were fancied out of a body. I spoke to your faithful little ones, my fellow citizens, from whom I was an exile, although I knew it not. Full of words and folly as I was, I said to them, "Why, then, does the soul, which God has created, fall into error?" But I did not want anyone to say to me, "Why, then, does God err?" I would rather argue that your unchangeable substance was necessitated to err than confess that my mutable nature had gone astray of its own accord and that to err was now its punishment.

(27) I was perhaps twenty-six or twenty-seven years old when I wrote those books, winding around within myself bodily figments that pounded upon my heart's ears, although I strained those ears towards your interior melody, sweet truth. I thought all the time upon the beautiful and the fitting: I desired to stand fast and to hear you, and to "rejoice with joy because of the bridegroom's voice."[9] I could not, because I was carried away outside myself by the voices of my error, and under the weight of my pride I sank down into the depths. You did not give to my hearing joy and gladness, nor did my bones rejoice, for they had not yet been humbled.[10]

Chapter 16
False Conceptions of God

(28) What did it profit me that when I was scarcely twenty years old certain writings of Aristotle called *The Ten Categories*[1] fell into my hands? I had gaped at the very name, as if in suspense at a thing somehow magnificent and divine, whenever my teacher, a rhetorician at Carthage, along with others who were considered learned men, had praised the work with cheeks bursting and booming with pride. What did it profit me that I read and understood these writings by myself alone? When I conferred with others, who said that they could hardly understand them, although taught by very learned teachers not only by lectures but also by many diagrams drawn in the dust, they were able to tell me no more than what I had grasped by myself. The book seemed to me to speak clearly enough of substances, such as a man is, and of what are in them, such as a man's figure; of what quality he is; his stature; how many feet tall he is; his relationships, as whose brother he is; where he is placed; when he was born; whether he stands or sits; whether he is shod with shoes or armed; whether he does something or has something done to him; and the innumerable things that are found in these nine categories, of which I have set down some examples, or in the category of substance.[2]

(29) What did all this profit me, since it came to be a hindrance to me? I thought that whatever existed had to be

Book 4. Augustine the Manichean

included under these ten predicaments. In this way, I attempted to understand even yourself, my God, who are most wonderfully simple and incommunicable, as if you were subject to your greatness and beauty in such wise that they would be in you as in a subject, just as they are in bodies. But you yourself are your greatness and your beauty.[3] On the other hand, a body is not great or beautiful in so far as it is a body, for even if it were smaller and less beautiful, it would yet remain a body. What I had conceived of you was falsity itself; it was not truth. It was a figment formed out of my own misery; it was not the firm reality of your happiness. For you had commanded it, and so it was done in me, that the earth should bring forth thorns and thistles for me and with labor should I earn my bread.[4]

(30) What did it profit me that I, who was then a most wicked servant of base lusts, should read and understand all the books on the liberal arts, as they are called, whatever of such books I could get to read? I found joy in those books, but I did not know the source of whatever was good and certain within them. I had my back to the light and my face turned towards the things upon which the light fell: hence my face, by which I looked upon the things that were lighted up, was not itself in the light. Whatever concerned the arts of speaking and reasoning, whatever there was on the dimensions of figures and on music and numbers, I understood without much difficulty and without instruction from men. You know this, O Lord my God, for quickness in understanding and keenness at analysis are your gift. But of that gift I made no sacrifice to you. Therefore it availed me not to my service but rather to my perdition, for I strove to keep so good a portion of my substance under my own power. I kept my strength[5] not for your purposes, but I wandered away from you into a far country, so that I might waste it all upon lust and harlots.[6] What did good gifts profit me if I did not put them to good use? I did not realize that those sciences are understood with great difficulty even by the studious and the intelligent, until I tried to expound them to such men, and found that he was best among them who followed me the least slowly as I explained the subjects.

(31) What did all this profit me when I thought that you, O Lord God of truth, were an immense shining body, and I a particle of that body? O deepest perversity! But such was I! My God, I do not blush to confess your mercies to me and to call upon you, I who once did not blush to profess before men all my blasphemies and to bark like a dog against you. What profited me then my abilities, so quick at all those studies, and so many most knotty books, their knots untied by me without help of human teaching, when I erred crookedly and with foul sacrilege against all holy doctrine? Or what great handicap to your little ones was a far slower mind? For they did not depart from you, but they grew their wings safe within the nest that is your Church and they strengthened the wings of charity on the food of a sound faith.

O Lord our God, under the shadow of your wings[7] let us hope, and do you protect us, and carry us. You will carry us, as little ones you will carry us, and even up to our gray hairs will you carry us.[8] For since you are our strength, then it is strength indeed; but when it is our own, then it is but weakness. With you our good lives forever, and because we have turned away from you, we have become perverted. Now let us return, O Lord, so that we be not overturned, for with you our good, which is yourself, lives beyond all decay. And we do not fear lest there be no place to return to, although we rushed headlong from it, for while we were far from you, our mansion, your eternity, fell not in ruin.

BOOK 5
AT ROME AND MILAN

Chapter 1
A Prayer

(1) Accept the sacrifice of my confessions from the hand that is my tongue, which you have formed and aroused to confess to your name. Heal all my bones, and let them say, "Lord, who is like to you?"[1] No man who makes confession to you teaches you what takes place within him, for a closed heart does not close out your eye, nor does man's hardness turn back your hand. You loose it when you will, either in mercy or in vengeance, and there is no one that can hide himself from your heat.[2] Let my soul praise you, so that it may love you, and let it confess your mercies before you, so that it may praise you. Your whole creation does not cease or keep silent from your praise, nor does every spirit through a mouth turned to you, nor do animals and corporeal things through the mouths of those who meditate upon them, so that our soul may arouse itself to you out of its weariness, resting first on the things that you have made, and passing on to you who made those things in so wonderful a way. For with you is refreshment and true strength.

Chapter 2
The Rugged Ways

(2) The wicked, who are without rest,[1] may go their way and flee from you, but you see them and pierce the shadows. Behold, all things about them are beautiful, but they themselves are vile. How have they done injury to you, and in what way have they disfigured your sway, which is just and perfect from the heavens even down to the lowest depths? Whither did they flee, when they would flee from your face? Or where

would you not find them out? But they fled away, so that they might not see you who see them always, and that, being blinded, they might stumble upon you—for you forsake nothing that you have made[2]—that they, the unjust, might stumble upon you, and thus be justly troubled, withdrawing themselves from your gentleness, stumbling against your righteousness, and falling upon your severity. In truth, they do not know that you are everywhere, for no place can enclose you, and that you alone are present even with those who have set themselves far from you. Let them be converted, then, and seek you, for you have not forsaken your creation, as they have forsaken you. Let them be converted, and behold, you are there within their hearts, within the hearts of those who confess to you, and cast themselves upon you, and weep upon your breast after all their rugged ways. When you gently wipe away their tears,[3] they weep the more and rejoice in their weeping, for you, O Lord, and not a mere man of flesh and blood, you, O Lord, who made them, can remake them and give them consolation. Where was I, when I sought you? You were before me, but I had departed even from myself, and I did not find myself, and how much less you!

Chapter 3

Faustus the Manichean and the Astronomers

(3) I speak out in the sight of my God of the twenty-ninth year of my age. There had come to Carthage at that time a certain bishop of the Manichees, Faustus[1] by name, a great snare of the devil,[2] and in that snare many were entangled by the lure of his smooth language. Although I praised this latter, yet I was able to distinguish it from the truth of the things I was avid to learn about. I was concerned not with what vessel of discourse but with what knowledge this Faustus, so renowned among them, would put before me to eat. Report had sent me beforehand the story that he was most highly instructed in all genuine studies and especially skilled in the liberal arts.

Since I had read many doctrines of the philosophers and retained them in my memory, I compared certain of them

Book 5. At Rome and Milan

with the long fables of the Manichees. I found much more probable the words of the philosophers who were "able to know so much as to make a judgment of the world," although its Lord they did not find.[3] For you are great, O Lord, and you look upon the lowly, but the high you know afar off.[4] You do not draw near to any but the contrite of heart,[5] and you are not found by the proud, not even if they could number with curious skill the stars and the sands, and measure the constellations, and plot the courses of the planets.

(4) By their own minds and by that ingenuity with which you endowed them, they investigated these matters and made many discoveries. Many years in advance they foretold eclipses of the great luminaries, the sun and the moon, telling on what day, at what hour, and to what extent they would be, and their calculations did not fail them. The event proved as they had foretold. The principles that they had discovered they put down in writing, and they are read to this day. According to these rules, predictions are made in what year, in what month of the year, on what day of the month, on what hour of the day, and in what part of its light the sun or moon is to be eclipsed, and so it comes to pass, as it is predicted. Men who do not understand such matters stand in amazement and wonder at all this; those who understand them exult and are elated. Out of an impious pride they fall back from you and suffer an eclipse of your light. So early can they foresee a coming eclipse of the sun, but their own present eclipse they do not see, for they do not seek with a devout mind whence it is that they possess this skill by which they seek out these things. But when they find this, because you have made them, they do not give themselves up to you, so that you may preserve what you have made, and they do not slay in sacrifice to you what they have made themselves to be. Nor do they slay their own prideful boasts, which are like the fouls of the air, or their selfish curiosity, which is like the fishes in the sea, by which they wander along the hidden paths of the deep, or their carnal indulgence, which is like the beasts of the field,[6] so that you, O God, who are a devouring[7] flame, may consume their dead cares and re-create them deathlessly.

(5) But they did not know the way, your Word, by which

you made the things[8] that they number off, and themselves who number, and the sense by which they discern what they number, and the intellect by which they number. To your wisdom there is no number.[9] The Only-begotten himself "is made unto us wisdom, and justice, and sanctification,"[10] and he has been numbered among us, and he has paid tribute to Caesar.[11] They have not known this way by which they may descend from themselves to him, and through him ascend up to him. They have not known this way, and they think themselves to be lifted up to the stars and to be shining lights, and lo, they plunge down to earth, "and their foolish heart is darkened over."[12] They say many true things of your creation, but he who is truth, the artificer of creation, they do not seek in piety, and therefore they do not find him. Or if they do find him, and acknowledge him to be God, they do not honor him as God, or give him thanks. They become vain in their thoughts and "profess themselves to be wise," by attributing to themselves the things that are yours. In this wise, in a most perverse blindness, they strive to attribute to you even their own deeds, that is, to put their lies upon you, who are the truth, to change "the glory of the incorruptible God into the likeness of an image of a corruptible man, and of birds and four-footed beasts, and of creeping things." They change your truth into a lie, and they worship and serve the creature rather than the creator.

(6) I kept in memory many true things said by these men concerning your creation, and I found proof for them, based on mathematical calculations, the orderly succession of the seasons, and the visible testimony of the stars. I compared them with the pronouncements of Mani,[13] who in the course of his ravings had written very extensively on these matters, but in his works I found no explanation of solstices, equinoxes, or the eclipse of the greater lights, and nothing such as I had learned in the books on natural philosophy. But I was ordered to believe the things he wrote and this belief did not agree with those proofs established by mathematics and by my own eyes, but was far different.

CHAPTER 4
Knowledge and Happiness

(7) Lord God of truth, is whoever knows these things by that fact pleasing to you? No, unhappy is the man who knows all this, but does not know you; happy is he who knows you, even if he does not know such things. Indeed, a man who knows both you and these things too is not the happier because of them, but because of you alone is he happy, if knowing you, he likewise glorifies you, gives thanks to you, and does not become vain in his own thoughts.[1] A man who knows that he owns a tree, and gives thanks to you for its fruit, even though he may not know how many cubits high it is or how wide it spreads, is better than one who measures it and counts all its branches, but does not own it and does not know or love its creator. It is thus with the man of faith, to whom this whole rich world belongs, who, by cleaving to you whom all things serve, is as one having nothing yet possessing all things,[2] although he does not know even the circles of the Great Bear. It is folly to doubt that he is far better than one who measures the skies, and counts the stars, and weighs the elements, but neglects you who have "ordered all things in measure, weight, and number."[3]

CHAPTER 5
The Character and Doctrine of Mani

(8) Who was it that requested someone called Mani to write even about such things? Apart from knowledge in these matters, true piety can yet be learned. You have said to man, "Behold, piety is wisdom."[1] Of this Mani could be ignorant, even though he knew the other matters perfectly. But in truth because he did not know these subjects, and yet brazenly presumed to teach them, he plainly could not attain to knowledge of piety. It is vanity to make profession of these worldly subjects even when they are known, but it is piety to make confession to you. Hence this devious character spoke at length on natural philosophy only to this effect, that when re-

futed by others who had learned the truth concerning such things, they would clearly recognize what sort of knowledge he had of other more difficult subjects. He did not wish to be thought of small account, but tried to convince men that the Holy Spirit, the consoler and enricher of your faithful, was with full authority personally present in him. Therefore, when he was found out to have taught falsely about the heavens and the stars and the movements of the sun and the moon, although such things do not belong to religious doctrine, it would be quite clear that his were sacrilegious presumptions. For he would make pronouncements not only on things of which he knew nothing but even on things he falsified, with such mad pride and vanity that he tried to attribute them to himself as to a divine person.

(9) When I hear this or that brother Christian who is ignorant of these subjects and thinks one thing in place of another, I can regard such a man with patience as he gives his opinion. I cannot see how it will harm him if he is perhaps in ignorance with regard to the position or condition of some corporeal creature, as long as he does believe things unworthy of you, O Lord, creator of all things.[2] However, it is harmful to him if he thinks that this belongs to the very essence of religious teaching and obstinately presumes to assert what he is ignorant of. Such weakness in the cradle days of a man's faith is put up with by charity, our mother, until this new man grows up into "a perfect man," no more "to be carried about with every wind of doctrine."[3] But as to that one[4] who dared to become the teacher, and the authority and the leader, and the prince of those whom he could persuade to such things, so that his followers thought that they followed not a mere man but your Holy Spirit, who would not deem that in him such madness should be detested and totally rejected, when once he had been convicted of making false statements? But I had not as yet clearly determined whether the changes of the longer and shorter days and nights, and of day itself and night itself, and the waning of the stars, and any other things of this kind that I had read in other books, could also be explained in keeping with his words. For if by any chance they could, it would still be uncertain to me whether the

things were so or not. However, because of the supposed sanctity of the man, I could advance his authority to support my belief.

Chapter 6
Faustus in Person

(10) For almost nine years, during which my errant mind had hearkened to those men, I awaited with intense longing the coming of this Faustus. Others among them whom I chanced to meet failed to answer my questions and objections on these subjects, but they promised me that when he came and took part in the discussions, these problems, and even harder ones that I might present, would be easily and clearly settled. When he came, then, I found that he was gracious and pleasant in his conversation, and that on the topics on which they usually speak he could talk along much more agreeably. But how could the most comely cup-bearer help to slake my thirst for more precious drinks? My ears already had had enough of such things. They did not seem the better to me because better expressed, nor true because eloquent, nor was his soul wise because he looked that way and had a suitable flow of words. The men who had made me such promises about him were not good judges of things, and therefore he appeared wise and prudent to them because his speech was pleasing to them.

I came to know another type of men who even hold the truth in suspicion and refuse to accept it if it is presented to them in an elegant and copious style. But you, my God, had already taught me in wonderful and secret ways, and therefore I believe because you taught me. For your teaching is true, and besides you there is no other teacher of the truth, no matter at what time or in what place he may have fame. Already, therefore, I had learned from you that nothing should be held true merely because it is eloquently expressed, nor false because its signs sound harsh upon the lips. Again, I learned that a thing is not true because rudely uttered, nor is it false because its utterance is splendid. I learned that wisdom is like wholesome food and folly like unwholesome food: they can be set forth in language ornate or plain, just as both kinds of food can be served on rich dishes or on peasant ware.

(11) Therefore, that greed of mine, with which I had so long awaited the man, found delight in his lively manner and feeling in disputation and with his language, which was so appropriate and arose so easily to clothe his thoughts. I was delighted with him, and together with many others, indeed more so than many of them, I praised and extolled him. But I took it amiss that in the midst of a crowd of listeners I could not bring forward and share with him my own worrisome questions in personal conferences and by offering and receiving arguments. When I was able to do this, I began, together with some friends, to lay siege to his ears at a time when mutual discussion was not out of place. I set forth certain things that were disturbing me, and I saw at once that the man was unskilled in the liberal arts, with the exception of grammar, and with that only in an elementary way. But he had read some of Cicero's orations, and a very few books of Seneca,[1] certain things of the poets, and whatever volumes of his own sect that were written in Latin and were well composed, and he had daily practice in speaking. By such means he acquired a certain eloquence that became the more acceptable and the more seductive because kept within the limits of his abilities and because of a certain natural grace. Is it not thus as I recall it, O Lord my God, judge of my conscience? My heart and my remembrance lie open before you, who at that time worked upon me, out of the secret mystery of your providence, and turned my shameful errors before my face,[2] so that I might see them and detest them.

Chapter 7
Faustus as Teacher

(12) After it had become quite clear to me that Faustus was not well equipped in those arts in which I had supposed him to be outstanding, I began to despair that he could ever explain and solve the things that perplexed me. A man ignorant of these subjects could yet hold fast to the truths of religion, but only on the condition that he were not a Mani-

chean. In fact, their books are filled with long-spun-out tales of the heavens, the stars, the sun, and the moon. Having compared their accounts with the mathematical solutions that I had read elsewhere, I did not think that he was able to explain these matters with exactness or—and this was what I greatly desired—to show that they are such as is found in Mani's books, or that an equally good solution could be drawn from those books. When I proposed these problems for consideration and discussion, he was properly modest and did not make bold to take up the burden. He knew that he did not know these subjects, and he was not ashamed to admit it. He was not one of those wordy fellows, from whom I had suffered much, who attempted to instruct me in these matters but said nothing. Although the man's heart was not rightly disposed towards you,[1] yet it was not altogether imprudent with regard to itself. He was not completely ignorant of his own ignorance, and he did not want to engage rashly in a discussion from which he had no way out or no easy way of retreat. He appealed to me the more for this: more beautiful than all those things I desired to know is the modest mind that admits its own limitations. Such I found him to be with regard to all the more difficult and abstruse questions.

(13) As a result, the zeal with which I had set out on the study of Mani's books was much dulled, and I despaired all the more of learning anything from the rest of their teachers, since as regards the many problems that troubled me the famous Faustus had appeared in this light. However, I was thereafter much in his company in consequence of the enthusiasm with which he was inflamed for literature, which I, as a professor of rhetoric, was teaching young men at Carthage. I began to read with him books such as he had heard of and desired to read, or such as I thought proper to his abilities. But all my efforts by which I had determined to advance in that sect collapsed utterly as I came to know that man. I did not as yet break completely with them, but as if unable to find anything better than what I had in some way stumbled upon, I resolved to be content with it for the time being, unless something preferable should chance to appear. So this Faustus, who had been a fatal snare to so many men, now began,

neither willing it nor knowing it, to loosen the snare in which I was caught. Your hands, my God, in the secret of your providence, did not forsake my soul. Out of the blood of my mother's heart, through the tears she poured out by day and night, a sacrifice was offered up to you in my behalf, and you dealt with me in a wondrous way.[2] This did you do, O my God. For "with the Lord are a man's steps directed, and he well likes his way."[3] For how shall we obtain salvation save from your hand, which makes anew what it has made?

Chapter 8

A Road to Rome

(14) You worked within me, then, so that I might be persuaded to go to Rome, and to teach there rather than at Carthage. How I was persuaded to do this I will not neglect to confess to you, for in all this both the most hidden depths of your providence and your mercy, most near at hand to give us help, must be thought upon and proclaimed. I did not want to go to Rome because greater stipends and greater honors were promised to me by friends who urged me on to this, although such things also influenced my mind at that time. The greatest and almost the sole reason was because I had heard that young men studied there in more a peaceful way and were kept quiet by the restraints of a better order and discipline.[1] They were not allowed to rush insolently and at random into the classroom of a teacher with whom they were not enrolled, nor were they let in at all unless he gave permission. On the other hand, at Carthage there is a foul, unrestrained license among the students. They break in boldly and, looking almost like madmen, they disrupt whatever order a teacher has established for his students' benefit. With strange recklessness they do many injurious things that would be punished by law, unless they had custom as their patron. This very custom displays them to be the more wretched in that they do, with permission as it were, what will never be permitted by your eternal law. They think that they act with impunity, whereas they are punished by the very blindness in which they act, and they suffer incomparably greater evils than

Book 5. At Rome and Milan

they inflict. Thus, manners that I did not want for myself as a student I was forced to endure in others when I became a teacher. Hence I was pleased to go where such things were not done, as all who knew the situation told me. But you, "my hope and my portion in the land of the living,"[2] to the end that I would change my residence on earth for the sake of my soul's salvation, put goads to me at Carthage by which I would be turned away from there, and at Rome you set allurements before me by which I would be drawn thither. All this you did by means of men who loved a dead life, and in the one case did senseless deeds and in the other made empty promises. To correct my steps[3] you secretly made use of both their perversity and my own. For those who disturbed my peace were blinded by a foul frenzy, and those who called me to another course savored of earth.[4] But I myself, who in the one city detested true misery, in the other sought false felicity.

(15) Why I went from the one place and went to the other you knew, O God, but you did not reveal it to me or to my mother, who bitterly bewailed my journey and followed me even down to the seashore. But I deceived her, although she held onto me by force, so that she might either call me back or make the journey with me. I pretended that I had a friend whom I would not leave until a fair wind came and he could sail away. Thus I lied to my mother—to such a mother!—and slipped away from her. This deed also you have forgiven me in your mercy, and you preserved me, all full of execrable filth, from waters of the sea and kept me safe for the waters of your grace.[5] For when I would be washed clean by that water, then also would be dried up those rivers flowing down from my mother's eyes, by which, before you and in my behalf, she daily watered the ground beneath her face.

Yet she refused to return without me, and I was hardly able to persuade her to spend the night in a place close by our ship, an oratory built in memory of Blessed Cyprian.[6] During the night I secretly set out; she did not, but remained behind, praying and weeping. What was it, my God, that she sought from you with so many tears, except that you would not let me sail away. But in your deepest counsels you heard the crux of her desire: you had no care for what she then sought, so that you might do for me what she forever sought. The wind blew and filled our sails, and the shore receded from our sight. On that shore in the morning she stood, wild with grief, and with complaints and groans she filled your ears. But you rejected such things, since you carried me away on my own desires so as to put an end to those desires, and thus the carnal affection that was in her was beaten by the just scourge of sorrow. For she loved me to be present with her, after the custom of mothers, but much more than many mothers. She did not know how great a joy you would fashion for her out of my absence. She knew nothing of this, and therefore she wept and lamented. By such torments the remnant of Eve within her was made manifest, and with groans she sought what she had brought forth with groans.[7] Yet after her denunciation of my falsity and cruelty, she turned again to beseech you in prayer for me. She went back home, and I went on to Rome.

Chapter 9
Sickness at Rome

(16) But behold, there I was caught under the scourge of bodily sickness, and I was on the verge of going down to hell, carrying with me all the sins that I had committed against you, against myself, and against others, many and great they were, and beyond that bond of original sin, in which we all die in Adam.[1] You had not yet forgiven me any of them in Christ, nor had he destroyed upon his cross the enmities[2] that I had contracted against you by my sins. How would he destroy them on the cross of a phantom, which was what I then believed him to be?[3] As false, therefore, as his bodily death seemed to me, so true was the death of my soul. As true as was the death of his body, so false was the life of my soul, which did not believe in his bodily death.

My fever grew worse within me: I was now about to depart and to perish. Where would I have gone, if I had then left this world, except into the fire and torment that were worthy of my deeds, according to the truth of your dispensation? Of all this my mother knew nothing, yet far away she continued

Book 5. At Rome and Milan

to pray for me. But you are present in all places, and you graciously heard her where she was, and you had mercy on me where I was, so that I regained my bodily health, although still diseased within my sacrilegious heart. Nor in so great a danger did I desire your baptism: I had been better disposed as a boy, when I had begged for it of my mother's piety, as I have already recorded and confessed. But I had grown in my shame, and, a very madman, I scoffed at the healing remedies of you who did not let me as such a man die a twofold death.[4] If my mother's heart had been struck by that wound, it would never have been healed. I cannot tell clearly enough what love she had for me, and how with greater anguish she brought me forth in spirit than she had given me birth in the flesh.[5]

(17) Hence, I cannot see how she would ever have been healed, if my death in such a state had pierced through and through the bowels of her love.[6] Where would have been such mighty prayers, sent up so often and without ceasing? Nowhere, except with you! But would you, O God of mercies, have despised the contrite and humbled heart[7] of so chaste and sober a widow, generous in almsgiving, faithful and helpful to your holy ones, letting no day pass without an offering at your altar, going without fail to church twice a day, in the morning and at evening, not for empty stories and old wives' tales, but that she might hear you in your instructions and that you might hear her in her prayers? Could you, by whose gift she was such, despise and reject from your help those tears, by which she sought from you not gold and silver or any changing, fleeting good but the salvation of her son's soul? By no means, O Lord! Yes, you were present to help her, and you graciously heard her, and you did this in the order in which you had predestined it to be done. Far be it that you would deceive her by those visions and by your answers to her, both those I have already recounted and those I have not recounted. She kept them faithfully in her breast, and, always at prayer, she would urge them upon you as if they were your own signed bonds. For since your mercy endures forever,[8] you vouchsafe, to those in whom you forgive all debts,[9] to become even a debtor by your promises.

Chapter 10
False Philosophy and False Theology

(18) Therefore, you caused me to recover from that illness, and then also you healed the son of your handmaid[1] for a time as to his body, so that he might live and you might give him a better and more certain health. Even then at Rome I associated with those false and falsifying holy ones: not merely with their hearers, among whom was numbered the man in whose house I had both fallen ill and recovered, but also with those whom they call the elect. I still thought that it was not ourselves who sin, but that some sort of different nature within us commits the sin. It gave joy to my pride to be above all guilt, and when I did an evil deed, not to confess that I myself had done it, so that you might heal my soul, since it had sinned against you.[2] I loved to excuse myself, and to accuse I know not what other being that was present with me but yet was not I. But in truth I was the one whole being, and my own impiety had divided me against myself.[3] That sin was the more incurable whereby I judged myself to be no sinner. Accursed is such iniquity, almighty God, by which I chose rather that you, you within me, should be overthrown unto my damnation, rather than that I should be conquered by you unto my salvation.

You had not yet "set a watch before my mouth, and a door" of continence "round about my lips," so that my heart would not decline "to evil words, to make excuses in sins with men that work iniquity,"[4] and therefore I still communicated with their elect. But since I despaired of making progress in that false doctrine, I now began to hold in a more loose and careless manner those very tenets with which, if I came upon nothing better, I had resolved to be content.

(19) The thought arose in me that those philosophers whom they call the Academics[5] were wiser than the rest. They were of the opinion that all things are doubtful, and they decreed that no truth can be apprehended by man. To me they clearly seemed to believe this, as is commonly held, although I did not yet understand their meaning. I did not fail to re-

Book 5. At Rome and Milan

strain my host from overcredulity, which I knew him to have concerning those fabled topics with which the Manichean books are filled. Yet I lived in closer friendship with them than with other men who did not belong to that heresy. However, I did not defend it with my former ardor, but close association with them—Rome concealed many of them—made me more slothful to seek something different. This was especially so because I despaired, O Lord of heaven and earth, creator of all things visible and invisible, of finding the truth within your Church, from which they had averted me.

To me it seemed a most base thing to believe that you have the shape of our human flesh and are bounded by the outward lines of our bodily members. I wished to meditate upon my God, but I did not know how to think of him except as a vast corporeal mass, for I thought that anything not a body was nothing whatsoever. This was the greatest and almost the sole cause of my inevitable error.

(20) As a result, I believed that evil is some such substance and that it possesses its own foul and hideous mass, either gross, which they styled the earth, or thin and subtle, as is the body of the air, which they imagine to be a malignant mind stealing through the earth. Because some sort of reverence forced me to believe that a good God would create no evil nature, I postulated two masses opposed to one another, each of them infinite, but the evil one on a narrower scale, the good one larger. From this pestilential beginning other blasphemies pursued me. When my mind attempted to have recourse to the Catholic faith, it was struck back again, for the Catholic faith was not such as I thought it to be. My God, to whom your own mercies make confession out of my mouth, I thought myself to be more truly religious if I believed you to be infinite in other parts, even though I was forced to admit that you are finite in that part where the evil mass stands in opposition to you, than if I thought that in all your parts you were bounded by the form of the human body.

I thought it better to believe that you created nothing evil —which in my ignorance appeared to be not only some kind of substance but even a corporeal thing, since I could not think of mind except as a subtle body diffused throughout space—

than to believe that a nature such as I thought evil to be could come from your hand. Our Savior himself, your Only-begotten, I so thought of as being something extruded out of the mass of your pellucid substance for our salvation, that I could believe nothing of him except what I could picture by my own vain powers. I judged that such a nature as his could never be born of the Virgin Mary, without becoming intermingled in the flesh. How such a thing as I had figured out for myself could be thus intermingled and yet undefiled I could not see. So I feared to believe that he was born in the flesh, lest I be forced to believe him defiled by the flesh. Now will your spiritual ones gently and lovingly smile at me if they should read these confessions of mine. But such was I at that time.

Chapter 11
Scriptural Problems

(21) Moreover, I did not think it possible to defend the things in your Scriptures to which those men had objected. Sometimes I desired greatly to discuss individual points with someone highly trained in those books and to find out what he thought of them. Already the statements of a certain Elpidius, who had spoken and disputed face to face against these same Manicheans, had begun to affect me even at Carthage, since he advanced such passages from the Scriptures as could not easily be refuted. I thought that their answer was a feeble one. They were not ready to state it publicly, but only to us in private, and then they would assert that the New Testament writings were falsified by some unknown persons who wished to implant the law of the Jews in the Christian faith.[1] However, they themselves did not produce any uncorrupted copies.

But those two masses weighed down on me, caught fast and as it were suffocated, as I lay thinking only of corporeal things. Beneath them I gasped for the pure, clear air that is your truth, but I was unable to breathe it in.

Chapter 12
Dishonest Students at Rome

(22) I began to devote myself busily to the purpose for which I had come to Rome, namely, to teach rhetoric. I first gathered together in the house some students with whom and through whom I began to gain a reputation. See now how I learned that certain things are done in Rome which I had not suffered from in Africa. It became manifest to me that the wreckage wrought there by abandoned young men was not done here. "But yet," men told me, "to evade paying their teacher, many young men conspire together and all at once transfer themselves from one teacher to another. They are false to their own word, and out of love for money they hold justice in contempt." My heart hated these men, but not with "a perfect hatred."[1] For perhaps I hated them because of what I was to suffer at their hands, rather than because they did unjust things to other men. In truth such men are vile in character; they fornicate against you[2] out of love for passing, temporary trifles and filthy lucre, which defiles the hand that seizes it, and by embracing a fleeting world, and by despising you who abide forever, who call back to yourself and forgive the human soul, which though once sunk in harlotries has now returned to you.

But now I hate such depraved and perverse men, although I can love them when they have been corrected, so that they may prize above money the doctrine itself which they learn, and above that last, yourself, O God, the truth, and the fullness of all sure good, and peace most chaste. But at that time, because of self-regard, I was more unwilling to suffer at the hands of evil men than I was willing that they become good men for your sake.

Chapter 13
A New Career at Milan

(23) Afterwards a message was sent from Milan[1] to Rome, addressed to the prefect of the city, asking that a rhetoric mas-

ter be secured for Milan and stating that his transportation would be at public expense. I applied for the position through the offices of those very men, drunk as they were with Manichean follies, to get free from whom I was leaving, although neither I nor they knew that. The result was that after I had been tested by a public discourse that had been prescribed, Symmachus,[2] who was then prefect, sent me there. I came to Milan, and to Ambrose,[3] its bishop, a man famed throughout the world as one of its very best men, and your devout worshiper. By his eloquent sermons in those days he zealously provided your people with the fat of your wheat,[4] the gladness of your oil,[5] and the sobering intoxication of your wine.[6] All unknowing, I was led to him by you, so that through him I might be led, while fully knowing it, to you.

That man of God[7] received me in fatherly fashion, and as an exemplary bishop he welcomed my pilgrimage. I began to love him, at first not as a teacher of the truth, which I utterly despaired of finding in your Church, but as a man who was kindly disposed towards me. I listened carefully to him as he preached to the people, not with the intention I should have had, but to try out his eloquence, as it were, and to see whether it came up to its reputation, or whether it flowed forth with greater or less power than was asserted of it. I hung eagerly on his words, but I remained uninterested in his subject matter or contemptuous of it. With the sweetness of his discourse I was delighted, which, although more learned, was less lively and entertaining than was that of Faustus. This applies to his style of speaking, for with regard to their subjects there was no comparison. The one man went wandering about among his Manichean fallacies, whereas the other taught salvation in a most salutary way. But "salvation is far from sinners,"[8] and such was I at that time. Yet little by little I was drawing closer to you, although I did not know it.

Chapter 14
The Influence of St. Ambrose's Preaching

(24) Although I was not anxious to learn what he said, but merely to hear how he said it—for such bootless concern re-

Book 5. At Rome and Milan

mained with me, although I had no hope that any way lay open for a man to come to you—yet at the same time with the words, which I loved, there also entered into my mind the things themselves, to which I was indifferent. Nor was I able to separate them from one another, and when I opened up my heart to receive the eloquence with which he spoke, there likewise entered, although only by degrees, the truths that he spoke. At first it began to appear that what he said could be defended. I now judged that the Catholic faith, for which I had thought nothing could be said against the Manichean objectors, could be maintained without being ashamed of it. This was especially the case after I had heard various passages in the Old Testament explained most frequently by way of allegory, by which same passages I was killed when I had taken them literally.[1] Hence when many passages in those books were explained spiritually, I now blamed my own despair, in which I had believed that the law and the prophets could in no way be upheld against those who hated them and scoffed at them.

(25) Yet for all that I did not think that the Catholic way must be held to by myself, even though it could have its learned defenders who would fully and not absurdly refute objections made to it. Nor did I think that what I had previously held was to be condemned, for both parties seemed to be equal in their defenses. Thus while the Catholic position did not seem to be overthrown, neither did it appear to be the victor. I then earnestly applied my mind to see if it were possible, by means of sure arguments, to convict the Manicheans of falsity. For if I were only able to conceive a spiritual substance, then forthwith all those stratagems would be foiled and cast out of my mind. But this I was unable to do.

But with regard to the structure of this world, and every nature that our bodily senses can perceive, as I more and more reflected on and compared things, I came to the conclusion that the philosophers had held much more probable opinions. After the manner of the Academics (as they supposedly are) I doubted everything and wavered in the midst of all things. Yet I resolved that the Manicheans must be abandoned. Even in my skeptical period I did not see how I could persist in a sect above which I now placed many philosophers. But because these philosophers were without the saving name of Christ, I refused utterly to commit the cure of my soul's sickness to them. Therefore, I determined to continue as a catechumen[2] in the Catholic Church, commended to me by my parents, until something certain would enlighten me, by which I might direct my course.

BOOK 6
YEARS OF STRUGGLE

Chapter 1
The Widow's Son

(1) "My hope from my youth,"[1] where were you, and where had you gone?[2] Was it not you who created me, and made me different from the beasts of the field, and made me wiser than the birds of the air?[3] But I walked in darkness, and upon a slippery way,[4] and I sought for you outside myself, but I did not find you, the God of my heart.[5] I went down into the depth of the sea,[6] and I lost confidence, and I despaired of finding the truth.

But now my mother, strong in her love, had come to me, for she had followed me over land and sea, kept safe by you through all her perils. In the midst of storms at sea, she reassured the sailors themselves, by whom inexperienced travelers upon the deep are accustomed to be comforted, and promised them that they would reach port in safety, for you had promised this to her in a vision.[7] She found me in great danger because of my despair at ever finding the truth. Yet when I told her that I was no longer a Manichean, although not a Catholic Christian, she did not leap with joy, as if she had heard something unexpected. The reason was that she had already been assured with regard to that aspect of my wretched state, in which she bewailed me as one dead, but yet destined to be brought back to life by you. In thought she put me before you on a bier, so that you might say to a widow's son, "Young man, I say to you, arise!"[8] Then would he revive, and begin to speak, and you would deliver him to his mother. Therefore, her heart did not pound in turbulent exultation when she heard that what she daily implored you with her tears to do was already done in so great a part. For although I had not yet attained to the truth, I had now been rescued from falsehood. Rather, she was all the more certain that you, who had promised the whole, would grant what still remained. Hence most calmly and with a heart filled with confidence, she replied to me how she believed in Christ that before she departed from this life she would see me a faithful Catholic. This much she said to me. But to you, O fountain of mercies, she multiplied her prayers and tears, so that you would speed your help[9] and enlighten my darkness.[10] More zealously still she would hasten to the church, and she would hang on the words of Ambrose, as on "a fountain of water springing up into life everlasting."[11] For she loved that man as though he were an angel of God,[12] because she had learned that through him I had been brought in the meantime to the wavering, doubtful state in which I then was. She felt sure that through this state I was to pass from sickness to health, with a more acute danger intervening, through that paroxysm, as it were, which doctors call the crisis.

Chapter 2

Outworn Customs

(2) One time when she had brought to the saints' memorial shrines pottage and bread and wine, as was her custom in Africa, she was forbidden to do this by the doorkeeper.[1] As soon as she learned that this prohibition came from the bishop, she accepted it in so devout and obedient a manner that I myself wondered at how easily she became an accuser of her custom rather than an objector to his command.[2] Addiction to wine did not capture her will, nor did a love of wine arouse her to a hatred of truth, as it does so many men and women who object to sober praise, just as the intoxicated object to a watery drink. But when she brought her basket of festival foods, which were to be merely tasted and then shared with others, she never set out more than a single small cup, diluted to suit her own sober taste, from which she would take a little for sake of courtesy. If there were many memorials of the dead that seemed fit to be honored in this manner, she carried around the same cup, which she would set out in all shrines. This cupful, which had become very watery and tepid, she

Book 6. Years of Struggle

would share in small portions with those present. In those places she sought devotion and not pleasure.

As soon as she found that by order of that famous preacher and patron of devotion such things were not to be done, not even by those who would do them in a sober fashion, so that no opportunity would be offered for sots to get drunk, and because such tributes to the dead were too much like Gentile superstitions, she most willingly gave them up. Instead of a basket filled with the fruits of the earth, she learned to bring to the martyrs' memorials a breast filled with purer oblations. Thus she would give what she could to the poor, and thus would the communication of the Lord's body be celebrated in those places where, in imitation of his passion, the martyrs were immolated and received their crowns.

Yet it seems to me, O Lord my God, and so stands my heart on this matter in your sight, that perhaps it would not have been easy for my mother to forego that custom, if it had been forbidden by someone whom she did not love as she loved Ambrose. She loved him greatly because of my salvation, while he loved her because of her most devout life, in which, so fervent in spirit[3] among her good works, she frequented the church. Hence when he saw me, he would often break forth in her praise, and congratulate me for having such a mother. But he did not know what sort of son she had, for I doubted all things, and I thought that the way to life[4] could not be found.

Chapter 3
The Example and Words of St. Ambrose

(3) I had not yet groaned in prayer for you to come to my help, but my mind was intent on questioning and restless for argument. Ambrose himself I believed to be a happy man, as the world judges such things, because so many powerful persons showed him honor. His celibacy alone appeared to me to be a hard thing. But what hopes he held, what struggles against temptations arising from his exalted station, what comforts amid adversities, how sweet the joys of that secret mouth within his heart as it fed upon and savored again the bread you

gave him—such things I could not guess at, nor had I any experience of them.

He did not know the passions that seethed within me, nor my pit of danger. Yet I was unable to ask of him what I wanted and in the way I wanted, for crowds of busy men, to whose troubles he was a slave, shut me away from both his ear and his mouth. When he was not with them, and this was but a little while, he either refreshed his body with needed food or his mind with reading. When he read, his eyes moved down the pages and his heart sought out their meaning, while his voice and tongue remained silent. Often when we were present—for no one was forbidden to entry, and it was not his custom to have whoever came announced to him—we saw him reading to himself, and never otherwise. After sitting for a long time in silence—who would dare to annoy a man so occupied? —we would go away. We thought that in that short time which he obtained for refreshing his mind, free from the din of other men's problems, he did not want to be summoned to some other matter. We thought too that perhaps he was afraid, if the author he was reading had expressed things in an obscure manner, then it would be necessary to explain it for some perplexed but eager listener, or to discuss some more difficult questions, and if his time were used up in such tasks, he would be able to read fewer books than he wished to. However, need to save his voice, which easily grew hoarse, was perhaps the more correct reason why he read to himself. But with whatever intention he did it, that man did it for a good purpose.[1]

(4) Certainly, no opportunity was given me to ask what I desired to ask of so holy an oracle of yours, his breast, unless the matter could be heard quickly. But my surging passions needed full leisure in him to whom they might be poured out, but this they never found. I heard him, indeed, every Sunday as he was "rightly handling the word of truth"[2] before the people. More and more was I convinced that all the knots of the wily calumnies that those men who had deceived us wove against the sacred books could be loosened. When I found that "man was made by you to your image,"[3] was understood by your spiritual sons, whom you had regenerated by grace in our Catholic Mother, not as though they believed and thought

of you as limited by the shape of the human body—although what a spiritual substance would be like I did not surmise even in a weak and obscure manner[4]—I blushed joyfully because I had barked for so many years, not against the Catholic faith but against the fantasies of a carnal imagination. Rash and irreverent had I been in that I talked about and condemned things I should have inquired into and learned about. But you, most high and most near at hand, most secret and most present, in whom there are no members, some greater and others smaller, who are everywhere whole and entire, who are never confined in place, and who surely are not in our corporeal shape, you have yet made man to your own image.[5] And behold, from head to foot he is contained in space!

Chapter 4
Errors Refuted; Truth not yet Found

(5) Therefore, since I did not understand how this, your image, should subsist, I should have knocked[1] and proposed the question, "How is this to be believed?" instead of insultingly opposing it, as if it were believed as I thought. So much the more sharply did concern over what I could hold with certainty gnaw at my very vitals, so much the more shame did I feel at being so long deluded and deceived by a promise of certainties and for gabbling in childish error and ardor over so many uncertainties as if they were certain.[2] That they were false afterwards became clear to me. Certain it was that they were uncertain, and that at one time they had been taken for certain by me, when with blind belligerence I would attack your Catholic Church, although I had not yet discovered that it teaches true doctrines, and that it does not teach those with which I had seriously charged it. Thus I was in the course of being refuted and converted. I rejoiced, my God, that the one only Church, the body of your Only-begotten Son,[3] in which the name of Christ had been put upon me as an infant, had no place for such infantile nonsense. Nor in its sound doctrine would it maintain one that would confine you, the creator of all things, in a space, however high and wide, yet bounded on every side by the shape of human members.

(6) I rejoiced also that the ancient scriptures of the law and the prophets were now set before me for reading, not with that eye which once looked on them as absurdities, when I argued as if your saints understood them in that way, whereas in truth they did not thus understand them. I was glad when I often heard Ambrose speaking in his sermons to the people as though he most earnestly commended it as a rule that "the letter kills, but the spirit quickens."[4] For he would draw aside the veil of mystery and spiritually lay open things that interpreted literally seemed to teach unsound doctrine. He would say nothing that caused me difficulty, although he would state things which I did not as yet know to be true. I held back my heart from all assent, fearing to fall headlong, and died all the more from that suspense.[5] I wished to be made just as certain of things that I could not see, as I was certain that seven and three make ten. I was not so mad as to think that even this last could not be known, but I wanted other things to be known with the same certainty, whether bodily things that were not present to my senses, or spiritual things, which I did not know how to conceive except in a corporeal way. By believing I could have been healed, so that my mind's clearer sight would be directed in some way to your truth, which endures forever[6] and is lacking in nothing. But as often happens, just as a man who has had trouble with a poor physician fears to entrust himself even to a good one, so it was with my soul's health. In truth, it could never be healed except by believing, but lest it believe what was false, it refused to be cured and it resisted the hands of you who have compounded the remedies of faith, and have applied them to the diseases of the whole world, and to them you have given great efficacy.

Chapter 5
The Authority of the Scriptures

(7) From that time forward I preferred Catholic teaching. I thought that on its part it was more moderate and not at all deceptive to command men to believe what was not demonstrated, either because it was a matter that could be demonstrated, but perhaps not to everyone, or because it was in-

Book 6. *Years of Struggle*

demonstrable, than for others to make a mockery of credulity by rash promises of sure knowledge, and then commanding that so many most fabulous and absurd things be accepted on trust because they could not be demonstrated. Then, little by little, O Lord, with a most mild and merciful hand you touched and calmed my heart. I considered how countless were the things that I believed, although I had not seen them nor was I present when they took place. Such were so many events in human history, so many things about places and cities that I had not seen, so many things about my friends, so many things about physicians, so many things about countless other men. Unless we believed these things, nothing at all could be done in this life. Lastly, I thought of how I held with fixed and unassailable faith that I was born of certain parents, and this I could never know unless I believed it by hearing about them. By all this you persuaded me that not those who believe in your books, which you have established with such mighty authority among almost all nations, but those who do not believe in them are the ones to be blamed, and not to be given a hearing, if they should perhaps say to me: "How do you know that these are the books of the one true and most truthful God, dispensed by his Spirit to the human race?" This truth most above all was to be believed, for no hostile and slanderous questions, so many of which I had read in philosophers who contradict one another, could extort from me the answer that I would at any time believe that you do not exist, whatsoever might be your nature (for this I did not know), or that the governance of human affairs did not belong to you.

(8) Sometimes I believed this more strongly and at other times in a more feeble way. But always I believed both that you are and that you have care for us, although I did not know either what must be thought concerning your substantial being or what way led up to you or back to you. Therefore, since we were too weak to find the truth by pure reason, and for that cause we needed the authority of Holy Writ, I now began to believe that in no wise would you have given such surpassing authority throughout the whole world to that Scripture, unless you wished that both through it you be believed in and through it you be sought. Now that I had heard

many things in those writings explained in a probable manner, I referred the absurdity that used there to cause me difficulty to the depths of their mysteries. To me, that authority seemed all the more venerable and worthy of inviolable faith, because they were easy for everyone to read and yet safeguarded the dignity of their hidden truth within a deeper meaning, by words completely clear and by a lowly style of speech making itself accessible to all men, and drawing the attention of those who are not light of heart.[1] Thus it can receive all men into its generous bosom, and by narrow passages lead on to you a small number of them,[2] although these are more numerous than if it did not stand out with such lofty authority and if it had not attracted throngs into the bosom of its holy humility.

I thought over these things, and you were present to me. I uttered sighs, and you gave ear to me. I wavered back and forth, and you guided me. I wandered upon the broad way[3] of the world, but you did not forsake me.

Chapter 6

False Happiness and Empty Joys

(9) I looked with longing at honors, wealth, and marriage, and you laughed at me. Amidst such desires I suffered most bitter troubles, but your mercy was so much the greater according as you let nothing prove sweet to me that was apart from yourself. Behold my heart, O Lord, for it is your will that I recall all this to memory and confess it to you! Now let my soul cleave to you, for you have freed it from so fast a snare of death. How wretched was my soul! Yet you pierced the very nerve within its wound, so that it might leave all things and be converted to you, who are above all things,[1] and without whom they would be nothing, so that it might be converted and healed. How wretched, then, was I, and how wonderfully did you deal with me, so that I might feel my own misery on the very day when I was preparing to make an address in praise of the emperor.[2] In it I would tell many a lie, and for my lies I would be applauded by men who knew that I was lying. My heart pounded over such causes of care and it burned with the wasting fever of my thoughts.

Book 6. Years of Struggle

While going along one of the streets of Milan, I noticed a poor beggar; he was, I believe, already drunk, as he was making jokes and feeling high. I gave a groan and spoke to the friends who were with me of the many sorrows arising from our own madness. For from all such efforts as I was then exerting, while under the good of my desires, as I dragged along the burden of my unhappiness and made it worse by dragging it along, what else did we want except to attain sure joy, which that beggar had already gained ahead of us, and which perhaps we would never come to? For what he had grasped, the joy of a temporary happiness, by means of a few coins that he had gained by begging, I was scheming for by many a troubled twist and turn. It was not true joy that he possessed, but by my ambitious plans I sought one much more false. Certain it was that he was in high humor, while I was troubled; he was free from care, while I was full of fear. If anyone had asked me whether I would prefer to be joyful or to suffer from fear, I would answer, "To be joyful." Again, if anyone should ask whether I preferred to be like the beggar, or such as I then was myself, I would prefer to be myself, charged with care and fear as I was. But I would speak perversely, for was it true? I ought not to have preferred myself because I was more learned, since I took no joy from that. I sought only to please men, not to instruct them, but only to please them. For that reason, you broke my very bones[3] under the rod of your discipline.

(10) Let them depart from my soul who say to it, "It makes a difference where a man finds his joy. That beggar found joy in drinking wine, but you find it in glory." Lord, in what sort of glory? In a glory that is not from you. For just as his was no true joy, so was mine no true glory, and it did the more to overthrow my mind. During that very night he would get rid of his drunkenness. But as for mine, I slept and got up again, and I was to continue to sleep and get up again with it for, see, how many days! It does indeed make a difference where a man finds his joy. This I know, and the joy from hope and faith are incomparably greater than such an empty thing. But at that time there lay a great distance between him and me, for he was happier than I, not only because he was soaked

through and through with high spirits, while my very vitals were torn by care, but also because he by wishing people good luck had got his wine, while by means of lies I sought satisfaction of my pride. At that time I said many things to my dear friends in this line of thought, and I often pointed out how things went with me in such matters. I found that things were ill with me, and I sorrowed over this and thus redoubled that very evil. If any good fortune smiled upon me, it was too much trouble to reach out for it, because almost before I could grasp it, it had flown away.

Chapter 7
Alypius of Thagaste

(11) Those of us who lived together as friends often lamented such things as these, and I especially discussed them with Alypius[1] and Nebridius.[2] Alypius was born in the same town as I was—his parents were among its leading citizens—but he was younger than I. He had studied under me when I first began to teach in our home town, and later at Carthage. He had a great devotion to me, because I seemed to be well disposed towards him and to be a learned man. For my part, I liked him because of his great natural virtue, which was outstanding in one who was not advanced in age. Yet the maelstrom of Carthaginian customs, among which idle spectacles are a violent rage, had sucked him down into a madness for the circus. While he was being miserably tossed about in this course, I was teaching rhetoric there in a public school. However, he had not as yet heard me as a teacher, by reason of a certain difference that had arisen between his father and me. I learned that he loved the circus with this fatal passion, and I was greatly disturbed, as I thought that he would ruin his promise, or had even ruined it already. I had no opportunity to warn him or to recall him by some check, whether out of friendly good will or by a teacher's authority. I thought that he felt the same as his father about me, but actually he did not. He put aside his father's attitude in this matter and began to greet me, to come into my school room, to listen to me for a while, and then go away.

Book 6. *Years of Struggle*

It had slipped from my memory that I should do something for him, so that he would not ruin such good abilities by a blind, headstrong love for worthless pastimes. But you, O Lord, who rule the course of all things, which you have created, had not forgotten that he was to be numbered among your sons as a bishop of your Church. Hence, that his amendment might clearly be attributed to you, you brought it about through me, although I knew it not. For on a certain day, as I sat in my usual place and my students were present with me, he came in, greeted me, sat down, and applied his mind to the subjects under discussion. By chance, there was a passage to be read lying in my hands. As I was explaining it, I thought that a comparison with the circus would be apropos, by which what I wished to say would become both clearer and more pleasant to those whom such madness held captive by means of some biting sarcasm at their expense. You know, O my God,[3] that at that time I had no thought of curing Alypius of his disease. But he applied it to himself, and believed that I had said it only because of him. What another man would take as an occasion for anger at me, this sincere young man took as a reason for becoming angry at himself and for loving me more ardently.

(12) Long ago you had said and had inserted it into your books, "Rebuke a wise man, and he will love you."[4] I had not rebuked him, but you who make use of all men, both the knowing and the unknowing, in the order that you know—and that order is just—out of my mouth and tongue made coals of fire by which you cauterized a mind of such high promise and healed it. Let the man who does not reflect upon your mercies keep silent in your praise, for those mercies confess to you[5] from the bottom of my heart. Upon hearing those words he burst forth from that deep pit in which he had willingly plunged himself and wherein he was blinded with its strange pleasures. He shook his mind with a vigorous self-control. All the filth of the circus fell off from him, and he never returned there again. Next he prevailed upon his unwilling father, so that he might have me as his teacher. He gave way and agreed to this plan. Beginning to attend my lectures again, he became involved with me in that superstition. He loved the Mani-

cheans' show of continence, which he thought to be true and genuine. However, it was a foolish and seductive thing that it captured precious souls as yet unable to touch the heights of virtue, and easy to deceive with the mere surface of a shadowy and bogus virtue.

Chapter 8
Alypius and the Gladiators

(13) Since of course he did not plan to give up the worldly career that had been dinned into him by his parents, he had gone on ahead of me to Rome to study law, and there he was carried off in an unbelievable way by the unbelievable passion for gladiatorial shows. Although he would have opposed such shows and detested them, certain of his friends and fellow students whom he chanced to meet as they were returning from dinner, in spite of the fact that he strongly objected and resisted them, dragged him with friendly force into the amphitheater on a day for these cruel and deadly games. All the while he was saying: "Even if you drag my body into this place, can you fasten my mind and my eyes on such shows? I will be absent, though present, and thus I will overcome both you and them."

When they heard this, they nevertheless brought him in with them, perhaps wanting to find out if he would be able to carry it off. When they had entered and taken whatever places they could, the whole scene was ablaze with the most savage passions. He closed his eyes and forbade his mind to have any part in such evil sights. Would that he had been able to close his ears as well! For when one man fell in the combat, a mighty roar went up from the entire crowd and struck him with such force that he was overcome by curiosity. As though he were well prepared to despise the sight and to overcome it, whatever it might be, he opened his eyes and was wounded more deeply in his soul than the man whom he desired to look at was in his body. He fell more miserably than did that gladiator at whose fall the shout was raised. The shout entered into him through his ears and opened up his eyes. The result was that there was wounded and struck down a spirit that was

Book 6. Years of Struggle

still bold rather than strong, and that was all the weaker because it presumed upon itself[1] whereas it should have relied upon you.

As he saw that blood, he drank in savageness at the same time. He did not turn away, but fixed his sight on it, and drank in madness without knowing it. He took delight in that evil struggle, and he became drunk on blood and pleasure. He was no longer the man who entered there, but only one of the crowd that he had joined, and a true comrade of those who brought him there. What more shall I say? He looked, he shouted, he took fire, he bore away with himself a madness that should arouse him to return, not only with those who had drawn him there, but even before them, and dragging along others as well.

From all that you rescued him with a hand that was most strong and yet most merciful, and you taught him to put his trust not in himself but in you.[2] But that was long afterwards.

Chapter 9
Alypius and the Thief

(14) All this was then laid up in his memory as a remedy in days to come. So also was what happened to him while he was still a student attending my lectures at Carthage.[1] One noon hour when he was in the market place, thinking over what he would be called upon to recite, as students are accustomed to do, you permitted him to be arrested as a thief by the officers of the market place. I do not think that you, our God, allowed this for any other reason except the following. He who was to become so great a man would even then begin to learn this: in cases up for judgment, no man is readily to be condemned with rash credulity by another man.

He was walking alone before the place of judgment, his notebooks and pen in hand, when, look, a certain young man, one of the students, who was the true thief, came, carrying a hidden hatchet—Alypius did not know all this—got in as far as the leaden gratings that cover the silversmiths' shops,[2] and started to cut through the lead. The noise of the hatchet was heard, and the silversmiths who were down below began to whisper among themselves, and sent out men to catch whomever they might find. When he heard their voices, he ran away, leaving behind the tool out of fear that he would be caught with it on him. Alypius, who had not seen him enter, watched him come out and noted how quickly he went away. Wanting to learn the reason for this, he went over to the place, found the hatchet, and stood there, looking at it and wondering what it was all about. At this point the men who had been sent up found him there alone, holding in his hand the hatchet, the sound of which had alarmed them into coming. They seized him and dragged him off, taking great glory before those dwellers in the market place who had crowded around at having caught a manifest thief. From there he was led off to be arraigned before the judges.

(15) But only this far was Alypius to be instructed. For immediately you, O Lord, stood present to prove his innocence, of which you were the sole witness. While he was being led off, either to prison or to be punished, a certain architect, who was in chief charge of public buildings, met them. As the men were often suspected by him of stealing goods that were lost from the market place, they were particularly glad to have met him, so that he might at length learn by whom the thefts were actually committed. However, the man had often seen Alypius in the home of a certain senator,[3] whom he used to visit. As soon as he recognized him, he took him by the hand, took him apart from the crowd, asked him the reason for so bad an affair, heard what had happened, and commanded all present—they were milling about and making great threats—to come with him.

They then went to the house of the young man who had committed the deed. At the door there was a boy who was so little that he would be likely to disclose the whole affair, without being afraid of harming his master, for he had followed him to the market place. As soon as Alypius recognized him, he told it to the architect. He showed the hatchet to the boy and asked him whose it was. Right away the boy said, "Ours," and on further questioning cleared up the rest of it. Thus the whole affair was charged against the master of the house, and the crowd, which had already started to triumph over Alypius, was put to shame. Alypius, who was to become a dispenser of your Word, and an examiner of many cases[4] in your Church, went away a more experienced and a better instructed man.

CHAPTER 10
Alypius as a Public Official

(16) Alypius, then, I found established in Rome. He attached himself to me by an exceedingly strong tie, and went with me to Milan. He did this so that he might not be separated from me and also that he might to some extent practice the law that he had studied, although he had done so more out of his parents' wishes than his own. He had already sat three times as an assessor, with an integrity that was a matter of wonder to other men, although he himself wondered more at those who preferred money to honesty. Moreover, his character was tested not only by the bait held out to avarice but also by the pressure of fear. At Rome he served as assessor to the Count of the Italian Treasury.[1] There was at that time a certain very powerful senator, to whose benefactions many men had obligations, while many others stood in fear of him. As was customary with such power as his, he desired that permission be given him for something or other which was forbidden by law. Alypius held out against it. Next, a bribe was offered. This he scorned with all his mind. Threats were made. He trod them underfoot. Everyone was amazed at so extraordinary a character, for he neither wanted the friendship nor feared the enmity of such a man, who was notorious for having countless ways both of helping others and of harming them. The very judge, whose counselor Alypius was, although he did not want the favor to be granted, did not openly refuse it. Saddling the whole case on Alypius, he asserted that Alypius would not permit him to do it, and truly, if the judge had done it, Alypius would have given up his place.[2]

Because of his zeal for study, he was almost led astray in one single matter, viz., he wanted to have books copied for him at "palace prices."[3] However, after consulting the principles of justice, he changed his decision for the better, as he concluded that equity, which restrained him from this, was more important to him than the power that permitted it. This is but a small matter, but "he who is faithful in what is little is faithful also in the great." Nor can what proceeds from the mouth of your truth be worthless in any way. For "if you have not been faithful in the unjust mammon; who will trust you with that which is the true? And if you have not been faithful with that which is another's, who will give you that which is your own?"[4] Such was he at that time who clung so close to me, and, together with me, wavered in thought as to what course in life was to be taken.

(17) There was Nebridius also who had left his native place near Carthage, and Carthage itself, where he lived most of the time, left his father's rich country estate, left home and mother, who did not wish to follow him, and had come to Milan. This he had done for no other purpose but to live with me in a most ardent search for truth and wisdom. Like me, he sighed, and like me, he vacillated, an ardent seeker after a happy life and a subtle critic of the most difficult questions. Thus there were the mouths of three men in want, who were sighing out their needs to one another and were waiting for you, that you might "give them meat in due season."[5] In all that bitterness, which in accordance with your mercy resulted from our worldly deeds, when we sought to know the reason why we should suffer such things, darkness confronted us. Groaning, we turned away, and we said, "How long shall these things last?" Often we said this, but even as we spoke, we did not give up our worldly ways. For as yet there shone forth nothing certain, which, such ways forsaken, we might reach out to and grasp.

Chapter 11
An Examination of Conscience

(18) Anxiously reflecting on these matters, I wondered most of all at how long was that time from my nineteenth year, when I had first been fired with a zeal for wisdom. For then I had determined, if wisdom were found, to abandon all the

Book 6. *Years of Struggle*

empty hopes and all the lying follies of my vain desires. But see, I was now in my thirtieth year, still caught fast in the same mire by a greed for enjoying present things that both fled me and debased me. All the while I would say to myself:

"Tomorrow I will find it! It will appear clearly to me, and I will accept it! Behold, Faustus will come, and he will explain everything! Ah, what great men are the Academic philosophers! Nothing certain can be discovered for the conduct of life! But no, we must search more diligently; we must not fall into despair! See, things in the Church's books that once seemed absurd do not seem absurd to us now, for they can be explained differently and can be interpreted in a reasonable way. I will fix my feet on that step where my parents placed me as a child, until the clear truth is discovered. But where shall it be sought? When shall it be sought? Ambrose has no leisure. There is no time for reading. Where do we look for the very books? Where or when can we get them? From whom can we borrow them? Times must be set and hours must be assigned to provide for our health of soul. One great hope has dawned: the Catholic faith does not teach what we once thought and what we vainly accused it of. Her learned men hold it blasphemy to believe that God is limited by the shape of the human body. Do we still hesitate to knock, so that all other things may be opened to us?[1] Our students take up the morning hours, but what do we do during the rest of the day? Why not do this? When then will we pay calls on our more powerful friends, whose help we need? When can we prepare books for students to buy? When can we repair[2] our strength by relaxing our minds from these persistent cares?"

(19) "Perish all such things! Let us put away these vain and empty concerns. Let us turn ourselves only to a search for the truth. Life is hard, and death is uncertain. It may carry us away suddenly. In what state shall we leave this world? Where must we learn what we have neglected here? Or rather, must we not endure punishment for our negligence? What if death itself should cut off and put an end to all care, along with sensation itself? This too must be investigated. Far be it, that this should be so! It is no vain, no empty thing that the lofty dignity and the authority of the Christian faith are spread

throughout the whole world. Never would such mighty things be wrought by God in our behalf if the soul's life ceased with the body's death. Why then do we delay to abandon worldly hopes and devote ourselves wholly to seeking God and a life of happiness? But wait! Such things are pleasing to us: they have no small sweetness of their own. A decision to abandon them is not easy, and it is a base thing to return to them again. See, too, how much is already done to obtain a place of honor. What more is there to wish for in these things? We have plenty of powerful friends, and if we do not rashly attempt too much, at least a governorship may be granted to us. I can marry a wife with some money, so that our expenses will not be too heavy, and this would be the limits of my desires. Many great men who have been most worthy of imitation have dedicated themselves to the pursuit of wisdom as married men."

(20) While I was saying all this to myself and the winds were shifting and driving my heart now this way and now that, time passed, and still I delayed to be converted to the Lord.[3] From day to day I deferred to live in you, but on no day did I defer to die in myself.[4] I loved the happy life, but I feared to find it in your abode, and I fled from it, even as I sought it. I thought that I would be too wretched, if I were kept from a woman's arms. I did not believe that the cure for this disease lay in your mercy, for I had had no experience with that cure. I believed that continence lay within a man's own powers, and such powers I was not conscious of within myself. I was so foolish that I did not know that, as it is written, no man can be continent unless you grant it to him.[5] This you would surely have given, if with inward groanings I had knocked at your ears and with a firm faith had cast all my cares upon you.

Chapter 12
A Discussion on Marriage

(21) Alypius in fact kept me from marrying, since he repeated over and over that if I did so, we would in no wise live together in unbroken leisure in love of wisdom, as we had long desired. In this regard, he was even then living a life of

Book 6. Years of Struggle

the strictest chastity, so that it was a source of admiration to me. In early adolescence, indeed, he had had some experience with sex, but had not persisted in it. On the contrary, he had repented of it, turned away from it, and from that time on had lived in complete continence. I opposed him with examples of married men who had cherished wisdom, had gained merit before God, and had faithfully kept and loved their friends. From their grandeur of mind I was far removed. Caught fast in a disease of the flesh with its deadly sweetness, I dragged along my chains and was fearful of being loosed from them. As if my wound had been struck, I repelled his good and persuasive words, as I would a hand unlocking my chains. Moreover, through me the serpent[1] spoke to Alypius: by my tongue he wove sweet snares and placed them upon his path, so that his free and virtuous feet might be entangled in them.

(22) He marveled that I, whom he esteemed in no slight way, would stick so fast in the birdlime of that pleasure as to affirm, whenever we discussed it among ourselves, that I could never lead a celibate life. When I saw that he was astonished at me, I urged in my defense that there was a great difference between what he had taken quickly and furtively, which he could scarce remember, and therefore might scorn easily and without regret, and my long-continued pleasure. Moreover, if the honored name of matrimony were added to it, he ought not to wonder why I could not despise that way of life. Then he also began to desire to marry, not because he was overcome by lust for such pleasure but out of curiosity. He said that he wanted to know what that might be, without which my life, which pleased him so, seemed to me not life but punishment. A mind free from that bondage wondered at my servitude, and from wonder it passed into a desire to experience it. Next he might go on to the experience itself, and then perhaps he would fall into that very slavery at which he wondered. For he was willing to make a pact with death,[2] and "he who loves danger perishes in it."[3]

For whatever conjugal dignity there is in the duty of well-ordered marriage and in raising children, it attracted neither of us, unless very lightly. For the most part, the habit of satisfying an insatiable appetite grievously tormented me, its captive, while an admiring wonder was dragging him into captivity. Thus were we, until you, O Most High, who never desert our clay, mercifully by marvelous and hidden ways come to aid us in our wretchedness.

CHAPTER 13
Arrangements for Marriage

(23) Steady pressure was put upon me to get married. Soon I asked for a girl's hand, and soon she was promised to me. This was principally through my mother's activity,[1] for she hoped that once I was married the baptism of salvation would wash me clean. Hence she rejoiced that day by day I was being prepared for it, and she noted that her prayers and your promises were being fulfilled by my faith. Then indeed, both at my pleading and by her own desire, each day with a mighty cry from her heart she besought you to give her in a vision some sign as to my coming marriage, but you never willed to do so. She saw certain vain and fantastic things, such as are wrought by the powers of the human spirit when concentrated on a matter like this, and she related them to me. However, this was not with the confidence she was wont to have when you showed anything to her, but she disparaged what she saw. She said that she could distinguish by some sort of savor,[2] which she could not explain in words, the difference between your revelations and her own dreaming soul. Yet the marriage was urged on me, and the girl was asked for. She lacked almost two years of the age of consent,[3] but since she appealed to me, I was willing to wait for her.

CHAPTER 14
Proposals for Community Life

(24) Many of us who were friends together discussed among ourselves the turmoils and troubles of man's life and had a common disgust for them. We deliberated about a life of quiet apart from the crowd, and had almost decided upon it. This life of retreat we would arrange for thus: whatever

Book 6. Years of Struggle

we possessed we would put into a common fund, and out of all these goods, we would establish a single household. Hence, through a sincere friendship, one thing would not belong to this man and another to that, but a single fund would be formed out of all the items. The whole would belong to each of us individually, and everything would belong to all of us. We thought that there would be about ten men in this society, some of whom were very rich, especially Romanianus,[1] our fellow citizen—grave difficulties in his business affairs had brought him up to court—who had been very close to me from my early years. He was extremely interested in this project, and he had great authority in persuading us to it, since his ample wealth much exceeded that of the others. We decided also that two men, both holding office for a year like magistrates, would take care of all necessary matters, the others being left at rest. Afterwards the question began to be raised whether the wives, whom some of us already had and we wished to have, would permit this. As a result, the whole project, which we had worked out so well, collapsed in our hands; it was completely broken up and thrown aside. Thereupon we returned to sighs and groans and turned our steps to following the broad and beaten ways[2] of the world. For many thoughts were in our hearts, but your counsel endures forever.[3] Out of that counsel you derided our plans and you prepared your own, according to which you were to give us meat in due season, and to open your hand and fill our souls with blessing.[4]

Chapter 15
The Mother of Adeodatus

(25) In the meantime my sins were multiplied. The woman with whom I was wont to share my bed was torn from my side as an impediment to my marriage. My heart still clung to her: it was pierced and wounded within me, and the wound drew blood from it. She returned to Africa, vowing that she would never know another man, and leaving with me our natural son.[1] But unhappy man that I was, no imitator of a woman and impatient of delay, since it would be two years before I

could have her whose hand I sought, and since I was not so much a lover of marriage as a slave to lust, I procured another woman, but not, of course, as a wife. By her my soul's disease would be fostered and brought safe, as it were, either unchanged or in a more intense form, under the convoy of continued use into the kingdom of marriage. Not yet healed within me was that wound which had been made by the cutting away of my former companion. After intense fever and pain, it festered, and it still caused me pain, although in a more chilling and desperate way.[2]

Chapter 16
In the Garden of Epicurus

(26) Praise be to you, glory to you, O fountain of mercies! I was becoming more wretched, and you drew closer to me. At that very moment your right hand was ready to help me, to lift me out of the mire,[1] and to wash me clean, but this I did not know. All that called me back from a deeper maelstrom of carnal pleasures was the fear of death and of your judgment to come, which never left my soul through all my changing opinions.

I disputed with my friends Alypius and Nebridius concerning the final causes of good and evil, and Epicurus[2] would have won the palm within my soul if I had not believed that after death there remain for the soul life and rewards and punishments, which Epicurus refused to believe. I asked, "If we were immortal and lived in perpetual bodily pleasure without any fear of loss, why should we not be happy, and what else would we ask for?" I did not know that this very fact belonged to my misery, that being drowned and blinded, I could not conceive the light of a virtue and beauty that must be embraced for their own sake. For this the body's eye does not see: it is seen only from within. In my wretchedness I did not consider from what source it flowed to me that I could discuss so sweetly with my friends these very things, foul as they were. For without friends I could not be happy, even in that frame of mind and with no matter how great a flood of carnal pleasures. In truth, I loved these friends for their own sakes, and I know that they in turn loved me for my own sake.

O tortuous ways! Woe to my proud soul,[3] which hoped that if it fell away from you, it would have something better! It turned and turned again upon its back and sides and belly, but all places were hard to it, for you alone are rest. Behold, you are present, and you deliver us from all wretched errors, and you put us on your way,[4] and you console us, and you say to us, "Run forward! I will bear you up, and I will bring you to the end, and there also will I bear you up!"[5]

BOOK 7
PROBLEMS OF THOUGHT AND BELIEF

Chapter 1
New Knowledge of God's True Nature

(1) My evil and abominable youth was now dead, and I was passing into early manhood.[1] But the more advanced I was in age, so much the more was I defiled by vain things. I could conceive of no substantial being except such as those that I was wont to see with my own eyes. Yet from the time that I first began to learn anything of wisdom[2] I did not think of you, O God, as being in the shape of the human body. Such a conception I always shunned, and I rejoiced to find that the faith of our spiritual mother, your Catholic Church, likewise shunned it. But what more I should think you to be, I did not know. I, a man—and such a man!—tried to think upon you, the supreme, the sole, and the true God,[3] and I believed with all my soul that you are incorruptible, and inviolable, and immutable. Not knowing whence or how, I clearly saw and was certain that what can be corrupted is inferior to what cannot be corrupted, and what cannot be violated I unhesitatingly placed above what is violable, and what suffers no change I saw to be better than what can be changed.

My heart cried out violently against all my phantasms,[4] and with one blow I tried to beat off the throng of unclean images fluttering[5] before my mind's eye. Yet they had scarcely been driven off, when, lo, in the twinkling of an eye, they came thronging back again, rushed before my sight, and clouded it over. Hence, although I did not think of you as being in the shape of a human body, I was forced to think of you as something corporeal, existent in space and place, either infused into the world or even diffused outside the world throughout infinite space. Even thus did I think of that very incorruptible and inviolable and immutable being which I set above the corruptible, the violable, and the mutable. For whatever I conceived as devoid of such spatial character seemed to me to be nothing, absolutely nothing, not even so much as an empty space. For if a body is removed from a place, and the place remains empty of any body whatsoever, whether earthly, watery, airy, or celestial,[6] yet there remains that empty space, as it were a spacious nothing.

(2) So gross of heart was I,[7] and I had no clear idea even of my own self, that whatever was not extended over, or diffused throughout, or compacted into, or projected up to definite measures of space, or did not or could not receive something of this kind, I thought to be completely non-existent. Just as my eyes were wont to move about among such forms, so also my heart moved about among similar images. I did not perceive that the mental power by which I formed these images was no such corporeal substance. Yet it could not form them unless it were itself some great thing. So also, I thought that you, the life of my life, were a great corporeal substance, existent everywhere throughout infinite space, which penetrates the whole world-mass, and spreads beyond it on every side throughout immense, limitless space. Thus the earth would have you, the heavens would have you, all things would have you: they would all be limited by you, but you would be limited nowhere. The body of the air—of that air which is above the earth—does not hinder the light of the sun from passing through it. The sun penetrates the air, not by breaking it up or cutting it apart, but by completely filling it. Just so, I thought that the bodies, not only of the heavens, and the air, and the sea, but even of the earth, are all subject to your passage and penetrable in all their parts, the greatest as well as the least, so that they may receive your presence, while all things, which you have created, are governed both inwardly and outwardly by your secret inspiration. Thus did I conjecture, because I could think of nothing different, but it was all false. In that theory, a larger part of the earth would hold a larger part of you, a lesser part, a smaller portion. Thus all things would be filled with you, in such wise that an elephant's body would receive more of you than would a sparrow's, in

so far as it was bigger and occupied a bigger place. Thus you would cause your parts to be present as fragments, large parts in the large parts of the world and small parts in the small parts of the world. It is not so with you, but as yet you had not enlightened my darkness.[8]

Chapter 2

A Refutation of the Manichees

(3) For me, O Lord, that was a sufficient answer to those men, themselves deceived and deceiving others, dumb yet talking much (for from them your Word did not sound forth)—that was indeed a sufficient answer which long ago, while we were still at Carthage, Nebridius used to propose, and which impressed all of us who heard it. He asked: "What would that unknown nation of darkness, which the Manichees are wont to postulate as a hostile mass, have done to you if you had refused to contend with it?" If it was answered that it would do you some injury, then you would be violable and corruptible. If it were said that it could not injure you, no reason would be offered for your fighting with it, fighting, too, in such wise that some portion and member of your being, or some offspring of your very substance, would be mingled with those opposing powers and natures which were not created by you. Thus it would be so far corrupted and changed for the worse, as to be turned from happiness to misery, and as to need some assistance by which it could be rescued and cleansed. They would hold that this offspring is the soul, to whose aid your Word would come: your utterance,[1] which is free, pure, and without defect, would bring aid to the enslaved, the defiled, and the corrupt. Yet your utterance would itself be corruptible because it came from the same substance. Therefore, if they should affirm that whatever you are, that is, your substance, by which you are, is incorruptible, this whole tale is false and execrable. But if they should say that you are corruptible, that too is known to be false and abominable as soon as it is uttered. Sufficient, therefore, was his argument against those who on every count deserved to be spewed forth by a sickened stomach. For the men who thought and spoke of such things of

Chapter 3
Free Will and the Problem of Evil

(4) Up to this time, although I affirmed and firmly believed that you, our Lord, the true God, who made not only our souls but also our bodies, and not only our souls and bodies, but all men and all things, are inviolable and inalterable and in no way mutable, I still had no explicit and orderly knowledge of the cause of evil. Yet whatever it was, I saw that it must be sought out in such wise that I would not be constrained to believe that the immutable God is mutable, lest I myself become the very thing I was seeking to explain.[1] Therefore, I felt safe in my search and certain that what those men,[2] whom I fled from with all my soul, said was not the truth. I saw that in their search for the cause of evil they had become full of malice,[3] and because of this they deemed that your substance is subject to evil, rather than that their own substance committed evil.

(5) I strove to understand what I often heard, that the will's free decision is the cause of our doing evil, and that your just judgment is the cause of our suffering evil, but this I could not discern clearly. When I attempted to withdraw my mind's eye out of those depths, I was plunged down into it again, and as often as I attempted it, I was plunged down again and again. But this raised me up towards your light; I knew just as surely that I had a will as that I was alive. I was absolutely certain when I willed a thing or refused to will it that it was I alone who willed or refused to will. Already I was beginning to see that therein lay the cause of my sin. I saw that what I did against my will was something done to me, rather than something I actually did. I concluded that it was not my fault, but my punishment, but I quickly confessed that I was not punished unjustly, for I thought of you as being just.

But then again I said: "Who made me? Was it not you, my God, who are not merely good, but goodness itself? Whence then comes it, then, that I will evil, and do not will the good?

Book 7. Problems of Thought and Belief

That there may be a reason why I should justly be punished? Who has placed this in me and ingrafted in me this seedbed of bitterness,[4] since I have been fashioned whole and entire by my most sweet God? If the devil is its author, whence comes the devil himself? If he by his own perverse will was changed from a good angel into a devil, whence came that evil will in him by which he became a devil, when the whole angel was made by a supremely good creator?"

By such thoughts I was again crushed and stifled, but I was not brought down even into that hell of error, where no one makes confession[5] to you, while they think that you suffer evil rather than that man commits it.

Chapter 4
God the Absolute Good

(6) In this manner I strove to establish further facts, just as I had already discovered that the incorruptible is better than the corruptible, and as a result confessed that you, whatever you are, are incorruptible. There never has been, nor will there be, a soul able to conceive anything better than you, who are the supreme and best good. But since it is of the utmost truth and certainty that the incorruptible is preferable to the corruptible, even as I already preferred it to be, I could now attain in thought to a being better than yourself, my God, if you were not incorruptible.[1] Therefore, where I perceived that the incorruptible must be preferred to the corruptible, there ought I to seek you. There, too, ought I to observe where evil itself is, that is, whence comes that corruption, by which your substance can in no way be violated. For absolutely no corruption defiles our God: none from the will, none from necessity, none from any unforeseen chance. He is God, and what he wills for himself is good, and he himself is that same good, whereas to be corrupted is not good. Nor are you forced to do anything against your will, because your will is not greater than your power. But it would be greater if you were greater than yourself. God's will and power are God himself. What is unforeseen by you who know all things? No nature exists, unless because you know it. But why should we ask many

times, "Why may not that substance which is God be corruptible?" If it were, it would not be God.

Chapter 5
God's Omnipotence and the Fact of Evil

(7) I sought an answer to the question, "Whence is evil?" but I sought it in an evil way, and I did not see the evil in my very search. I placed before my spirit's gaze the whole creation, whatever we can see in it, such as earth, and sea, and air, and stars, and trees, and mortal animals, and likewise whatever we do not see therein, such as the firmament of heaven above, and all the angels, and all its spiritual beings, but I set out even such things as if they were bodies arranged in such and such places, as my imagination dictated. I made your creation into a single great mass, arrayed with a variety of bodies, whether they were true bodies or bodies that I had feigned for the spiritual beings. I formed this huge mass, not as great as it actually was, which I could not know, but as great as I thought proper, yet finite in its every aspect. I imagined, Lord, that you encircled it on every side and penetrated it, but you remained everywhere infinite. It was as if there were a sea, one single sea, that was everywhere and on all sides infinite over boundless reaches. It held within itself a sort of sponge, huge indeed, but yet finite, and this sponge was filled in every part by that boundless sea.[1] Thus did I conjecture that your finite creation was filled by you, the infinite, and I said:

"Behold God, and behold what God has created! God is good. Most mightily and most immeasurably does he surpass these things. But being good, he has created good things. Behold how he encircles and fills all things! Where then is evil, and whence and by what means has it crept in here? What is its root, and what is its seed? Or has it no being whatsoever? Why then do we fear and shun what does not exist? If we fear it without cause, that very fear is evil. By it our stricken hearts are goaded and tortured, and that evil is all the more serious in so far as what we fear does not exist, and still we are fearful of it. Therefore, either there is an evil that we fear,

Book 7. Problems of Thought and Belief

or the fact that we fear is itself an evil. Whence, therefore, is evil, since God the good has made all these things good? He, the greater, the supreme good, has made these lesser goods, yet both creator and all created things are good. Whence comes evil? Was there a certain evil matter, out of which he made these things? Did he form and fashion it, but yet leave within it something that he would not convert into good? Why would he do this? Was he powerless to turn and change all this matter, so that no evil would remain in it, even though he is all-powerful? Lastly, why should he will to make anything at all out of it, and not rather by that same omnipotence cause that it should not exist at all? Or forsooth, did it have the power to exist against his will? If it were eternal, why did he permit it to exist so far back throughout infinite ages of time? Why was he pleased so long after to fashion something out of it? Or if he now suddenly willed to take some action, would not the omnipotent cause rather it not to exist, and for himself alone to exist, the whole true and supreme and infinite good? Or if it were not good for him who is good to refrain from fashioning and creating something good, then, after that evil matter had been removed and reduced to nothing, would he not establish good matter, out of which he would create all things? He would not be omnipotent, if he were unable to create anything good, unless he were assisted by that matter which he had not created."

Such things I turned over within my unhappy breast, overladen with gnawing cares that came from the fear of death and from not finding the truth. Yet the faith of your Christ, our Lord and Savior,[2] the faith that is in the Catholic Church, was firmly fixed within my heart. In many ways I was as yet unformed and I wavered from the rule of doctrine. But my mind did not depart from it, nay, rather, from day to day it drank in more and more of it.

Chapter 6
Astrologists and Horoscopes

(8) By this time also I had rejected the deceitful divinations and impious ravings of the astrologists. For this too, O

my God, let your own mercies confess to you from the deepest depths of my soul. For you, you alone—for who else calls us back from the death of every error except that life which cannot die, that wisdom which needs no light itself but enlightens every mind that needs it, by which the whole world is ruled, down even to the quivering leaves on the trees?—you alone had concern for my obstinacy, by which I struggled against Vindicianus,[1] that keen old man, and Nebridius, a young man admirable in mind. The first affirmed vehemently and the second said frequently, although with some hesitation, that there is no art of foreseeing the future, and that men's conjectures are often assisted by chance: for since they say many things, some of them actually come to pass, and apart from any knowledge in the speakers, they hit upon these things by the mere fact that they do not remain silent.

You provided me with a friend who was neither a foolish client of the astrologers nor one well versed in their studies, but, still, as I said, a curious consultor of them. Furthermore, he had some knowledge, which he said he had heard from his father, but he did not know how it would serve to topple over his belief in that art. This man, Firminus by name, who was possessed of a liberal education and well trained in rhetoric, consulted me, as one of his dearest friends, as to what I might think, in the light of his so-called constellations, about certain of his affairs, upon which his worldly ambitions were taking rise. I had already begun to incline towards Nebridius's opinion in this matter, but I did not refuse to interpret them and to tell him what came into my mind, still undecided as it was. However, I submitted that I was now almost persuaded that these are empty and ridiculous fables. He then told me that his father was very much addicted to such books, and had a friend who studied them at the same time and with equal passion. By joint study and discussion they so fanned in their hearts the desire for such trifles that they even made observations on the moments when their dumb animals were born, if they were brought forth at home, and noted the position of the heavens at those times. From these things they would gather proofs for their so-called art.

He told me that he had heard from his father that, when

Book 7. Problems of Thought and Belief

his mother was carrying himself, Firminus, a servant of one of his father's friends was likewise pregnant. This fact did not escape her master, who even took pains to know by very careful examination the time when his dogs littered. Thus, while the two men, one for his own wife, the other for his servant, by most painstaking observations, figured out the day, the hour, and the most minute particles of the hour, both women were delivered at the same time. As a result, they were compelled to draw up identical horoscopes, right down to the same minute, for each of the newborn infants, one man for his son, the other for his tiny slave. For when the women began to be in labor, each man indicated to the other what was happening in his home. They arranged to send messengers to each other, as soon as the expected birth was announced to them. Each man in his own estate easily provided for word to be sent immediately. The messengers sent by the two men met, he said, exactly at the midpoint between their houses, so that neither of them could determine a different position for the stars or different moments of time. However, Firminus, who was born to an ample estate within his own family, ran his course on life's brighter paths, increased in wealth, and rose to places of honor, whereas that slave served his masters with never a lightening of the yoke of his condition, as I was told by Firminus, who knew him.

(9) After I had listened to and believed this story, for such a man had related it, all that reluctance of mine was dissolved and gave way. First, I attempted to recall Firminus from that fond study. I said to him that, after I had inspected his horoscope, if I were to make true predictions, I would surely have to see therein his parents, eminent among their fellow citizens, a family nobly placed in its city, gentle birth, good education, and liberal learning. But if that slave had consulted me about the same horoscope, for the two were identical, I ought again, so as to speak truly to him also, see therein a family most abjectly poor, a servile condition of life, and other things far different and far removed from the first. Hence it would be that from an inspection of the same horoscope I would state different things, if I were to speak the truth, but if I made identical statements, I would speak falsely. From this I gath-

ered with absolute certainty that any true statements made after an inspection of such horoscopes would be uttered not by art but by luck, while false statements would be made not out of ignorance of the art but by the trickery of chance.

(10) Having taken this approach to the problem, I ruminated within myself upon related things. So that none of the dotards following such a trade, whom I longed to attack right off and to refute with ridicule, might object to me that either Firminus had given me a false account or his father had given him one, I turned my attention to those who are born twins. For the most part, one issues from the womb so close upon the other that that brief difference in time, however great the power they may claim it to have in the nature of things, cannot be determined by human observation, nor can it be written down at all in those tables which the astrologer must inspect in order to make true predictions. Yet they will never be true, for after inspecting the same tables, he must say the same things of both Esau and Jacob, although the same things did not befall both men. Therefore, he would make false statements; or if he made true ones, he would not be saying the same things. Yet he inspected the same tables. Not by art, therefore, but by chance would he make true statements.

For you, O Lord, most just ruler of the universe, while both those who consult and those who are consulted in this way know nothing of it, by a hidden inspiration bring it about that, according to the secret merits of men's souls, the consultor may hear what he ought to hear out of the depths of your just judgment.[2] Let no man say to you, "What is this?"[3] or "Why is that?" Let him not say it, let him not say it, for he is man.

Chapter 7
A Soul Still Tormented

(11) But now, O my helper,[1] you had freed me from my chains, and still I asked, "Whence is evil?" but there was no way out. Yet in none of those wavering thoughts did you let me be carried away from that faith in which I believed both that you exist, and that your substance is unchangeable, and that you have care over men and pass judgment on them, and

Book 7. Problems of Thought and Belief

that in Christ, your Son, our Lord, and in the Holy Scriptures, which the authority of your Catholic Church approves, you have placed the way of man's salvation unto that life which is to be after this death. These truths being made safe and fixed immovably in my mind, I asked uncertainly "Whence is evil?" What torments there were in my heart in its time of labor, O my God, what groans! Still were your ears turned to me, although I knew it not! When I sought an answer, bravely but in silence, the unspoken sufferings of my soul were mighty cries for your mercy. You knew what I suffered, but no man knew of it. How much of that torment did my tongue direct from there into the ears of my closest friends! Did my soul's tumult, for which neither time nor my tongue sufficed, ever resound in their ears? But all that "I roared with the groaning of my heart"[2] went into your ears, and "my desire was before you, but the light of my eyes was not with me."[3] It was within; I was outside, but it was not in any place. I was intent on the things that are contained in places, but among them I found no place of rest, nor did they receive me, so that I might say, "It is enough, and it is well." Nor did they permit me to return to where it would indeed be well with me. I was superior to those things, but inferior to you, for you are the true joy for me who am subject to you, and all those things which you have created inferior to me you have made subject to me.

This was the right mean, and the middle region of my salvation, to remain in your image, and by serving you to subdue my body. But when I would rise up in pride against you, and run against the Lord with the thick boss of my shield,[4] even those lowest things were set against me and pressed down upon me, and there was never relief or breathing spell. From all sides they rushed upon me in hordes and heaps as I gazed at them, and as I took thought and turned back from them, the images of bodily things set upon me, as if to say, "Where are you going, O foul and unworthy man?" Such things grew out of my wound, for you humble the proud man, like one who has been wounded.[5] By my swelling wound I was separated from you, and my badly bloated face closed up my eyes.

Chapter 8
God's Healing Hand

(12) But you, O Lord, abide forever,[1] and you will not be angry with us forever,[2] for you have mercy on earth and ashes,[3] and it has been pleasing in your sight to reform my deformities. By inner goads you aroused me,[4] so that I did not rest until you stood plain before my inner sight. By the secret hand of your Physician[5] my swelling wound subsided, and day by day my mind's afflicted and darkened eyes grew sounder under the healing salve[6] of sorrow.

Chapter 9
Sacred Scripture and Pagan Philosophy[1]

(13) It was first your will to show me how you resist the proud and give grace to the humble,[2] and how great is your mercy in showing men the way of humility, for the reason that "the Word was made flesh, and dwelt among" men.[3] Therefore, by means of a certain man[4] puffed up with most unnatural pride, you procured for me certain books of the Platonists[5] that had been translated out of Greek into Latin.[6] In them I read, not indeed in these words but much the same thought, enforced by many varied arguments, that

"In the beginning was the Word, and the Word was with God, and the Word was God. The same was in the beginning with God. All things were made by him, and without him nothing was made. What was made, in him is life, and the life was the light of men. And the light shines in darkness, and the darkness did not comprehend it."[7]

I read that the soul of man, although it gives testimony of the light, is not itself the light, but the Word, God himself, is "the true light, which enlightens every man that comes into this world," and that "he was in the world, and the world was made by him, and the world knew him not."

But that "he came unto his own, and his own did not receive him, but as many as received him, to them he gave power

Book 7. Problems of Thought and Belief

to be made the sons of God, to them that believe in his name,"[8] this I did not read in those books.

(14) Again, I read there that the Word, God, was born, not of the flesh, nor of blood, "nor of the will of man, nor of the will of the flesh, but of God." But I did not read there that "the Word was made flesh, and dwelt among us."[9]

I found out in those books, though it was said differently and in many ways, that the Son, "being in the form of the Father, thought it not robbery to be equal with God," for by nature he is the same with him. But those books do not have it that he "emptied himself, taking the form of a servant, being made in the likeness of men, and in habit found as a man," and that "he humbled himself, becoming obedient unto death, even to the death of the cross. For which cause God also has exalted him" from the dead, "and has given him a name which is above all names: that in the name of Jesus every knee shall bend down of those that are in heaven, on earth, and under the earth: and that every tongue should confess that the Lord Jesus is in the glory of God the Father."[10]

That before all times and above all times your Only-begotten Son remains unchangeably coeternal with you; and that souls receive "of his fulness,"[11] so that they may be blessed; and that they are renewed by participation in the wisdom "remaining in herself,"[12] so as to be wise: these truths are found in those books.

But that "according to the time, he died for the ungodly," and that "you spared not your only Son, but delivered him up for us all"[13] is not there. For "you have hidden these things from the wise, and have revealed them to little ones," so that they who labor and are burdened might come to him and he would refresh them. For he is meek and humble of heart,[14] and he guides the meek in judgment, and he teaches the mild his ways, seeing our abjection and our labor, and forgiving all our sins.[15] But those men who are raised up on the heights of some toplofty teaching do not hear him as he says, "Learn of me, for I am meek and humble of heart, and you shall find rest to your souls."[16] "Although they know God, they do not glorify him, or give thanks, but become vain in their thoughts, and their foolish heart is darkened; for professing themselves to be wise, they became fools."[17]

(15) Therefore I also read there that "they changed the glory of your incorruption" into idols and various images, "into the likeness of the image of a corruptible man, and of birds, and of fourfooted beasts, and of creeping things," namely, into the Egyptian food by which Esau lost his birthright. For the first-born people worshiped the head of a fourfold beast instead of you, "and in their hearts turned back into Egypt,"[18] and bent your image, their own souls, before "the likeness of a calf that eats hay."[19] These things I found there, but I did not feed upon them.

It pleased you, Lord, to remove the reproach of a lesser status from Jacob, so that "the elder should serve the younger," and you called the Gentiles into your inheritance.[20] I had come to you from among the Gentiles, and I set my mind on that gold which you willed your people to take out of Egypt, for it was yours wherever it was. To the Athenians you said through your Apostle that in you "we live, and move, and have our being," as indeed some of them have said.[21] In truth these books were from the Gentiles. But I did not set my mind upon the idols of the Egyptians, which they served with your gold, they "who changed the truth of God into a lie; and worshipped and served the creature rather than the Creator."[22]

Chapter 10
The Infinite Light

(16) Being thus admonished to return to myself, under your leadership I entered into my inmost being. This I could do, for you became my helper.[1] I entered there, and by my soul's eye, such as it was, I saw above that same eye of my soul, above my mind, an unchangeable light. It was not this common light, plain to all flesh, nor a greater light, as it were, of the same kind, as though that light would shine many, many times more bright, and by its great power fill the whole universe. Not such was that light, but different, far different from all other lights. Nor was it above my mind, as oil is above water, or sky above earth. It was above my mind, because

it made me, and I was beneath it, because I was made by it. He who knows the truth, knows that light, and he who knows it knows eternity. Love knows it, O eternal truth, and true love, and beloved eternity! You are my God, and I sigh for you day and night!

When first I knew you, you took me up,[2] so that I might see that there was something to see, but that I was not yet one able to see it. You beat back my feeble sight, sending down your beams most powerfully upon me, and I trembled with love and awe. I found myself to be far from you in a region of unlikeness, as though I heard your voice from on high: "I am the food of grown men. Grow, and you shall feed upon me. You will not change me into yourself, as you change food into your flesh, but you will be changed into me." I knew that "you have corrected man for iniquity, and you have made my soul to waste away like a spider,"[3] and I said, "Is truth nothing, because it is diffused neither through finite nor through infinite space?" From afar you cried to me, "I am who am."[4] I heard, as one hears in his heart; there was no further place for doubt, for it would be easier for me to doubt that I live than that there is no truth, which is "clearly seen, being understood by the things that are made."[5]

Chapter 11
Finite and Infinite

(17) I beheld other things below you, and I saw that they are not altogether existent nor altogether non-existent: they are, because they are from you; they are not, since they are not what you are. For that truly exists which endures unchangeably. "But it is good for me to adhere to my God,"[1] for if I do not abide in him, neither will I be able to abide in myself. But he abides in himself, and he renews all things.[2] "You are my Lord, for you have no need of my goods."[3]

Chapter 12
Every Being Is Good

(18) It was made manifest to me that beings that suffer corruption are nevertheless good. If they were supremely good, they could not be corrupted, but unless they were good, they could not be corrupted. If they were supremely good, they would be incorruptible, and if they were not good at all, there would be nothing in them to be corrupted. Corruption damages a thing, and it would not suffer damage unless its good were diminished. Therefore, either corruption damages nothing, and this cannot be, or whatever suffers corruption is deprived of some good, and this fact is most certain. If things are deprived of all good whatsoever, they will not exist at all. If they continue to be, and still continue incapable of suffering corruption, they will be better than before, because they will remain forever incorruptible.

What is more monstrous than to claim that things become better by losing all their good? Therefore, if they are deprived of all good, they will be absolutely nothing. Hence, as long as they exist, they are good. Therefore, whatsoever things exist are good. But evil, of which I asked "Whence is it?" is not a substance, for if it were a substance, it would be good. Either it would be an incorruptible substance, a great good indeed, or it would be a corruptible substance, and it would not be corruptible unless it were good. Hence I saw and it was made manifest to me that you have made all things good, and that there are no substances whatsoever that you have not made. Since you have not made all things equal, it follows that all things, taken one by one, are good, and all things, taken together, are very good. For our God has made all things very good.[1]

Chapter 13
Universal Good

(19) To you, nothing whatsoever is evil, and not only to you but also to your whole creation, for outside of it there is

nothing that can break in and disrupt the order that you have imposed upon it. Among its parts, certain things are thought to be evil because they do not agree with certain others. Yet these same beings agree with others still, and thus they are good, and they are also good in themselves. All these beings, which do not harmonize with one another, nevertheless are in keeping with that lower part of things, which we call the earth, which has a cloudy and windy sky of its own that is congruous to itself.

Let me never say, "These things should not be!" If I considered them alone, I might desire better things; but still for them alone I ought to praise you. That you must be praised all these show forth: from the earth, dragons, and all the deeps, fire, hail, snow, ice, stormy winds, which fulfill your word, mountains and all hills, fruitful trees and all cedars, beasts and all cattle, serpents and feathered fowls; kings of the earth and all people, princes and all judges of the earth, young men and maidens, the old with the younger; let them praise your name.[1] And from the heavens also let these praise you, let these praise you, our God, in the high places, all your angels, all your hosts, the sun and the moon, all stars and light, the heavens of heavens, and the waters that are above the heavens, let them praise your name.[2]

No more did I long for better things, because I thought of all things, and with a sounder judgment I held that the higher things are indeed better than the lower, but that all things together are better than the higher things alone.

Chapter 14
A Return to Idolatry

(20) There is no health[1] in them to whom any part of your creation is displeasing, nor was there health in me, when many of the things that you had made displeased me. Since my soul did not dare to be displeased at my God, it would not admit that anything displeasing to it was your work. From there it turned to the theory of two substances, but it found no rest in it, and uttered the errors of other men. Turning away from that belief, my soul fashioned for itself a god that filled all the

places in infinite space. It thought that this god was you, and set it up in its heart. Thus it again became the temple of its own idol, a thing abominable before you. But afterwards you soothed my head, unknown to me, and closed my eyes, lest they see vanity,[2] I turned[3] a little from myself, and my madness was lulled to sleep. I awoke in you, and I saw that you are infinite, although in a different way, and this vision was not derived from the flesh.

Chapter 15
The Temporal and the Eternal

(21) I looked back over other things, and I saw that they owe their being to you, and that all finite things are in you. They are there, not as though in a place, but in a different fashion, because you contain all things in your hand by your truth. All things are true, in so far as they have being, nor is there any falsity, except when that is thought to be which is not. I saw that all things are in harmony not only with their proper places, but also with their seasons. I saw that you, who alone are eternal, did not make a beginning to your works after innumerable ages had passed, because all ages, both those which have passed, and those which will come to pass, neither depart nor come to be except by your activity and your abiding presence.

Chapter 16
The Relative and the Absolute

(22) From experience, I knew it is no strange thing that the bread that pleases a healthy appetite is offensive to one that is not healthy, and that light is hateful to sick eyes, but welcome to the well. Your justice offends the wicked, much more do the viper and the worm, which you have created good and in keeping with those lower parts of your creation, to which the wicked themselves are adapted. For they are in harmony with those lower things in so far as they are unlike you, but they are in harmony with higher things, in so far as they become liker to you.

I asked, "What is iniquity?" and I found that it is not a substance. It is perversity of will, twisted away from the supreme substance, yourself, O God, and towards lower things, and casting away its own bowels,[1] and swelling beyond itself.

CHAPTER 17

A Momentary Vision

(23) I marveled that now I loved you, and not a phantom in your stead. Yet I was not steadfast in enjoyment of my God: I was borne up to you by your beauty, but soon I was borne down from you by my own weight, and with groaning, I plunged into the midst of those lower things. This weight was carnal custom. Still there remained within me remembrance of you: I did not doubt in any way that there was one to cleave to, nor did I doubt that I was not yet one who would cleave to him. "For the corruptible body is a load upon the soul, and the earthly habitation presses down upon the mind that muses upon many things."[1] Yet I was most certain that your "invisible things, from the foundation of the world, are clearly seen, being understood by the things that are made," your "eternal power also, and divinity."[2]

Searching into why it was that I gave approval to the beauty of bodies, whether in the heavens or on earth, and what helped me to make sound judgments, and to say, "This should be thus and so, and that not," searching, then, into why I passed such judgments, for I did pass them, I had found that immutable, true, and eternal truth which exists above my changeable mind. Thus I gradually passed from bodies to the soul, which perceives by means of the body, and thence to its interior power, to which the bodily senses present exterior things—beasts too are capable of doing this much—and thence again to the reasoning power, to which what is apprehended by the bodily senses is referred for judgment. When this power found itself to be in me a variable thing, it raised itself up to its own understanding. It removed its thought from the tyranny of habit, and withdrew itself from the throngs of contradictory phantasms. In this way it might find that light by which it was sprinkled, when it cried out, that beyond all doubt the immutable must be preferred to the mutable. Hence it might come to know this immutable being, for unless it could know it in some way, it could in no wise have set it with certainty above the mutable. Thus in a flash of its trembling sight it came to that which is. Then indeed I clearly saw your "invisible things, understood by the things which are made." But I was unable to fix my gaze on them. In my frailty I was struck back, and I returned to my former ways. I took with me only a memory, loving and longing for what I had, as it were, caught the odor of, but was not yet able to feed upon.[3]

Chapter 18
The Way of Humility

(24) I sought for a way of gaining strength sufficient for me to have joy in you, but I did not find it until I embraced "the mediator between God and man, the man Christ Jesus, who is over all things, God blessed forever."[1] He called to me, and said, "I am the way of truth, and the life."[2] He mingled that food,[3] which I was unable to receive, with our flesh, for "the Word was made flesh,"[4] so that your Wisdom, by which you created all things, might provide milk for our infant condition. I did not hold fast to Jesus my God, a humble man clinging to him who was humble, nor did I know in what thing his lowliness would be my teacher. Your Word, eternal truth, surpassingly above the highest parts of your universe, raised up there to himself those who had been brought low. Amid the lower parts he has built for himself out of our clay a lowly dwelling, in which he would protect from themselves those ready to become submissive to him, and bring them to himself. He heals their swellings, and nourishes their love, so that they may not go on further in self-confidence, but rather become weak. For at their feet they see the Godhead, weak[5] because of its participation in our "coats of skin,"[6] and in their weariness they may cast themselves upon it, while it arises and lifts them up.

Chapter 19
The Divinity of Jesus Christ

(25) But I had other thoughts:[1] I conceived my Lord Christ only as a man of surpassing wisdom, whom no other man could equal. Above all, because he was born in a wondrous manner of the Virgin, to give us an example of despising temporal things in order to win immortality, he seemed by the godlike care that he had for us, to have merited such great authority as a teacher. But what mystery was contained within those words, "The Word was made flesh,"[2] I could not conceive. But of what has been handed down in writing concerning him, namely, that he ate and drank, slept, walked about, was joyful, grew sad, and preached, I had learned only that that flesh did not cleave to your Word except together with a human soul and mind. Any man who has knowledge of the immutability of your Word knows this: I knew it at that time, as far as I could know it, and had no doubt whatsoever concerning it. Now to move one's bodily members at the command of the will, and now not to move them; now to be affected by some emotion, and now not to be affected; now to utter wise judgments by means of signs, and now to remain silent —such things belong to a soul and a mind that are subject to change. If these things were written falsely of him, then all else would be in danger of being false, and no saving faith for mankind would remain in those Scriptures. But since the things written are true, I acknowledged that in Christ there was a complete man: not merely a man's body, nor an animating principle in the body but without a mind, but a true man.[3] I accounted him a person to be preferred above all other men, not as the person of Truth, but because of some great excellence of his human nature and a more perfect participation in wisdom.[4]

Alypius, on the other hand, thought that Catholics believed that God was clothed in flesh in such wise that in Christ there was no soul, in addition to his divinity and his body. Nor did he think that a human mind was attributed to him. Because he was firmly convinced that the deeds recorded of him could only be done by a creature possessed of life and reason, he moved more slowly towards the Christian faith. However, he learned later that this was the error of the Apollinarian heretics,[5] and he was pleased with the Catholic faith and better disposed towards it. It was somewhat after this, I admit, that I learned how, with regard to those words, "The Word was made flesh," Catholic truth is distinguished from the false teaching of Photinus.[6] In fact, the refutation of heresies causes what your Church thinks, and what sound doctrine holds, to stand out.[7] "For there must be heresies, so that those who are approved may become manifest among the weak."[8]

Chapter 20
The Soul's True Country

(26) At that time, after reading those books of the Platonists and being instructed by them to search for incorporeal truth, I clearly saw your invisible things which "are understood by the things that are made."[1] Although pushed backwards in my search, I perceived what that was which, because of my mind's darkness, I was not permitted to contemplate. I was made certain that you exist, that you are infinite, although not diffused throughout spaces, either finite or infinite, that you are truly he who is always the same, with no varied parts and changing movements, and that all other things are from you, as is known by one single most solid proof, the fact that they exist. Of these truths I was most certain, but I was too weak to find my joy in you. I prated as if I were well instructed, but I did not know enough to seek your way in Christ our Savior. I had not perished, but I was on the road to perdition.

Now I began to desire to appear wise. Filled up with punishment for my sins,[2] I did not weep over them, but rather was I puffed up with knowledge. Where was that charity which builds upon the foundation of humility, which is Christ Jesus? When would those books teach it to me? It is for this reason, I believe, that you wished me to come upon those books before I read your Scriptures, so that the way I was affected by them might be stamped upon my memory. Hence, later on, when I was made gentle by your books, and my wounds had been treated by your soothing fingers, I would be able to detect and distinguish how great a difference lies between presumption and contrition, and between those who see where they must travel, but do not see the way, and those who see the way that leads not only to beholding our blessed fatherland but also to dwelling therein. If I had first been formed by your Sacred Scriptures and if you had grown sweet to me by my familiar use of them, and I had afterwards happened on those other volumes, they might have drawn me away from the solid foundation of religion. Or else, even if I had persisted in those salutary dispositions which I had drunk in, I might have thought that if a man studied those books alone, he could conceive the same thoughts from them.[3]

Chapter 21
The Pilgrim Way

(27) So it was with the most intense desire that I seized upon the sacred writings of your Spirit, and especially the Apostle Paul. Those difficult passages,[1] where at one time he seemed to me to contradict himself, and where the text of his discourse appeared to be at variance with the testimonies of the law and the prophets, melted away. I saw those pure writings as having one single aspect, and I learned to exult with joy.[2] I made a beginning, and whatever truths I had read in those other works I here found to be uttered along with the praise of your grace, so that whosoever sees may not glory, as if he had not received[3] not merely what he sees but also his very ability to see. For what does he possess which he has not received?[4] Also, it is that he may be admonished not only to see you who are always the same,[5] but also that he may be made strong to hold fast to you. Again, it is that he who cannot see from afar off may yet walk upon that way whereby he may come to you, and see you, and hold fast to you. For although a man may be delighted with the law of God, according to the inward man, what shall he do with that other law in his members, fighting against the law of his mind, and making him captive in the law of sin, which is in his members?[6]

For you are just, O Lord, but we have sinned, and committed iniquity, and have acted wickedly,[7] and your hand is heavy upon us,[8] and we have been justly delivered over to that ancient sinner, the lord of death,[9] because he persuaded our wills to be like his will, whereby he stood not in the truth.[10]

What shall an unhappy man do? "Who shall deliver me from the body of this death," unless it is by your grace, "through Jesus Christ, our Lord,"[11] whom you have begotten coeternal with yourself, and created in the beginning of your ways,[12] in whom the prince of this world found nothing worthy of death,[13] and yet killed him? And the handwriting of the decree that was against us was blotted out.[14]

All this those writings of the Platonists do not have. Their pages do not have this face of piety, the tears of confession, your sacrifice, a troubled spirit, a contrite and a humbled heart,[15] the salvation of your people, the city that is like a bride,[16] the pledge of the spirit,[17] the cup of our redemption. In those books no one sings: "Shall not my soul be subject to God? For he is my God and my savior, my protector. I shall be moved no more."[18] In them no man hears him calling to us: "Come unto me, all you that labor."[19] They scorn to learn of him because he is meek and humble of heart. "For you have hid these things from the wise and prudent, and have revealed them to little ones."[20]

It is one thing to behold from a wooded mountain peak the land of peace,[21] but to find no way to it, and to strive in vain towards it by unpassable ways, ambushed and beset by fugitives and deserters, under their leader, the lion and the dragon.[22] It is a different thing to keep to the way that leads to that land, guarded by the protection of the heavenly commander, where no deserters from the heavenly army lie in wait like bandits. They shun that way, like a torture. In a wondrous way all these things penetrated my very vitals, when I read the words of that least of your apostles,[23] and meditated upon your works, and trembled at them.[24]

BOOK 8
THE GRACE OF FAITH

Chapter 1
Truth Seen but not Followed

(1) With thanksgiving let me remember, O my God, all your mercies to me and let me confess them to you. Let my bones be filled with your love, and let them say to you: "Lord, who is like unto you?"[1] You have broken my bonds. I will sacrifice to you the sacrifice of praise."[2] I will narrate how you broke them asunder. And when they hear these things, let all who adore you say: "Blessed be the Lord, in heaven and on earth. Great and wonderful is his name."[3]

Your words had stuck fast in the depths of my heart, and on every side I was encompassed by you. I was now certain that you are eternal life, although I saw it only "in a glass, in a dark manner."[4] Yet all my doubts concerning incorruptible substance, and that every other substance comes from it, had been removed from me. It was not to be more certain concerning you, but to be more steadfast in you that I desired. But in my temporal life all things were uncertain, and my heart had to be cleansed of the old leaven.[5] The way, the Savior himself, had become pleasing, but as yet I was loath to tread its narrow passes. You put it into my mind, and it seemed good to my sight, to turn to Simplicianus,[6] who appeared to me to be a good servant of yours, for in him your grace shone bright. I had also heard that from his youth he had lived most devoutly in your service. At that time he had grown old, and because of long years spent in following your way with such good zeal, I thought that he was one who had experienced many things and learned many things. In truth, he was such a one. Hence I wished that after I had discussed my problems with him, he would show me the proper manner for one affected like me to walk in your way.

(2) I saw that the Church was full of men, of whom one went this way, another that. I was displeased with the course I followed in the world, and with my desires no longer aflame with hope of honor and wealth, as they had been, to bear so grievous a bondage was a very great burden to me. In comparison with your sweetness and the beauty of your house, which I loved,[7] those things no longer gave me delight, but I was still tightly bound by love of women. However, your apostle did not forbid me to marry, although he exhorted me to something better, especially wishing that all men would be like himself.[8] But I was weaker and chose the softer place. For this one thing I was tossed all about in other ways: I was faint and I wasted away with withering cares. For in other matters, which I had no wish to endure, I was forced to adapt myself to that conjugal life, which I had given myself to and by which I was therefore restricted.

From the mouth of your truth I had learned that there are eunuchs who made themselves such for the kingdom of heaven, but he also says, "He that can take it, let him take it."[9] Surely "all men are vain in whom there is not the knowledge of God: and who by these good things that are seen could not understand, could not find, him who is."[10] I was no longer in that vanity! I had passed beyond it, and by the testimony of the whole creation I had found you our creator, and your Word, who is God with you, and who is one God with you, through whom you created all things.

There is another class of impious men, who "knowing God, have not glorified him as God, or given thanks."[11] Into this group also I had fallen, but your right hand[12] raised me up, and took me out of it, and you placed me where I might grow strong again. For you have said to man: "Behold, piety is wisdom,"[13] and "Do not desire to appear wise,"[14] "for professing themselves to be wise, they became fools."[15] But I had now found the good pearl, and this I must buy, after selling all that I had.[16] Yet still I hesitated.

Chapter 2
The Conversion of Victorinus

(3) I went, then, to Simplicianus, the father, as to his reception of grace,[1] of Ambrose, the then bishop, and by him loved as a father. To him I recounted the winding ways of my errors. When I recorded how I had read certain books of the Platonists, translated into the Latin language by Victorinus,[2] sometime professor of rhetoric at Rome, who, I had heard, had died a Christian, he congratulated me because I had not fallen in with the writings of other philosophers, full of fallacies and deceits according to the elements of this world,[3] whereas in the works of the Platonists God and his Word are introduced in all manners. Thereupon, in order to exhort me to accept Christ's humility, "hidden from the wise and revealed to little ones,"[4] he spoke of Victorinus himself, whom he had known intimately when he was in Rome. He told me certain things about him that I will not pass over in silence, as they involve an instance of that great praise of your grace[5] which must be confessed to you. For that aged man, most learned and most highly skilled in all liberal studies, had read through and passed judgment on many philosophical works and had been the teacher of many noble senators. He had even merited and obtained a statue in the Roman forum as a memorial of his outstanding teaching, which citizens of this world deem a great honor. Right up to his old age, he had been a worshiper of idols and a communicant in sacrilegious rites, with which almost the entire Roman nobility was then inflated. By such rites they inspired the people with the cult of Osiris,[6] and every kind of god, monsters, and barking Anubis, which at one time had borne arms against Neptune and Venus, and against Minerva.[7] These gods, whom Rome had once conquered, she now adored. Over the course of many years, the aged Victorinus himself had defended them with thunderous and terrifying eloquence. But now he did not blush to become the child of your Christ and a newborn infant at your font,[8] to bend his neck under the yoke of humility, and to lower his brow before the reproach of the cross.[9]

(4) Lord, Lord, you who have bowed down the heavens and have descended, you who have touched the mountains and they have smoked,[10] by what means did you wend your way into his breast? He used to read Holy Writ, as Simplicianus has said, and he studiously searched into and examined all Christian writings. He said to Simplicianus, not openly, but privately and as a friend, "You should know that I am already a Christian." But he answered, "I will not believe it, nor will I reckon you among Christians, unless I see you in the Church of Christ." The other laughed and said, "Is it walls, then, that make men Christians?" He often said that he was already a Christian; Simplicianus just as often made his reply; and just as often he made his joke about the walls. He was afraid of offending his friends, the proud worshipers of demons. He thought that from their lofty seat of honor in Babylon,[11] as from cedars of Lebanon, which the Lord had not yet broken down,[12] the heavy weight of their enmity would rush down upon him.

Afterwards, through reading and longing, he drank in strength. He feared that he would be denied by Christ before the angels if he now feared to confess him before men.[13] He saw himself as guilty of a great crime by being ashamed of the mysteries of the humility of your Word, while not being ashamed of the sacrilegious rites of proud demons, which he had proudly imitated and accepted. He put aside shame from vanity and became modest before the truth. Suddenly and unexpectedly, he said to Simplicianus, who has himself described it, "Let us go to the church. I wish to become a Christian." Unable to contain himself for joy, Simplicianus went with him. There he was granted the initial sacraments of instruction,[14] and not long after he gave in his name, so that he might be reborn in baptism. Rome stood in wonder, and the Church rejoiced. The proud saw, and were angry; they gnashed their teeth, and pined away.[15] But the Lord God was the hope of his servant, and he had no regard for vanities and lying follies.[16]

(5) At length the hour came for him to make his profession of faith.[17] At Rome, those who are about to approach your grace usually deliver this profession from an elevated place,

in the sight of your faithful people, in set words which they have learned and committed to memory. To Victorinus, he said, the priests gave permission to make the profession in private, as it was the custom to allow this to those who looked as if they would be self-conscious and upset. However, he preferred to make profession of his salvation in the sight of that holy throng. What he taught in his school of rhetoric was not salvation, and yet he taught it publicly. How much less, then, should he dread your meek flock when he affirmed your Word, since he had never dreaded to pronounce his own words before throngs of madmen! Hence, when he arose to make his profession, all who knew him uttered his name to one another with a murmur of congratulation. And who among them did not know him? A suppressed sound issued from the mouths of all those who rejoiced together, "Victorinus! Victorinus!" Suddenly, as they saw him, they gave voice to their joy, and just as suddenly they became silent in order to hear him. He pronounced the true faith with splendid confidence, and they all desired to clasp him to their hearts. By their love and joy they clasped him to themselves. Those were the hands by which they clasped him.

Chapter 3
The Law of Contrasts

(6) O God the good, what goes on within a man that he should rejoice more over the salvation of a soul that had been despaired of, and was then set free of a greater peril, than if there had always been hope for him, or if his danger had been less? Merciful Father, you too rejoice more over one man who does penance than over ninety-nine just men who do not need penance. We listen with great gladness as we hear how the sheep that had strayed away is brought back on the joyful shepherd's shoulders, and how the drachma is restored to your treasure house, while the neighbors rejoice with the woman who has found it. The joyous festivities within your home wring tears from our eyes when the story is read in your house of how your younger son was dead and is come to life again, was lost and is found.[1] In truth, you rejoice in us and in your

angels, who are holy in holy charity. For you are always the same, but things that do not exist forever or in the same way, all these you know forever and in the same way.

(7) What is it, therefore, that goes on within the soul, since it takes greater delight if things that it loves are found or restored to it than if it had always possessed them? Other things bear witness to this, and all are filled with proofs that cry aloud, "Thus it is!" The victorious general holds his triumph: yet unless he had fought, he would never have won the victory, and the greater was the danger in battle, the greater is the joy in the triumph. The storm tosses seafarers about, and threatens them with shipwreck: they all grow pale at their coming death. Then the sky and the sea become calm, and they exult exceedingly, just as they had feared exceedingly. A dear friend is ill, and his pulse tells us of his bad case. All those who long to see him in good health are in mind sick along with him. He gets well again, and although he does not yet walk with his former vigor, there is joy such as did not obtain before when he walked well and strong.

Men gain these very pleasures of human life, not merely from any unexpected and unwanted troubles that happen to them, but from those that are planned and voluntary. There is no pleasure in eating and drinking unless the discomfort of hunger and thirst comes first. Men addicted to liquor eat certain salty foods so as to produce an annoying dryness, and when a drink allays this, pleasure results. It is the custom for affianced brides not to be given immediately in marriage, lest as husband a man hold in low esteem the woman given to him, whom as her betrothed he did not long for because she was kept from him.

(8) This same rule holds for foul and accursed joys; it holds for those that are permitted and lawful; it holds for the most sincere and virtuous friendship; it holds for him who was dead but now lives again, and for him who was lost and is now found. Everywhere a greater joy is preceded by a greater suffering. Why is this, O Lord my God, since you are eternal unto yourself, since you yourself are joy, and since there are beings that forever rejoice in you and about you?[2] Why is it that this particular rank of beings alternates between decline

and advance and between strife and harmony? Is this their proper measure? Is it so much only that you have given to them, when from the heights of heaven[3] down to the depths of the earth, from the beginning to the end of time, from the angel even to the worm, from the first movement up to the last, you seated, each in its proper place, all varieties of good things and all your just works, and caused them to be each in its proper season?

Woe is me! How high are you in the highest, and how deep are you in the depths? Nowhere do you depart from us, and we scarcely return to you.

Chapter 4
Mutual Joy

(9) Lead us, O Lord, and work within us: arouse us, and call us back; enkindle us, and draw us to you; grow fragrant and sweet to us. Let us love you, and let us run to you.[1] Are there not many men who, out of a deeper hell of blindness than Victorinus, have turned back to you and drawn near to you? Are they not enlightened, as they receive your light? For if they receive it, they also receive from you power to become your sons.[2] Yet if they are known to fewer people, so also those who know them rejoice less over them. For when many men rejoice together, there is a richer joy in each individual, since they enkindle themselves and they inflame one another.[3] Again, if they are well known to many men, they exercise authority towards salvation for many others, and they lead the way on which many others follow. Therefore, those also who have preceded them rejoice because of them, for the reason that they do not rejoice over them alone.[4]

Far be it from me to think that in your tabernacles there should be acceptance of persons,[5] of the rich before the poor, or of the noble before the baseborn. Rather, you have chosen the weak things of the world, that you may confound the strong, and the contemptible things, and those that are not, as if they are, that you might bring to naught things that are.[6] Yet even that same man, the least of your apostles,[7] by whose tongue you have uttered these words of yours, when Paulus the proconsul, whose pride had been conquered through that other's warfare, was sent to pass under the easy yoke of your Christ, and was made a private citizen of the great King, then, instead of his former name of Saul, was pleased to be called Paul as a token of so great a victory.[8]

A greater victory is won over the enemy in the case of a man upon whom he has a firmer hold and by means of whom he has hold on many others. He has more hold on the proud because of their lofty titles, and because of their name and authority, he has hold on many others. Hence the more grateful were their thoughts with regard to Victorinus's heart, which the devil had held as an impregnable fortress, and with regard to Victorinus's tongue, with which as a keen and powerful weapon he had slain so many, so much the more abundantly did it behoove your sons to rejoice because our King bound up the strong man,[9] and because they saw his vessels taken from him, and cleansed, and rendered fit for your honor, and made profitable to the Lord for every good work.[10]

Chapter 5
The Inner Conflict

(10) When Simplicianus, your servant, related to me all this concerning Victorinus, I was on fire to imitate him, and it was for this reason that he had told it to me. Afterwards he added to it how in Emperor Julian's time a law was passed by which Christians were forbidden to teach literature and oratory, and how he obeyed the law, and chose rather to give up his school for words than your Word, by which you make eloquent the tongues of infants.[1] Then he appeared to me to have been no more courageous than fortunate, since he found opportunity to devote himself to you alone. For this very thing did I sigh, bound as I was, not by another's irons but by my own iron will. The enemy[2] had control of my will, and out of it he fashioned a chain and fettered me with it. For in truth lust is made out of a perverse will, and when lust is served, it becomes habit, and when habit is not resisted, it becomes necessity. By such links, joined one to another, as it were—for this reason I have called it a chain—a harsh bondage held me

Book 8. The Grace of Faith

fast. A new will, which had begun within me, to wish freely to worship you and find joy in you, O God, the sole sure delight, was not yet able to overcome that prior will, grown strong with age. Thus did my two wills, the one old, the other new, the first carnal, and the second spiritual, contend with one another, and by their conflict they laid waste my soul.

(11) Thus I understood from my own experience what I had read, how "the flesh lusts against the spirit, and the spirit against the flesh."[3] I was in both camps, but I was more in that which I approved within myself than in that other which I disapproved within me. For now, in the latter, it was not so much myself, since in large part I suffered it against my will rather than did it voluntarily. Yet it was by me that this habit had been made so warlike against me, since I had come willingly to this point where I now willed not. Who can rightly argue against it, when just punishment comes upon the sinner? Nor did I any longer have that former excuse, in which I used to look upon myself as unable to despise the world and to serve you, because knowledge of the truth was still uncertain to me. Now indeed it was certain to me. Yet I was still bound to the earth, and I refused to become your soldier.[4] I was afraid to be lightened of all my heavy burden, even as I should have feared to be encumbered by it.

(12) Thus by the burdens of this world I was sweetly weighed down, just as a man often is in sleep. Thoughts wherein I meditated upon you were like the efforts of those who want to arouse themselves but, still overcome by deep drowsiness, sink back again. Just as no man would want to sleep forever, and it is the sane judgment of all men that it is better to be awake, yet a man often defers to shake off sleep when a heavy languor pervades all his members, and although the time to get up has come, he yields to it with pleasure even although it now irks him. In like manner, I was sure that it was better for me to give myself up to your love than to give in to my own desires. However, although the one way appealed to me and was gaining mastery, the other still afforded me pleasure and kept me victim. I had no answer to give to you when you said to me, "Rise, you who sleep, and arise from the dead, and Christ will enlighten you."[5] When on

all sides you showed me that your words were true, and I was overcome by your truth, I had no answer whatsoever to make, but only those slow and drowsy words, "Right away. Yes, right away." "Let me be for a little while." But "Right away—right away" was never right now, and "Let me be for a little while" stretched out for a long time.

In vain was I delighted with your law according to the inward man, when another law in my members fought against the law of my mind, and led me captive in the law of sin which was in my members.[6] For the law of sin is force of habit, whereby the mind is dragged along and held fast, even against its will, but still deservedly so, since it was by its will that it had slipped into the habit. Unhappy man that I was! Who would deliver me from the body of this death, unless your grace through Jesus Christ our Lord?[7]

Chapter 6
The Story of Ponticianus

(13) I will now recount and confess to your name,[1] "O Lord, my helper and my redeemer,"[2] how you delivered me from the fetters of desire for concubinage, by which I was held most tightly, and from the slavery of worldly concerns. I went about my accustomed tasks with ever increasing anxiety, and each day I sighed for you. I frequented your church whenever I was free from the burden of the tasks under which I groaned. Alypius was with me, since now, after his third term as assessor, he was relieved of his legal duties and was looking for clients to whom he might again sell his counsel, just as I sold skill at speech, if such skill can be imparted by teaching. By reason of our friendship, Nebridius had consented to teach under Verecundus, a citizen and grammarian of Milan and a very close friend to all of us, who urgently desired, and by right of friendship demanded from our group, the reliable assistance he needed so much. Nebridius was not attracted to this by desire for profit; if he wished for that, he could have gained greater rewards from his learning. But he was a very kind and agreeable friend, and out of duty to friendship he would not reject our request. He acted in a very prudent manner, as he

Book 8. The Grace of Faith

was on guard against becoming known to men who were great according to this world,[3] and he avoided among them all mental disturbance. He wished to keep his mind free and to have as much time as possible open to engage in study, to read, or to hear things concerning wisdom.

(14) One day when Nebridius was absent, for what reason I do not recall, there came to our home to visit me and Alypius a certain Ponticianus,[4] a countryman of ours, in so far as being from Africa, who held a high office at court. I do not know what he wanted from us, but we sat down to talk together. He chanced to notice a book lying upon a game table that stood before us. He took it up, opened it, and much to his surprise found that it was by the apostle Paul. He had thought that it was one or another of the books that I was wearing myself out in teaching. Whereupon he smiled and looked at me as if to congratulate me, and expressed surprise that he had suddenly found these writings and these alone before my eyes. For he was a faithful Christian, and often he prostrated himself before you, our God, in many long prayers within the church. When I told him how I expended very great pains upon those Scriptures, a discussion arose in which he narrated the story of Anthony, an Egyptian monk.[5] His name was famous among your servants, but up to that very hour it had been unknown to us. When he discovered this, he dwelt all the more on the subject, introducing this great man to us who were ignorant of him, and wondering at this same ignorance. We in turn stood in amazement on hearing such wonderful works[6] of yours, deeds of such recent memory, done so close to our own times, and most fully testified to, in the true faith and in the Catholic Church. All of us marveled at it, we because there had been such great wonders, and he because they had not been heard of by us.

(15) From this subject his discourse turned to the flocks within the monasteries and to their way of life, which is like a sweet-smelling odor to you, and to the fruitful deserts in the wilderness, of all of which we knew nothing. There was a monastery at Milan, filled with good brothers, situated outside the walls, under the fostering care of Ambrose, but we had not known about it. He proceeded with his account, and

we kept silent and attentive. Then it came about that he told us how he and three of his associates—just when I do not know, but it was at Trier[7]—one afternoon, when the emperor was attending the games at the circus, went out for a walk in the gardens along the walls. As they chanced to walk in pairs, one went apart with him and the other two wandered off by themselves. While wandering about, these two others came upon a certain house, where dwelled some of your servants, "poor in spirit, of whom is the kingdom of heaven,"[8] and there they found a little book in which was written the life of Anthony.

One of them began to read this book, to marvel at it, and to be aroused by it. As he read it, he began to meditate on taking up such a life, and to give up his worldly career and serve you. These two men were numbered among those whom they style special agents.[9] Then the reader, suddenly filled with holy love and by sober shame made angry with himself, turned his eyes upon his friend and said, "Tell me, I ask you, where will we get by all these labors of ours? What are we seeking for? To what purpose do we serve in office? What higher ambition can we have at court than to become friends of the emperor?[10] In such a position what is there that is not fragile and full of peril? By how many perils do we arrive at a greater peril? When will we get there? But to become God's friend, if I wish it, see, I become one here and now."

He spoke these words, and in anguish during this birth of a new life, he turned his eyes again upon those pages. He read on and was changed within himself, where your eye could see. His mind was stripped of this world, as soon became apparent. For as he read, and turned about on the waves of his heart, he raged at himself for a while, but then discerned better things and determined upon them. Already belonging to you, he said to his friend, "I have now broken away from our former hopes, and I have determined to serve God, and from this very hour and in this very place I make my start. If it is too much for you to imitate me, do not oppose me." The other answered that he would join him as a comrade for so great a reward and in so great a service. Both of them, being now yours, began to build a tower at that due cost[11] of leaving all that they had and following you.

Book 8. *The Grace of Faith*

By then Ponticianus and the man with him, who had walked in other parts of the garden, came in search of them in the same place, and on finding them, warned them that they must return, as the day was already late. The men told them of their resolution and purpose and how such a determination had sprung up and become established within them, and begged the others not to trouble them, even if they would refuse to join them. Ponticianus and his companion, although in no wise changed from their former state, nevertheless wept over it, as he affirmed, congratulated them devoutly, and recommended themselves to their prayers. Then, with hearts dragging along upon the earth, they returned to the palace, while the other two fixed their hearts on heaven and remained in the house. Both men had affianced brides, and when these women heard the story, they also dedicated their virginity to you.

Chapter 7
The Naked Self

(16) Ponticianus told us this story, and as he spoke, you, O Lord, turned me back upon myself. You took me from behind my own back, where I had placed myself because I did not wish to look upon myself. You stood me face to face with myself, so that I might see how foul I was, how deformed and defiled, how covered with stains and sores. I looked, and I was filled with horror, but there was no place for me to flee to away from myself. If I tried to turn my gaze from myself, he still went on with the story that he was telling, and once again you placed me in front of myself, and thrust me before my own eyes, so that I might find out my iniquity and hate it.[1] I knew what it was, but I pretended not to; I refused to look at it, and put it out of my memory.

(17) At that time, in truth, the more ardently I loved those men whose healthful affections I was hearing about, because they had given themselves wholly to you for healing, the more detestably did I hate myself as compared to them. Many, perhaps twelve, of my years had flown by since that nineteenth year when by reading Cicero's *Hortensius* I was aroused to a

zeal for wisdom. Yet still I delayed to despise earthly happiness, and thus devote myself to that search. For the bare search for wisdom, even when it is not actually found,[2] was preferable to finding treasures and earthly kingdoms and to bodily pleasures swirling about me at my beck. But I, a most wretched youth, most wretched from the very start of my youth, had even sought chastity from you, and had said, "Give me chastity and continence, but not yet!" For I feared that you would hear me quickly, and that quickly you would heal me of that disease of lust, which I wished to have satisfied rather than extinguished. I had wandered along crooked ways[3] in a sacrilegious superstition, not indeed because I was certain of it, but as though I preferred it to other teachings which I did not seek with piety but opposed with hatred.

(18) I thought that the reason I deferred from day to day[4] to reject worldly hopes and to follow you alone was because there seemed nothing certain by which I could direct my course. But the day had come when I stood stripped naked before myself, and my conscience upbraided me. "Where is my tongue? You said, forsooth, that you would not cast off your burden of vanity for the sake of an uncertain truth. See, now it is certain, and yet that burden still weighs you down, while men who neither wore themselves out in search of truth, nor meditated for ten years and more on such things, win wings for their readier shoulders."[5]

Thus was I gnawed within myself, and I was overwhelmed with shame and horror, while Ponticianus spoke of such things. When he had brought an end to his story, and to the business for which he had come, he departed and I went into myself. What was there that I did not say against myself? With what scourges of self-condemnation did I not lash my soul, so that it would follow me as I strove to follow after you? Yet it drew back; it refused to go on, and it offered no excuses for itself. All arguments were used up, and all had been refuted. There remained only speechless dread and my soul was fearful, as if of death itself, of being kept back from that flow of habit by which it was wasting away unto death.

Chapter 8
In the Garden

(19) Then, during that great struggle in my inner house, which I had violently raised up against my own soul in our chamber,[1] in my heart, troubled both in mind and in countenance, I turn upon Alypius and cry out to him: "What is the trouble with us? What is this? What did you hear? The unlearned rise up and take heaven by storm,[2] and we, with all our erudition but empty of heart, see how we wallow in flesh and blood! Are we ashamed to follow, because they have gone on ahead of us? Is it no shame to us not even to follow them?" I said some such words, and my anguish of mind tore me from him, while astounded he looked at me and kept silent. I did not speak in my usual way. My brow, cheeks, eyes, color, and tone of voice spoke of my state of mind more than the words that I uttered.

Attached to our lodging there was a little garden; we had the use of it, as of the whole house, for our host, the owner of the house, did not live in it. The tumult within my breast hurried me out into it, where no one would stop the raging combat that I had entered into against myself, until it would come to such an end as you knew of, but as I knew not. I suffered from a madness that was to bring health, and I was in a death agony that was to bring life: for I knew what a thing of evil I was, but I did not know the good that I would be after but a little while. I rushed, then, into the garden, and Alypius followed in my steps. Even when he was present, I was not less alone—and how could he desert me when I was reduced to such a state? We sat down as far as we could from the house. Suffering from a most fearful wound, I quaked in spirit, angered by a most turbulent anger, because I did not enter into your will and into a covenant with you,[3] my God. For all my bones cried out[4] to me to enter into that covenant, and by their praises they lifted me up to the skies. Not by ships, or in chariots, or on foot do we enter therein; we need not go even so far as I had gone from the house to the place where we were sitting. For not only to go, but even to go in thither was naught else but the will to go, to will firmly and finally, and not to turn and toss, now here, now there, a struggling, half-maimed will, with one part rising upwards and another falling down.

(20) Finally, in the shifting tides of my indecision, I made many bodily movements, such as men sometimes will to make but cannot, whether because they lack certain members or because those members are bound with chains, weakened by illness, or hindered in one way or another. If I tore my hair, and beat my forehead, if I locked my fingers together and clasped my knees, I did so because I willed it. But I could have willed this and yet not done it, if the motive power of my limbs had not made its response. Therefore I did many things in which to will was not the same as the ability to act. Yet I did not do that which I wanted to do with an incomparably greater desire, and could have done as soon as I willed to act, for immediately, when I made that act of will, I would have willed with efficacy. In such an act the power to act and the will itself are the same, and the very act of willing is actually to do the deed. Yet it was not done: it was easier for the body to obey the soul's most feeble command, so that its members were moved at pleasure, than for the soul to obey itself and to accomplish its own high will wholly within the will.

Chapter 9
The Two Wills

(21) Whence comes this monstrous state?[1] Why should it be? Let your mercy shine forth, and let me inquire, if perchance man's hidden penalties and the darkest sufferings of the sons of Adam may be able to give me an answer. Whence comes this monstrous state? Why should it be? Mind commands body, and it obeys forthwith. Mind gives orders to itself, and it is resisted. Mind gives orders for the hand to move, and so easy is it that command can scarce be distinguished from execution. Yet mind is mind, while hand is body. Mind commands mind to will: there is no difference here, but it does not do so. Whence comes this monstrous state? Why should

it be? I say that it commands itself to will a thing: it would not give this command unless it willed it, and yet it does not do what it wills.

It does not will it in its entirety: for this reason it does not give this command in its entirety. For it commands a thing only in so far as it wills it, and in so far as what it commands is not done, to that extent it does not will it. For the will commands that there be a will, and that this be itself, and not something else. But the complete will does not give the command, and therefore what it commands is not in being. For if it were a complete will, it would not command it to be, since the thing would already be in being. Therefore, it is no monstrous thing partly to will a thing and partly not to will it, but it is a sickness in the mind. Although it is supported by truth, it does not wholly rise up, since it is heavily encumbered by habit. Therefore there are two wills, since one of them is not complete, and what is lacking in one of them is present in the other.

Chapter 10
Man's Single Nature

(22) Let them perish from before your face,[1] O God, even as vain talkers and seducers[2] of men's minds perish who detect in the act of deliberation two wills at work, and then assert that in us there are two natures of two minds, one good, the other evil.[3] They themselves are truly evil, when they think such evil things. They will become good, if they come to know true doctrines and assent to the truth, so that your apostle may say to them, "For you were heretofore darkness, but now light in the Lord."[4] But they wish to be light, not in the Lord, but in themselves, and they think the soul's nature to be that which God is. Thus they are made into a deeper darkness, for in horrid pride they have turned back farther from you, from you who are "the true light which enlightens every man that comes into this world."[5] Take heed of what you say, and blush for shame, but "come to him and be enlightened, and your faces shall not be confounded."[6]

As for me, when I deliberated upon serving the Lord my

God, as I had long planned to do, it was I myself who willed it and I myself who did not will it. It was I myself. I neither willed it completely, nor did I refrain completely from willing it. Therefore, I was at war within myself, and I was laid waste by myself. This devastation was made against my will indeed, and yet it revealed not the nature of a different mind within me, but rather the punishment of my own nature. Therefore, it is no more I that did it, but sin that dwells in me,[7] sin that issues from punishment of a more voluntary sin, for I was Adam's son.[8]

(23) If there are as many contrary natures as there are conflicting wills, there will now be not only two natures but many of them. If a man deliberates whether he should go to the Manicheans' meeting place or to the theater, they cry out: "See, there are two natures: the good one draws him this way, while the evil one leads him back there! For whence else is this hesitation between the opposing wills?" I answer that both of them are evil, both that which draws him to them and that which draws him back to the theater. But they do not believe a will that leads to them to be anything but good. What results? If one of us debates with himself and wavers between two contending wills—whether he should go to the theater or to our church—must not those men likewise waver as to their answer? Either they will admit what they do not want to, viz., that he goes to our church out of a good will, as those who receive its sacraments and are obligated by them enter into it, or else they will suppose that two evil natures and two evil minds conflict within one man. But then what they are accustomed to say, that one nature is good and the other evil, will not be true. Or else they will be converted to the truth, and they will not deny that when a man deliberates, a single soul wavers between different wills.

(24) Therefore, when they perceive two conflicting wills within one man, let them no longer say that two contrary minds, deriving from two contrary substances and from two contrary principles, contend together, one good, the other evil. For you, the God of truth, condemn them, and contradict and refute them, as in cases where both wills are bad. For instance, a man deliberates whether he should murder another by poi-

son or with a sword; whether he should seize this or that part of another man's land, when he cannot take both; whether he should purchase pleasure out of lust or save his money out of avarice; whether he should go to the circus or to the theater, if both are showing on the same day. To this last I add a third choice, whether he should rob another man's house, if he has the chance. And I add a fourth, whether he should commit adultery, if an opportunity opens up at the same time. Let us suppose that all these occur together at exactly the same time, and that all are equally desired but cannot be carried out simultaneously. They rend asunder the mind, with these four wills opposing one another, or even with many more, in accordance with the great range of things that are desired. Yet the Manicheans are not accustomed to assert that there is such a great multitude of diverse substances.

So also with regard to wills that are good. I ask of them whether it is good to find delight in reading the apostle, whether it is good to take delight out of a sober psalm, whether it is good to discourse on the Gospel? To each of these questions they will answer, "It is good." What now? If, therefore, all these offer delight at one and the same time, do not diverse wills perplex a man's heart while it deliberates which thing we would seize upon before all others? All of them are good, but all strive with one another, until one is chosen, and there is fixed upon it a single complete will, whereas it had been divided into many wills. So also, when eternity above delights us and the pleasure found in a temporal good holds us fast from below, it is the same soul that wills this course or that, but not with its whole will. Therefore, it is rent asunder by grievous hurt as long as it prefers the first because of its truth but does not put away the other because of habit.

Chapter 11
The Voice of Continence

(25) Thus I was sick and tormented, and I upbraided myself much more bitterly than ever before.[1] I twisted and turned in my chain, until it might be completely broken, although now I was scarcely held by it, but still held by it I was. Within

the hidden depths of my soul, O Lord, you urged me on. By an austere mercy you redoubled the scourges[2] of fear and shame, lest I should give in again, and lest that thin little remaining strand should not be broken through but should grow strong again and bind me yet more firmly.

Within myself I said: "Behold, let it be done now, now let it be done," and by those words I was already moving on to a decision. By then I had almost made it, and yet I did not make it. Still, I did not slip back into my former ways, but close by I stood my ground and regained my breath. Again I tried, and I was but a little away from my goal, just a little away from it, and I all but reached it and laid hold of it. Yet I was not quite there, and I did not reach it, and I did not catch hold of it. I still hesitated to die to death and to live to life, for the ingrown worse had more power over me than the untried better. The nearer came that moment in time when I was to become something different, the greater terror did it strike into me. Yet it did not strike me back, nor did it turn me away, but it held me in suspense.

(26) My lovers of old, trifles of trifles and vanities of vanities,[3] held me back. They plucked at my fleshly garment, and they whispered softly: "Do you cast us off?" and "From that moment we shall no more be with you forever and ever!" and again, "From that moment no longer will this thing and that be allowed to you, forever and ever!" What did they suggest by what I have called "this thing and that," what, O my God, did they suggest? May your mercy turn away all that from your servant's soul! What filth did they suggest! What deeds of shame! But now by far less than half did I hear them. For now it was not as if they were openly contradicting me, face to face, but as if they were muttering behind my back, and as if they were furtively picking at me as I left them, to make me look back again. Yet they did delay me, for I hesitated to tear myself away, and shake myself free of them, and leap over to that place where I was called to be. For an overpowering habit kept saying to me, "Do you think that you can live without them?"

(27) But now it asked this in a very feeble voice. For from that way in which I had set my face and where I trembled to

pass, there appeared to me the chaste dignity of continence, serene and joyous, but in no wanton fashion, virtuously alluring, so that I would come to her and hesitate no longer. To lift me up and embrace me, she stretched forth her holy hands, filled with varied kinds of good examples. Many were the boys and girls, there too a host of youths, men and women of every age, grave widows and aged virgins, and in all these continence herself was in no wise barren but a fruitful mother[4] of children, of joys born of you, O Lord, her spouse.

She smiled upon me with an enheartening mockery, as if to say: "Cannot you do what these youths and these maidens do? Or can these youths and these maidens do this of themselves, and not rather in the Lord their God? The Lord their God gave me to them. Why do you stand on yourself, and thus stand not at all? Cast yourself on him. Have no fear. He will not draw back and let you fall. Cast yourself trustfully on him: he will receive you and he will heal you." I felt great shame, for I still heard the murmurings of those trifles, and still I delayed and hung there in suspense. Again she smiled, as if to say: "Turn deaf ears to those unclean members of yours upon the earth, so that they may be mortified. They tell you of delights, but not as does the law of the Lord your God."[5] This debate within my heart was solely of myself against myself. But Alypius, standing close by my side, silently awaited the outcome of my strange emotion.

CHAPTER 12

The Voice as of a Child

(28) But when deep reflection had dredged out of the secret recesses of my soul all my misery and heaped it up in full view of my heart, there arose a mighty storm, bringing with it a mighty downpour of tears. That I might pour it all forth with its own proper sounds, I arose from Alypius's side—to be alone seemed more proper to this ordeal of weeping—and went farther apart, so that not even his presence would be a hindrance to me. Such was I at that moment, and he sensed it, for I suppose that I had said something in which the sound of my voice already appeared to be choked with weeping. So I had

arisen, while he, in deep wonder, remained there where we were sitting. I flung myself down, how I do not know, under a certain fig tree, and gave free rein to my tears.[1] The floods burst from my eyes, an acceptable sacrifice to you.[2] Not indeed in these very words but to this effect I spoke many things to you: "And you, O Lord, how long?[3] How long, O Lord, will you be angry forever?[4] Remember not our past iniquities."[5] For I felt that I was held by them, and I gasped forth these mournful words, "How long, how long? Tomorrow and tomorrow? Why not now? Why not in this very hour an end to my uncleanness?"

(29) Such words I spoke, and with most bitter contrition I wept within my heart. And lo, I heard from a nearby house, a voice like that of a boy or a girl, I know not which, chanting and repeating over and over, "Take up and read. Take up and read." Instantly, with altered countenance, I began to think most intently whether children made use of any such chant in some kind of game, but I could not recall hearing it anywhere. I checked the flow of my tears and got up, for I interpreted this solely as a command given to me by God to open the book and read the first chapter I should come upon. For I had heard how Anthony had been admonished by a reading from the Gospel at which he chanced to be present, as if the words read were addressed to him: "Go, sell what you have, and give to the poor, and you shall have treasure in heaven, and come, follow me,"[6] and that by such a portent he was immediately converted to you.

So I hurried back to the spot where Alypius was sitting, for I had put there the volume of the aspostle when I got up and left him. I snatched it up, opened it, and read in silence the chapter on which my eyes first fell:[7] "Not in rioting and drunkenness, not in chambering and impurities, not in strife and envying; but put you on the Lord Jesus Christ, and make not provision for the flesh in its concupiscences."[8] No further wished I to read, nor was there need to do so. Instantly, in truth, at the end of this sentence, as if before a peaceful light streaming into my heart, all the dark shadows of doubt fled away.

(30) Then, having inserted my finger, or with some other

mark, I closed the book, and, with a countenance now calm, I told it all to Alypius. What had taken place in him, which I did not know about, he then made known to me. He asked to see what I had read: I showed it to him, and he looked also at what came after what I had read for I did not know what followed. It was this that followed: "Now him that is weak in the faith take unto you,"[9] which he applied to himself and disclosed to me. By this admonition he was strengthened, and by a good resolution and purpose, which were entirely in keeping with his character, wherein both for a long time and for the better he had greatly differed from me, he joined me without any painful hesitation.

Thereupon we went in to my mother; we told her the story, and she rejoiced. We related just how it happened. She was filled with exultation and triumph, and she blessed you, "who are able to do above that which we ask or think."[10] She saw that through me you had given her far more than she had long begged for by her piteous tears and groans. For you had converted me to yourself, so that I would seek neither wife nor ambition in this world, for I would stand on that rule of faith where, so many years before, you had showed me to her.[11] You turned her mourning into a joy[12] far richer than that she had desired, far dearer and purer than that she had sought in grandchildren born of my flesh.[13]

BOOK 9
THE NEW CATHOLIC

Chapter 1
A Soul Set Free

(1) "O Lord, I am your servant; I am your servant and the son of your handmaid. You have broken my bonds: I will sacrifice to you the sacrifice of praise."[1] Grant that my heart and my tongue may praise you. Grant that all my bones may say, "Lord who is like unto you?"[2] Grant that they may speak, and deign to answer me and "say to my soul: I am your salvation."[3]

Who am I, and what am I? Is there any evil that is not found in my acts, or if not in my acts, in my words, or if not in my words, in my will? But you, O Lord, are good and merciful, and your right hand has had regard for the depth of my death, and from the very bottom of my heart it has emptied out an abyss of corruption. This was the sum of it: not to will what I willed and to will what you willed.

But throughout these long years where was my free will? Out of what deep and hidden pit was it called forth in a single moment, wherein to bend my neck to your mild yoke and my shoulders to your light burden,[4] O Christ Jesus,[5] "my helper and my redeemer?"[6] How sweet did it suddenly become to me to be free of the sweets of folly: things that I once feared to lose it was now joy to put away. You cast them forth from me, you the true and highest sweetness, you cast them forth, and in their stead you entered in, sweeter than every pleasure, but not to flesh and blood, brighter than every light, but deeper within me than any secret retreat, higher than every honor, but not to those who exalt themselves. Now was my mind free from the gnawing cares of favor-seeking, of striving for gain, of wallowing in the mire, and of scratching lust's itchy sore. I spoke like a child to you, my light, my wealth, my salvation, my Lord God.

CHAPTER 2
End of a Worldly Career

(2) In your sight I resolved not to make a boisterous break, but gently to withdraw the service of my tongue from the language marts. Thus youths who did not meditate on your law,[1] or on your peace, but on foolish lies and court quarrels, would no longer pry from my mouth weapons for their madness. Happily, very few days still remained before the vintage vacation.[2] I resolved to endure them, so that I might leave in correct fashion, and, since I had now been ransomed by you, not to put myself up for sale again. Hence our plan was known to you, but it was not known to men, with the exception of our friends. We had agreed among ourselves, that it should not be spread everywhere, even though to us who were now mounting up from the vale of tears[3] and were singing a gradual canticle[4] you had given sharp arrows and consuming coals against a deceitful tongue.[5] For such a tongue, while seeming to counsel us, would oppose us, and out of fondness would devour us, as it does its food.

(3) Your love pierced our heart like an arrow,[6] and we bore within us your words, transfixing our inmost parts. The examples set by your servants, whom you had turned from black to shining bright, and from death to life, brought together in the bosom of our thought, set fire to our heavy torpor and burned it away, so that we would not turn towards lower things. So strong a fire did they enkindle in us that all the hostile blasts from deceitful tongues would only inflame us more fiercely and not put out that fire.

But truly for your name's sake, which you have hallowed throughout the earth, our vow and our resolution might even find men to give them praise. Therefore, it seemed like outward show if we would not wait for the vacation time that was now so near, but would leave early a public profession, practiced before the eyes of all men. The result would be that all who regarded my act and noted how close was that day of

Book 9. The New Catholic

the vintage holidays which I wished to anticipate, would do a great deal of talking, to the effect that I wanted to look like a big man. Further, what would it have profited me for them to think and argue about my state of mind and "for our good to be evil spoken of?"[7]

(4) Moreover, it happened that in that very summer, because of too much literary work, my lungs had begun to weaken and it was difficult for me to breathe deeply. By pains in my chest they showed that they were injured, and it was impossible to make clear or extended use of my voice. This fact first disturbed me, as it was forcing me almost of necessity to put down my burden of teaching, or surely, to interrupt it, even if I were to be cured and recover. But when a complete will to remain still and see that you are the Lord[8] arose and was made firm in me—you know all this, my God—I even began to be glad that this not untrue excuse was at hand. It would lessen the opposition of men who, for the sake of their freeborn sons, were willing that I should never be free. Full of such joy, then, I endured that space of time until it had run its course—whether there were twenty days I am not sure—yet they were endured by sheer strength. The desire for profit, by which I used to bear this heavy trial, was gone from me, and I would have continued in it completely crushed if patience had not succeeded to it. Some of your servants, my brethren, may say that I sinned in this matter, in that, with a heart now completely in your service, I allowed myself to sit for even a single hour in that chair of lies. I do not debate with them on this. But have not you, most merciful Lord, by your sacred waters pardoned and wiped away this sin along with my other horrid and deadly deeds?

Chapter 3
Conversion and Death of Verecundus and Nebridius

(5) At the time this boon was granted to us, Verecundus was tortured with anxiety. Because of bonds by which he was most strictly held, he perceived that he would be bereft of our companionship. Not yet a Christian, but with a wife who was one of the faithful, he was held back from the path we were

entering upon, by fetters more binding than any of the others. Nor would he be a Christian, he said, under any other condition than that which was impossible to him. However, he graciously allowed us to live in his house as long as we wished to remain there. Lord, you will reward him with the reward of the just, for you have already rewarded him with their lot. Although we were absent, for by then we were in Rome, he was seized by bodily illness and during it he became a Christian and one of the faithful, and he departed from this life. So you had mercy not only on him but also on us. For if we thought of this friend's outstanding courtesy to us, and yet could not count him within your flock, we should have been tormented by unbearable grief. Thanks be to you, our God! We are yours. Your encouragement and your consolation have told us so. Faithful to your promises, in return for that country place of his at Cassiciacum,[1] where far from the madding world we found rest in you, you gave to Verecundus delights in your paradise that are eternally fresh, for you forgave him his sins upon earth,[2] in that mountain flowing with milk, your mountain, that richest mountain.[3]

(6) Therefore, at that time he was in anguish, but Nebridius rejoiced with us. Although he too was not yet a Christian and had fallen into that pit of most pernicious error, wherein he believed that the flesh of your Son, truth itself, was but a phantasm, yet he had emerged from it. He was thus placed: he had not as yet received any of your Church's sacraments, but he was a most ardent searcher for the truth. This man, not long after our conversion and regeneration by your baptism, also became a faithful Catholic and served you in perfect chastity and continence among his own people in Africa, for his whole household through him became Christian, and you freed him from the flesh. Now he lives in Abraham's bosom.[4] Whatever is that abode signified by the word "bosom," in it lives my Nebridius, my sweet friend, who from a freedman became your adopted son. There he lives. What other place is there for such a soul? There he lives, in that place of which he asked so many questions of me, a poor, ignorant man. No longer does he put his ear to my mouth, but he puts his spiritual mouth to your fountain, and in accordance with his desire

Book 9. The New Catholic

he drinks in wisdom, as much as he can, endlessly happy. Nor do I think that he is so inebriated by that fountain of wisdom as to become forgetful of me, for you, O Lord, of whom he drinks, are mindful of us.

Such, then, were we. We consoled Verecundus, saddened because of our conversion, but with his friendship kept whole, and we exhorted him to accept the faith in his own station, namely, in married life. We looked forward to when Nebridius would follow us. The time when he would do so was near at hand, and now he was about to do it, for lo, those days rolled by at length. Many and long they seemed to be, because of my desire for liberty and leisure in which to sing to you out of my very marrow: "My heart has said to you: I have sought your face: your face, O Lord, will I require."[5]

Chapter 4
At Cassiciacum

(7) The day came when I was actually set free from teaching rhetoric, although I had already been free from it in thought. Now it was done. You set free my tongue, as you had already freed my heart from that profession. I blessed you, and joyfully, together with all my household,[1] I started out for that country place. As to what I did there by way of literary work, which was already in your service, although during this period as it were of rest it still breathed forth the school of pride, my books bear witness, both the ones that resulted from discussion with those present there[2] and the ones made by myself alone before you.[3] Letters record what things I discussed with Nebridius, who was absent.[4] But when will there be time enough for me to commemorate all the great benefits that you showed to us at that time, especially since I now hasten on to other still greater benefits? For my memory calls me back, and it becomes sweet to me, O Lord, to confess to you by what inward goads you mastered me, and how you leveled me down by making low the mountains and the hills[5] of my thoughts, how you made straight my crooked paths and smoothed the rough, and how you likewise subdued my heart's brother, Alypius himself, to the name of your Only-begotten,

"our Lord and Savior Jesus Christ."[6] For at first he disdained to put that name into our writings,[7] but wished rather to have them smell of those cedars of the schools which the Lord had now broken down,[8] than of those healthful herbs which the Church provides against serpents.

(8) What cries did I send up to you, my God, when I read the psalms of David, those canticles of faith, those songs of devotion, which exclude a boastful mind, I who was but an uncouth beginner in your faithful love, a catechumen, having a season of rest in that country place, together with Alypius, another catechumen, and my mother, in a woman's garb but with a man's faith, clinging to us with an aged woman's sure trust, a mother's love, and a Christian's devotion! What cries did I send up to you when reading those psalms! How was I set on fire for you by them and how did I burn to repeat them, if I but could, throughout the whole world against mankind's pride! Yet they are sung through the whole world, and "there is no one that can hide himself from your heat."[9] With what strong and bitter sorrow did I wax angry at the Manicheans, yet I had pity on them again, because they did not know of those sacraments, those medicines, and raged madly against the antidote by which they could become sane! I wish that they had been somewhere near me at that time, while I did not know that they were there, so that they could see my face and hear my voice as I read Psalm 4 at that time of rest, and perceive what that psalm wrought within me. "When I called upon you, you heard me, O God of my justice! when I was in distress, you have enlarged me. Have mercy on me, and hear my prayer."[10] Would that they could have heard me, while I did not know that they heard me, so that they would not think that I said for their benefit the things that I uttered along with the words of the psalm. For in truth I would not say those same words, nor would I say them in the same way, if I knew that I was being heard and seen by them. Even if I said them, they would not understand them in the way that I spoke them in your presence, by myself and to myself out of the closest feelings of my mind.

(9) I shook with fear, and at the same time I grew ardent with hope and exultation in your mercy,[11] O Father. All these

Book 9. The New Catholic

things issued from my eyes and my voice when your good Spirit turned towards us and said to us: "O you sons of men, how long will you be dull of heart? Why do you love vanity, and seek after lying?"[12] For I had loved vanity and I had sought after lying. But you, O Lord, had already made your holy one great,[13] raising him from the dead, and setting him at your right hand,[14] from where he shall send from on high his promise, the Paraclete, the spirit of truth.[15] He had already sent him, but I did not know it. He had sent him, because he had already been made great, rising from the dead and ascending into heaven. But before that, "as yet the Spirit was not given, because Jesus was not yet glorified."[16] And the prophet cried out: "How long will you be dull of heart? Why do you love vanity, and seek after lying?" And, "Know you that the Lord has made great his holy one."[17] He cries out, "How long," he cries out, "Know you," but for so long a time I did not know, and I loved vanity, and I sought after lying. Therefore, I heard and I trembled, because this was said to such men as I remembered myself to have been. For in those phantoms which I had held for truth there were vanity and lying, and grievously and strongly did I utter many things in my sorrowful remembrance. Would that they who still love vanity and seek after lying could have heard these things. Perchance they would have been troubled and would have vomited it all forth, and you would have heard them when they cried out to you. For by a true death in the flesh did he die for us, "who makes intercession for us with you."[18]

(10) I read on: "Be angry, and sin not."[19] How moved was I, my God, for I had now learned to be angry at myself for my past deeds, so that I would not sin in the future. With justice was I angry, for it was not another nature belonging to a race of darkness that sinned in me, as say those who do not grow angry at themselves, and thus treasure up for themselves "wrath against the day of wrath and revelation of your just judgment!"[20] Now my good things were not in the outward world, nor were they sought with fleshly eyes under that outward sun. For those who wish to find joy in outward things quickly grow vain and spend themselves on the things that are seen and are temporal. In their hungry thoughts they lick

the images of these things. Oh, if they would only grow weary of their hunger, and say, "Who will show us good things?"[21] Then we would say, and then they would hear, "The light of your countenance, O Lord, is signed upon us,"[22] for we are not "the light that enlightens every man,"[23] but we are enlightened by you, so that we who were heretofore darkness may be light in you.[24] Oh, if they would only see that inner eternal light, which I had tasted. I was sore grieved because I was not able to show it to them, even if they brought me their heart in those eyes of theirs that looked away from you, and if they said, "Who will show us good things?"

For there, within my chamber, where I was angry with myself, where I suffered compunction, where I made sacrifice, slaying my old self and, with initial meditations on my own renewal of life, hoping in you, there you began to grow sweet to me, and you "gave joy to my heart."[25] I cried out, as I read those things outwardly and found them within myself. Nor did I wish to have earthly things made manifold for me, thus consuming time away and being consumed by time. For in your eternal simplicity I would possess other "corn, and wine, and oil."[26]

(11) At the next verse I cried out with a deep cry from my heart, "Oh, in peace, oh, in the Selfsame!"[27] Oh, why did he say: "I will fall asleep and I will take my sleep?"[28] For who will hinder us when there "shall come to pass the saying that is written, 'Death is swallowed up in victory.'"[29] You are surpassingly the Selfsame,[30] you who change not, and in you there is rest, forgetful of all labor. For there is none other with you. Nor have you fashioned me to seek after those many other things, which are not what you are, but "you, O Lord, singularly have settled me in hope."[31] This I read, and I burned with ardor, but I did not find what I should do for those deaf and dead, among whom I once had been, a diseased thing, a blind and bitter yapper against those writings which are honied over with the honey of heaven, which are luminous with your light,[32] and I wasted away because of the enemies of this Scripture.[33]

(12) When shall I recall to mind all the things of those days of rest? I have not forgotten, nor will I keep silent concerning

the sharpness of your scourge and the wonderful speed of your mercy. At that time you tortured me with pain in my teeth, and when it became so grievous that I could not speak, there rose up in my heart the thought of urging all my friends there present to beseech you, the God of every kind of health, in my behalf. I wrote this on wax and gave it to them to read. Immediately, when we bent our knees in devout supplication, that pain fled away. But what kind of pain was it? How did it flee away? I admit to you, my Lord, my God,[34] that I was terrified. For from the first years of my life I had never felt such pain.[35] Your decrees wound their way into the depths of my being: I rejoiced in the faith and I gave praise to your name. Nor did that faith let me be without care because of my past sins, for they had not yet been forgiven to me through your baptism.

Chapter 5
Resignation of a Professorship

(13) When the vintage vacation was ended, I sent word to the citizens of Milan that they should arrange for another seller of words for their students. This was both because I had chosen to serve you and because I was no longer equal to that profession by reason of difficulty in breathing and the pain in my chest. By letters I made known to your bishop, Ambrose, that holy man, both my former errors and my present intention, so that he could advise me as to which of your books it would be best for me to read, to the end that I would become more prepared and better fitted to receive so great a grace. He recommended the prophet Isaias: I believe it was because he is a more manifest prophet of the gospel and of the calling of the Gentiles than are the other writers. But in fact I did not understand the first lesson in this book, and thinking the whole work to be similar, I put it aside to be taken up again when I was better accustomed to the Lord's mode of speech.

Chapter 6
Baptism, Easter 387

(14) When the time arrived for me to give in my name,[1] we left the country and returned to Milan.[2] Alypius likewise resolved to be born again in you, in company with me, for he was now clothed with that humility which befits your sacraments. Valiantly had he brought his body into subjection, even to the point that, with unusual daring, he would tread the icy Italian ground with bare feet. We also joined to ourselves the boy Adeodatus, born of me in the flesh out of my sin. Well had you made him: he was almost fifteen years old, and in power of mind he surpassed many grave and learned men. O Lord my God, creator of all things and most powerful to reform our deformities, to you do I confess your gifts. For in that boy I owned nothing but the sin. That he was brought up by us in your discipline, to that you and none other inspired us. Your gifts I confess to you. There is one of our books which is entitled *On the Teacher*,[3] and in it he speaks with me. You know that his are all the ideas which are inserted there, as from the person of the one talking with me, when he was in his sixteenth year. I had experience of many still more wonderful things in him. To me his power of mind was a source of awe. Who except you is the worker of such marvels?

Quickly you took his life away from the earth,[4] and now I remember him with a more peaceful mind, for I have no fear for anything in his childhood or youth, and none at all for him as a man. We joined him to us, of equal age in your grace, to be instructed in your discipline. We were baptized,[5] and anxiety over our past life fled away from us. In those days I could not take my fill of meditating with wondrous sweetness on the depths of your counsel concerning the salvation of mankind. How greatly did I weep during hymns and canticles, keenly affected by the voices of your sweet-singing Church! Those voices flowed into my ears, and your truth was distilled into my heart, and from that truth holy emotions overflowed, and the tears ran down, and amid those tears all was well with me.

Chapter 7
Saints Gervase and Protase

(15) The Church in Milan had not long before begun to worship with this form of consolation and exhortation, wherein with great fervor the brethren sing together in voice and heart. For it was only a year, or not much more, since Justina, the mother of the boy king,[1] Valentinian, had persecuted your man Ambrose in favor of her heresy, to which she had been seduced by the Arians.[2] A devout people, who were prepared to suffer death together with their bishop, your servant, kept watch in the church. Therein, living in prayer, my mother, your handmaid, held a first place amid these cares and watchings. Ourselves, still cold to the warmth of your Spirit, were nevertheless stirred by the astonished and disturbed city. At that time it was established that, after the custom of the Eastern lands, hymns and canticles should be sung, so that the people would not become weak through the tedium and sorrow. From then up to the present day that custom has been maintained, with many, or almost all, of your congregations taking it up throughout other parts of the world.

(16) At that same time you revealed by a vision to your aforenamed prelate the place in which the bodies of the martyrs Protase and Gervase[3] lay hidden, which for so many years you had stored away uncorrupted in your secret treasure house. In due time you would bring them forth from that place so as to restrain the mad rage of a woman, yes, a woman of royal rank. When they were discovered and dug up, and with fitting honors transferred into the Ambrosian basilica, not only were those tormented by unclean spirits healed, while those same demons confessed themselves, but also a certain citizen,[4] very well known throughout the city, who had been blind for many years, asked and heard the reason for the people's joy and tumult, and then leaped up and demanded that his guide lead him thither. Brought there, he begged to be admitted so that he might touch the bier with his handkerchief, for precious in your sight is the death of your saints.[5] When he had done this and touched the cloth to his eyes, they

were immediately opened. From that place the story spread abroad. From there, your praises grew bright and shone forth. From there, the mind of that hostile woman, although not turned to sound belief, was yet restrained from the fury of persecution. "Thanks be to you, my God."[6] Whence and whither have you led my recollection so that I confess also these things to you, mighty deeds that I had almost passed over in forgetfulness? Yet even then, when the odor of your ointments was so fragrant, we did not run after you.[7] Therefore, I wept the more at the singing of your hymns. For long had I sighed after you, and at length I breathed in you, as far as breath may enter into this house of grass.[8]

Chapter 8
Monica's Youth

(17) You "who make men to dwell of one mind in a house,"[1] joined with us Evodius,[2] a young man of our own city, who had served as a special agent. He had been converted to you before we were, and he had been baptized. Having given up his secular service, he girded himself for yours. We were together, and we planned to dwell together in our holy resolution. We made investigations as to what place would be best fitted to us for your service, and together we were returning back to Africa.[3] When we were at Ostia on the Tiber, my mother died.[4]

I omit many things, as I am making great haste. Accept my confessions and acts of thanksgiving, O my God, for countless things, even those I pass over in silence. But I will not pass over whatever my soul brings to birth concerning that handmaiden of yours, who brought me to birth, both in her flesh, so that I was born into this temporal light, and in her heart, that I might be born into eternal light. Not of her gifts, but of your gifts in her, will I speak. She neither made herself nor did she educate herself: you created her. Neither her father nor her mother knew what sort of woman would be made from them. The rod of your Christ, the rule of your only Son, in a faithful home, in a good member of your Church, instructed her "in your fear."[5] But for her training she was wont

Book 9. The New Catholic

to praise not so much her mother's diligence as that of a certain age-worn maidservant who had carried her father about when he was an infant, as little ones are usually carried on the backs of older girls. Because of this service and because of her advanced age and excellent habits, she was held in high esteem by the masters of a Christian house. For these reasons also she was put in charge of her master's daughters and she took diligent care of them. When necessary, she restrained them strictly with a holy severity, and she taught them with prudence and sobriety. Outside the hours when they were properly fed at their parents' table, she did not permit them to drink water, even though they were parched with thirst. She thus forestalled a bad habit, and she added these sound words: "You drink water now, because you cannot get at the wine. When you come to be married, and are made mistresses of storerooms and cellars, water will be distasteful to you, but the habit of drinking will persist." By this form of teaching and by her authority to give orders, she restrained the greediness of their tender age and turned the girls' thirst towards a virtuous moderation, so that even then they would not want to do what they should not do.

(18) Nevertheless, there crept on her, as your handmaid told me, her son, there crept on her a love of wine. For when her parents, according to custom, ordered her as a sober girl to fetch wine out of the cask, she would dip a cup into the opening at the top before she poured the wine into a pitcher. Then she would take just a little sip with the tip of her lips, since the taste kept her from taking more. She did this not out of a desire for drink, but from a sort of excess of those youthful spirits which blow off in absurd actions and which parental firmness usually suppresses in our childhood years. Thus by adding to that daily little bit each day another little bit—for "he who contemns small things falls by little and little"[6]—she had fallen into the habit of greedily drinking her little cups almost full up with wine. Where then was the wise old woman, and where was her stern prohibition? Did anything avail against a secret disease, Lord, unless your medicine kept watch over us?[7] Father and mother and protectors are absent, yet you are present, you who have created us, who have called us,

who work good towards the salvation of souls even through men placed over us. My God, what did you do at that time? How did you cure her? Whence did you heal her? Was it not that you brought out of another soul, a hard and sharp reproach, like a surgeon's knife out of your secret stores, and by one stroke you cut away all that foul matter? A maidservant, with whom she used to go down to the cellar, quarreled with her little mistress, the two being all alone, as it so happened. She threw this fault at her with most bitter insults, and called her a winebibber. Wounded through and through by this taunt, she beheld her own foul state, and immediately condemned it and cast it off. Just as fawning friends pervert us, so also quarrelsome enemies often correct us. Yet you repay them, not according to what you did through them, but according to what they themselves had a will to do. For that wrathful servant desired to provoke her little mistress, not to cure her. Therefore, she did this in private, either because the time and place of the quarrel so found them or perhaps because she was afraid that she would get into trouble for reporting it so late. But you, O Lord, ruler of things in heaven and on earth, who turn to your uses the deeps of the torrent, and give order to the turbulent flood of the ages, by means of madness in one soul you even heal another. This is to the end that no man who observes this may attribute it to his own powers, when some other man, whom he wishes to correct, is corrected by his words.

Chapter 9
Monica, Wife of Patricius

(19) Brought up modestly and soberly in this manner, and made subject by you to her parents rather than by her parents to you, when she arrived at a marriageable age, she was given to a husband and served "him as her lord."[1] She strove to win him to you,[2] speaking to him about you through her conduct, by which you made her beautiful, an object of reverent love, and a source of admiration to her husband. She endured offenses against her marriage bed in such wise that she never had a quarrel with her husband over this matter. She looked

Book 9. The New Catholic

forward to seeing your mercy upon him, so that he would believe in you and be made chaste. But in addition to this, just as he was remarkable for kindness, so also was he given to violent anger. However, she had learned to avoid resisting her husband when he was angry, not only by deeds but even by words. When she saw that he had curbed his anger and become calm and that the time was opportune, then she explained what she had done, if he happened to have been inadvertently disturbed.

In fine, when many wives, who had better-tempered husbands but yet bore upon their faces signs of disgraceful beatings, in the course of friendly conversation criticized their husbands' conduct, she would blame it all on their tongues. Thus she would give them serious advice in the guise of a joke. From the time, she said, they heard what are termed marriage contracts read to them, they should regard those documents as legal instruments making them slaves. Hence, being mindful of their condition, they should not rise up in pride against their lords. Women who knew what a sharp-tempered husband she had to put up with marveled that it was never reported or revealed by any sign that Patricius[3] had beaten his wife or that they had differed with one another in a family quarrel, even for a single day. When they asked her confidentially why this was so, she told them of her policy, which I have described above. Those who acted upon it, found it to be good advice and were thankful for it; those who did not act upon it, were kept down and abused.

(20) By her good services and by perseverance in patience and meekness, she also won over her mother-in-law who at first was stirred up against her by the whispered stories of malicious servants. She told her son about the meddling tongues of the servants, by which peace within the house had been disturbed between herself and her daughter-in-law, and asked him to punish them. Afterwards, both to obey his mother and to improve discipline within his household and promote peace among its members, he punished by whippings the servants who had been exposed, in accordance with the advice of her who had exposed them. Afterwards she promised that the same reward might be expected by whoever tried to please her

by telling any evil tale about her daughter-in-law. Since nobody thereafter dared to do this, they lived together with extraordinary harmony and good will.

(21) Moreover, upon that good handmaiden of yours, in whose womb you created me, "my God, my mercy,"[4] you bestowed this great gift: wherever she could, she showed herself to be a great peacemaker between persons who were at odds and in disagreement. When she heard from either side many very bitter things, like something a swollen, undigested discord often vomits up, when a rough mass of hatred is belched out in biting talk to a present friend about an absent enemy, she would never betray a thing to either of them about the other except what would help towards their reconciliation. This might have seemed a small thing to me, if from sad experience I had not known unnumbered throngs who, through some kind of horrid wide-spreading sinful infection, not only report the words of angry enemies to angry enemies, but even add things they did not say. On the contrary, to a man who is a man it should be a little thing not to stir up or increase men's enmities by evil speaking, or else he even strives to extinguish them by speaking well of others. Such was she, and she had you as her inward teacher in the school of her heart.

(22) Finally, towards the very end of his earthly life, she gained her husband for you. After he became one of the faithful, she did not have to complain of what she had endured from him when he was not yet a believer. She was also a servant of your servants.[5] Whosoever among them knew her greatly praised you, and honored you, and loved you in her, because they recognized your presence in her heart, for the fruit of her holy life bore witness to this. She had been the wife of one husband; she repaid the duty she owed to her parents; she had governed her house piously; she had testimony for her good works;[6] she had brought up children, being as often in labor in birth of them[7] as she saw them straying from you. Lastly, Lord, of all of us, your servants—for out of your gift you permit us to speak—who, before she fell asleep[8] in you already lived together, having received the graces of your baptism, she took care as though she had been mother to

Book 9. The New Catholic

us all, and she served us as though she had been a daughter to all of us.

Chapter 10
The Vision at Ostia

(23) With the approach of that day on which she was to depart from this life, a day that you knew, although it was unknown to us, it came about, as you yourself ordered it, so I believe, in your secret ways, that she and I stood leaning out from a certain window, where we could look into the garden within the house we had taken at Ostia on the Tiber, where, removed from crowds, we were resting up, after the hardships of a long journey, in preparation for the voyage. We were alone, conversing together most tenderly, "forgetting those things that are behind, and stretching forth to those that are before."[1] We inquired of one another "in the present truth,"[2] which truth you are, as to what the eternal life of the saints would be like, "which eye has not seen, nor ear heard, nor has it entered into the heart of a man."[3] But we were straining out with the heart's mouth for those supernal streams flowing from your fountain, "the fountain of life," which is "with you,"[4] so that, being sprinkled with it according to our capacity, we might in some measure think upon so great a subject.

(24) When our discourse had been brought to the point that the highest delight of fleshly senses, in the brightest corporeal light, when set against the sweetness of that life seemed unworthy not merely of comparison with it, but even of remembrance, then, raising ourselves up with a more ardent love to the Selfsame, we proceeded step by step through all bodily things up to that heaven whence shine the sun and the moon and the stars down upon the earth. We ascended higher yet by means of inward thought and discourse and admiration of your works, and we came up to our own minds. We transcended them, so that we attained to the region of abundance that never fails,[5] in which you feed Israel[6] forever upon the food of truth, and where life is that Wisdom by which all these things are made, both which have been and which are to be. And this Wisdom itself is not made, but it is such as it

was, and so it will be forever. Nay, rather, to have been and to be in the future do not belong to it, but only to be, for it is eternal. And while we discourse of this and pant after it, we attain to it in a slight degree by an effort of our whole heart. And we sighed for it, and we left behind, bound to it, "the first-fruits of the spirit,"[7] and we turned back again to the noise of our mouths, where a word both begins and ends. But what is there like to your Word, our Lord, remaining in himself without growing old, and yet renewing all things?[8]

(25) Therefore we said: If for any man the tumult of the flesh fell silent, silent the images of earth, and of the waters, and of the air; silent the heavens; silent for him the very soul itself, and he should pass beyond himself by not thinking upon himself; silent his dreams and all imagined appearances, and every tongue, and every sign; and if all things that come to be through change should become wholly silent to him—for if any man can hear, then all these things say to him, "We did not make ourselves,"[9] but he who endures forever made us[10] —if when they have said these words, they then become silent, for they have raised up his ear to him who made them, and God alone speaks, not through such things but through himself, so that we hear his Word, not uttered by a tongue of flesh, nor by an angel's voice,[11] "nor by the sound of thunder,"[12] nor by the riddle of a similitude,[13] but by himself whom we love in these things, himself we hear without their aid,—even as we then reached out and in swift thought attained to that eternal Wisdom which abides over all things—if this could be prolonged, and other visions of a far inferior kind could be withdrawn, and this one alone ravish, and absorb, and hide away its beholder within its deepest joys, so that sempiternal life might be such as was that moment of understanding for which we sighed, would it not be this: "Enter into the joy of your Lord?"[14] When shall this be? When "we shall all rise again, but we shall not all be changed."[15]

(26) Such things I said, although not in this manner and in these words. Yet, O Lord, you know that on that day when we were speaking of such things, and this world with all its delights became contemptible to us in the course of our words, my mother said: "Son, for my own part, I now find no delight

in anything in this life. What I can still do here, and why I am here, I do not know, now that all my hopes in this world have been accomplished. One thing there was, for which I desired to linger a little while in this life, that I might see you a Catholic Christian before I died. God has granted this to me in more than abundance, for I see you his servant, with even earthly happiness held in contempt. What am I doing here?"

CHAPTER 11
The Death of St. Monica

(27) What I said to her in answer to this I do not entirely recall, for scarcely five days later, or not much more, she fell sick of fever. One day, as she lay ill, she lost consciousness and for a little while she was withdrawn from all present things. We rushed to her, but she quickly regained her senses. She looked at me and my brother as we stood there, and said to us, after the manner of one seeking something. "Where was I?" Then, gazing at us who were struck dumb with grief, she said, "Here you put your mother."[1] I remained silent and stopped my weeping. But my brother said, as if wishing a happier lot for her, that she should die not in a foreign land but in her own country. When she heard this, she stared reproachfully at him with an anxious countenance, because he was concerned about such things. Then she looked at me and said, "See what he says!" Presently she said to both of us: "Put this body away anywhere. Don't let care about it disturb you. I ask only this of you, that you remember me at the altar of the Lord, wherever you may be." When she had expressed this wish in what words she could manage, she fell silent and was racked with increasing sickness.

(28) I thought of your gifts, O God unseen,[2] which you instill into the hearts of your faithful and from which come wonderful fruits, and I rejoiced and gave thanks to you. I recalled what I already knew, how concerned she had always felt over her burial place, which she had arranged and prepared for herself next to her husband's body. They had lived together in great harmony, and hence she wished—so little is the human mind able to grasp the things of God—this too to

be added to her happiness and remembered by men: that after a journey across the sea it had been granted to her that the earth of the two wedded ones have a joint covering of earth.

At what time, out of the fullness of your bounty, this vain wish began to fade from her heart I do not know. I marveled and rejoiced over the fact that she had thus revealed it to me, although in our conversation at the window, when she said, "What do I still do here?" it did not appear that she wanted to die in her native land. I also heard later on that already, while we were at Ostia, one day when I was absent, she talked with a mother's confidence to certain friends of mine about contempt of this life and the advantages of death. They were amazed at the woman's strength, which you had given to her, and asked if she did not fear leaving her body so far from her own city. She replied, "Nothing is far from God. I need not fear that he will not know where to raise me up at the end of the world."

So, on the ninth day of her illness, in the fifty-sixth year of her life and in the thirty-third year of mine, this devout and holy soul was set loose from the body.

Chapter 12
Monica's Burial; Augustine's Grief

(29) I closed her eyes, and a mighty sorrow welled up from the depths of my heart and overflowed into tears. At the same time, by a powerful command of my mind, my eyes drank up their source until it was dry. Most ill was it with me in such an agony! When she breathed her last, the boy Adeodatus burst out in lamentation, but he was hushed by all of us and fell silent. In like manner, something childish in me, which was slipping forth in tears, was by a youthful voice, my heart's own voice, checked, and it grew silent. We did not think it fitting to solemnize that funeral with tearful cries and groans, for it is often the custom to bewail by such means the wretched lot of those who die, or even their complete extinction. But she did not die in misery, nor did she meet with total death.[1] This we knew by sure evidence and proofs given by her good life and by her "unfeigned faith."[2]

Book 9. The New Catholic

(30) What was it, therefore, that grieved me so heavily, if not the fresh wound wrought by the sudden rupture of our most sweet and dear way of life together? I took joy indeed from her testimony, when in that last illness she mingled her endearments with my dutiful deeds and called me a good son. With great love and affection she recalled that she had never heard me speak a harsh or disrespectful word to her. Yet, O my God who made us! what comparison was there between the honor she had from me and the services that she rendered to me? When I was bereft of such great consolation, my heart was wounded through and my life was as if ripped asunder. For out of her life and mine one life had been made.

(31) After the boy had been stopped from weeping, Evodius took up the psalter and began to sing a psalm. The whole household answered him in the psalm, "I will sing of mercy and judgment unto you, O Lord."[3] When they heard what had happened, many of the brethren and devout women gathered there. According to custom, those whose duty it was made ready the burial. At the same time, in that part of the house where I could do so, I discussed a subject suitable to such a time with those who thought that I should not be left alone. By so true a salve I soothed a torment known to me alone. The others knew nothing of it; they listened attentively to me, and they thought that I was free from all sense of sorrow. But in your ears, where none of them could hear, I upbraided the weakness of my affection, and I held back the flood of sorrow. It gave way a little before me, but I was again swept away by its violence, although not as far as to burst into tears, nor to any change of expression. But I knew what it was I crushed down within my heart. Because it distressed me greatly that these human feelings had such sway over me, for this needs must be according to due order and our allotted state, I sorrowed over my sorrow with an added sorrow,[4] and I was torn by a twofold sadness.

(32) Lo, when her body was carried away, we went out,[5] and we returned without tears. Not even in those prayers we poured forth to you when the sacrifice of our redemption was offered up in her behalf, with the corpse already placed beside the grave before being lowered into it, as is the custom of that

place,[6] not even during those prayers did I shed tears. But all day long in secret, heavy was my sorrow, and with a troubled mind I besought you as best I could to heal my anguish. You did not do so, and it was, I think, to impress upon my memory by this one lesson how strong is the bond of any habit, even upon a mind that no longer feeds upon deceptive words. I also thought it good to go and bathe, as I had heard that the baths (*balnea*) are so-called because the Greeks say βαλανεῖον, meaning that it drives anxiety from the mind. See, O Father of orphans, this fact too do I confess to your mercy, for after I had bathed I was the same as before I bathed. Bitter grief did not pour like sweat out of my heart. But then I slept, and I woke up, and I found that my sorrow had in no small part been eased. As I lay alone on my bed, I remembered those truthful verses of your own Ambrose. For you are

God, creator of all things, ruler of the sky,
Who clothe the day with beauteous light, the night with grateful sleep,
That rest may weakened limbs restore for labor's needs,
And ease our weary minds, and free our worried hearts from grief.

(33) Little by little, I regained my former thoughts about your handmaid, about the devout life she led in you, about her sweet and holy care for us, of which I was so suddenly deprived. I took comfort in weeping in your sight over her and for her, over myself and for myself. I gave way to the tears that I had held back, so that they poured forth as much as they wished. I spread them beneath my heart, and it rested upon them, for at my heart were placed your ears, not the ears of a mere man, who would interpret with scorn my weeping.

Now, Lord, I confess to you in writing. Let him read it who wants to, let him interpret it as he wants. If he finds a sin in it, that I wept for my mother for a small part of an hour, for that mother now dead to my eyes who for so many years had wept for me so that I might live in your eyes, let him not laugh me to scorn. But rather, if he is a man of large charity, let him weep over my sins before you, the Father of all brothers of your Christ.

Chapter 13
Remembrance in Prayer

(34) But now, with a heart healed from that wound, for which afterwards I blamed my merely natural feelings, I pour out to you, our God, in behalf of her who was your handmaid, a far different kind of tears. These tears flow from a spirit shaken by thought of the dangers besetting every soul "that dies in Adam." She had been made to live in Christ[1] even while not yet released from the flesh, and she had so lived as to give praise of your name by her faith and conduct. Still, I dare not say that from the time you regenerated her by baptism no word had issued from her mouth contrary to your commandment. By the Truth, your Son, it has been said, "Whosoever shall say to his brother, 'Thou fool,' shall be in danger of hell fire."[2] Woe even to such life of men as can be praised if you should set aside mercy and examine that life carefully.[3] But because you are not rigorous in searching out sins, we confidently hope to find a place with you. Yet if a man numbers his true merits before you, what else does he number before you except your own gifts? Ah, if men would know themselves to be but men, and if he who glories would glory in the Lord.[4]

(35) Therefore, O my praise[5] and my life, O God of my heart,[6] I put aside for a while her good deeds, for which I give thanks to you with joy, and I now beseech you in behalf of my mother's sins. Hear me for the sake of him who is the medicine of our wounds, of him who hung upon the tree, of him who now sits at your right hand and makes intercession for us.[7] I know that she was merciful to others and that from her heart she forgave her debtors their debts. Do you also forgive her her debts,[8] if she contracted any in so many years after receiving the water of salvation. Forgive her, Lord, forgive her, I beseech you. Enter not into judgment with her.[9] Let your mercy be exalted above your justice,[10] for your words are true, and you have promised mercy to the merciful.[11] Such you made them to be, for you will have mercy on whom you will have mercy, and you will show mercy to whom you will show mercy.[12]

(36) I believe that you have already done what I ask, but

accept, O Lord, "the free offerings of my mouth."[13] For when the day of her dissolution was at hand,[14] she did not think of having her body richly clothed or embalmed with spices. She did not desire a carefully chosen monument, nor did she care for a grave in her own land. Such things she did not enjoin upon us, but she desired only that she be remembered at your altar, which she had served without the loss of a single day. For she knew that from it would be dispensed that holy Victim by whom "the handwriting of the decree that was against us, which was contrary to us,"[15] was blotted out, through whose sacrifice was vanquished that enemy who counted up our offenses and sought what he could lay against us, but found nothing in him[16] in whom we conquer. Who shall pour back into him his innocent blood? Who shall repay him the price by which he bought us, so as to take us from him? By the bond of faith your handmaid bound her soul to this sacrament of our redemption. Let no one sever her from your protection. Let neither the lion nor the dragon[17] put himself between you and her by force or fraud. She will not answer that she owes no debt, lest she be convicted and seized by her crafty accuser. She will answer that her sins have been forgiven by him to whom no one can return that price which he who owed nothing returned for us.

(37) Therefore, may she rest in peace, together with that husband before whom and after whom she had no other, whom she obeyed with patience, bringing forth fruit[18] to you so that she might win him also to you. Inspire, O my Lord, my God, inspire your servants my brethren, your sons my masters, whom with voice and heart and pen I serve, so that as many of them as read these words may at your altar remember Monica,[19] your handmaid, together with Patricius, sometime her husband, by whose flesh you brought me into this life, how I know not. May they with devout affection remember them who were my parents in this passing light, my brethren under you our Father in our Catholic Mother, and my fellow citizens in that eternal Jerusalem, which your pilgrim people sigh after from their setting forth even to their return,[20] so that, more abundantly than through my own prayers, my mother's last request of me may be granted through the prayers of many, occasioned by these confessions.

BOOK 10
A PHILOSOPHY OF MEMORY

Chapter 1
Joy and Hope

(1) I shall know you, my knower, I shall know you, "even as I am known."[1] Power of my soul, enter into it and fit it for yourself, so that you may have it and hold it "without spot or wrinkle."[2] This is my hope. Therefore I speak out, and in this hope I rejoice[3] when I rejoice in a wholesome way. As for other things in this life, so much the less should they be wept for, the more they are wept over, and all the more must they be wept over, the less we weep when among them. "For behold, you have loved truth,"[4] since "he who does truth comes to the light."[5] This I wish to do in my heart, before you in confession, and in my writing before many witnesses.

Chapter 2
The Soul Seen Plain

(2) Lord, before whose eyes the abyss of man's conscience lies naked,[1] what thing within me could be hidden from you, even if I would not confess it to you? I would be hiding you from myself, not myself from you. But now, since my groans bear witness that I am a thing displeasing to myself, you shine forth, and you are pleasing to me, and you are loved and longed for, so that I may feel shame for myself, and renounce myself, and choose you, and please neither you nor myself except because of you.

Therefore, before you, O Lord, am I manifest, whatever I may be. With what profit I may confess to you, I have already said. Nor do I this with bodily words and sounds but with words uttered by the soul and with outcry of thought, of which your ear has knowledge. When I am evil, to confess to you is naught else but to be displeased with myself; when I am up-

The Confessions of St. Augustine

...e, naught else is it to confess to you but to attribute... in no wise to myself. For you bless the just man,[2] O ...d, but first you justify him as one who has been ungodly.[3] Hence my confession is made in silence before you, my God, and yet not in silence. As to sound, it is silent, but it cries aloud with love. Nor do I say any good thing to men except what you have first heard from me; nor do you hear any such thing from me but what you have first spoken to me.

Chapter 3
The Ears of Men

(3) What have I to do with men, that they should hear my confessions, as if they were to "heal all my diseases?"[1] A race eager to know about another man's life, but slothful to correct their own! Why do they seek to hear from me what I am, men who do not want to hear from you what they themselves are? When they hear me speak about myself, how do they know if I speak the truth, since none among men knows "what goes on within a man but the spirit of man which is in him?"[2] But if they should hear about themselves from you, they cannot say, "The Lord lies!" What else is it for them to hear from you about themselves except to know themselves? Who knows anything and yet says, "It is false," unless he is a liar? But because "charity believes all things"[3] among them whom it unites by binding them to itself, I too, O Lord, will confess to you in such manner that men may hear, although I cannot prove to them that I confess truly. But those men whose ears charity opens to me believe me.

(4) Do you, my inmost physician, make clear to me with what profit I do these things. For when they are read and heard, these confessions of my past sins—which "you have forgiven and covered over,"[4] so that you may make me blessed in you, changing my soul by faith and your sacrament—stir up the heart. Then it will not sleep in despair and say, "I cannot," but it will awaken in love of your mercy and in your sweet grace. Through this grace whosoever is weak is strong,[5] when by its means he comes to know his own weakness. Good people like to hear about the past misdeeds of others who are now rid

of such things, not because those deeds are present evils, but because once they were but no longer are.

With what fruit, then, O my Lord, to whom my conscience each day makes confession—more secure in its hope of your mercy than from any innocence of its own—with what fruit, I ask, do I confess, not only in your presence but to men also by these writings, what I now am, not what once I was? That other advantage I have seen and spoken of. But as to what I am now, at this very time when I make my confessions, many men wish to know about this, both men who have known me and others who have not known me. They have heard something from me or about me, but their ear is not placed close to my heart, where I am whatever I am. Therefore, they wish to hear me confess what I am within myself, where they can extend neither their eye nor ear nor mind. This they desire, as men ready to believe; how otherwise could they know it? Charity, by reason of which they are good men, tells them that I do not lie when I make my confession: it is charity in them that believes in me.

Chapter 4
Help Men to Hear Me Aright

(5) But with what benefit do they wish to hear me? Do they wish to share my thanksgiving, when they hear how close it is by your gift that I approach to you, and to pray for me, when they hear how I am held back by my own weight? To such men I will reveal myself. It is no small benefit, O Lord my God, that "thanks may be given to you by many in our behalf,"[1] and that many should pray to you for us. Let a brother's mind love in me what you teach us must be loved, and lament in me what you teach us must be lamented. Let a brother's mind do this, not a stranger's mind, not the mind "of strange children, whose mouth has spoken vanity, and their right hand is the right hand of iniquity."[2] Let it be that brotherly mind which, when it approves me, rejoices over me, and when it disapproves of me, is saddened over me, for the reason that, whether it approves or disapproves, it loves me. To such men will I reveal myself. May they sigh for my good

deeds, and may they sigh over my evil deeds. All my goods are things that you have established and they are your gifts; my evils are my own misdeeds and your judgments upon me. May they sigh for the one, and sigh over the other. May hymns and weeping ascend in your sight from the hearts of my brethren, your censers.[3] Be pleased, O Lord, with the odor of your holy temple, and "have mercy on me according to your great mercy"[4] for your name's sake. Do not abandon in any way what you have begun in me, but make perfect my imperfections.

(6) Such is the benefit from my confessions, not of what I have been, but of what I am, that I may confess this not only before you in secret exultation with trembling[5] and in secret sorrow with hope, but also in the ears of believing sons of men, partakers of my joy and sharers in my mortality, my fellow citizens and pilgrims with me, those who go before me and those who follow me, and those who are companions on my journey. They are your servants, my brothers, whom you will to be your sons; my masters, whom you have commanded me to serve if I would live by you. Yet this your Word would be but little to me, if he had given his precepts in speech alone and had not gone on before me by deeds.[6] I do this service by deeds as well as by words: I do this "under your wings,"[7] with too grave a peril unless "under your wings" my soul had been subdued to you and my infirmity made known to you. I am but a little one, but my Father lives forever, and my protector is sufficient for me. He is the Selfsame, who begot me and watches over me. You are all my goods, you the almighty, who are with me even before I am with you. Therefore, to such as you command me to serve I will reveal not what I have been but what I now am and what I still am. "But neither do I judge myself."[8] In this manner, then, let me be heard.

Chapter 5
God's Knowledge and Man's Ignorance

(7) You judge me, O Lord, for, although no one "knows the things of a man but the spirit of man which is in him,"[1] there is something further in man which not even that spirit of man

which is in him knows. But you, Lord, who made him, know all things that are in him. Although I despise myself before your sight, and account myself but dust and ashes,[2] yet I know something of you which I do not know about myself. In truth, "we see now through a glass in a dark manner," and not yet "face to face."[3] Therefore, as long as I journey apart from you,[4] I am more present to myself than to you. Yet I have known that you are in no wise subject to violation, whereas for myself, I do not know which temptations I can resist and which I cannot. Even so, there is hope, for you are "faithful, who will not suffer" us "to be tempted above that which" we "are able to bear," but you "make also with temptation issue, that" we "may be able to bear it."[5] Let me confess, then, what I know about myself. Let me confess also what I do not know about myself, since that too which I know about myself I know because you enlighten me. As to that which I am ignorant of concerning myself, I remain ignorant of it until my "darkness shall be made as the noonday in your sight."[6]

Chapter 6
The Life of Life

(8) Not with doubtful but with sure knowledge do I love you, O Lord. By your Word you have transfixed my heart, and I have loved you. Heaven and earth and all things in them, behold! everywhere they say to me that I should love you. They do not cease from saying this to all men, "so that they are inexcusable."[1] But in a deeper way you will have mercy on him on whom you will have mercy, and you will show mercy to him to whom you will show mercy,[2] for otherwise heaven and earth proclaim your praises to the deaf. What is it then that I love when I love you? Not bodily beauty, and not temporal glory, not the clear shining light, lovely as it is to our eyes, not the sweet melodies of many-moded songs, not the soft smell of flowers and ointments and perfumes, not manna and honey, not limbs made for the body's embrace, not these do I love when I love my God.

Yet I do love a certain light, a certain voice, a certain odor, a certain food, a certain embrace when I love my God: a light, a voice, an odor, a food, an embrace for the man within me, where his light, which no place can contain, floods into my soul; where he utters words that time does not speed away; where he sends forth an aroma that no wind can scatter; where he provides food that no eating can lessen; where he so clings that satiety does not sunder us. This is what I love when I love my God.

(9) And what is this? I asked the earth, and it said, "I am not he!" And all things in it confessed the same. I asked the sea and the deeps, and among living animals the things that creep, and they answered, "We are not your God! Seek you higher than us!" I asked the winds that blow: and all the air, with the dwellers therein, said, "Anaximenes[3] was wrong. I am not God!" I asked the heavens, the sun, the moon, and the stars: "We are not the God whom you seek," said they. To all the things that stand around the doors of my flesh I said, "Tell me of my God! Although you are not he, tell me something of him!" With a mighty voice they cried out, "He made us!"[4] My question was the gaze I turned on them; the answer was their beauty.

I turned then to myself, and I said to myself, "Who are you?" I answered, "A man!" See, body and soul await my service, one without, the other within. From which of these ought I to have sought my God, whom I had already searched for through bodily things, from the earth up to the heavens, as far as I could project the radiant messengers of my eyes? Better indeed is that inner being. For to it, as that which rules over other things and passes judgment upon them, all those bodily messengers reported back answers of heaven and earth and all things that are in them, as they said: "We are not God!" and again, "He made us!" The inner man knows such things through the ministry of the outer man. I, the inner man, know these things; I, I, the mind, by means of my bodily senses. I asked the whole fabric of the world about my God, and it answered me, "I am not he, but he has made me!"

(10) Is not this beauty apparent to all men whose senses are sound and whole? Why then does it not speak the same to all men? Animals both great and small see it, but they cannot question it. In them, reason has not been placed in judg-

ment over the senses and their reports. But men can ask questions, so that they may clearly see the invisible things of God, "being understood by the things that are made."[5]

However, through love for such things they become subject to them, and in subjection they cannot pass judgment on them. Nor do things answer those who ask unless they are men of judgment. They do not change their voice, that is, their beauty, when one man merely looks at them and another both looks and questions, so as to appear one thing to this man, another to that. It appears the same to both: it is silent to one, but speaks to the other. Nay rather, it speaks to all, but only those understand who compare its voice taken in from outside with the truth within them. Truth says to me: "Your God is not heaven and earth, nor any bodily thing." Their very nature proclaims this. Men see that the world is a vast mass, smaller in any part than in its whole. But I say to you, O my soul, that you are already my better part, for you quicken the body's mass and give it life, and this a body cannot give to a body. But your God is for you even the life of life.

Chapter 7
The Power of Sensation

(11) What, therefore, do I love when I love my God? Who is he who is above the head of my soul? By my soul itself will I ascend to him. I will pass beyond that power of mine by which I adhere to the body and fill the body's frame with life. Not by that power do I find my God. For "the horse and the mule in which there is no understanding"[1] would likewise find him, since in them there is that same power, and by it their bodies also live. But there is another power, by which I not only give life but sensation as well to my flesh, which the Lord has fashioned for me, commanding the eye that it should not hear, and the ear that it should not see, but giving to the first power so that I may see by it, and the other power so that I hear by it, and singly to each of the other senses powers proper to their organs and purposes. I, who am one single mind, perform these diverse things through the senses.[2] But I will pass beyond this power of mine, for this too the horse

and the mule possess. They too sense things by means of the body.

Chapter 8
The Fields of Memory

(12) Therefore, I will pass also beyond this power of my nature, and ascending by steps to him who made me, I come into the fields and spacious palaces of my memory, where are treasures of countless images of things of every manner, brought there from objects perceived by sense. Hidden away in that place is also whatever we think about, whether by increasing or by lessening or somehow altering the things that sense attains to. There also is whatever else has been entrusted to it and stored up within it, which forgetfulness has not yet swallowed up and buried away.

When I am in that realm, I ask that whatsoever I want be brought forth. Certain things come forth immediately. Certain other things are looked for longer, and are rooted out as it were from some deeper receptacles. Certain others rush forth in mobs, and while some different thing is asked and searched for, they jump in between, as if to say, "Aren't we perhaps the ones?" By my heart's hand I brush them away from the face of my remembrance until what I want is unveiled and comes into sight from out of its hiding place. Others come out readily and in unbroken order, just as they are called for: those coming first give way to those that follow. On yielding, they are buried away again, to come forth when I want them. All this takes place when I recount anything by memory.

(13) In memory, all things are kept distinct and according to kind. Each is brought in through its own proper entrance: as light and all colors and bodily shapes through the eyes; all varieties of sound through the ears; all odors by the portal of the nostrils; all tastes by the portal of the mouth; and, by the sense diffused throughout the whole body, what is hard, what is soft, what is hot or cold, smooth or sharp, heavy or light, whether outside or inside the body. The great cave of memory, and I know not what hidden and inexpressible recesses within it, takes in all these things to be called up and brought forth

when there is need for them. All these enter in, each by its own gateway, and are laid away within it. The things themselves do not enter there, but images of things perceived by sense are kept ready there for the thought of the one recalling them. Although it is apparent by which senses they are seized and stored away there, who can say how these images are formed? For even when I dwell in darkness and silence, I bring forth colors in my memory, if I wish, and I distinguish between white and black and between what others as I will. Nor do sounds rush in and disturb the thing drawn in by the eyes as I reflect upon it, although sounds too are there and lie hidden and set apart, as it were. These also I call for, if I please, and immediately they are there on the spot. Although my tongue is at rest and my throat silent, yet I sing as much as I wish. Those images of color, although they are nonetheless there, do not interpose or interrupt, when another stock of images, which flowed in through the ears, is drawn forth. So also other things, which were carried in and heaped up by other senses, I recall at pleasure. I distinguish the breath of lilies from violets, although smelling neither one. I prefer honey to must,[1] the smooth to the sharp, although not tasting and touching them at the time, but simply by recalling them in memory.

(14) These acts I perform within myself in the vast court of my memory. Within it are present to me sky, earth, and sea, together with all things that I could perceive in them, aside from all the things I have forgotten. There too I encounter myself and recall myself, and what, and when, and where I did some deed, and how I was affected when I did it. There are all those things which I remember either as experienced by me or as taken on trust from others. From that same abundant stock, also, I combine one and another of the likenesses of things, whether things actually known by experience or those believed in from those I have experienced, with things past, and from them I meditate upon future actions, events, and hopes, and all these again as though they were actually present. "I will do this or that," I say to myself within that vast recess of my mind, filled with images, so many and so great, and this deed or that then follows. "Oh, that this or

that could be!" "May God forbid this or that!" I say such things within myself, and as I speak, the images of all the things I name are ready at hand, out of that same treasure house of memory. Nor would I utter any of them, if their images were absent.

(15) Great is the power of memory, exceeding great is it, O God, an inner chamber, vast and unbounded! Who has penetrated to its very bottom? Yet it is a power of my mind and it belongs to my nature, and thus I do not comprehend all that I am. Is the mind, therefore, too limited to possess itself? Must we ask, "Where is this power belonging to it which it does not grasp?" "Is it outside it, and not within it?" "How then does it not comprehend it?" Great wonder arises within me at this. Amazement seizes me. Men go forth to marvel at the mountain heights, at huge waves in the sea, at the broad expanse of flowing rivers, at the wide reaches of the ocean, and at the circuits of the stars, but themselves they pass by. They do not marvel at the fact that while I was speaking of all these things, I did not look upon them with my own eyes. Yet I would never have spoken of them, unless within me, in my memory, in such vast spaces as though I were looking at them outside, I could gaze upon mountains, waves, rivers, and stars, which I have seen, and that ocean, which I believe to be. Yet when I saw them with my eyes I did not draw them into myself by looking at them. Nor are the things themselves present to me, but only their images, and in each instance I have known what has been impressed on me by each bodily sense.[2]

Chapter 9
A Higher Memory

(16) But not these things alone does that immeasurable capacity of my memory encompass. Here also are all those things learned from the liberal studies which have not yet slipped away, and are put back as it were into an interior place that is yet not a place. Of these things it is not images that I carry about, but the things themselves. For what literature is, what skill in disputation is, how many kinds of ques-

tions there are, and whatever else of such subjects I know, all this is in my memory in such wise that I have not retained the image while leaving the reality outside. Nor is it a sound that has passed away, after the manner of an utterance that makes its impression through the ears, leaving some trace of itself, whereby it may be recalled, as if to make sound although it no longer does make sound. It is not like an odor, which, as it passes and vanishes with the wind, affects the sense of smell, and thence conveys into memory an image of itself, which we repeat by remembrance of it. Nor is it like food, which surely has no taste when once in the stomach, but still has a sort of taste in memory. Nor is it like anything perceived by bodily touch, which is imaged in memory even when the object is kept apart from us. These things indeed are not themselves transmitted into memory: only images of them are seized with marvelous speed and are put away as if into wondrous cells, and are wonderfully brought forth by acts of memory.

CHAPTER 10

Learning as Remembrance

(17) But when I hear that there are three kinds of questions—Does a certain thing exist? What is it? What are its properties?[1]—I retain the images of the sounds out of which these words have been fashioned, and I know that they passed with ordered sound through the air, and that they no longer exist. But as to the things themselves which are signified by those sounds, I neither attained to them by any bodily sense nor did I descry them anywhere except in my mind. Yet I stored away in my memory not their images but the things themselves. Let such things tell how they entered into me if they can. For I check over all the portals of my flesh, and I do not discover any through which they have entered.

The eyes indeed say, "If those images were colored, we reported them to you." The ears say, "If they had sound, they have been declared by us." The nostrils say, "If they had odor, they passed through us." The sense of taste says, "If there was no savor in them, do not ask me." Touch says, "If the thing had no bodily shape, I have not handled it. If I have not handled it, I have not reported it." Whence and how did these things enter into my memory? How, I do not know, for when I learned them I did not give credence to another's heart, but I recognized them within my own, and I approved them as true, and I entrusted them to my heart. It was as if I stored them away there, whence I would bring them forth when I wanted them. Therefore they were there even before I learned them, but they were not in memory. Where, then, or why, when they were uttered, did I recognize them, and say, "So it is; it is true," if not because they were already in memory, but so removed and pushed back as it were in more hidden caverns that, unless they were dug up by some reminder, I would perhaps have been unable to conceive them.[2]

Chapter 11
Thought and Memory

(18) For this reason, we find that to learn such things, images of which we do not take in through the senses, and which apart from images we discern within us, just as they are in themselves, is simply this: by acts of thought we gather together and collect as it were things that memory contained here and there and without any order, and then observe them and see to it that they be placed near at hand as it were in that very memory, where they previously lay scattered and neglected. Thus they will occur easily to a mind already made familiar with them.

How numerous are the things of this kind that my memory contains! Things that have already been discovered, and, as I said, placed ready at hand, as it were, things which we are said to have learned and to have come to know! If I cease to recall these things for a short space of time, they are again submerged and slip down into still deeper hiding places, so that they must again be thought of as if new, and again from that same place—there is no other region for them—they must be brought together (*cogenda*) so that they may be known. That is, they must be collected together (*colligenda*) as it were out of a sort of scattered state. Hence it is termed cogitation. For *cogo* (I bring together) and *cogito* (I cogitate) have the same mutual relation as *ago* (I do) and *agito* (I do constantly) and *facio* (I make) and *factito* (I make often). But the mind has appropriated this word to itself, so that what is collected together (*colligitur*), that is, brought together (*cogitur*), in the mind but in no other place, is now properly said to be cogitated.

Chapter 12
Mathematics and Memory

(19) Again, memory contains the principles and countless laws of numbers and dimensions, none of which any bodily sense has impressed upon it, since they are not colored, nor do they give out sound or odor, nor are they tasted or touched. I have heard the sound of the words by which such things are signified when they are discussed, but the sounds are one thing and the things are another. The sounds are of one kind in Greek and of another in Latin, but the things are neither Greek, nor Latin, nor any other kind of language. I have seen lines drawn by builders, even lines so fine as to be like a spider's threads. But those other lines are different: they are not images of things of which the fleshly eye has told me. Anyone who perceives them within himself, without the conception of any body whatsoever, knows those things. Also, by means of all the bodily senses I have perceived the numbers that we enumerate, but those numbers with which we enumerate are something different.[1] They are not the images of the other ones, and yet they truly exist. Let him who does not perceive them laugh at me for making these statements; I will pity him for laughing at me.

Chapter 13
Memory of Memories

(20) I retain these things in memory, and in memory I retain how I learned them. Again, I have heard many things that have been most fallaciously argued against them, and I

retain them in memory. Even if those things are false, it is not false that I have remembered them. Further, I remember that I distinguished between those true doctrines and the false things said against them. It is one thing that I now perceive that I make this distinction and another to remember that I often made the distinction when I thought about them. Therefore, I both remember that I have often understood these things, and I store away in memory what I now discern and understand, so that hereafter I may remember that I have understood at the present time. I have remembered that I have remembered, just as hereafter, if I shall recall that I have now been able to remember these things, I shall in truth recall it by the power of memory.

Chapter 14
Problems of Memory

(21) This same memory likewise contains the affections of my mind, not in that manner in which the mind itself has them at the time it experiences them, but in a far different manner, after the fashion in which the power of memory retains memory itself. For without being actually joyful, I remember myself to have been joyful; without being actually sad, I recall my past sorrow. Without fear, I recollect that I was at one time fearful; and without desire, I am mindful of previous desire. Contrariwise, at times I remember with joy my bygone sorrow, and with sorrow I remember past joy. This is not to be wondered at, as far as the body is concerned, for mind is one thing, and body is another. Hence it is not so strange a thing if I remember with joy past bodily pain. But in the present case, the mind is even memory itself. For when we order that a thing be committed to memory, we say, "See that you keep this in mind," and when we forget something, we say, "It was not in my mind," and "It slipped out of my mind." Thus we give the name of mind to memory itself. Therefore, since this is so, how is it that when I remember with joy my past sorrow, the mind contains joy, while the memory contains sadness, and that the mind rejoices from the fact that there is joy within it, whereas memory is not saddened by the fact

Book 10. A Philosophy of Memory   243

that there is sadness within it? Is it perhaps because memory does not belong to the mind? Who would admit such a thing? No doubt, therefore, memory is the mind's stomach, as it were, and joy and sadness are like sweet and bitter food. When they are committed to memory, they are as it were passed into the stomach and they can be stored away there, but they cannot be tasted. It is absurd to think that these things are like one another, and yet they are not entirely different.

(22) But note, when I say that there are four passions of the mind, I bring forth from memory desire, joy, sadness, and fear. From memory I bring forth whatever I say in disputation concerning them, by dividing the individual instances into species belonging to their own genus, and by defining them. Whatever I say about them I discover in memory and it is from memory that I produce it. Yet I am disturbed by none of these passions when I call them back to mind by remembrance of them. Even before they were recalled and brought back by me, they were there, and for that reason they could be brought back from there by recollection.

Perhaps, then, just as food is brought up from the stomach by rumination, so such things are brought up from memory by recollection. Why then are not the sweetness of joy and the bitterness of sorrow tasted in the mouth of thought by one discoursing, that is, reminiscing, upon these matters? Or is it in this that these two, which are not completely alike, really differ? Which of us would willingly speak of such matters if, whenever we name sadness or fear, we would be constrained to be sad or fearful? Yet we could not speak of this unless we found within our memory not only the sounds of their names, in keeping with the images impressed by bodily senses, but also conceptions of the things themselves, which we did not receive through any fleshly door. The mind itself, perceiving them by experience of its own passions, committed them to memory, or memory itself retained them for itself, even though they had not been committed to it.

Chapter 15
Image and Reality

(23) But who can easily say whether this is by means of images or not? I name a stone, for instance, or I name the sun, and although the things themselves are not present to my senses, certainly their images are present within my memory. I name bodily pain; it is not present to me as long as nothing is causing me pain. However, if its image were not present in my memory, I would not know what word to use, nor could I distinguish it from pleasure when discussing it. I name bodily health, when I am sound in body. The reality itself is present to me, but truly unless its image were also in my memory, I could in no wise recollect what the sound of this name should signify. When the word health is used, the sick would not understand what was said unless the same image were retained by force of memory, even though the reality itself is absent from the body.

I name the numbers by which we calculate, and note that not their images but they themselves are present in my memory. I name the image of the sun, and it is present in my memory. I do not recall the image of its image, but the image itself. It is present to me as I engage in reminiscence. I name memory, and I recognize what I name. Where do I recognize it unless in memory itself? Is it also present to itself by means of its own image, and not by itself?

Chapter 16
The Problem of Forgetting

(24) When I name forgetfulness and at the same time recognize what I name, how do I recognize the reality unless I remember it? I do not speak of the name's sound but of the thing that it signifies. If I had forgotten that, I would surely be unable to recognize what the sound should impart. When I remember memory, memory itself is present to itself through itself. But when I remember forgetfulness, both memory and

forgetfulness are present: memory by which I remember and forgetfulness which I remember.

What is forgetfulness, unless it be privation of memory? How then is it present so that I can remember it, since when it is present I am unable to remember? But if we retain in memory what we remember, and unless we remember forgetfulness, when we hear the word we are in no wise able to recognize the thing signified by the word, then forgetfulness is retained in memory. Therefore it is present, so that we are not forgetful of it, yet when it is present we are actually forgetful. Or do we understand from this fact that when we remember it, it is not present in memory in itself, but by means of its image? For if forgetfulness were present in itself, would it not cause us not to remember but to forget? What man will search this out? Who can comprehend how it is?

(25) Lord, I truly labor at this task, and I labor upon myself. I have become for myself a soil hard to work and demanding much sweat.[1] We do not now explore the regions of the sky; we do not measure the distances of the stars; nor do we search out the weight of the earth. It is I who remember, I the mind. It is no matter for wonder that what I am not is far distant from me; but what is closer to me than I myself? Consider: the power of my own memory is not understood by me, and yet apart from it I cannot even name myself. What shall I say when it is certain to me that I have remembered forgetfulness? Am I to assert that what I remember is not in my memory? Am I to say that forgetfulness is in my memory to the end that I do not forget? Both answers are most absurd. What third answer is there? How can I say that the image of forgetfulness is retained in my memory, but not forgetfulness itself, when I remember it?

How could I say this, since, when the image of anything is impressed on memory, it is first necessary that the thing itself be present, whence that image may be impressed? Thus do I remember Carthage, thus all places where I have been, thus men's faces that I have seen, and things reported by the other senses, thus health or pain in the body itself. When these things were present, memory acquired images from them, which as present with me I could look upon and turn about in my mind when I would remember those things in their absence.

Therefore, if forgetfulness is retained in memory not through itself but through its image, surely it was itself once present so that its image might be acquired. But when it was present, how did it inscribe its image on memory, since by its very presence forgetfulness wipes away whatever it finds already noted there? Yet in some manner, although this manner is incomprehensible and inexplicable, I am certain that I have remembered forgetfulness itself, whereby what we remember is destroyed.

Chapter 17
Beyond Memory

(26) Great is the power of memory! An awesome thing, my God, deep and boundless and manifold in being! And this thing is the mind, and this am I myself: What then am I, O my God? What is my nature? A life varied and manifold and mightily surpassing measurement. Behold! in the fields and caves and caverns of my memory, innumerable and innumerably filled with all varieties of innumerable things, whether through images, as with all bodies, or by their presence, as with the arts, or by means of certain notions and notations, as with the passions of the mind—for these memory retains even when the mind does not experience them, although whatever is in memory is also in the soul—through all these I run, I fly here and there, and I penetrate into them as far as I can, and there is no end to them. So great is the power of memory! So great is the power of life, even in man's mortal life!

What then shall I do, O you who are my true life, my God? I will pass beyond even this power of mine which is called memory, desiring to reach you, where you may be reached, and to cling to you there where you can be clung to.

Even the beasts of the field and the birds have memory. Elsewise they could not seek out again their dens and nests, nor the many other places which they have grown to know. Indeed, they could not grow used to any other things except through memory. Therefore, I will pass beyond even memory, so that I may attain to him who has set me apart from four-footed animals and made me wiser than the birds of the air.[1] Even beyond memory will I pass, so that I may find you—where? O truly good and certain delight, so that I may find you where? If I find you apart from memory, I am unmindful of you. How then shall I find you, if I do not remember you?

Chapter 18
Lost Things Found Again

(27) The woman who had lost the drachma and searched for it with a lamp would not have found it unless she had remembered it.[1] When it was found, how would she know whether it was the same one if she had not remembered it? I remember that I have looked for many lost articles and have found them again. I know this from the fact that if, while I was looking for something and someone would say to me, "Is this it?" or "Is that it?" I kept saying "It is not," until what I was looking for was brought to me. Unless I remembered it, whatever it was, even if it were brought to me, I would not have found it because I could not identify it. This is always the way when we search for a lost article and find it again.

If a thing, such as any visible body, should happen to disappear from sight, but not from memory, its image is retained within us, and the thing is searched for until it is restored to sight. When it is found, it is recognized by the image which is within. We do not say that we have found what was lost, unless we recognize it, and we cannot recognize it, if we do not remember it. It was lost to sight but kept in memory.

Chapter 19
The Forgotten Name

(28) What? When memory itself loses a thing, as happens when we forget and try to remember it, where after all do we look except in memory itself? There, if one thing chances to be offered instead of the other, we reject it until what we are looking for occurs to us, and when it does occur, we say, "This is it." We would not say this unless we recognized it, and we

would not recognize it unless we remembered it. But surely we had forgotten it. Or was it that the entire matter had not slipped from us, but because of a part that was retained, the other part was looked for? Was memory thus conscious that it did not retain all it was accustomed to, and limping as it were from this loss of familiar knowledge, did it demand the return of what was lacking? For instance, we see or think of some man we know, and as we have forgotten his name, we try to recall it. Any other name that occurs is not assigned to him, because it is not associated with him in thought. Hence, each one is rejected, until that name presents itself which our knowledge without objection accepts as familiar to it. Whence does this name present itself, unless from memory itself? For even when we recognize the name after being reminded of it by another person, it is from there that it presents itself. We do not assent to it as it were something new, but since we remember it, we agree that the one spoken is the name. If it had been completely wiped out of the mind, we would not remember it even when reminded of it. For we have not as yet completely forgotten what we still remember to have forgotten. Therefore, what we have completely forgotten we cannot even look for if it is lost.

Chapter 20
What All Men Seek

(29) How then do I seek you, O Lord? For when I seek you, my God, I seek the happy life. Let me seek you "so that my soul may live."[1] My body lives by my soul, and my soul lives by you. How then do I seek the happy life? For I do not possess it until I can say, "Enough! It is there!" Here I ought to tell how I seek it, whether through remembrance, as if I had forgotten it but still held to the fact that I had forgotten it, or out of desire to learn a thing unknown, whether one I never knew or one I had forgotten so completely that I did not remember I had forgotten it. Is not the happy life that which all men will to have, and no man entirely wills against? Where have they known it, that they in such wise will to pos-

sess it? Where have they seen it, so that they love it? Truly, we have it, but how I do not know.

There is a certain other way by which a man is happy when he has the happy life, and there are also those who are happy because of hope. These last have happiness in a lower way than do those who already are happy in very reality, but they are better than those who are happy neither in fact nor in hope. Yet even these latter men would not thus desire to be happy unless they possessed it in some fashion, and that they do desire it is most certain. They have known it, how I do not know, and therefore they have it with I know not what kind of knowledge. Concerning this knowledge, I am perplexed as to whether it is in memory, for if it is there, then all of us have already been happy at some period, either each of us individually, or all of us together in that man[2] who first sinned, in whom we all died,[3] and from whom we are all born in misery. Of this last I do not now inquire, but I inquire whether the happy life is in the memory.

Unless we knew it, we would not love it. We have heard this name, and we all confess that we all desire the reality: we do not take delight in the mere sound of the word. When a Greek hears it in Latin, he finds no delight in it, since he does not know what has been said. We are delighted, just as he is also if he hears it in Greek. For neither Greek nor Latin is that reality which Greeks and Latins and men of other tongues long to possess. Therefore, it is known to all men, for if they could be asked in one language whether they wish to be happy, they would answer without hesitation that they wish this. This could not be unless that very thing for which this is the name were retained in their memory.

Chapter 21
The Longed-for Life

(30) Is this just as one who has seen Carthage remembers it? No, for the happy life is not seen by the eyes, since it is not a body. Is it like the way we remember numbers? No, for one who holds them in knowledge does not still seek to acquire them, whereas we possess the happy life in knowledge,

and therefore love it, but still wish to obtain it so that we may be actually happy. Is it like the way we remember the arts of speech? No, for even those who are not skilled speakers recall the thing itself when they hear the word. Also, many men desire to be eloquent: hence it is apparent that this is in their knowledge. However, by means of their bodily senses they have taken note of other men who are finished speakers, have been pleased by them, and desire to be such themselves. At the same time, they would not have been pleased unless because of some inner knowledge, nor would they have wanted to be eloquent unless they had been pleased, whereas we do not perceive the happy life in others by means of any bodily sense.

Is it like the way we remember joy? Perhaps so, for even when I am sad, I remember my joys, just as when wretched I remember the happy life. But I never saw, or heard, or smelled, or tasted, or touched joy by a bodily sense. I have experienced it in my mind, when I have rejoiced, and knowledge of it has clung to my memory. Hence I could remember it, sometimes with disgust, sometimes with desire, in keeping with the different things in which I recalled myself to have taken joy. For I have been plunged into a sort of joy even from foul deeds, which joy I now abhor and execrate as I recall it, and at other times from good and virtuous things. This latter joy I recall with desire, although perhaps the things are no longer present. Therefore, with sadness do I recall past joy.

(31) Where, then, and when did I have experience of my happy life, so that I remember it, and love it, and long for it? It is not merely myself along with a few others, but all of us without exception want to be happy. Unless we knew this with sure knowledge, we would not want it with so sure a will. But what is this? If two men are asked whether they want to serve as soldiers, it may well be that one of them will reply that he wants to, while the other will reply that he does not. However, if they are asked whether they want to be happy, both will say immediately and without hesitation that they want to. Moreover, one man wants to be a soldier and the other does not want to be one for no reason except that they may be happy. Is it perhaps because one finds joy in one course and

the other in a different one? Just so, all men agree that they want to be happy, just as they would agree, if they were asked, that they want to be joyful, and this very joy they call the happy life. Although one man seeks it in one way and the other in a different way, there is one thing that they all strive to attain, that is, to have joy. Since this is the case, and no one can deny that he has felt this way, it is therefore found in memory and recognized when the words "happy life" are heard.

Chapter 22
The Only Happiness

(32) Far be it, Lord, far be it from the heart of your servant who confesses to you, far be it that, no matter with what joy I may rejoice, I should think myself happy. There is a joy that is not granted to the wicked, but only to those who worship you for your own sake, and for whom you yourself are joy. This is the happy life, to rejoice over you, to you, and because of you: this it is, and there is no other. Those who think that there is another such life pursue another joy and it is not true joy. Yet their will is not turned away from a certain image of joy.

Chapter 23
Truth and Happiness

(33) Is it uncertain, then, that all men desire to be happy, seeing that they do not truly desire the happy life, who do not desire to have joy in you, which is the only happy life? Or do all men indeed desire this? But, since "the flesh lusts against the spirit, and the spirit against the flesh,"[1] so that they do not do what they wish, do they fall down to what they are able to take, and are they satisfied with that? Is this because what they are unable to do they do not desire with sufficient strength to accomplish?

Of each and every man I ask, whether he would rather have joy in truth or in falsity. They no more hesitate to say they prefer to have joy in truth than they hesitate to say they desire to be happy. In fact, joy in the truth is the happy life. This is joy in you who are the truth,[2] O God, "my light,"[3] "the salvation of my countenance, my God."[4] This happy life all men desire; this life which alone is happy all men desire; all men desire joy in the truth.

I have known many men who would like to deceive, but none who wants to be deceived. Where then have they known this happy life, except where they knew truth as well? They love it too because they do not want to be deceived. When they love the happy life, which is no different from joy in the truth, then indeed they love the truth as well. They would not love it unless there were some knowledge of it in their memory. Why then do they not rejoice in it? Why are they unhappy? It is because they are more strongly taken up with other things, which have more power to make them wretched, than has that which they remember so faintly to make them happy. Yet a little while there is light among men. Let them walk, let them walk, lest the darkness overtake them.[5]

(34) Why is it, then, that "truth begets hatred?"[6] Why is your man who preaches truth to men become an enemy in their eyes,[7] even though there is love for the happy life, which is naught else but joy in the truth? Can such things be except because truth is loved in such wise that men who love some other object want what they love to be the truth, and because they do not want to be deceived, they refuse to be convinced that they have been deceived? Therefore, they hate the truth for the sake of that very thing which they have loved instead of the truth. They love the truth because it brings light to them; they hate it in as much as it reproves them. Because they do not wish to be deceived but wish to deceive, they love it when it shows itself to them, and they hate it when it shows them to themselves.[8]

Thus does it repay them, so that those who do not desire to be made manifest by it, it makes manifest as unwilling, while it is not itself made manifest to them. Thus, thus, yea, thus does the human soul, even thus blind and diseased and foul and degraded, desire to lie hidden, but it does not desire that anything lie hidden from itself. Against it judgment is rendered, that while it does not lie hidden from the truth, the truth can be hidden from it. Yet even so, while man's soul is thus wretched, it prefers to have joy in true things rather than in false. Happy, therefore, will it be, when no obstacle stands between and it shall find joy in that sole truth by which all things are true.

Chapter 24
God, Truth Itself

(35) Behold, how far within my memory have I traveled in search of you, Lord, and beyond it I have not found you! Nor have I found anything concerning you except what I have kept in memory since I first learned of you. For since I learned of you, I have not forgotten you. Wheresoever I found truth, there I found my God, truth itself, and since I first learned the truth I have not forgotten it. Therefore, ever since I learned about you, you abide in my memory, and I find you there when I recall you to mind and take delight in you. These are my holy delights which you have given to me out of your mercy, having regard for my poverty.

Chapter 25
Lord of Mind and Memory

(36) But where within my memory do you abide, Lord, where do you abide? What kind of abode have you fashioned for yourself? What manner of sanctuary have you built for yourself? So great an honor have you given to my memory as to abide within it. In what part of it you abide, this do I now consider. As soon as I brought you up in memory, I passed beyond such parts of it as the beasts also possess, for I did not find you there amid images of bodily things. I came to those of its parts to which I entrusted my mind's affections, and yet I did not find you there.

I entered even into the very seat of my mind, which lies within my memory, since the mind also remembers itself. You were not there. For you are not a bodily image, nor are you an affection of a living thing, such as obtains when we rejoice, feel sad, desire, fear, remember, forget, or do anything of that kind. Nor are you the mind itself, because you are the Lord God of the mind. All these things undergo change, but you remain unchangeable above all things. And you have deigned to dwell in my memory, whence I have learned of you. Why then do I seek in what place you dwell therein, as if forsooth there were places there? Truly, you dwell in my memory, since I have remembered you from the time I learned of you, and I find you there when I call you to mind.

Chapter 26
The First Petition

(37) Where then did I find you, so that I might learn to know you? You were not in my memory before I learned to know you. Where then have I found you, if not in yourself and above me? There is no place, both backward do we go and forward, and there is no place. Everywhere, O Truth, you give hearing to all who consult you, and at one and the same time you make answer to them all, even as they ask about varied things. You answer clearly, but all men do not hear you clearly. All men ask counsel about what they wish, but they do not all hear what they wish. Your best servant is he who looks not so much to hear from you what he wants to hear, but rather to want what he hears from you.

Chapter 27
The Everlasting Love

(38) Too late have I loved you, O Beauty so ancient and so new, too late have I loved you! Behold, you were within me, while I was outside: it was there that I sought you, and, a deformed creature, rushed headlong upon these things of beauty which you have made. You were with me, but I was not with you. They kept me far from you, those fair things which, if they were not in you, would not exist at all. You have called to me, and have cried out, and have shattered my deafness. You have blazed forth with light, and have shone upon me, and you have put my blindness to flight! You have sent forth fragrance, and I have drawn in my breath, and I pant

after you. I have tasted you, and I hunger and thirst after you. You have touched me, and I have burned for your peace.

CHAPTER 28
Life Is a Warfare

(39) When I shall cleave to you with all my being, no more will there be pain and toil for me. My life will be life indeed, filled wholly with you. But now, since you lift up him whom you fill with yourself, and since I am not yet filled with you, I am a burden to myself. Joys that I should bewail contend with sorrows at which I should rejoice, but on which side victory may rest I do not know. My evil sorrows contend with my virtuous joys, and on which side victory may rest I do not know. Alas for me! Lord, have mercy on me![1] Alas for me! See, I do not hide my wounds. You are the physician; I am a sick man. You are merciful; I am in need of mercy. Is not "the life of man upon earth a trial?"[2]

What man wants trouble and hardship? You command that they be endured, not that they be liked. No man likes what he endures, although he likes to endure it. Yet, even though he may rejoice that he endures hardship, he prefers rather that there be nothing to endure. In the midst of adversities, I desire prosperous days; in the midst of prosperity, I dread adversity. Between these two, is there no middle ground where the life of man is not a trial? Woe to the prosperity of this world, once and again, both from fear of adversity and from corruption of joy! Woe to the adversities of this world, once and again, and a third time, from desire for prosperity, and because adversity itself is hard, and because it can make wreck of endurance! Is not the life of man upon earth a trial, without any relief whatsoever?

CHAPTER 29
Command What You Will

(40) All my hope is found solely in your exceeding great mercy. Give what you command, and command what you will. You enjoin continence. "And as I knew," says a certain man,

"that no one could be continent except God gave it, and this also was a point of wisdom to know whose gift it was."[1] By continence we are gathered together and brought back to the One, from whom we have dissipated our being into many things.[2] So much the less does he love you who loves anything else, even together with you, which he does not love for your sake. O Love, who are forever aflame and are never extinguished, O Charity, my God, set me aflame! You enjoin continence: give what you command, and command what you will.

Chapter 30
Persistence of Temptation

(41) In truth, you command me to be continent with regard to "the concupiscence of the flesh, and the concupiscence of the eyes, and the ambition of the world."[1] You have commanded me to abstain from concubinage, and in place of marriage itself, which you permit, you have counseled something better.[2] Since you granted this to me, it has been fulfilled even before I became a dispenser of your sacrament.[3] Yet in my memory, of which I have said many things, there still live images of such things as my former habits implanted there. When I am awake, they assail me but lacking in strength; in sleep they assail me not only so as to arouse pleasure, but even consent and something very like the deed itself. So great a power have these deep images over my soul and my flesh that these false visions persuade me when asleep to do what true sights cannot persuade me to when awake.

At such times am I not myself, O Lord my God? Yet so great a difference is there between myself and that same self of mine within the moment when I pass from waking to sleep or return hither from sleep! At such times where is reason, by which a man awake resists those suggestions, and remains unshaken even if the very deeds themselves are urged upon him? Is it closed, together with my eyes? Is it asleep, together with the body's senses? How is it that even in sleep we often resist, and mindful of our resolution, persist in it most chastely, and yield no assent to such allurements? Yet so great a difference obtains that, when it happens otherwise, we return on awaking to peace of conscience. By that very contrast we discover that it was not ourselves who did what we yet grieve over as in some manner done within us.

(42) Is not your hand, O God all-powerful, powerful to heal all diseases[4] of my soul, and, by your more abundant grace,[5] to quench even the lustful movements of my sleep. Lord, more and more will you increase in me your gifts, so that my soul, freed from the clinging mire of concupiscence, may follow me to you, so that it may not rebel against itself, so that even in sleep it will not commit those base corrupting deeds, brought on through corporeal images even to bodily pollution, so that it will not even consent to them. For that such a thing may give no pleasure at all, or so little as may be curbed easily even in the chaste affection of one asleep, not only in this life but even at my present age—this is no great thing to the Almighty, for you are "able to do more than we desire and understand."[6]

But what I still may be in this type of evil I have now said to my good Lord, "rejoicing with trembling"[7] for what you have given to me, lamenting in that in which I remain incomplete, hoping that you will make perfect in me your mercies even unto the fullness of peace, which my inward and outward members will have with you, when "death is swallowed up in victory."[8]

Chapter 31
Problems of Food and Drink

(43) There is another evil of the day, and would that it were sufficient for the day![1] We rebuild each day's decay within the body by eating and drinking, until that time when "you shall destroy both the food and the stomach,"[2] when you shall kill my hunger by a wondrous satiety, and "clothe this corruptible with an incorruption"[3] that will last forever. But now this need is sweet to me, and against such sweetness I fight, lest I be captured by it, and I wage daily warfare by fastings, more frequently "bringing my body into subjection,"[4] and my pains are driven out by pleasure. For hunger and thirst are a kind of pain: they burn and they kill like fever, unless

the medicine that is food brings them relief. Since this medicine is at hand, out of the consolation of your gifts, in which earth and water and sky come to help our infirmity, our very misfortune is called delight.

(44) You have taught me this, so that I may come to take food just as I take medicine. But while I pass from the discomfort of hunger to repletion and content, a snare of concupiscence is laid for me in that very process. For the passage itself is pleasurable, and there is no other way whereby we can make that passage which our need forces us to make. Since good health is the reason for eating and drinking, a dangerous pleasure makes herself my companion. Frequently she strives to go on ahead, so that for her sake I may do what I either say I do or wish to do for reasons of health. Nor is there one standard for both of them: for what is enough for health is too little for pleasure. Often it becomes a matter of doubt whether it is the care needed by the body that seeks help or a deceitful desire for pleasure that demands service. The unhappy soul finds cheer in this uncertainty, and in it prepares an excuse and a self-defense. It rejoices that what suffices to maintain health is not evident, so that under pretense of health it may disguise a pursuit of pleasure. Each day I strive to resist such temptations, and I call upon your right hand for help. To you do I refer all my doubts, because as yet I have no settled counsel upon this problem.

(45) I hear the voice of my God as he commands me, "Let not your hearts be overcharged with surfeiting and drunkenness."[5] Drunkenness is far from me: you will be merciful so that it does not come close to me. But sometimes gluttony creeps upon your servant: you will be merciful so that it may be put far from me. "No one can be continent unless you give it."[6] Many things you give to us when we pray for them, and whatever good we have received before we prayed for it, we have received from you. This too we have received from you, that we should afterwards know that we received it from you. I was never a drunkard, but I have known drunkards made into sober men by you. Therefore, you have accomplished this, that men who have never been drunkards might be what they are; and this also have you done, that men who were drunkards

should cease to be such; and this further you have done, that both classes might know by whom all this has been wrought.

I have heard another word of yours: "Do not go after your lusts, but turn away from your own will."[7] By your gift, I have heard that word which I have much loved: "For neither if we eat shall we have the more, nor if we do not eat shall we have the less."[8] This is to say: neither will the one course make me richer nor will the other make me wretched. I have heard another word: "For I have learned in whatever state I am to be constant therein . . . and I have known both to abound and to suffer need . . . I can do all things in him who strengthens me."[9] Behold a soldier of the heavenly encampments, not the dust that we are! But remember, Lord, "that we are dust,"[10] and that you have made man of dust,[11] and that "he was lost and is found."[12] Nor was that man able to do anything of himself, for he himself was dust, he whom I loved, when through the breath of your inspiration, he said these words, "I can do all things," he said, "in him who strengthens me."[13] Strengthen me, so that I can do all things! Grant what you command, and command what you will! He confesses that he has received this from you, and that "when he glories, he glories in the Lord."[14] I have heard another man as he prayed that he might receive help from you: "Take from me," he said, "the greediness of the belly."[15] Hence it is apparent, O holy God, that you give it all when men accomplish what you command to be done.

(46) You have taught me, good Father, that "all things are clean to the clean," "but it is evil for the man who eats with offense,"[16] and that "every creature of God is good, and nothing is to be rejected that is received with thanksgiving,"[17] and that "meat does not commend us to God,"[18] and that "no man should judge" us "in food or drink,"[19] and that "he who eats should not despise him who does not eat, and he who does not eat should not judge him who eats."[20] I have learned these things, praise to you, my God, my teacher, who knock upon my ears, who enlighten my heart. Deliver me from all temptation!

I do not fear uncleanness of food, but uncleanness of desire. I know that Noah was permitted to use every kind of flesh that could be used for food,[21] and that Elias was fed with flesh,[22] and that John, who was gifted with wondrous abstinence, was not defiled by the living things, the locusts, that he fed upon.[23] I know that Esau was deceived by his lust for lentils,[24] that David blamed himself for desiring a drink of water,[25] and that our King was tempted not by flesh meat but by bread.[26] Therefore the people in the desert deserved to be reproved, not because they desired flesh meat, but because out of desire for food they murmured against the Lord.[27]

(47) Set in the midst of such temptations, I struggle each day against concupiscence in eating and drinking. It is not something that I can resolve to cut off once and for all and touch no more, as I could concubinage. The bridle put upon the throat must be held with both moderate looseness and moderate firmness. Who is it, Lord, who is not carried a little beyond the limits of his need? Whoever he is, he is great indeed: let him magnify your name. Not such a one am I, "for I am a sinful man."[28] Yet I too magnify your name, and he who has overcome the world[29] intercedes with you for my sins,[30] numbering me among the weak members of his body. For "your eyes have seen my imperfect being, and in your book shall all be written."[31]

Chapter 32
Inner Doubt and Darkness

(48) With the allurements of sweet odors I am not much troubled: when they are absent, I do not seek them, and when they are present, I do not reject them, but I am prepared to do entirely without them. So do I seem to myself, but perhaps I am deceived. Within me are those lamentable dark areas wherein my own capacities lie hidden from me. Hence, when my mind questions itself about its own powers, it is not easy for it to decide what should be believed.[1] For even what is within it is for the most part hidden away unless brought to light by some experience. In this life, the whole of which is termed a trial,[2] no man should be sure whether one who can pass from worse to better might not also pass from better to worse. One hope, one trust, one firm promise—your mercy!

Chapter 33
Music as Means and End

(49) The delights of the ear had more firmly entangled and subdued me, but you broke them and set me free.[1] I confess that when melodies that your words bring to life are sung by a sweet and well-trained voice, I now find therein a little rest, not such that I cling to them, but such that I may rise up when I wish. But along with the words from which they take life, so that they are granted entry into me, they call for a place of some honor in my heart, and I can hardly offer one that is suitable to them.

Sometimes I think that I grant them more honor than is proper. This is when I feel our spirits aroused to a flaming piety more devoutly and ardently by such sacred words when they are sung well than if they are not so chanted, and when I see that all our spiritual affections, in keeping with their diversity, have corresponding modes of voice and song and are stirred up by a kind of secret propriety. But this sensual pleasure, to which the soul must not be delivered so as to be weakened, often leads me astray, when sense does not accompany reason in such wise as to follow patiently after it, but, having won admittance for reason's sake, even tries to run ahead and lead reason on. Thus in such things I unconsciously sin, but later I am conscious of it.

(50) Sometimes I avoid this very error in an intemperate fashion, and I err by an excess of severity. Then I strongly desire that all the melodies and sweet chants with which David's psalter is accompanied should be banished from my ears and from the Church itself. Then I think that the safer course is what I remember has often been related to me about Athanasius, Bishop of Alexandria. He made the reader of the psalm utter it with so slight a vocal inflection that it was more like speaking than singing. But again, when I recall the tears I poured out on hearing the Church's songs in those first days of my recovered faith, and how even now I am not moved by the singing but by the things sung, when they are sung with

clear voices and fitting modulation, I again recognize the great utility of this institution.

Thus do I waver between the danger of sensual pleasure and wholesome experience. I am inclined rather to approve the practice of singing in church, although I do not offer an irrevocable opinion on it, so that through the pleasure afforded the ears the weaker mind may rise to feelings of devotion. However, when it so happens that I am moved more by the singing than by what is sung, I confess that I have sinned, in such wise as to deserve punishment, and at such times I should prefer not to listen to a singer.

See how I stand! Weep with me, and weep for me, you who in this matter bring about within yourselves some good from which like deeds issue. For you who do not do this, these problems do not affect you.[2] But do you, O Lord my God, graciously hear me, and turn your gaze upon me, and see me, and have mercy on me, and heal me.[3] For in your sight I have become a riddle to myself, and that is my infirmity.

Chapter 34

Custody of the Eyes

(51) There remains the pleasure of these fleshly eyes of mine, concerning which I voice confessions to which the ears of your temple,[1] ears devout and brotherly, may listen. Thus may we conclude the temptations arising from concupiscence of the flesh that still assail me, groaning and "desiring to be clothed upon with my habitation that is from heaven."[2] The eyes love fair and varied forms and bright and beauteous colors. Let not such things possess my soul: may God who made these things good, yea, very good,[3] may he possess it. He is my good, not they. Each day they affect me all the while I am awake. No rest from them is granted to me, such as is granted at times of silence from singing voices, sometimes from all voices. For this queen of colors, this light which bathes all the things we look upon, drops down in many ways wherever I may be throughout the day, and beguiles me while engaged in some other task and not even observing it. So strongly does it entwine itself about me, that if it is suddenly withdrawn,

Book 10. A Philosophy of Memory 263

it is sought for with longing, and if it is long absent, it causes mental depression.

(52) O Light, which Tobias saw, when with closed bodily eyes he taught his son the way of life, and never straying, went before him on the feet of charity![4] O Light which Isaac saw with fleshly eyes burdened down and closed by old age, when he unknowingly blessed his sons, but by blessing them merited to know them![5] O Light, which Jacob saw, although he too was bereft of sight because of old age, and with an enlightened heart beheld tribes of men yet to come prefigured in his sons, and laid hands mystically crossed upon his grandchildren by Joseph, not as their father outwardly corrected them but as he himself inwardly perceived them![6] This is the Light! It is one, and all who see it and love it are one!

But that corporeal light of which I spoke seasons for its blind lovers this world's life with an alluring and perilous sweetness. But they who know how to praise you for it, O God, creator of all things,[7] take over this light when they sing your hymn, and they are taken over by it in their sleep. Such do I desire to be. I resist these seductions of the eyes, lest my feet, wherewith I walk upon your path, be ensnared, and I raise up my unseen eyes to you so that you may "pluck my feet out of the snare."[8] Again and again do you pluck them out, for they become ensnared. You never cease to pluck them out, for I often get caught in the snares scattered on every side, for "you do not sleep, nor will you sleep, you who keep Israel."[9]

(53) Beyond count are the things made by various arts and crafts in garments, shoes, utensils, and implements of every sort, in pictures, too, and divers images, far exceeding all necessary and temperate use and devout purpose! Men have added all these to the allurements of the eyes, outwardly pursuing the things they make, but inwardly forsaking him by whom they themselves have been made, and destroying what they themselves have been made to be. But I, O my God and my glory, I also proclaim a hymn to you, and I sacrifice praise to him who is my sacrificer, for the beautiful things transmitted through the artists' souls into their hands all come from that beauty which is above their souls,[10] and for which my soul sighs by day and by night.

The makers and pursuers of external beauties derive therefrom a norm of judging, but they do not derive therefrom a norm for use. It is present there, although they do not see it, so that they do not wander farther away but keep their strength for you,[11] and they do not scatter it on delights that weary. I say these things and see their truth, yet I too entangle my steps in such outward beauties. But you pluck me out, Lord, you pluck me out, "for your mercy is before my eyes."[12] For I am caught most wretchedly, and you mercifully pluck me out. Sometimes I feel nothing, because I had not fallen deep into those snares; sometimes it is with pain, because I was already caught firmly therein.

Chapter 35
Empty Curiosity and Frivolous Interests

(54) To this is joined another form of temptation, perilous in many ways. In addition to that concupiscence of the flesh present in delight in all the senses and in every pleasure—and its slaves put themselves far from you and perish utterly—by reason of those same bodily senses, there is present in the soul a certain vain and curious desire, cloaked over with the title of knowledge and science, not to take pleasure in the flesh but to acquire new experiences through the flesh. Since this is rooted in the appetite for knowledge, and since the eyes are the princely sense,[1] it is called in God's Scriptures concupiscence of the eyes.[2]

Seeing belongs properly to the eyes. However, we also apply this word to other senses when we set them to the acquisition of knowledge. We do not say, "Listen how it sparkles," or "Smell how red it glows," or "Taste how it shines," or "Feel how it gleams." All these are said to be seen. But we say not only, "See how it shines," which the eyes alone can see, but we also say, "See how it sounds," "See how it smells," "See how it tastes," "See how hard it is." Hence, as has been noted, sense experience in general is called concupiscence of the eyes, because the function of sight, in which the eyes hold primacy, even the other senses appropriate in an analogous way when they investigate any object of knowledge.

Book 10. *A Philosophy of Memory*

(55) From this fact we can have a clearer perception of the place of pleasure and curiosity in sense activity: pleasure seeks things that are beautiful, melodious, fragrant, tasty, and soft, while curiosity seeks even their opposites, with a view to trying them out, not in order to suffer disgust but out of a desire for experience and knowledge. What pleasure is there in looking at a mangled corpse that causes you to shudder? Yet if one lies somewhere or other, men rush there to be made sad and to turn pale. They are even afraid of seeing the same object in their sleep—as if someone were forcing them to look at it while they are awake, or some report of its beauty had drawn them there!

Thus also with regard to the other senses, but it is a long task to review them all. Because of this morbid curiosity, monstrous sights are exhibited in the show places. Because of it, men proceed to search out the secrets of nature, things beyond our end, to know which profits us nothing, and of which men desire nothing but the knowing. Such curiosity is also the motive when things are investigated by magic arts and with the same purpose of perverted science. Because of this, God is tempted in religion itself, when signs and wonders are demanded of him, and are desired not for some wholesome purpose but only for experience of them.

(56) In this vast forest, filled with snares and dangers, see how many of them I have cut away and thrust out of my heart, even as you have granted me to do, O God of my salvation.[3] Yet when may I dare to say, while so many things of this kind make uproar around our daily life on its every side, when dare I say that nothing of this sort makes me intent to gaze at it or to be captured by idle interest? True it is, the theater no longer sweeps me away.[4] I do not care now to know the courses of the stars, nor has my soul ever sought answers from the shades of the dead.[5] I detest all sacrilegious rites. But, O Lord my God, to whom I owe humble and single-minded service, by how many tricks and suggestions does the enemy work upon me, so that I might seek some sign from you![6] I beseech you by our King, and by our pure and chaste fatherland, Jerusalem, that even as consent to such things is far from me, so may it ever be far and still farther away. But

when I pray to you for the salvation of any man, far different is my end and purpose, and you grant, and you will continue to grant me to follow you freely, while you do what you will.

(57) Even so, who can number in how many trivial and contemptible things our curiosity is daily tempted, and how often we fall! How often we do first as it were tolerate tellers of empty tales, so as not to offend the weak, and then little by little listen willingly to them. I no longer watch a dog running after a rabbit when it is put on at the circus, but out in the field, if I happen to be passing, such a chase will perhaps draw me away from some important thought and draw me to itself. It does not force me to deviate by the body of the beast I am riding, but rather by an inclination within my heart. Unless you show me my weakness and quickly warn me, either to rise up to you from the sight through some reflection, or to spurn the whole incident and pass it by, I stand there vacant-minded. When I am sitting at home and a lizard is catching flies or a spider is trapping them as they blunder into its web, how often does this catch my attention![7] Is the activity any different, merely because the animals are small? From these incidents I advance to praising you, O wondrous creator and orderer of all things, but I did not begin by being concerned with this. It is one thing to rise quickly, another thing not to fall. My life is filled with such incidents, and my one hope is your exceeding great mercy. For when our heart is made a receptacle for such things, and carries about throngs of abundant vanity, then our prayers are often interrupted and disturbed, and while in your sight we direct our heart's voice into your ears, so great a project is broken off by worthless thoughts rushing in from I know not where.[8]

Chapter 36
The Pride of Life

(58) Shall we therefore account this also among things to be despised? Or shall anything restore us to hope, unless it be your known mercy, since you have begun to change us? You know how greatly you have already changed me, you who first healed me from the passion for self-vindication, so

that you might also forgive all my other iniquities, and heal all my diseases, and redeem my life from corruption, and crown me with mercy and compassion, and satisfy my desires with good things,[1] you who subdued my pride by your fear and tamed my neck to your yoke?[2] Now I bear that yoke, and it is light upon me, for this have you promised, and thus have you made it be. Truly, it was this, but I did not know it when I was afraid to submit to it.

(59) Lord, you who alone dominate over others without pride, for you are the sole true God,[3] you who have no lord, I ask you, has this third kind of temptation ceased for me, or can it cease throughout all my life, this wish to be feared and to be loved by men, for no reason but that from it there may come a joy that is yet no joy? A miserable life is this, and a foul boast! Hence most of all it comes that I neither love you nor have a chaste fear of you. Therefore, you "resist the proud, but give grace to the humble,"[4] and you thunder down upon the ambitions of the world, and the foundations of the mountains tremble.[5]

But now, since by reason of certain official positions in human society, it is necessary for us to be both loved and feared by men, the adversary of our true happiness keeps after us, and on every side amidst his snares he scatters the words, "Well done! Well done!" He does this so that, as we greedily gather up these words, we may be caught unawares, displace our joy from the truth, and place it among the deceits of men, and so that it may afford us pleasure to be feared and to be loved, not because of you but in place of you. In such wise would he possess for himself those who have become like himself, not for a union in charity but for comradeship in punishment. This is he who has decreed to put his throne to the north, so that, darkling and cold, such men may serve him who in a perverse and tortured way imitates you.[6]

But we, Lord, behold, we are your little flocks:[7] keep us for your own! Spread forth your wings, and let us flee under them. Be our glory! Let us be loved for your sake, and in us let only your Word be held in fear. Whosoever wishes to be praised by men, while you hold him worthy of blame, is not defended by men when you judge him, nor will he be rescued by men when you condemn him. But there are times when it is not "the sinner that is praised in the desires of his soul, nor the unjust man who is blessed,"[8] but a man is praised for some gift that you have given to him, and he rejoices more because he is praised for his own sake than because he possesses that gift for which he is praised. In this case also is a man praised while you blame him, and better then is he who gave the praise than he who received it. For the one is pleased at God's gift to a man, whereas the other is more pleased by a man's gift than by God's.

Chapter 37
Problems of Praise

(60) By these temptations are we tempted daily, Lord, without ceasing we are tempted. Our daily furnace is the human tongue.[1] In this way, too, you impose continence upon us. Give what you command, and command what you will! You know the groans of my heart[2] with regard to this matter, and the tears that flood from my eyes. For I do not gather with ease to what extent I have been made more clean of this disease, and I much fear my secret sins,[3] which your eyes know but mine do not.

For other types of temptation I have some kind of ability for self-examination, but for this scarcely any. With regard to fleshly pleasures and curiosity to know idle things, I perceive to what extent I have attained the power of restraining my mind when I am free of such things, either voluntarily or because they are not present. Then I ask myself whether not having them is more annoying or less annoying to me. Riches, again, are sought for the purpose of providing for one or another of these three lusts, or for two of them, or for all of them. If the mind cannot perceive distinctly whether it despises them when it possesses them, they can be rejected and it may thus put itself to the test.

But to be without any praise whatsoever, and to test ourselves in this condition, how can we manage it? Must we not live an evil life, so abandoned and so inhuman a life that no one can know us without detesting us? What greater madness

Book 10. A Philosophy of Memory

can be named or conceived than this? If praise usually is, and should be, companion to a good life and good deeds, we should no more abandon such accompaniment than the good life itself. Yet I do not know whether I can do without a thing with a calm or with a distressed mind unless by its being absent.[4]

(61) What, then, do I confess to you with regard to this kind of temptation? What else, except that I find delight in being praised, but more with truth than with praise. For if the question is put to me whether I would prefer to be a madman or a man at fault in everything and yet be praised by men, or to be steady and absolutely right in truth but yet reviled by all men, I see which I should choose. Yet I should not wish the approval of another man's mouth to increase my joy over any good that may be in me. But I admit not only that it increases it, but that condemnation lessens it.

When I am distressed at this misery of mine, an excuse steals into my mind. What its value is, you know, O God, although it leaves me uncertain. You have commanded upon us not only continence, that is, to withhold our love from certain things, but also justice, that is, whereon we are to bestow our love. You have willed not only that you yourself be loved by us, but our neighbor also. Often, when I am pleased by the praises of someone who clearly understands a matter, I think that I am pleased at my neighbor's progress or promise. Again, when I hear him condemn something that he does not understand or that is good, I think that I am made sad by his wrong deed. Sometimes I am depressed at my own praises, either when things are praised in me over which I am displeased with myself, or when lesser or trifling goods are rated higher than they should be. Again, how do I know whether I am thus affected because I do not like the man praising me to differ from me concerning myself, not because I am motivated by his advantage but because those very goods which please me in myself are all the sweeter to me when they please another man also? In some fashion, I am not praised when my own opinion of myself is not praised, whenever things that displease me are praised, or else things that please me less are praised more highly. Am I not therefore doubtful of myself concerning this matter?

(62) Behold, O Truth, I see in you that I ought not to be moved by my praises on account of myself, but for my neighbor's good. Whether I am so, I do not know. Concerning this matter I know less about myself than you do. I beseech you, my God, show me to myself, so that to my brothers, who will pray for me, I may confess what wounds I find in me. Let me examine myself once again, and more diligently. If in my own praises I am moved by the utility of my neighbor, why am I less moved if someone else is unjustly reviled than if it is I who am reviled? Why am I hurt more by abuse cast upon myself than by that cast in my presence with the equal injustice upon another? Am I in ignorance of this also? Does it amount to this, that I deceive myself,[5] and do not do the truth[6] before you in my heart and on my tongue? Put this madness far from me, Lord, lest my own mouth be to me "the sinner's oil to make fat my head."[7]

Chapter 38
False Humility

(63) "I am needy and poor,"[1] but I am a better man so long as by secret groans I displease myself and seek your mercy, until my defect is made over again and is made whole again, unto that peace which the proud man's eye does not perceive.

But words coming out of man's mouths and deeds known to men contain a most perilous temptation. This arises from love of praise which, to build up a sort of private superiority, begs for and hoards up marks of approval. Even when this is rebuked within myself by myself, it affords temptation by the very fact that it is rebuked. Often, out of very contempt of glory a man derives an emptier glory.[2] No longer, therefore, does he glory in contempt of vainglory: he does not despise it, in as much as he glories over it.

Chapter 39
Presumption and Selfishness

(64) There is a further evil within us included in this same type of temptation. By it those men grow in conceit who are complacent with themselves and because of themselves, although they either do not please others or displease them, and even make no effort to please them. While they please themselves, they are greatly displeasing to you, not only by reason of things not good that are looked upon as good, but also by reason of goods belonging to you that they think to be their own, and even by reason of goods seen to be yours but looked upon as due to their own merits, or by reason of things known to be your free gifts but not rejoiced over with brotherly love and begrudged by them to other men. In all such things and in like perils and hardships, you behold my trembling heart. Over and over, I feel my wounds, not so much as inflicted upon me, but rather as healed by you.

Chapter 40
Light and Love

(65) When is it that you have not walked with me, O Truth, teaching me what to shun and what to seek, while I would refer to you the baser things that I have seen, as far as I could, and would consult you about them? By means of sense I gazed upon the outside world, as far as I could, and I looked upon this bodily life of mine, and so too upon these very senses of mine. From there I entered into the recesses of my memory, those manifold and spacious chambers filled with marvelous varieties of countless rich stores. I considered them, and I stood aghast; I could discern nothing of these things without you, and I found nothing of these things to be you.

And I myself, who found all this, who went over all these things, and strove to mark off and value each thing in accordance with its excellence, taking some things as senses reported them, questioning about others that I felt were intermingled with myself, numbering off and distinguishing the very messengers of sense, and then in the wide treasuries of memory scanning certain things, laying away certain others, and drawing forth others still—I myself was not you. Not even when I did these deeds, that is, not even that power of mine by which I did them, not even that was you. For you are that abiding light which I consulted concerning all these things, as to whether they were, as to what they were, and as to what value they possessed. I heard you as you directed and commanded me. This I often do; this brings me delight, and as far as I can be relieved of necessary duties, in this delight I take refuge. In all these things which I review as I consult you, I can find no safe place for my soul except in you. In you may my scattered longings be gathered together, and from you may no part of me ever depart. Sometimes you admit me in my innermost being into a most extraordinary affection, mounting within me to an indescribable sweetness. If this is perfected in me, it will be something, I know not what, that will not belong to this life. But under my burdens of misery I sink down to those other things, and I am drawn back again by former ways and held fast by them. Much do I weep over them, but much am I caught by them. Such is the strength of onerous habit! Here I can abide, although I would not; there I wish to be, but cannot; in both ways am I wretched.

Chapter 41
Truth and the Lie

(66) Thus, therefore, I have considered the sicknesses of my sins in that threefold concupiscence,[1] and I have called your right hand to bring me health. With a wounded heart I have looked upon your splendor, and struck back by it, I have said: Who can attain to it? "I am cast away from before your eyes."[2] You are the truth who preside over all things. In my greed, I did not want to lose you, but together with you I wanted to possess a lie, just as no one wants to speak falsehood such that he himself does not know the truth. Thus did I lose you, because you disdain to be possessed together with a lie.

Chapter 42
A False Mediator

(67) Whom could I find to reconcile me to you? Was I to turn to angels? By what prayers? By what rites?[1] Many men who strive to return to you, and are unable to do so by their own strength, have tried such things, so I have heard, and have fallen victim to desire for curious visions, and have been accounted fit for delusions. Lifted aloft, they have sought you by pride of learning, thrusting out their chests rather than smiting their breasts. By similarity of heart they have attracted to themselves fellow conspirators and partners in their pride, "the powers of this air,"[2] by whose potent magic they have been deceived. For they were seeking a mediator by whom they might be cleansed, and none such was there. "For the devil was transforming himself into an angel of light."[3] Much did it entice proud flesh that he was not embodied in flesh. For they were mortal and sinners, but you, Lord, to whom they sought to be reconciled, are immortal and without sin. But "the mediator between God and man"[4] must have something like to God and something like to men, lest being in both things like to men, he should be far from God, or being in both ways like to God, he should be far from men, and so not be a mediator.

Therefore, that false mediator, by whom in your secret judgments pride merited to be deluded, had one thing in common with men, which is sin. He wishes to appear as if he had the other thing common with God, so that, since he is not clothed with mortal flesh, he might show himself as an immortal. But because "the wages of sin is death,"[5] he has in common with men that for which he is condemned to death along with them.

Chapter 43
The One Mediator

(68) The true mediator, whom in your secret mercy you have shown to the humble, whom you have sent to them, that by his example they also might learn humility, that "me-

diator of God and man, the man Christ Jesus,"[1] appeared between mortal sinners and the immortal just one, mortal with men, just with God. Because the wages of justice is life and peace,[2] he thus appeared that, being joined through justice to God, he might make void[3] the death of sinners now justified, which death he willed to have in common with them. He was shown forth to saints of old, so that they might be saved through faith in his coming passion, even as we are saved by faith in his passion now past. For as man, he is mediator, but as the Word, he is in no middle place, since he is equal to God, and God with God, and together one God.[4]

(69) How have you loved us, O good Father, who did not spare your only Son, but delivered him up for us sinners.[5] How have you loved us, from whom he who "did not think it robbery to be equal to you" became "obedient even unto death, even to the death of the cross,"[6] he alone being "free among the dead,"[7] having power of laying down his life, and having power of taking it up again.[8] For us, he is before you both victor and victim, and therefore victor for the reason that he is victim. For us, before you, he is both priest and sacrifice, and therefore priest because sacrifice, making us your sons instead of servants, by being born of you, and by becoming servant to us.

Rightly is my hope strong in him, because you will heal all my diseases,[9] through him "who sits at your right hand and makes intercession for us,"[10] elsewise I would despair. Many and great are those infirmities of mine, many they are and great, but more potent is your medicine. We could think that your Word is far from union with men, and we could despair of ourselves, unless he had been "made flesh and dwelt amongst us."[11]

(70) Struck with terror at my sins and at the burden of my misery, I had been tormented at heart and had pondered flight into the desert. But you forbade me, and comforted me, saying: "Therefore Christ died for all: that they who live may now live not to themselves but to him who died for them."[12] Behold, Lord, I cast my cares upon you,[13] so that I may live, and "I will consider the wondrous things of your law."[14] You know my lack of wisdom and my infirmity, teach me, and heal

me.[15] He, your only Son "in whom are hid all the treasures of wisdom and knowledge,"[16] has redeemed me by his blood. "Let not the proud calumniate me,"[17] for I think upon my ransom, and I eat and drink, and share it with others,[18] and as a pauper I desire to be filled from him amid those who eat and are filled, "and they shall praise the Lord that seek him."[19]

BOOK 11
TIME AND ETERNITY

Chapter 1
For Love of Love

(1) Lord, since eternity is yours, are you ignorant of the things that I say to you, or do you see only at a certain time what is done in time? Why then do I set out in order before you this account of so many deeds? In truth, it is not that you may learn to know these matters from me, but that I may rouse up towards you my own affections, and those of other men who read this, so that all of us may say: "The Lord is great, and exceedingly to be praised."[1] I have already said this, and I will say it again: for love of your love I perform this task.

For we pray, although Truth has said, "Your Father knows what is needful for you before you ask him."[2] Therefore, when we confess to you our miseries and your mercies upon us, we lay bare before you our condition, so that you may set us wholly free. For you have begun to do this, so that we may cease to be wretched in ourselves and become happy in you. And you have called us to the end that we may be poor in spirit, and meek, and mourners, and hungry and thirsty for justice, and merciful, and clean of heart, and peacemakers.[3] Behold, I have recounted many things to you, such things as I could and as I wished to recount. For, first of all, it was your will that I confess to you, my Lord God, because you are good, and your mercy endures forever.[4]

Chapter 2
The Treasures of Scripture

(2) When shall I suffice to proclaim by the tongue of my pen[1] all your exhortations, and all your warnings, consolations,

and acts of guidance, by which you have led me to preach your Word and dispense your sacrament to your people?[2] If I am sufficient to declare all these in due order, the drops of time[3] are precious to me. For a long time I have burned to meditate upon your law, and therein to confess to you both my knowledge and my lack of wisdom, the first beginnings of your enlightenment and the last remains of my darkness, until my infirmity be swallowed up by your strength. On nothing else would I want those hours to flow away which I find free from need of replenishing my body and my mental powers and the demands of such service as we owe to other men, and such as we do not owe but yet render.

(3) O Lord my God, "be attentive to my prayer,"[4] and in your mercy graciously hear my desire,[5] for it burns not for me alone but desires to be for the use of fraternal charity. You see that in my heart it is so. I will sacrifice to you the service of my thought and tongue; give me what I may offer to you. For "I am needy and poor," and "you are rich to all that call upon you,"[6] who, although free from care, yet care for us. From all temerity and all lying circumcise my lips, both my interior and my exterior lips. May your Scriptures be my chaste delights! May I never fall into error in my reading of them, may I never deceive others by misuse of them.

Lord, hearken to me, and have mercy on me, O Lord my God, light of the blind and strength of the weak, at once light of those who see and strength of the strong, give ear to my soul, and hear me as I cry out of the depths.[7] For unless your ears are present with us in the depths, where shall we go? Where shall we cry to? "Yours is the day, and yours is the night."[8] At your command the minutes fly away. From them, bestow upon us a time for meditation on the hidden things of your law; do not close up that law against those knocking upon it.[9]

Not for nothing, have you willed that these dark secrets be written on so many pages. Nor are those forests to lack their harts, who will retire therein, and regain their strength, walk about and feed, lie down and ruminate.[10] Lord, perfect me, and open those pages to me. Behold, your voice is my joy, your voice is above a flood of pleasures.[11] Grant me what I love, for I love in truth, and this too have you given to me! Do not forsake your gifts, and do not despise this your plant which thirsts for you. Let me confess to you whatsoever I shall find in your books, and let me "hear the voice of praise,"[12] and drink you in, and consider "the wonderful things of your law,"[13] from that beginning, wherein you made heaven and earth, even to an everlasting kingdom together with you in your holy city.

(4) Lord, have mercy on me, and graciously hear my desire.[14] I do not think that it is for things of earth, for gold and silver, for gems or rich garments, for honors and power, for fleshly pleasure, not even for the needs of the body and of this our life of pilgrimage, for "all these things shall be added unto us if we seek your kingdom and your justice."[15] See, O my God, whence arises my desire. "The wicked have told me their pleasures, but not as your law,"[16] O Lord. See, whence springs my desire! See, Father, look down, and see, and approve, and let it be pleasing in the sight of your mercy for me to find grace before you,[17] so that the inner meaning of your words may be opened up to me when I knock.

I beseech you by your Son, our Lord Jesus Christ, "the man of your right hand, whom you have confirmed for yourself,"[18] as your mediator and ours, through whom you have sought us when we did not seek you, and sought us so that we might seek you, your Word, through whom you have made all things, among them myself also, through whom you have called to adoption a people of believers, among them me also. I beseech you by him who "sits at your right hand, and makes intercession with you for us,"[19] "in whom are hid all the treasures of wisdom and knowledge."[20] These same treasures I seek in your books. Moses wrote of him: He himself says this. Truth says this.[21]

CHAPTER 3

The Language of Truth

(5) Let me hear and understand how "in the beginning" you "made heaven and earth."[1] Moses wrote these words: he wrote them, and he passed away. He passed from this world,

from you to you,[2] and he is not now here before me. If he were, I would catch hold of him, and I would ask him, and through you I would beseech him to make these things plain to me. I would lay my body's ears to the sounds breaking forth from his mouth. If he spoke in Hebrew, in vain would his voice strike upon my senses, and none of it would touch my mind. But if he spoke in Latin, I would know what he said.

Yet how would I know whether he spoke the truth? Even if I knew this, would I know it from him? Truly, within me, within the dwelling place of thought, Truth, neither Hebrew nor Greek nor Latin nor barbaric in speech, without mouth or tongue as organ, and without noise of syllables, would say to me, "He speaks the truth." Forthwith I would be certain of it, and I would say confidently to that man, "You speak the truth." Therefore, since I cannot question him who was filled by you, and thus spoke true words, I entreat you O Truth, I entreat you, O my God, "spare my sins."[3] Do you who granted to him, your servant, to speak these true words, grant to me that I may understand them.

Chapter 4
Evidence of Creation

(6) Lo, heaven and earth exist: they cry out that they have been created, for they are subject to change and variation. Whatever has not been made, and yet exists, has nothing in it which was not previously there, whereas to have what once was not is to change and vary. They also cry out that they did not make themselves: "For this reason, do we exist, because we have been made. Therefore, before we came to be, we did not exist in such wise as to be able to make ourselves."[1]

Self-evidence is the voice with which these things speak. You, therefore, O Lord, who are beautiful, made these things, for they are beautiful; you who are good made them, for they are good; you who are made them, for they are. Yet they are not so good, nor are they so beautiful as you, nor do they even be in such wise as you, their creator. Compared to you, they are neither good, nor beautiful, nor real. We know all this, thanks be to you, but our knowledge compared to your knowledge is ignorance.[2]

Chapter 5
Creator of All Things

(7) How did you make heaven and earth? What was your engine for doing this mighty work? You did not work as does the human artist, who transforms one body into another according to the purposes of a soul able somehow to imprint forms that it perceives by its inner eye. How could he do this unless you had first created his mind? The artist imprints a form on something already existing and having power to be, such as earth, stone, wood, or gold, or something of that sort. From what source would they be, unless you had decreed them to be? You made the artist's body; you, the soul that gives orders to his members; you, the matter out of which he fashions things; you, the intellect by which he controls his creative imagination and sees within it what he fashions outside himself. You made his bodily senses by which, as through an interpreter, he transfers his work from mind to matter, and then reports back to mind what he has made, so that he may consult therein the truth presiding over him, so as to know whether it was well made.

All these praise you, the creator of all things. But how do you make them? O God, how have you made heaven and earth? Truly, neither in heaven nor upon earth have you made heaven and earth. Nor was it in the air, nor in the waters, for these too belong to heaven and earth. Nor was it in the one wide world that you made that one wide world, for before it was caused to be, there was no place where it could be made. You did not hold in your hand anything out of which to make heaven and earth: whence would you obtain this thing not made by you, out of which you would make a new thing? What exists, for any reason except that you exist? You spoke, therefore, and these things were made, and in your Word you made them.[1]

Chapter 6
God's Voice

(8) But how did you speak? Was it in the way that the voice came out of the cloud, saying, "This is my beloved Son?"[1] That voice went forth and went away; it began and it ceased. The syllables were sounded and they passed away, the second after the first, the third after the second, and the rest in order, until the last one came after all the others, and silence after the last. Whence it is clear and evident that a creature's movement,[2] a temporal movement, uttered that voice in obedience to your eternal will. These words of yours, formed for a certain time, the outer ear reported to the understanding mind, whose interior ear was placed close to your eternal Word. Then the mind compared these words sounding in time with your eternal Word in its silence, and said, "It is far different; it is far different. These words are far beneath me. They do not exist, because they flee and pass away. The Word of my God abides above me forever."[3]

Therefore, if you had said in audible and passing words that heaven and earth should be made, and had so made heaven and earth, then before heaven and earth, there was already some corporeal creature by means of whose temporal movements that voice would run in time. But before heaven and earth, there was no bodily thing. Or if there were one, you surely had made it without using a passing voice by which you would say, "Let heaven and earth be made." Whatsoever that thing might be, from which such a voice could be made, it could not be at all unless it were made by you. By what word, then, did you speak, so that there might be a body from which these words[4] would be uttered?

Chapter 7
The Word of God

(9) So you call us to understand the Word, God with you, O God,[1] which is spoken eternally, and in which all things are spoken eternally. Nor is it the case that what was spoken is

ended and that another thing is said, so that all things may at length be said: all things are spoken once and forever. Elsewise, there would already be time and change, and neither true eternity nor true immortality. I know this, my God, and "I give thanks for it."[2] I know this, I confess to you, O Lord God, and together with me whoever is grateful to the sure Truth knows this and blesses you.

We know, O Lord, we know, since in so far as anything which once was now no longer is, and anything which once was not now is, to that extent such a thing dies and takes rise. Therefore, no part of your Word gives place to another or takes the place of another, since it is truly eternal and immortal. Therefore, you say once and forever all that you say by the Word, who is coeternal with you. Whatever you say shall be made, then it is made. But while you do not make anything otherwise than by speaking, yet not all things which you make by speaking are made simultaneously and eternally.

Chapter 8
Christ Our Teacher

(10) Why, I beseech you, O Lord my God, is this? In a way, I see it, but how I am to express it I do not know, unless it is because whatever begins to be, and then ceases to be, does then begin to be and then cease to be when it is known in your eternal reason, wherein nothing begins or ceases, that it must begin or cease. This is your Word, which is also the beginning[1] because it also speaks to us. Thus in the Gospel he speaks through the flesh, and this word sounded outwardly in the ears of men, so that it might be believed, and sought inwardly, and found in the eternal Truth where the sole good Master[2] teaches all his disciples. There, O Lord, I hear your voice speaking to me, since he who teaches us speaks to us. But a man who does not teach us, even though he speaks, does not speak to us. Who teaches us now, unless it be stable Truth? Even when we are admonished by a changeable creature, we are led to stable Truth, where we truly learn "while we stand and hear him" and "rejoice with joy because of the bridegroom's voice"[3] restoring us to him from whom we are.

Therefore, he is a beginning, for unless he abided when we went astray, he would not be there when we returned. But when we return from error, we truly return by knowing that we do so, and that we may know this, he teaches us, because he is the beginning and he speaks to us.

Chapter 9
Wisdom Itself

(11) In the beginning, O God, you made heaven and earth in your Word, in your Son, in your Power, in your Wisdom, in your Truth, speaking in a wondrous way and working in a wondrous way. Who shall comprehend it? Who shall declare it? What is that which shines through me and strikes my heart without injuring it? I both shudder and glow with passion: I shudder, in as much as I am unlike it; I glow with passion in as much as I am like to it.

It is Wisdom, Wisdom itself, which shines through me, cutting through my dark clouds which again cover me over, as I fall down because of that darkness and under the load of my punishments. For thus is my strength weakened in poverty,[1] so that I cannot support my good, until you, O Lord, "who have been gracious to all my iniquities," likewise "heal all my diseases." For you will "redeem my life from corruption," you will "crown me with mercy and compassion," and you will "satisfy my desire with good things," because my "youth shall be renewed like the eagle's."[2] For in hope we are saved, and we wait for your promises through patience.[3]

Let him who can hear you inwardly as you speak to us. I will cry out boldly in words from your oracle: "How great are your works, O Lord; you have made all things in wisdom!"[4] That wisdom is the beginning, and in that beginning you have made heaven and earth.[5]

Chapter 10
A Skeptical Objection

(12) Lo, are not those men full of their old carnal nature who say to us, "What was God doing before he made heaven

and earth?" "For if," they say, "he took his ease and did nothing, why did he not continue in this way henceforth and forever, just as previously he always refrained from work? If any new motion arise in God, or a new will is formed in him, to the end of establishing creation, which he had never established previously, how then would there be true eternity, when a will arises that previously was not there? The will of God is not a creature, but it is before the creature, for nothing would be created unless the creator's will preceded it. Therefore God's will belongs to his very substance. But if anything has appeared in God's substance that previously was not there, then that substance is not truly called eternal. Yet if it were God's sempiternal will for the creature to exist, why is not the creature sempiternal also?"

CHAPTER 11

Past, Present, and Future

(13) Men who say such things do not yet understand you, O Wisdom of God,[1] O light of minds. They do not yet understand how those things are made which are made through you and in you. They attempt to grasp eternal things, but their heart flutters among the changing things of past and future, and it is still vain.[2] Who will catch hold of it, and make it fast, so that it stands firm for a little while, and for a little while seize the splendor of that ever stable eternity, and compare it with times that never stand fast, and see that it is incomparable to them, and see that a long time cannot become long except out of many passing movements, which cannot be extended together, that in the eternal nothing can pass away but the whole is present, that no time is wholly present? Who will see that all past time is driven back by the future, that all the future is consequent on the past, and all past and future are created and take their course from that which is ever present?

Who will hold the heart of man, so that it may stand still and see how steadfast eternity, neither future nor past, decrees times future and those past? Can my hand do this, or does the hand of my mouth by its little words effect so great a thing?

Chapter 12
A Frivolous Answer

(14) See, I answer the man who says,[1] "What did God do before he made heaven and earth?" I do not give the answer that someone is said to have given, evading by a joke the force of the objection: "He was preparing hell," he said, "for those prying into such deep subjects." It is one thing to see the objection; it is another to make a joke of it. I do not answer in this way. I would rather respond, "I do not know," concerning what I do not know rather than say something for which a man inquiring about such profound matters is laughed at, while the one giving a false answer is praised.

I say that you, our God, are the creator of every creature, and, if by the phrase heaven and earth all creation is understood, I boldly say, "Before God made heaven and earth, he did not make anything." If he made anything, what else did he make except a creature? Would that I knew all I want to know that is for my good in the same way that I know that no creature was made before any creature was made.[2]

Chapter 13
Before All Time

(15) If any flighty mind wanders among mental pictures of past times, and wonders that you, the all-great, all-creating, and all-sustaining God, maker of heaven and earth, should for countless ages have refrained from doing so great a work before actually doing it, let him awake and realize that he wonders at falsities. How could they pass by, those countless ages, which you had not made, although you are the author and creator of all ages?[1] Or what times would there be, times not been made by you? Or how did they pass by, if they never were? Therefore, since you are the maker of all times, if there was a time before you made heaven and earth, why do they say that you rested from work?[2] You made that very time, and

no times could pass by before you made those times. But if there was no time before heaven and earth, why do they ask what you did then? There was no "then," where there was no time.

(16) It is not in time that you precede time: elsewise you would not precede all times. You precede all past times in the sublimity of an ever present eternity, and you surpass all future times, because they are to come, and when they come, they shall be past, "but you are the Selfsame, and your years shall not fail."[3] Your years neither come nor go, but our years come and go, so that all of them may come. Your years stand all at once, because they are steadfast: departing years are not turned away by those that come, because they never pass away. But these years of ours shall all be, when they all shall be no more. Your years are one day,[4] and your day is not each day, but today, because with you today does not give way to tomorrow, nor does it succeed yesterday. With you, today is eternity. Therefore you begot the coeternal, to whom you said, "This day have I begotten you."[5] You have made all times, and you are before all times, and not at any time was there no time.[6]

Chapter 14
What Is Time?

(17) At no time, therefore, did you do nothing, since you had made time itself. No times are coeternal with you, because you are permanent, whereas if they were permanent, they would not be times. What is time? Who can easily and briefly explain this? Who can comprehend this even in thought, so as to express it in a word? Yet what do we discuss more familiarly and knowingly in conversation than time? Surely we understand it when we talk about it, and also understand it when we hear others talk about it.

What, then, is time? If no one asks me, I know; if I want to explain it to someone who does ask me, I do not know.[1] Yet I state confidently that I know this: if nothing were passing away, there would be no past time, and if nothing were coming, there would be no future time, and if nothing existed, there would be no present time. How, then, can these two kinds of time, the past and the future, be, when the past no longer is and the future as yet does not be? But if the present were always present, and would not pass into the past, it would no longer be time, but eternity. Therefore, if the present, so as to be time, must be so constituted that it passes into the past, how can we say that it is, since the cause of its being is the fact that it will cease to be? Does it not follow that we can truly say that it is time, only because it tends towards non-being?

Chapter 15
Can Time Be Long or Short?

(18) Yet we say "a long time" and "a short time," and do not say this except of the past or the future. For example, we call a hundred years ago a long time in the past, and a hundred years from now we call a long time in the future. On the contrary, we term ten days ago, let us say, a short time past, and ten days to come, a brief future time. But in what sense is something non-existent either long or short? The past no longer exists, and the future is not yet in being. Therefore we should not say, "It is long," but we should say of the past, "It was long," and of the future, "It will be long." My Lord, my light,[1] shall not your truth here also jest at man?[2] That past time which was so long, was it long when it was already past, or before that, when it was still present? It could be long at the time when that existed which could be long. Once past, it did not exist, hence it could not be long, since it in no wise existed. Therefore, let us not say, "Past time was long." We will not find anything which was long, since from the very fact that it is past, it is no more. Let us say, "That time once present was long," because it was long when it was present. It had not yet passed away, so as not to be, and therefore there existed that which could be long. On the other hand, after it passed away, it instantly ceased to be long, because it ceased to be.

(19) Let us see, then, O human soul, whether present time can be long, for it has been granted to you to perceive and to measure tracts of time. What answer do you make me? Are a

hundred years, when present, a long time? See first whether a hundred years can be present. If the first of these years is going on, it is present, but the other ninety-nine are still in the future, and therefore as yet are not existent. If the second year is current, one is already past, another is present, and the rest are in the future. So it is if we posit any of the intervening years of the hundred as the present: before it will be past years, and after it, future years. For this reason, a hundred years cannot be present.

But see, at least, if the year now going on is itself present. If the first month is current, then all the rest are to come; if it is the second, then the first is already past and the others are not yet here. Therefore the current year is not wholly present, and if it is not wholly present, then the year is not present. A year is made up of twelve months, of which any one month, which is current, is the present, and the others are either past or future. However, not even the current month is present, but only a single day. If it is the first day, the others are to come; if the last day, the others are past; if any intervening day, it is between those past and those to come.

(20) See how the present time, which alone we found worthy to be called long, is contracted to hardly the space of a single day. But let us examine it also, because not even a single day is present in its totality. It is completed in twenty-four hours of night and day, and of these the first has the others still to come, the last has them past it, and each of the intervening hours has those before it in the past and those after it in the future. That one hour itself goes on in fleeting moments; whatever part of it has flown away is past, whatever remains is future. If any point of time is conceived that can no longer be divided into even the most minute parts of a moment, that alone it is which may be called the present. It flies with such speed from the future into the past that it cannot be extended by even a trifling amount. For if it is extended, it is divided into past and future. The present has no space.

Where then is the time that we may call long? Is it to come? We do not say of it that it is long, because it does not yet exist, so as to be long. We say that it will be long. When, therefore, will it be? Even then, if it will still be to come, it will not be long, since that which will be long does not yet be. But suppose it will be long, at that time when out of the future, which does not yet be, it will first begin to be and will have become present, so that what may be long can actually exist. Then immediately present time cries out in the words above that it cannot be long.

Chapter 16
Time and Measurement

(21) Still, O Lord, we perceive intervals of time. We compare them to one another and say that some are longer and some shorter. Also, we measure how much longer or shorter this time may be than that, and answer that this is twice or three times as long as another, or that that one is identical with or just as much as this. But it is passing times that we measure, and we make these measurements in perceiving them. As to past times, which no longer exist, or future, which as yet do not exist, who can measure them, except perhaps a man rash enough to say that he can measure what does not exist? Therefore, as long as time is passing by, it can be perceived and measured, but when it has passed by, it cannot be measured since it does not exist.

Chapter 17
Prophecy and History

(22) Father, I ask questions; I do not make assertions. My God, govern me and guide me.[1] Who is it that will tell me, not that there are three times, just as we learned as boys and as we have taught to boys,[2] namely, past, present, and future, but that there is only present time, since the other two do not exist? Or do they too exist, but when the present comes into being from the future, does it proceed from some hidden source, and when past comes out of the present, does it recede into some hidden place? Where did they who foretold things to come see them, if they do not exist? A thing that does not exist cannot be seen. If those who narrate past events did not perceive them by their minds, they would not give true ac-

counts. If such things were nothing at all, they could not be perceived in any way. Therefore, both future and past times have being.

Chapter 18
Induction and Prediction

(23) Give me leave, "O Lord, my hope,"[1] to make further search: do not let my purpose be diverted. If future and past times exist, I wish to know where they are. But if I am not yet able to do this, I still know that wherever they are, they are there neither as future nor as past, but as present. For if they are in that place as future things, they are not yet there, and if they are in that place as past things, they are no longer there. Therefore, wherever they are, and whatever they are, they do not exist except as present things. However, when true accounts of the past are given, it is not the things themselves, which have passed away, that are drawn forth from memory, but words conceived from their images. These images they implanted in the mind like footsteps as they passed through the senses.

My boyhood, indeed, which no longer is, belongs to past time, which no longer is. However, when I recall it and talk about it, I perceive its image at the present time, because it still is in my memory. Whether there may be a like cause of predicting future events as well, namely, that actually existent images of things which as yet do not exist are perceived first, I confess, O my God, I do not know. But this I surely know, that we often premeditate our future actions and such premeditation is present to us, but the action that we premeditate does not yet exist, because it is to be. As soon as we have addressed ourselves to it and have begun to do what we were premeditating, then action will be existent. Then it will not be future, but present.[2]

(24) Howsoever this secret foresight of things to come takes place, nothing can be seen except what is present. But what now is is not future but present. Hence, when future things are said to be seen, it is not the things themselves, which are not yet existent, that is, the things that are to come, but their

causes, or perhaps signs of them, which already exist, that are seen. Thus they are not future things, but things already present to the viewers, and from them future things are predicted as conceived in the mind. Again, these conceptions are already existent, and those who predict the future fix their gaze upon things present with them.

Let the vast multitude of such things offer me some example of this. I look at the dawn; I foretell the coming sunrise. What I look at is present; what I foretell is future. It is not the sun that is about to be, for it already exists, but its rising, which as yet is not. Yet if I did not picture within my mind this sunrise, just as when I now speak of it, I would be unable to predict it. Still that dawn, which I see in the sky, is not the sunrise, although it precedes the sunrise, nor is the picture in my mind the sunrise. Both these are perceived as present to me, so that the future sunrise may be foretold. Therefore, future things do not yet exist; if they do not yet exist, they are not; if they are not, they can in no wise be seen. However, they can be predicted from present things, which already exist and are seen.

Chapter 19
A Prayer for Light

(25) O you, the ruler of your creation, in what manner do you teach souls those things which are to come? You have taught your prophets. What is that way by which you teach things to come, you to whom nothing is future? Or is it rather that you teach things present concerning what is to come? What does not exist surely cannot be taught. Too distant is this way for my sight. It is too strong for me, and of myself I will not be able to attain it.[1] But with your help I will be able to attain to it, when you will give it to me, you, the sweet light of my hidden eyes.[2]

Chapter 20
Three Kinds of Time

(26) It is now plain and clear that neither past nor future are existent, and that it is not properly stated that there are

three times, past, present, and future. But perhaps it might properly be said that there are three times, the present of things past, the present of things present, and the present of things future. These three are in the soul, but elsewhere I do not see them: the present of things past is in memory; the present of things present is in intuition; the present of things future is in expectation. If we are permitted to say this, then I see three times, and I affirm that there are three times. It may also be said that there are three times, past, present, and future, as common usage incorrectly puts it. This may be stated. Note that I am not concerned over this, do not object to it, and do not criticize it, as long as we understand what we say, namely, that what is future is not now existent, nor is that which is past. There are few things that we state properly, and many that we speak improperly,[1] but what we mean is understood.

CHAPTER 21

Measures of Time

(27) I said just a while ago that we measure passing times, so that we can say that this tract of time is double that single one, or that this one is just as long as the other, and whatever else as to periods of time we can describe by our measurements. Therefore, as I was saying, we measure passing times. If someone says to me, "How do you know this?" I may answer, "I know this because we make such measurements, and we cannot measure things that do not exist, and neither past nor future things exist." Yet how do we measure present time, since it has no extent? Therefore, it is measured as it passes by, but once it has passed by, it is not measured, for what would be measured will no longer exist. But from where, and on what path, and to what place does it pass, as it is measured? From where, except from the future? By what path, except by the present? To what place, except into the past? Therefore, it is from that which does not yet exist, by that which lacks space, and into that which no longer exists.

But what do we measure if time is not in a certain space? We do not say single, or double, or threefold, or equal, or anything else of this sort in the order of time, except with regard to tracts of time. In what space, then, do we measure passing time? In the future, out of which it passes? But we do not measure what does not yet exist. Or in the present, by which it passes? We do not measure what is without space. Or in the past, into which it passes? We do not measure what no longer exists.

Chapter 22
A New Task

(28) My mind is on fire to understand this most intricate riddle. O Lord my God, good Father, I beseech you in the name of Christ, do not shut off, do not shut off these things, both familiar and yet hidden, from my desire, so that it may not penetrate into them, but let them grow bright, Lord, with your mercy bringing the light that lights them up. Of whom shall I inquire concerning them? To whom shall I more fruitfully confess my ignorance than to you, to whom my studies, strongly burning for your Scriptures, are not offensive.

Give me what I love, for in truth I love it, and this you have given to me. Give this to me, Father, for "truly you know how to give good gifts to your children."[1] Give it to me, for "I studied that I might know this thing; it is a labor in your sight,"[2] until you open it up. I beseech you in the name of Christ, in the name of him, the saint of saints, let no man interrupt me. "I have believed, therefore do I speak."[3] This is my hope, for this I live, "that I may contemplate the delight of the Lord."[4] "Behold, you have made my days old,"[5] and they pass away, but how I do not know. We talk of time and time, of times and times: "How long ago did he say this?" "How long ago did he do this?" "How long a time since I saw that?" "This syllable takes twice the time of that short simple syllable." We say these things, and we hear them, and we are understood, and we understand. They are most clear and most familiar, but again they are very obscure, and their solution is a new task.

Chapter 23
Bodily Motion as Time

(29) I have heard from a certain learned man that the movements of the sun, moon, and stars constitute time, but I did not agree with him.[1] Why should not rather the movement of all bodies be times? In fact, if the lights of heaven should stop, while a potter's wheel was kept moving, would there be no time by which we might measure those rotations? Would we say either that it moved with equal speeds, or, if it sometimes moved more slowly and sometimes more swiftly, that some turns were longer and others shorter? Or while we were saying this, would we not also be speaking in time? Or would there be in our words some long syllables and others short, except for the fact that some were sounded for a longer and others for a shorter time? Grant to men, O God, that they may see in a little matter evidence[2] common to things both small and great. The stars and the lights of heaven are "for signs, and for seasons, and for days, and for years."[3] Truly they are such. Yet I should not say that the turning of that little wooden wheel constitutes a day, nor under those conditions should that learned man say that there is no time.

(30) I desire to know the power and the nature of time, by which we measure bodily movements, and say, for instance, that this movement is twice as long as that. I put this question: "Since a day is defined not only as the sun's time over the earth—according to which usage, day is one thing and night another—but also as its entire circuit from east to east—and accordingly we say 'So many days have passed,' for they are termed 'so many days' with their nights included and are not reckoned as days apart from the night hours—since, then, a day is completed by the sun's movement and its circuit from east to east, I ask whether the movement itself constitutes a day, or the period in which the movement is performed, or both together?"

If the first were a day, then there would be a day even if the sun completed its course in a period of time such as an hour. If the second, then there would not be a day, if from one sunrise to another there were as brief a period as an hour, whereas the sun would have to go around twenty-four times to complete a day. If both, it could not be called a day if the sun ran its entire course in the space of an hour, nor if, while the sun stood still, just so much time passed by as the sun usually takes to complete its entire course from morning to morning.

Therefore, I will not now ask what is it that is called a day, but rather what is time, by which we would measure the sun's circuit and say that it was completed in half the time it usually takes, if it were finished in a period like twelve hours. Comparing both times, we should call the one a single period, the other a double period, even if the sun ran its course from east to east sometimes in the single period and sometimes in the double.

Let no man tell me, then, that movements of the heavenly bodies constitute periods of time.[4] When at the prayer of a certain man,[5] the sun stood still until he could achieve victory in battle, the sun indeed stood still, but time went on. That battle was waged and brought to an end during its own tract of time, which was sufficient for it. Therefore, I see that time is a kind of distention. Yet do I see this, or do I only seem to myself to see it? You, O Light, will show this to me.

Chapter 24
Measures of Movement

(31) Do you command me to agree with someone who says that time is the movement of a body? You do not command this. I hear that a body is never moved except in time: this you yourself affirm.[1] But I do not hear that the movement of a body constitutes time: this you do not say. When a body is moved, I measure in time how long it is moved, from when it begins to be moved until it ceases. If I did not see when it began, and if it continues to be moved, so that I cannot see when it stops, I am unable to measure it, except perhaps from the time I begin to see it until I stop. If I look at it for long, I can merely report that it is a long time, but not how long. When we say how long, we say so by making a comparison,

such as, "This is as long as that," or "Twice as long as that," or something of the sort.

But if we can mark off the distances of the places from which and to which the body that is moved goes—or its parts, if it is moved as on a lathe—then we can say in how much time the movement of that body, or its part, from this place to that, is completed. Since the movement of a body is one thing and that by which we measure how long it takes another, who does not perceive which of the two is better called time? For if a body is sometimes moved in different ways and sometimes stands still, then we measure in time not only its movement but also its standing still. We say, "It stood still just as long as it was moved," or "It stood still twice or three times as long as it was moved," and whatever else our measurements either determine or reckon, more or less, as the saying goes. Time, therefore, is not the movement of a body.

Chapter 25
The Deepening Problem

(32) I confess to you, O Lord, that I do not yet know what time is, and again I confess to you, O Lord, that I know that I say these things in time, and that I have now spoken at length of time, and that that very length of time is not long except by a period of time. How, then, do I know this, when I do not know what time is? Or perhaps I do not know how to express what I know? Woe is me, who do not even know what I do not know![1] Behold, O my God, before you I do not lie.[2] As I speak, so is my heart. "You will light my lamp, O Lord, my God, you enlighten my darkness."[3]

Chapter 26
The Definition of Time

(33) Does not my soul confess to you with a true confession that I measure tracts of time? Yes, O Lord my God, I measure them, and know not what I measure, I measure the motion of a body in time. But again, do I not measure time itself? In fact, could I measure a body's movement, as to how long it is and

how long it takes from this place to that, unless I could measure the time in which it is moved? How, then, do I measure time itself? Do we measure a longer time by a shorter one, just as we measure the length of a rod by the length of a cubit?[1] It is thus that we seem to measure the length of a long syllable by the length of a short syllable, and to say that it is twice as long. So also we measure the length of poems by the length of verses, the length of verses by the length of feet, the length of feet by the length of syllables, and the length of long syllables by the length of short ones. This is not as they are on the page—in that manner we measure spaces, not times—but as words pass by when we pronounce them. We say: "It is a long poem for it is composed of so many verses; the verses are long, for they consist of so many feet; the feet are long, for they extend over so many syllables; the syllable is long, for it is double a short one."

But a reliable measure of time is not comprehended in this manner, since it can be that a shorter verse, if pronounced more slowly, may sound for a longer stretch of time than a longer but more hurried verse. So it is for a poem, so for a foot, so for a syllable. For this reason it seemed to me that time is nothing more than distention:[2] but of what thing I know not, and the marvel is, if it is not of the mind itself. For what do I measure, I beseech you, my God, when I say either indefinitely, "This time is longer than that," or even definitely, "This time is twice as long as that?" I measure time, I know. Yet I do not measure the future, because it does not yet exist; I do not measure the present, because it is not extended in space; I do not measure the past, because it no longer exists. What, then, do I measure? Times that pass, but are not yet past? So I have stated.

Chapter 27
Where Time Is Measured

(34) Be steadfast, O my mind, and attend firmly. "God is our helper."[1] "He made us, and not we ourselves."[2] Look to where truth begins to dawn.[3] See, as an example, a bodily voice begins to sound, and does sound, and still sounds, and

Book 11. *Time and Eternity*

then, see, it stops. There is silence now: that voice is past, and is no longer a voice. Before it sounded, the voice was to come, and could not be measured because it did not yet exist, and now it cannot be measured because it no longer is. Therefore, the time it was sounding, it could be measured, because at that time it existed. Even at that time it was not static, for it was going on and going away. Was it for that reason the more measurable? While passing away it was being extended over some tract of time, wherein it could be measured, for the present has no space. Therefore, if it could be measured at that time, let us suppose that another voice has begun to sound and still sounds on one continuous note without any break. Let us measure it while it is sounding, since when it has ceased to sound, it will be already past and there will be nothing that can be measured. Let us measure it exactly, and let us state how long it is. But it is still sounding, and it cannot be measured except from its beginning, when it begins to sound, up to its end, when it stops. We measure, in fact, the interval from some beginning up to some kind of end. Hence a voice that is never brought to a stop cannot be measured, so that one may say how long or short it is. Nor can it be said to be equal to another, or single or double or anything else with reference to something. But when it will be ended, it will no longer be. In what sense, then, can it be measured? Yet we do measure tracts of time, although not those which as yet are not, not those which no longer are, not those which are prolonged without a break, not those which have no limits. Neither future, nor past, nor present, nor passing times do we measure, and still we measure tracts of time.

(35) *Deus creator omnium*[4]—"God, creator of all things" —this verse of eight syllables alternates between short and long syllables. Hence the four short syllables, the first, third, fifth, and seventh, are simple with respect to the four long syllables, the second, fourth, sixth, and eighth. Each long syllable has a double time with respect to each of the others. This I affirm, this I report, and so it is, in so far as it is plain to sense perception. In so far as sense perception is clear, I measure the long syllable by the short one, and I perceive that it is exactly twice as long. But when one syllable sounds after another, and

if the first is short and the second long, how will I retain the short syllable and how will I apply it to the long syllable while measuring it, so as to find that the latter is twice as long? For the long syllable does not begin to sound until the short one has ceased to sound. Do I measure the long syllable itself while it is present, since I do not measure it until it is completed? Yet its completion is its passing away. Therefore, what is it that I measure? Where is the short syllable by which I measure? Where is the long syllable that I measure? Both of them have sounded, have flown off, have passed away, and now they are not. Yet I make measurements, and I answer confidently—in so far as sense activity is relied upon—that this syllable is single and that one double, namely, in length of time. Yet I cannot do this, unless because they have passed away and are ended. Therefore, I do not measure the syllables themselves, which no longer are, but something in my memory that remains fixed there.

(36) It is in you, O my mind, that I measure my times. Do not interrupt me by crying that time is. Do not interrupt yourself with the noisy mobs of your prejudices. It is in you, I say, that I measure tracts of time. The impression that passing things make upon you remains, even after those things have passed. That present state is what I measure, not the things which pass away so that it be made. That is what I measure when I measure tracts of time. Therefore, either this is time, or I do not measure time.

How is it when we measure stretches of silence, and say that this silence has lasted for as much of time as that discourse lasted? Do we not apply our thought to measurement of the voice, just as though it were sounding, so that we may be able to report about the intervals of silence in a given tract of time? Even though both voice and mouth be silent, in our thought we run through poems and verses, and any discourse, and any other measurements of motion. We report about tracts of time: how great this one may be in relation to that, in the same manner as if we said them audibly.

If someone wished to utter a rather long sound and had determined by previous reflection how long it would be, he has in fact already silently gone through a tract of time. After committing it to memory, he has begun to utter that sound and he voices it until he has brought it to his proposed end. Yes, it has sounded and it will sound. For the part of it that is finished has surely sounded; what remains will sound. So it is carried out, as long as his present intention transfers the future into the past, with the past increasing by a diminution of future, until by the consumption of the future the whole is made past.

Chapter 28
The Mental Synthesis

(37) But how is the future, which as yet does not exist, diminished or consumed, or how does the past, which no longer exists, increase, unless there are three things in the mind, which does all this? It looks forward, it considers, it remembers, so that the reality to which it looks forward passes through what it considers into what it remembers. Who, then, denies that future things are not yet existent? Yet there is already in the mind an expectation of things to come. Who denies that past things no longer exist? Yet there is still in the soul the memory of past things. Who denies that present time lacks spatial extent, since it passes away in an instant? Yet attention abides, and through it what shall be present proceeds to become something absent. It is not, then, future time that is long, but a long future is a long expectation of the future. Nor is past time, which is not, long, but a long past is a long memory of the past.

(38) I am about to recite a psalm that I know. Before I begin, my expectation extends over the entire psalm. Once I have begun, my memory extends over as much of it as I shall separate off and assign to the past. The life of this action of mine is distended into memory by reason of the part I have spoken and into forethought by reason of the part I am about to speak. But attention is actually present and that which was to be is borne along by it so as to become past. The more this is done and done again, so much the more is memory lengthened by a shortening of expectation, until the entire expectation is exhausted. When this is done the whole action is com-

pleted and passes into memory. What takes place in the whole psalm takes place also in each of its parts and in each of its syllables. The same thing holds for a longer action, of which perhaps the psalm is a small part. The same thing holds for a man's entire life, the parts of which are all the man's actions. The same thing holds throughout the whole age of the sons of men, the parts of which are the lives of all men.

Chapter 29
The One and the Many

(39) But since "your mercy is better than lives,"[1] behold, my life is a distention, or distraction.[2] But "your right hand has upheld me"[3] in my Lord, the Son of man, mediator between you, the One, and us, the many, who are dissipated in many ways upon many things; so that by him "I may apprehend, in whom I have been apprehended," and may be gathered together again from my former days, to follow the One; "forgetting the things that are behind" and not distended but extended, not to things that shall be and shall pass away, but "to those things which are before"; not purposelessly but purposively, "I follow on for the prize of my supernal vocation,"[4] where "I may hear the voice of your praise,"[5] and "contemplate your delights,"[6] which neither come nor go.

But now "my years are wasted in sighs,"[7] and you, O Lord, my comfort, my Father, are eternal. But I am distracted amid times, whose order I do not know, and my thoughts, the inmost bowels of my soul, are torn asunder by tumult and change, until being purged and melted clear by the fire of your love, I may flow altogether into you.

Chapter 30
God Alone Is Eternal

(40) I will stand and be firm in you, in your Truth, which is my mold. I will not endure the questions of men, who by a disease that is their punishment, thirst for more than they can hold, and say, "What did God do before he made heaven and

earth?" or "How did it come to his mind to make anything, since he had never before made anything?"

Give them, O Lord, to think well on what they say, and to learn that the word "never" cannot be used where there is no time. Therefore, when a man is said never to have made anything, what else is said except that he made it at no time? Let them see, therefore, that there can be no time without creation, and let them cease to speak vanity.[1] May they also reach out forth "to those things which are before,"[2] and understand that you are before all times, the eternal creator of all times, and that times are not coeternal with you, nor is any creature such, even if there were a creature above time.[3]

CHAPTER 31

Unchanging Thought, Unchanging Act

(41) O Lord my God, how deep are your secret places, and how far from them have the consequences of my sins cast me! Heal my eyes, and let me share in the joy of your light. Surely, if there is a mind possessed of such great knowledge and foreknowledge, so that to it are known all things past and future, just as I know one well-known psalm, then supremely marvelous is that mind and wondrous and fearsome. From it whatever there is of ages past and of ages to come is no more hidden than there are hidden from me as I sing that psalm what and how much preceded from its beginning and what and how much remains to the end.

But far be it that you, creator of the universe, creator of souls and bodies, far be it that in such wise you should know future and past. Far, far more wonderfully, far more deeply do you know them! It is not as emotions are changed or senses filled up by expectation of words to come and memory of those past in one who sings well-known psalms or hears a familiar psalm. Not so does it befall you who are unchangeably eternal, that is, truly eternal, the creator of minds. Therefore, just as in the beginning you have known heaven and earth without change in your knowledge, so too "in the beginning you made heaven and earth"[1] without any difference in your activity.

Whosoever understands this, let him confess it to you, and whosoever does not understand it, let him confess it to you. O how exalted are you, and yet the humble of heart are your dwelling place![2] You "lift up them that are cast down,"[3] and they do not fall down, whose place aloft is you!

BOOK 12
FORM AND MATTER

Chapter 1
A Creature of Needs[1]

(1) Smitten by the words of your Holy Scripture, my heart is much concerned over many things, amid this poverty which is my life. Most often on this account the poverty of man's understanding is spendthrift of words, because searching speaks more than does finding, pleading takes longer than acceptance, and the hand that knocks is busier than the hand that receives. We hold the promise: who shall destroy it? "If God is for us, who is against us?"[2] "Ask, and you shall receive."[3] "Seek, and you shall find; knock, and it shall be opened to you. For everyone who asks receives, and he who seeks finds, and to him who knocks, it shall be opened."[4] The promises are yours, and who fears deception, when Truth makes the promise?

Chapter 2
The Two Heavens

(2) The lowliness of my tongue confesses to your highness[1] that you have made heaven and earth, this heaven which I see, this earth on which I tread and from which comes this earth[2] I bear about with myself. You have made them. But where is that heaven of heaven,[3] O Lord, which we hear of in the words of the psalm: "The heaven of heaven is the Lord's, but the earth he has given to the children of men?"[4] Where is the heaven that we do not see, before which all this which we see is earth? For this corporeal whole, since it is not everywhere whole, has in such wise received form and beauty in its least parts, of which the very lowest is our earth, but to that heaven of heaven even our earth's heaven is but

earth. Not unreasonably are both these great bodies but earth before that indescribable heaven which is the Lord's and not the sons' of men.

Chapter 3
Matter and Form

(3) Assuredly, this earth was invisible and without order, and there was I know not what profound abyss, upon which there was no light, because there was no form in it. Whence you commanded it to be written that "darkness was upon the deep."[1] What else was this but absence of light? If there were light, where else would it be except up above, standing visible and shedding its rays? Therefore, where there was yet no light, what was the presence of darkness except the absence of light? So darkness was upon it, because there was no light upon it, just as where there is no sound, there is silence. What does it mean that silence is in a place, except that sound is not there? Lord, have you not taught this soul which confesses to you? Lord, have you not taught me[2] that before you formed this unformed matter[3] and fashioned it into kinds, there was no separate being, no color, no shape, no body, no spirit? Yet there was not absolutely nothing: there was a certain formlessness devoid of any specific character.

Chapter 4
A Proper Name

(4) What then should it be called, if not by some familiar word, so that it may also be instilled in some way even into our more sluggish minds? Among all the parts of the world, what can be found closer to utter formlessness than earth and the deep? Because they occupy the very lowest place, they are less beautiful than the other higher parts, all of them transparent and brilliant. Why, then, may I not perceive that the formlessness of matter, which you made without beauty, but from which you made this beauteous world, is effectively indicated to men when called "earth invisible and without form"?

Chapter 5
The Problem of Matter

(5) Hence, when thought seeks what mind may attain to in it, and says to itself, "It is not an intelligible form, like life, or like justice, because it is the matter of bodies. Nor is it a sensible form, because what may be seen and what may be sensed is not found in what is invisible and unordered," when human thought says such things to itself, does it not strive either to know it by not knowing it, or to be ignorant by knowing it?

Chapter 6
An Appeal to Reason

(6) Truly, Lord, if by my mouth and my pen I may confess to you whatsoever you yourself have taught to me concerning such matter—the very name of which I heard but did not understand when men[1] who themselves did not understand it repeated it to me—I formerly conceived it as having countless different forms, and therefore I did not conceive it at all. My mind turned over forms foul and horrid in confused array, but still forms. I called it formless, not because it lacked all form, but because it had such form that, if it ever showed itself, my senses would have turned away from it as from something strange and improper, and man's frail powers would be disturbed by it. But what I was thus thinking about was formless not from lack of all form, but by comparison with better formed things. Right reason[2] persuaded me that I must divest it utterly of every remnant of every form, if I desired to conceive it as completely formless. This I could not do. It was easier for me to conclude that it lacked all form than to conceive of something between form and nothing, neither formed nor nothing, an unformed near-nothing.

My mind ceased to question my imagination on this subject, for it was filled with pictures of formed bodies, and it was arbitrarily shifting and changing them about. I fixed my thought on the bodies themselves, and peered more deeply into their mutability, by reason of which they cease to be what they once were and begin to be what they were not. This same transition from form to form I suspected to be made through something formless and not by means of absolute nothing. But I desired to know this, not merely to guess at it. If my voice and hand were to confess to you all the knots that you have untied for me concerning this question, what one among my readers will persevere so as to grasp it all? But not for that fact will my heart cease from giving you honor and from raising a hymn of praise for those things which it cannot dictate. The mutability of mutable things is itself a capacity for all the forms into which mutable things are changed. What is this? Is it mind? Is it body? Is it a variety of mind or body? If it could be said, "a nothing-something," "an is-is-not," I would say that it is such. Yet it already somehow existed, so that it might receive these visible and ordered forms.

Chapter 7
Heights and Depths

(7) Whence and in what manner was it, if it was not from you, from whom are all things, in so far as they are? But so much more distant is anything from you, in so far as it is more unlike you, and this distance is not of place. Therefore, Lord, you who are not one thing at one time and a different thing in another, but the Selfsame, and the Selfsame, and the Selfsame,[1] "holy, holy, holy, Lord God almighty,"[2] in the Beginning,[3] which is of you, in your Wisdom, which is born of your own substance, you created something, and that something out of nothing. You made heaven and earth, not out of yourself, for then they would have been equal to your Onlybegotten, and through this equal also to you. But in no way was it just that anything which was not of you should be equal to you.

There was nothing beyond you from which you might make them, O God, one Trinity and trinal Unity. Therefore, you created heaven and earth out of nothing, a great thing and a little thing. For you are almighty and good, to make all things good, the great heaven and the little earth. You were, and there was naught else out of which you made heaven and earth: two beings, one near to you, the other near to nothingness, one to which you alone would be superior, the other to which nothing would be inferior.

Chapter 8
Darkness over the Deep

(8) But that "heaven of heaven is yours, O Lord,"[1] but the earth, which you gave to the sons of men to be seen and felt, was not such as we now see and touch. It was invisible and not set in order, and it was an abyss above which there was no light. Or else the words "darkness was upon the deep" mean that there was more darkness above the deep than in it. For in fact the watery deep now visible to us has even in its lowest parts a light that is proper to its character and can in some way be sensed by the fishes and the animals creeping on its bottom. But that entire abyss was close to non-being, since it was still altogether devoid of form. Still, it was already something that could be given form. Lord, you made the world out of formless matter;[2] this letter you made out of nothing into a near-nothing, thereof to make the great things that we, the sons of men, wonder at.

Truly wonderful is this, the corporeal heaven, this firmament between water and water, of which, on the second day after the creation of light, you said: "Let it be made," and so it was made.[3] You called this firmament heaven, namely, heaven of this earth and sea. These you made on the third day by giving visible form to formless matter, which you made before the beginning of all days. Already, before all days, you had made a heaven, but it was heaven of this heaven, for in the beginning you made heaven and earth. The earth itself, which you made, was formless matter, because it was invisible and not set in order, and darkness was above the deep. Out of this unordered and invisible earth, out of this formlessness, out of this almost-nothing, you made all things, of which this mutable world stands firm, and yet does not stand firm,[4] in which mutability itself is apparent, in which tracts of time can be perceived and numbered off. For tracts of time result from the changes of things, according as the forms, for which the aforesaid invisible earth is the matter, are varied and turned about.

Chapter 9
The Highest Heaven

(9) Therefore, when the Spirit, the teacher of your servant,[1] recounts that in the beginning you made heaven and earth, he says nothing of times and is silent of days. Doubtless, that heaven of heaven, which you made in the beginning, is some kind of intellectual creature. Although in no manner coeternal with you, the Trinity, it is yet a partaker of your eternity, and because of its most sweet and happy contemplation of you, it firmly checks its own mutability. Without any lapse from its first creation, it has clung fast to you and is thus set beyond all the turns and changes of time. This formlessness, this earth invisible and without form, is not numbered among the days. Where there is no form, no order, nothing comes or passes away. Where this does not take place, surely there are no days and no change of time.

Chapter 10
The Fountain of Life

(10) O may it be the Truth, the light of my heart, not my own darkness, that speaks to me. I fell away to those material things, and I became darkened over, but from there, even from there, I loved you. I went astray, but I did not forget you.[1] "I heard your voice behind me,"[2] calling me to return, but because of the tumult of men hostile to peace,[3] I scarcely heard it. But now, see, I return, burning and yearning for your fountain. Let no man forbid me! I will drink at this fountain, and I will live by it. Let me not be my own life: badly have I lived from myself: I was death to myself: in you I live again. Speak to me, speak with me. I have believed in your books, and their words are most full of mystery.

Chapter 11
The Soul a Pilgrim

(11) Already you have said to me with a strong voice into my interior ear that you are eternal, you who alone have immortality,[1] since you can be changed by no kind of motion and your will is not varied with time, for no will is immortal which is now one thing, now another. In your sight this is clear to me, and may it become more and more clear, I beseech you, and under your wings let me persevere soberly in what you have made manifest. You have also told me with a strong voice within my interior ear, O Lord, that you have made every nature and every substance, things that are not what you are but yet exist. The only thing that does not come from you is what does not exist, together with any movement of the will away from you who are and towards that which is in a lesser way, for such movement is crime and sin. You have told me that no man's sin either hurts you or disrupts the order of your government, whether in the beginning or in the end. In your sight this is clear to me: may it become more and more clear, I beseech you, and in this which you have made manifest let me persevere soberly under your wings.

(12) Again, you have told me with a strong voice within my interior ear that not even that creature is coeternal with you, whose delight you alone are, and who with most persevering chastity, drawing its nourishment from you, has nowhere and never asserted its own mutability, and with you yourself ever present with it, to whom it clings with all its powers, having neither future to look forward to nor transferring to the past what it remembers, is neither altered by any change nor distended into any times. O happy creature, if there be such, for cleaving to your happiness, happy in you, its eternal dweller and enlightener! I do not find anything which I may more fittingly judge should be called "the heaven of heaven, which is the Lord's,"[2] than your own house, which contemplates your delight[3] without any fault of going to another, a pure mind, most harmoniously one by the established peace of holy

spirits, citizens of your city in heavenly places above these present heavens.

(13) From this may the soul, whose pilgrimage has become long, understand that if she now thirsts for you, if her tears are now made her bread, while it is said to her each day, "Where is your God?"[4] if she now seeks of you one thing,[5] and desires it, that she may dwell in your house all the days of her life—and what is her life except yourself? and what are your days except eternity, just as are your years, which do not fail, because you are ever the same?[6]—from this, then, may that soul, which can do so, understand how far above all times are you, the Eternal. For your house, which is not on pilgrimage, even though it is not coeternal with you, yet unceasingly and unfailingly clings to you and thus suffers no change in time. In your sight this is clear to me: may it become more and more clear, I beseech you, and in this which you have made manifest let me persevere soberly under your wings.

(14) See, there is I know not what formlessness in those mutations of the latest and lowest things! Who will tell me, unless it be such a one as through his inanity of heart wanders about and tosses up and down amid his own fantasies? Who but such a one will tell me, if all form be lessened and consumed away and there remain formlessness alone, through which a thing was changed and turned from one kind to another kind, that it could exhibit temporal change? In no way could it do so, because without variety of motions there are no times, and there is no variety where there is no form.

Chapter 12
Things Immune to Time

(15) These things I have considered in so far as you have given it to me to do so, O my God, in so far as you have aroused me to knock, and in so far as you have opened up to my knocking. I find two things which you have made immune to time, although neither one is coeternal with you. One of them has been so formed that, without any interruption of its contemplation, without any interval of change, subject to

change yet never changed, it enjoys eternity and immutability. The other was so formless that it could not be changed from one form into another form whether of motion or of rest, and thus be made subject to time. But you did not abandon this second being to remain formless. For before all days, "in the beginning you made heaven and earth,"[1] those two things of which I was speaking. The earth was invisible and without order, and darkness was above the deep. By these words you have instilled the idea of formlessness, so that gradually aid might be given to minds that could not conceive complete privation of form without arriving at nothing. From it would be made another heaven and earth, visible and set in order, and beautiful bodies of water, and whatever else is recorded as being made thereafter, but not without days, in the creation of this world. For such things exist, so that in them temporal changes may take place because of ordered alterations of movements and forms.

Chapter 13

In a Glass, Darkly

(16) Meanwhile, I conceive this, O my God, when I hear your Scripture saying, "In the beginning God made heaven and earth, and the earth was invisible and without form, and darkness was upon the deep," and making no mention of the day on which you made these things. Meanwhile, I interpret the heaven of heaven as the intellectual heaven, where it belongs to intellect to know all at once, not in part, not in a dark manner, not through a glass, but as a whole, in plain sight, face to face,[1] not this thing now and that thing then, but, as has been said, it knows all at once, without any passage of time. By the earth invisible and without form, I understand an earth without any change of time, which change is wont to have now this thing, now that. For where there is no form, there is nowhere separation of this from that.

Because of these two, the one formed from the very beginning and the other completely unformed, the first heaven, but the heaven of heaven, the second earth, but the earth invisible and without form, because of these two I meanwhile understand what your Scripture says, without mention of days, "In the beginning God made heaven and earth." For immediately it subjoins which earth it spoke of. Also, since it is recorded that on the second day the firmament was made and was called heaven, it indicates which heaven was previously spoken of as being without days.

CHAPTER 14

The Two-edged Sword

(17) Wondrous is the depth of your words, for see, their surface lies before us, giving delight to your little ones. But wondrous is their depth, O my God, wondrous is their depth! It is awesome to look into that depth: an awe owed to honor, and a trembling arising from love! Strongly do I hate its enemies! Oh, that you would slay them with a two-edged sword,[1] that they would no longer be its enemies! Thus do I love them, that they be slain to themselves, so that they might live for you.

But see, there are others, not objectors to the book of Genesis but praisers of it, and they say: "The Spirit of God, who by his servant Moses wrote down these things, did not will that all this be understood from these words. He would not have what you say taken from them, but something different which we say."

To these men I thus make answer as follows, with you, O God of us all, as our judge.

CHAPTER 15

Answers to Objectors

(18) Will you claim that those things are false which Truth with a strong voice speaks into my inner ear concerning the true eternity of the creator, that his substance is in no wise changed in time, and his will is not outside his substance? For this reason, he does not will now this, now that, but once, and all at once, and forever he wills all that he wills. It is not again and again, now these things, now those. He does not will later on what he once willed against, nor does he will

Book 12. Form and Matter 315

against what he previously willed to do. Such a will is mutable, and no mutable thing is eternal. But our God is eternal.[1]

Again, truth speaks into my inner ear that expectation of things to come becomes complete intuition when those things come to pass, and this same contuition* becomes memory after they pass away. Now all thought that varies in this manner is mutable, and no mutable thing is eternal. These things I gather up and fit together, and I find that my God, the eternal God, did not establish all his creation by any new act of will, nor did his knowledge suffer any transmutation.

(19) What, then, will you say, O contradictors? Are these things false? "No," they say. What then? Is it false that every formed nature, or matter capable of formation, exists only from him who is supremely good because he supremely is? "We do not deny this," they say. What then? Do you deny this, that there is a certain sublime creature that cleaves with so chaste a love to the true and truly eternal God that, although not coeternal with him, it still does not detach from him and does not dissolve away into any variation and change of times, but finds rest in a most veracious contemplation of him alone? For you, O God, reveal yourself to a being that loves you as much as you command, and you are sufficient to it. Therefore, he does not fall away from you and to himself. This is the house of God, not earthly, and yet not of celestial, corporeal shape, but spiritual and partaking of your eternity, because it is forever without defect. For you have "established it forever and for ages of ages." You have "made a decree, and it shall not pass away."[2] Yet it is not coeternal with you, because it is not without beginning, for it was made.

(20) Although we do not find time before it, for "wisdom has been created before all things,"[3] surely it is not that wisdom which is altogether coeternal and equal with you, its Father, O our God, through which wisdom all things were created, and in whom, as the Beginning, you created heaven and earth. Rather it is that wisdom which is created, namely,

---

* Contuition: A word fashioned by the translator from the Latin *contuitus* as a stronger expression of St. Augustine's thought rendered by "complete intuition" immediately preceding.—*Editor's note.*

an intellectual nature, which, through contemplation of the Light, is light. For this is also called wisdom, although a created wisdom.

But great as is the difference between the Light which brings light and that light which is brought, just so great is the difference beween the Wisdom which creates and that which is created, even as there is between justice that justifies and justice that is brought about by justification. For we are also called by your justice. A certain servant of yours has said: "That we might be made the justice of God in him."[4] Therefore, a certain created wisdom was created before all things, the rational and intellectual mind of your chaste city, our mother, which is above, and is free and eternal in the heavens.[5] In what heavens was it, if not those which praise you, the heaven of heavens, for this is also the heaven of heaven for the Lord?[6] Although we find no time in it, for that which was created before all things also precedes the creation of time, yet the eternity of the creator himself is before it. For being made by him, it took its beginning from him, not indeed in time, for time itself was not yet, but in its very creation.

(21) Hence it is in such wise from you, our God, that it is completely other than you and not the Selfsame. Not only do we find no time before it, but not even in it, because it is adapted always to behold your face and is never turned away from it. Thus it comes about that it is never varied by any change. Yet there is in it a certain mutability, from which it would become dark and cold, unless it clung to you with a mighty love so as to shine and glow from you as at eternal noontide. O lightsome and beautiful house! I have loved your beauty and the dwelling place of the glory of my Lord,[7] your builder and possessor! May my pilgrimage sigh after you! I speak to him who made you, so that he may also possess me in you, because he has likewise made me. "I have gone astray, like a sheep that is lost."[8] Yet upon the shoulders of my shepherd,[9] your builder, I hope to be borne back to you.

(22) What do you say to me, O contradictors to whom I was speaking, who yet believe that Moses was a devout servant of God and that his books are the oracles of the Holy

Spirit? Is not this house of God, although not coeternal with God, nevertheless according to its condition eternal in the heavens, where in vain you seek for changes of time, because you do not find them there? This house, for which it is good ever to adhere to God,[10] surpasses all distention and all turning tracts of time. They say, "It is." What then of all those things that my heart cried out to my God,[11] when inwardly it heard the voice of his praise,[12] what part of them do you contend is false? Is it that matter was without form, wherein, since there was no form, there was no order? But where there was no order there could be no change of time. Yet this "almost nothing," in as much as it was not completely nothing, was surely from him, from whom is whatever is, whatever is anything in any way. They say, "This also we do not deny."

Chapter 16
The City of God

(23) I desire to converse for a little while in your presence, O my God, with these men who grant that all these things, of which your truth is not silent inwardly in my mind, are true. For those who deny these things, let them bark as much as they wish, make only a din for themselves. I will attempt to persuade them, so that they may become quiet and leave open a way into themselves for your Word. But if they refuse and repel me, I beseech you, my God, "do not be silent to me."[1] Speak in my heart, with truth, for you alone speak thus. I will leave them outside, blowing into the dust and raising up dirt into their own eyes. I will enter into my chamber[2] and there I will sing songs of love to you, groaning with unspeakable groanings[3] on my pilgrimage, and remembering Jerusalem, with heart lifted up towards it, Jerusalem my country, Jerusalem my mother,[4] and you who over her are ruler, enlightener, father, guardian, spouse, pure and strong delight, solid joy, all good things ineffable, all possessed at once, because you are the one and the true good. I will not be turned away until out of this scattered and disordered state you gather all that I am into the peace of her, the mother most dear, where are the first fruits[5] of my spirit, whence these

things are certain to me, and you conform and confirm me into eternity my God, my mercy.

But with those who do not assert to be false all these things which are true, but honor your holy Scripture put forth by holy Moses, and like us place it on the summit of authority that must be followed, and yet contradict me in some matter, I speak thus: Do you, our God, be judge between my confessions and their contradictions.

Chapter 17
Other Theories

(24) They say: "Although these words are true, yet Moses was not considering the two things you name when by the revelation of the Spirit he said, 'In the beginning God made heaven and earth.' By the term 'heaven,' he did not mean that spiritual or intellectual creature which forever contemplates God's face, nor by the term 'earth' did he mean formless matter." What then? They say: "That man meant what we say. He stated this in those words." What is that? They answer: "By the terms 'heaven' and 'earth,' he first wanted to signify in an all-inclusive and brief manner, the whole visible world, so that afterwards by enumeration of days[1] he could point out, in detail as it were, all the things which the Holy Spirit was pleased to announce in this manner. That rude and carnal people to which he spoke was made up of such men that he judged only the visible works of God should be set down for them." However, they agree that the invisible and unformed earth and the darksome deep, out of which, as is later shown, all these visible things were made and set in order during those various days, things which are known to all men, are not unfittingly interpreted as being that formless matter.

(25) But what if another man says that this same formless and confused matter was first indicated to us by the terms "heaven" and "earth," because out of it there was established and perfected this visible world, together with all the natures which most manifestly appear in it, which visible world is often accustomed to be called by the terms "heaven" and "earth?" What if another man says that invisible and visible

nature is not improperly called heaven and earth, and hence the universal creation which God made in his wisdom, that is, "in the beginning," was comprehended in two words of this sort? Nevertheless, all things have been made, not out of the very substance of God, but out of nothing, since they are not the same as he is, and because there is a certain mutability in all things, whether they stand fast, as does God's eternal house, or are subject to change, as are men's soul and body. Therefore, it follows that the common matter of all things visible and invisible, still unformed but certainly capable of being formed, out of which heaven and earth would be made, that is, the visible and invisible creature when actually formed, was designated by those names, by which "the earth invisible and without form" and "the darkness over the deep," are called. But it was with this difference, that "the earth invisible and without order" would be understood as corporeal matter before being qualified by any form, and "darkness above the deep" as spiritual matter before any restraint was put upon its almost unbounded fluidity and any enlightenment from wisdom.

(26) If any other man[2] so wishes, the following may still be stated. The natures, both visible and invisible, of heaven and earth, already perfected and formed, are not meant by the phrase "heaven and earth" when we read, "In the beginning God made heaven and earth." Rather, the still formless commencement of things, matter capable of form and creation, was called by these names, because contained in it in a confused manner, and not yet distinguished by qualities and forms, were those things now arranged in order and called heaven and earth, the one being a spiritual and the other a corporeal creature.

Chapter 18
Interpretation of Scripture

(27) Having heard and considered all these problems I do not wish to "contend in words, for it is to no profit, but to the subversion of the hearers."[1] But "the law is good" to edify, "if a man use it lawfully."[2] For the end of it "is charity, from

a pure heart, and a good conscience, and an unfeigned faith."[3] Our Master[4] has known upon which two commandments he would make the whole law and the prophets depend.[5] What harm comes to me, O my God, "light of my eyes"[6] in secret, if I zealously confess these things to you, what harm comes to me, if various meanings may be found in these words, all of which are true? What harm comes to me, I say, if I think differently than another thinks as to what he who wrote these words thought?[7] All of us who read strive to trace out and understand what he whom we read actually meant, and since we believe him to speak the truth, we dare not assert that he spoke anything we know or think to be false. Therefore, while every man tries to understand in Holy Scripture what the author understood therein, what wrong is there if anyone understand what you, O light of all truthful minds, reveal to him as true, even if the author he reads did not understand this, since he also understood a truth, though not this truth?

Chapter 19

A Recapitulation

(28) True it is, O, Lord, that you made heaven and earth. True it is that the beginning is your Wisdom, in which you made all things.[1] True it is also that this visible world has as its greater parts heaven and earth, by way of brief description of all made and created natures. True it is, too, that every mutable being suggests to our mind a certain formlessness, by reason of which it receives a form, or is transmuted or changed about. True it is that that being suffers no temporal changes which so clings to the immutable form that, although itself mutable, it is not changed. True it is that that formlessness which is almost nothing cannot have changes in time. True it is that that out of which a thing is made may already bear, in a certain figure of speech, the name of the thing made out of it. Hence a certain formlessness, out of which heaven and earth were made, could be called heaven and earth. True it is that of all formed beings, none is closer to unformed being than earth and the deep. True it is that you, from whom are

all things,[2] have made not only created and formed being, but also whatsoever is capable of being created and formed. True it is that every being that is formed out of that without form is itself first unformed and then formed.

CHAPTER 20
Exegesis of Genesis 1:1

(29) Out of all these truths, concerning which they do not doubt whose inward eye you have granted to see such things, and who steadfastly believe that your servant Moses spoke in the Spirit of Truth,[1] out of all these, then, he selects one who says: "'In the beginning, God made heaven and earth,' that is, in his Word, coeternal with himself, God made intelligible and sensible, or spiritual and corporeal, creation." He takes another who says: "'In the beginning, God made heaven and earth,' that is, in his Word, coeternal with himself, God made this universal mass of this corporeal world, together with all the manifest and known natures that it contains." He takes another who says: "'In the beginning, God made heaven and earth,' that is, in his Word, coeternal with himself, God made the formless matter of spiritual and corporeal creation." He takes another who says: "'In the beginning God made heaven and earth,' that is, in his Word, coeternal with himself, God made the formless matter of corporeal creation, wherein, still confused, lay heaven and earth, which we perceive now distinct and formed in the mass of this world." He takes another who says: "'In the beginning God made heaven and earth,' that is, in the very beginning of his making and working, God made that formless matter, confusedly containing within itself heaven and earth, from which matter they now stand forth fully formed and are apparent, together with all things that are in them."

CHAPTER 21
Interpretations of Genesis 1:2

(30) This holds also for an understanding of the words following. Out of all these truths, a man chooses one meaning

for himself when he says: "'But the earth was invisible and without form, and darkness was upon the deep.' That is, that corporeal thing which God made was as yet the formless matter of corporeal things, without order, without light." He chooses another who says: "'But the earth was invisible and without form, and darkness was upon the deep.' That is, this whole being, which is called heaven and earth, was as yet formless and darksome matter, out of which would be made the corporeal heaven and the corporeal earth, together with all things in them known to bodily senses." He takes another who says: "'But the earth was invisible and without form, and darkness was upon the deep.' That is, this whole, which is called heaven and earth, was as yet formless and darksome matter, out of which would be made the intelligible heaven—which elsewhere is called the heaven of heaven—and earth, namely, all corporeal nature, under which name may be understood likewise this corporeal heaven, that is, that from which would be made all invisible and visible creation." He takes another who says: "'The earth was invisible and without form, and darkness was upon the deep.' Scripture has not called that formlessness by the name of heaven and earth, but there already was formlessness itself," he says, "which Moses named 'the earth invisible and without form' and 'the darksome deep,' out of which, as he had said before, God made heaven and earth, namely, spiritual and corporeal creation." He takes another who says: "'But the earth was invisible and without form, and darkness was upon the deep.' That is, formlessness was already a certain matter, out of which, as Scripture said before, God made heaven and earth, namely, the whole corporeal mass of the world, divided into two immense parts, higher and lower, together with all the usual and familiar creatures in them."

Chapter 22
Objections and Answers

(31) Someone might attempt to oppose these two last opinions in this fashion: "If you will not grant that this formless matter seems to be called by the names of heaven and earth,

Book 12. Form and Matter

then there was something which God did not make, out of which he made heaven and earth. Scripture has not recounted that God made this matter, unless we understand that it was signified by the phrase heaven and earth, or earth alone, when it was said, 'In the beginning God made heaven and earth.' Hence by what follows, 'But the earth was invisible and without form'—although it pleased him to describe formless matter in this way—we are to understand no other matter but that which God made in it, whereof it is written above, 'He made heaven and earth.'"

The proponents of these two opinions which we placed last, whether of one or of the other, will respond, when they hear these things, and they will say: "We do not deny that this formless matter was made by God, from whom are all things exceeding good,[1] because, just as we have asserted that that is a greater good which is created and formed, so we admit that that is a lesser good which is made creable and formable, but yet a good. However, we say that Scripture has not recorded that God made this formlessness, just as it has not recorded many other things, like the Cherubim and the Seraphim, and those which the Apostle distinctly names, Thrones, Dominations, Principalities, and Powers.[2] Yet it is manifest that God made all of these. Or if in the words, 'He made heaven and earth,' all things are comprehended, what shall we say of the waters above which moved the Spirit of God? For if they are all to be understood together when earth is named, how then can formless matter be understood by that term earth, since we see the waters to be so beautiful? Or if it is taken in this sense, why then is it written that the firmament was made out of this same formlessness and was called heaven, and why is it not written that the waters were made from it? For the waters, which we see flowing in so fair a form, are not still formless and invisible. But if they received that beauty, when God said, 'Let the water which is under the firmament be gathered together,' so that this gathering together is itself a formation, what will they answer with regard to those 'waters which are above the firmament'? For if they are formless, they would not merit to receive so honorable a seat, and it is not written by what word they have been formed. Hence if Genesis is silent as to anything that God made—and that God did make it neither sound faith nor sure reasoning doubts—no sober teaching will dare to affirm that these waters are coeternal with God, merely because we hear them mentioned in the book of Genesis but we do not find when they were made. Why should we not understand, with Truth teaching us, that also formless matter, which Scripture calls earth invisible and unformed and darksome deep, was made by God out of nothing, and therefore is not coeternal with him, although this narrative may omit to state when those things were made?"

Chapter 23
Meaning and Reality

(32) Therefore, when all these views have been heard and considered according to my feeble capacities, which I confess to you, my God, who know them well, I see that two types of disagreement may arise when anything is uttered by means of signs by truthful reporters. One concerns the truth of things; the other is argument about the intention of the speaker. In one way we inquire what may be true with regard to the process of creation; in the other way as to what Moses, that excellent servant of your faith, wished the reader and hearer to understand by his words. With regard to the first kind of objection, may they depart from me all those who deem that they know things that are false. With regard to the second kind, let all those also depart from me who deem that Moses spoke things that are false. May I be united to them, O Lord, in you, and in you may I rejoice with them who feed upon your truth in breadth of charity. Let us together approach the words of your book, and let us seek in them for your will by means of the will of your servant, by whose pen you have dispensed those words.

Chapter 24
Truths Seen and Stated

(33) Among the many truths that occur to investigators as these words are interpreted in different ways, which of us finds

Book 12. Form and Matter

an answer such that he may say with equal confidence that Moses meant this and wished this to be understood from his account as he says that this meaning is true, whether Moses meant this or something different? For behold, O my God, I, your servant,[1] who have vowed to you a sacrifice of confession in these writings, and pray that by your mercy I may pay my vows to you,[2] behold with what confidence I say that in your immutable Word you made all things, visible and invisible. Can I say with the same confidence that Moses meant nothing else than this when he wrote, "In the beginning God made heaven and earth?" I do not see him thinking this within his mind as he wrote those words, in the way that I see this for a certainty in your truth.

He could have thought about the very start of God's creative action when he said, "In the beginning." He could have wished that the words "heaven and earth" in this passage be interpreted not as meaning a nature already formed and perfected, whether spiritual or corporeal, but as meaning both as just started and still unformed. I see that the truth could have been spoken, whichever of these was said. But which of them he meant by these words, this I do not see in the same manner. However, whether it was either of these, or some further meaning which I have not mentioned, that this so great a man gazed at in his mind, when he uttered these words, I have no doubt that he saw the true meaning and stated it correctly.

Chapter 25
A Reduction to First Principles

(34) Let no man attack me by saying to me: "Moses did not think as you say, but as I say." If he should say to me, "How do you know that Moses thought what you infer from his words?" I ought to take this calmly and perhaps respond to him in the way I have already answered him, or somewhat more fully, if he were stubborn. But when he says, "Moses did not mean what you say, but what I say," and still does not deny that what each of us says is true, then O my God, O life of the poor, in whose bosom there is no contradiction, rain down into my heart soothing drops, so that I may patiently

put up with such men. They do not say this to me because they have a divine spirit and have seen in the heart of your servant what they assert, but because they are proud and have not known Moses's meaning, but love their own, not because it is true, but because it is their own. Otherwise, they would have an equal love for another man's true opinion, just as I love what they say when they speak the truth, not because it is theirs but because it is true. Therefore, because it is true, it is by that very fact not theirs. Therefore, if they love it because it is true, then it is both theirs and mine, since it is the common property of all lovers of the truth.

But in so far as they contend that Moses did not mean what I say but what they say, this I do not like, this I do not love. For even if it is so, this is the temerity not of knowledge but of rash judgment: not insight but pride begot it. Therefore, O Lord, your judgments are terrible, since your truth is not mine, nor his, nor any other man's, but belongs to all of us whom you publicly call to its communion, warning us in a terrible manner that we must not will to keep it for ourselves lest we be deprived of it. Whosoever arrogates completely to himself that which you propose for the enjoyment of all men, and desires that to be his own which belongs to all men, is driven from what is common to all men to what is really his own, that is, from truth to a lie. For he who "speaks a lie speaks of his own."[1]

(35) Give heed,[2] O God, best judge, truth itself, give heed to what I shall say to this contradictor, give heed. I speak before you, and before my brethren, who lawfully use the law unto the end of charity.[3] Give heed, and see, if it pleases you, what I shall say to him. For I return this fraternal and peaceful word to him: "If we both see that what you say is true, and if we both see that what I say is true, where, I ask you, do we see it? Surely, I do not see it in you, nor do you see it in me, but both of us see it in that unchangeable truth which is above our minds. Therefore, since we do not contend about the light itself of the Lord our God, why do we contend about our neighbor's thought, which we cannot see in the same manner? If Moses himself appeared before us and said, 'This I have thought,' would we see it in this way or rather believe him?

Therefore, 'Let us not be puffed up one for another against another, above that which is written.'[4] 'Let us love the Lord our God, with our whole heart, and with our whole mind, and with our whole mind, and our neighbor just as ourselves.'[5] By reason of these two commandments[6] of charity, if we do not believe that Moses meant whatsoever he did mean in these books, we shall make the Lord a liar,[7] since we opine otherwise of our fellow servant's mind than he taught. See now how stupid it is, amid such an abundance of true meanings as can be taken out of these words, rashly to affirm which of them Moses chiefly meant, and with pernicious quarrels to offend against charity, for the sake of which he spake everything, whose words we strive to expound."

Chapter 26
Had I Been Moses

(36) Yet I, O my God, loftiest height above my lowliness and rest from my labor, who hear my confessions and forgive my sins, since you command me to love my neighbor as myself,[1] I cannot believe that to Moses, your most faithful servant, you would grant a lesser gift than I would will and desire from you for myself, had I been born in the same time as he, and had you established me in that office, so that by ministry of my heart and tongue there might be promulgated those books of yours which for so long after were to profit all nations, and by such supreme authority were to vanquish the words of all false and proud teachings throughout the whole world.

In truth, I should have wished, had I then been Moses—for we all come from the same clay,[2] and what is man, unless because you are mindful of him?[3]—I should have wished, if I had then been what he was and had been enjoined by you to write the book of Genesis, that such power of eloquence be given to me, and such ways to fashion words that not even they who cannot yet understand how God creates things would reject my words as beyond their powers; while they who can already understand, no matter what true interpretation they have arrived at in their thought, would not find it passed over in your servant's few words; and if some other man by the light of truth had perceived a further meaning, it should not fail to be understood from those same words.

CHAPTER 27
Two Analogies

(37) It is like a fountain, which in its narrow confines is more fruitful and supplies the flow of many streams over wider expanses than any of those rivers which take rise from it and flow through many regions. So also, the account given by the dispenser of your words, which was to provide material for many future commentators, out of a small amount of words pours forth floods of clear truth. From them each man for himself may draw the truth he can attain to concerning these matters, one man this truth, another man that, through their longer and more involved discussions.

When they read or hear these words, some men think that God, like a man, or like some power infused into an immense mass, by some new and sudden decision, operating outside himself and as it were, in distant regions, made heaven and earth, two great bodies, one up above, one below, in which all things would be contained. When they hear, "God said, 'Let this be made,' and that thing was made," they think of words that began and ended, sounding out at certain times and then passing away, and they think that after their departure there forthwith came into being what had been commanded to exist. They conjecture other things of this sort in accordance with ordinary sense operations. In such men, still little ones and wholly sense-conscious, while their infirmity is carried in this most lowly way of speech as if in their mothers' bosom, faith is strengthened in a healthful manner. Through it, they have and hold with certainty that God made all the natures that in wondrous variety their senses view about them. If any man despises your words, as if they were of little worth, and if with prideful weakness he stretches out too far beyond the mother's nest, alas! he will fall. O Lord God, have mercy,[1] lest they who pass along the way trample[2] upon the featherless birdling! Send your angel[3] to put it back into the nest, so that it may live until it can fly!

Chapter 28
Various Valid Interpretations

(38) But other men, for whom these words are no longer a nest but shady bowers, see the fruits that lie therein and joyously fly about, and pipe songs and look carefully at them and pluck them. When they read or hear your words, eternal God, they see that all times past and future are surpassed by your stable perduration, and yet that there is no temporal creature which you have not made; that by your will, since it is identical with you, not by any change of that will and not by an assertion of will which before did not obtain, you made all things; that these things were not out of yourself, in your own likeness, the form of all things, but out of nothing, a formless unlikeness, which would be formed to your likeness, returning to you, the One, according to its appointed capacity, in so far as it is given to each thing in its kind; and that all things were made exceeding good, whether they abide around you, or being removed from you in gradation throughout time and space, produce beautiful variations or are fashioned into them. These things they see, and they rejoice in the light of your truth, to the little degree that they can in this world.

(39) Another of them concentrates on what is said, "In the beginning God made heaven and earth," and therein beholds Wisdom, the Beginning, because it also speaks to us.[1] Another likewise concentrates on the same words, and by beginning he understands the commencement of things created, and takes the passage thus: "In the beginning he made," as if to say, "At first he made."[2] Among them who understand "In the beginning" to mean, "In Wisdom he made heaven and earth," one believes that the words "heaven and earth" mean the matter from which they would be created, and are thus named; another, natures already formed and made distinct; another, one formed nature, a spiritual nature, given the name of heaven, and a second formless nature of corporeal matter, with

the name of earth. Nor do those who by the names of heaven and earth understand matter as yet formless, out of which heaven and earth were to be formed, understand it in a single manner. One means that out of which both intelligible and sensible creation would be perfected. Another means only that out of which would be fashioned this sensible, corporeal mass, containing in its mighty womb natures now visible and lying before us.[3] Those too who believe that creatures already arranged and organized are in this passage called heaven and earth do not understand it in one single way. One means both invisible and visible creation; the other only visible creation in which we perceive the luminous heavens and the darksome earth and the things that are in them.

Chapter 29
Four Kinds of Priority

(40) But he who understands "In the beginning he made heaven and earth" as if it meant, "At first he made," has no valid interpretation of "heaven and earth" except as meaning the matter of heaven and earth, namely, of universal creation, that is, both intelligible and corporeal creation. If he wished to understand by it the universe as already formed, it could rightly be asked of him, "If he made this first, what did he make later on?" As he will find nothing after the universe, he must perforce hear another question, "How was this at first if there was nothing later on?" But if he says that God first made formless and later formed matter, he does not contradict himself,[1] if he is able to discern what precedes by eternity, what in time, what by choice, and what in origin: by eternity, as God precedes all creatures; in time, as the flower precedes the fruit; by choice, as the fruit precedes the flower; in origin, as the sound precedes the melody.

Of these four, the first and the last that I have mentioned are understood with great difficulty, the two in between very easily. It is a rare and exceedingly arduous vision, O Lord, to behold your eternity, immutably making mutable things, and for this reason prior to them. Again, who can mentally perceive so subtle a thing as to be able to distinguish without

Book 12. Form and Matter

great labor how sound may be prior to a melody? The reason is that a melody is formed sound, and, whereas an unformed thing can exist, what does not exist cannot be formed. In this way, matter is prior to what is made out of it: it is not prior because it makes the thing, for contrariwise it is itself made, and it is not prior by any interval of time. We do not at an earlier time utter formless sounds without the melody, and at a later time adapt or fashion them into the form of a song, like wood, out of which a chest is fashioned, or silver, out of which a vessel is made. Such materials, of course, precede even in time the forms of the things made out of them, but in a melody this is not the case. When it is sung, its sound is heard, for there is not first a formless sound that is afterwards formed into a melody. What first in some manner sounds forth passes away, and there is nothing of it that you can find, gather up, and put together by art.

Hence the melody depends for its being on its own sound, and this sound is its matter. This same sound, of course, is formed, so that there may be a melody. Therefore, as I was saying, the matter of sounding is prior to the form of singing.[2] It is not prior because of any power to make the melody, nor is the sound the artist producing the song, but it is supplied out of the body to the soul of the singer, and out of it he can make the melody. It is not prior in time, but it is uttered simultaneously with the melody. Nor is it prior by choice: a sound is not better than a melody, since a melody is not only a sound, but a beautiful sound as well. But it is prior in origin, for a melody is not formed so that there may be sound, but sound is formed so that there may be a melody.

By this example,[3] let him who can do so understand how the matter of things was first made and called heaven and earth, because heaven and earth were made out of it, and that it was not first made in time, since the forms of things give rise to times. It was formless, and now, in tracts of time, it is perceived together with them. Yet nothing can be told of that matter, unless it is described as prior in time. It is the lowest thing in value, for things formed are obviously superior to things without form. It is preceded by the eternity of the creator, so that that from which something would be made would itself be made from nothing.

Chapter 30
A Test of Truth

(41) Amid this diversity of true opinions, let truth itself beget concord. "May our God have mercy on us,"[1] so that we may lawfully use the law, according to the end of the commandment, in pure charity.[2] By this, if a man requests of me which of these interpretations Moses, your servant, meant, these are not words proper to my confessions, if I do not confess to you, "I do not know." Yet I know that these opinions are true, with the exception of the carnal ones, concerning which I have stated the judgment that I passed. May these words of your book, lofty but humble and few but abundant, not terrify those little ones who have good hope. But all of us whom I affirm to discern and to speak the truths found in those words, let us love one another[3] and let us likewise love you, our God, the fountain of truth, if we thirst for it and not for vain things. Let us so honor this same servant of yours, dispenser of this scripture and filled with your Spirit, as to believe that when he wrote these words by your inspiration he intended that sense in them which supremely excels both in the light of truth and in the fruit of profit.

Chapter 31
Levels of Truth

(42) So when one man says, "He meant what I say," and another, "No, what I say," I deem that I speak more reverently when I say, "Why not rather as both, if both be true?" If there is a third, and a fourth, and any other truth that any man sees in these words, why may we not believe that Moses saw all these truths? For through him[1] the one God has adapted the sacred writings to many men's interpretations, wherein will be seen things true and also diverse. Surely I myself—and I speak this fearlessly from my heart—if I were to write anything for the summit of authority, I would prefer to write in such

manner that my words would sound forth the portion of truth each one man could take from these writings, rather than to put down one true opinion so obviously that it would exclude all others, wherein there was no falsity to offend me. Therefore, O my God, I do not want to be so hasty as to disbelieve that this man did not merit this from you. Assuredly, when he wrote those words, he perceived in them and conceived whatever truth we here have been able to find, and also whatever we have been unable to find, or have not yet been able to find, although it can be found in them.

Chapter 32
What God Wants Us to Know

(43) Lastly, O Lord, who are God and not flesh and blood, even if man saw less than is there, could anything lie hidden from your good Spirit, who shall lead me into the land of righteousness,[1] anything which you yourself by those words were about to reveal to later readers, even though he through whom they were spoken perhaps had in thought but a single meaning among the many that were true! If this is so, may that which he thought about be higher than all others! But to us, Lord, you point out either that meaning or such other true meaning as pleases you. Hence, whether you uncover the same meaning to us as to that servant of yours, or some other meaning on the occasion of those words, you will still nourish us and error will not delude us.

Behold, O Lord my God, I beseech you, how many things we have written concerning these few words, how many! What strength of ours, what tracts of time would suffice to treat all your books in this manner? Permit me, then, in these words more briefly to confess to you, and to choose some single true, certain, and good meaning which you shall inspire, even though many should occur, where many can occur, in this faith of my confession, that if I should say that which your minister intended, I will say what is right and best. For this should I strive, and if I do not attain to it, I would still say that which your Truth willed by his words to say to me, which also spoke to him what it willed.

BOOK 13
THE CREATION OF THE WORLD

Chapter 1
Without You I Am Nothing

(1) I call upon you, my God, my mercy,[1] who made me, and did not forget me, although I forgot you. I call you into my soul, which you prepare to accept you by the longing that you breathe into it. Do not desert me now when I call upon you, for before I called upon you, you went ahead and helped me,[2] and repeatedly you urged me on by many different words, so that from afar I would hear you, and be converted, and call upon you as you called to me. For you have wiped away all my evil deserts, O Lord, so as not to return them to these hands of mine, whereby I fell away from you, and you went ahead and helped me in all my good deserts, so that you could restore them to your own hands, whereby you made me.

For before I was, you were, and I was nothing to which you could grant being. Yet, behold! I am, because of your goodness, which preceded all that you made me to be, and all out of which you made me. You did not need me, nor am I not such a good as you would put to use, O my Lord and my God. I am not such as would serve you in such wise that you would not tire out, so to speak, from activity, or that your strength would be the less for lack of my services. Nor am I such as to cultivate you like a land that would be untilled unless I tilled it. I am such a one as may serve you and cultivate you, so that because of you it may be well with me, for from you comes the fact that I am one with whom it may be well.

Chapter 2
The Source of Being and Value

(2) Your creation subsists out of the fullness of your goodness, to the end that a good that would profit you nothing, and that was not of your substance and thus equal to you,[1] would nevertheless not be non-existent, since it could be made by you. What claim on you had heaven and earth, which you made in the beginning? And those spiritual and corporeal natures which you made in your Wisdom,[2] that on it might depend even things inchoate and formless, each in its own genus, whether spiritual or corporeal, running off into immoderation and unlikeness far distant from you—the formless spiritual being more excellent than if a formed body; the formless corporeal being more excellent than if there were nothing whatsoever—and as formless things might thus depend upon your Word, let them tell me what claim they had on you unless they were recalled by that same Word to your unity and given form and, from you, the one and supreme good, would all be very good. What claim did they have on you even to be thus formless, these things which apart from you would not even be such as they are?

(3) What claim did corporeal matter have upon you, merely to be invisible and without form, since it would not even be such except because you made it? Hence, since it did not exist, it could have no claim on you to exist. What claim did inchoate spiritual creation have on you, even to float and flow about, darksome like the deep, but all unlike you, unless it were converted by that same Word to the same Word by whom it was made, and were enlightened by him and made into light, although not equal to the form equal to you, yet conformed to it? Just as for a body, to be is not the same as to be beautiful, otherwise it could not exist devoid of beauty; so also for a spiritual creature, to live is not the same as to live wisely, otherwise it would be immutably wise. But it is good for it always to adhere to you,[3] lest by aversion from you it lose the light gained by conversion, and fall back into a life similar to the darksome deep. For we also, who are spiritual

as to the soul, being turned away from you, our light, were sometimes darkness[4] in this life. Still do we labor amid the remains of our obscurity, until in your Only-begotten we may be your justice, as the mountains of God. For we have been your judgments, which are like a great deep.[5]

Chapter 3
Let There Be Light

(4) What you said at the first foundation of things, "Be light made, and light was made,"[1] I not improperly understand as applying to spiritual creation, since there was already some sort of life which you might illuminate. But just as it had no claim on you to be such a life as could be illuminated, so also, now that it existed, it had no claim on you to be given light. Nor would its formlessness be pleasing to you unless it were made light, not by merely existing but by beholding the light-giving light and adhering to it. Hence the fact that it lives in some way, and that it lives happily, it owes entirely to your grace, for by a better change it has been converted into that which can be changed neither into better nor into worse. This you alone are, because you alone exist absolutely. For with you to live is not other than to live in blessedness, because you are your own blessedness.

Chapter 4
Diffusive Good

(5) Therefore what would be wanting in you for that good which you yourself are for yourself, even if none of these things existed in any way or remained without form? These things you have made, not out of any need, but out of the fullness of your goodness, restraining them and converting them to a form, although not as if your joy were to be fulfilled by them. To you who are perfect, their imperfection is displeasing, and therefore they were perfected by you and are now pleasing to you. However, this is not as if you had been imperfect and were to be made perfect by their perfection. For your good "spirit was borne over the waters;"[1] it was not borne up by

them, as though it rested upon them. For those on whom your good Spirit is said to rest[2] he causes to rest upon himself. But your incorruptible and immutable will, itself sufficient in itself unto itself, was borne upon that life which you made. For it, to live is not identical with living happily, because it likewise lives as it floats about in its own darkness. It remains for this life to be converted to him by whom it was made, and more and more to live by the fountain of life, and in his light to see light,[3] and to be perfected, and enlightened, and made happy.

Chapter 5
The Trinity

(6) Behold, there appears to me in a dark manner[1] the Trinity, which is you, my God, since you, the Father, in the Beginning of our Wisdom, because he is your Wisdom, born of you, equal to you, and coeternal with you, that is, in your Son, you made heaven and earth. Many things have we said of the heaven of heaven, and of the earth "invisible and without form," and of the deep, darksome according to the inconstant downflow of its spiritual formlessness, unless it had been converted to him, from whom was life of some kind, and by his illumination made a beauteous life and become his heaven of heaven, which afterwards was made between the water and water.[2] By the name of God, who made these things, I now understood the Father, and by the name of Beginning the Son, in whom he made them. And believing my God to be the Trinity, as I did believe, I searched into his holy words, and behold, your "Spirit was borne above the waters." Behold, the Trinity, my God, Father, and Son, and Holy Spirit, creator of all creation!

Chapter 6
The Spirit over the Waters

(7) But what was the reason, O truthful Light? I move my heart up to you, lest it teach me vanities: dispel its darkness, and tell me, I beseech you, by charity, our mother, tell me

what was the reason, why, after heaven, and earth, "invisible and without form," and darkness upon the deep were named, your Scripture should finally name your Spirit? Was it because it was fitting for him to be introduced thus, so that he would be described as "borne over"? This could not be stated unless mention were first made of what your Spirit might be understood to be borne over. He was borne above neither the Father nor the Son, and he could not rightly be said to be borne above if he were borne above nothing. Therefore, what he would be borne over first had to be named, and then he who could not be properly mentioned otherwise, if he were not said to be one borne above. Why, then, was it unfitting that no other indication be made of him, except the statement that he was borne above?

Chapter 7
Lift up Your Hearts

(8) Let him who can now follow in his mind your apostle when he says that because your "charity is poured forth in our hearts, by the Holy Spirit, who is given to us,"[1] and when he teaches us about spiritual things,[2] and points out to us "a more excellent way"[3] of charity, and bows his knees before you in our behalf, so that we may know the supereminent knowledge of the love of Christ.[4] Therefore, supereminent from the very first, he was borne above the waters. To whom shall I say this? How shall I speak of the weight of lust, dragging downward into the steep abyss, and of charity lifting up through your Spirit, who was borne above the waters? To whom shall I say this? How shall I say it? These are places into which we are plunged and from which we emerge. What is more like them, and yet what is more unlike them? They are affections; they are loves: the filthiness of our spirit, flowing away downwards with a love that brings but care. But here too is the holiness of your Spirit, raising us aloft by a love that is free from care, so that we may lift up our hearts[5] to you, where your Spirit was "borne above the waters," and come to supereminent rest, when our souls shall have passed through the waters which are without substance.[6]

Chapter 8
Fall and Rise

(9) The angel fell away; man's soul fell away. They pointed out the abyss of all spiritual creation with its darksome depths, unless you had said from the beginning, "Be light made," and light was made, and every obedient intelligence in your heavenly city had cleaved to you and found rest in your Spirit, which is borne unchangeably over every changeable thing. Otherwise even the heaven of heaven would be a darksome deep within itself, but now it is light in the Lord.[1] For in that very restless misery of spirits flowing away and displaying their own darkness, when stripped of the garments of your light, you sufficiently reveal how great you made the rational creature. For in no wise is any being less than you sufficient to give it rest and happiness, and for this it is not sufficient to itself. For you, O our God, will enlighten our darkness.[2] From you arise our garments, and our darkness shall be as the noonday.[3]

Give me yourself, O my God! Restore yourself to me! Behold, I love you, and if it be too little, let me love you more strongly. I cannot measure so as to know how much love may be wanting in me to that which is sufficient so that my life may run to your embrace, and not be turned away, until it be hidden "in the secret of your face."[4] This alone I know, that apart from you it is evil with me, not only outside myself but also in myself, and that for me all abundance that is not my God is but want.

Chapter 9
The Upward Steps

(10) But was neither the Father nor the Son borne above the waters? If this means as a body is moved in place, then neither was the Holy Spirit. But if the supremacy of the unchangeable divinity over all mutable things is meant, then Father and Son, as well as Holy Spirit, were borne above the waters. Why, then, has this been said of the Holy Spirit alone?

Why has a sort of place, where he might be, which is yet not a place, been affirmed only of him, of whom alone it has been said that he is your gift?[1]

In your gift do we rest, and there we have joy in you. Our rest is our peace. Love lifts us up to it, and your good Spirit lifts up our lowliness "from the gates of death."[2] For us, peace is in a good will.[3] By reason of its weight the body strives towards its own place. Yet a weight strives not so much to sink to the very lowest depths, but rather to its proper place. Fire tends upwards; a stone downwards. They are impelled by their own weights; they seek their own places. Oil poured out beneath water is raised up above the water. Water poured on top of oil sinks down beneath the oil. They are impelled by their own weights; they seek their own places. Not put in proper order, they are without rest; when they are set in due order, they are at rest. My love is my weight! I am borne about by it, wheresoever I am borne. By your gift we are enkindled, and we are borne upwards. We glow with inward fire, and we go on. We ascend steps within the heart,[4] and we sing a gradual psalm.[5] By your fire, by your good fire, we glow with inward fire, and we go on, for we go upwards to "the peace of Jerusalem," for "I am gladdened in those who said to me, 'We will go into the house of the Lord.'"[6] There will good will find us a place, so that we may desire nothing further but to abide therein forever.[7]

CHAPTER 10

The Happiness of Pure Spirits

(11) O blessed creature that knew no other state, although it would have been different from what it is, unless as soon as it was made, without any intervening time, it was raised up by your gift, which is borne over every mutable being, through that call wherein you said, "Be light made," and so it was made light.[1] In us there is a distinction in time, because we were first darkness, and then were made light. But of that being it was stated what it would be if it were not made light. This was stated as if it had previously been in a state of flux and darkness, so that there would be made manifest the cause

whereby it was effected that it would be different, namely, that being converted to the unfailing light, it would itself be light. Let him who can do so understand this: let him ask it of you. Why does he trouble me, as if I could enlighten any man that comes into the world.[2]

Chapter 11
The Greatest Mystery

(12) Who among us understands the almighty Trinity? Yet who among us does not speak of it, if it indeed be the Trinity he speaks of? Rare is the soul that knows whereof it speaks, whatsoever it says concerning the Trinity. They contend and they quarrel, but without peace no man sees that vision. I would that men would reflect upon these three certain things within themselves. Far different are these three from that Trinity, but I indicate where it is men may consider them, weigh them, and perceive how far different they are.

I speak of these three: to be, to know, and to will. For I am, and I know, and I will: I am a knowing and a willing being, and I know that I am and that I will, and I will to be and to know. Therefore, in these three, let him who can do so perceive how inseparable a life there is, one life and one mind and one essence, and finally how inseparable a distinction there is, and yet there is a distinction. Surely a man stands face to face with himself. Let him take heed of himself, and look there, and tell me. But when he has discovered any of these and is ready to speak, let him not think that he has found that immutable being which is above all these, which is immutably, and knows immutably, and wills immutably.

But whether there is a Trinity in God, because of these three acts; or whether these acts are in each Person, so that all three belong to each Person; or whether both hold, so that the Selfsame exists immutably by its great and plenteous unity, in some marvelous way both simple and multiple, with an infinite end in and for itself, whereby it is, and is known to itself, and suffices to itself—who could conceive such things with any ease? Who could state them in any manner? Who could rashly pronounce thereon in any way?[1]

CHAPTER 12
The Body of Christ

(13) Proceed with your confession, O my faith. Say to your Lord God: Holy, holy, holy,[1] O Lord my God. In your name we were baptized,[2] O Father, and Son, and Holy Spirit. In your name we baptize, O Father, and Son, and Holy Spirit.

For also among us, in his Christ, has God made heaven and earth, the spiritual and the carnal parts of his Church. And before it received the form of doctrine, our earth[3] was invisible and without order, and we were covered over by the darkness of ignorance, for "you have corrected man for his iniquity,"[4] and "your judgments are a great deep."[5] But because your Spirit was borne over the water, your mercy did not abandon our misery, and you said, "Be light made. Do penance. The kingdom of heaven is at hand. Do penance. Be light made."[6] Since our soul was troubled within us, we remembered you, O Lord, "from the land of Jordan," and from the mountain, equal to you but made small in our behalf.[7] Our darkness displeased us, and we were converted to you, and light was made. Behold, we "were heretofore darkness, but now light in the Lord."[8]

CHAPTER 13
Thirst for the Living God

(14) Yet with us it is still by faith and not yet by sight.[1] "For we are saved by hope. But hope that is seen is not hope."[2] As yet, "deep calls unto deep," but now "in the voice of your floodgates."[3] And as yet he who says, "I could not speak to you as to spiritual, but only as to carnal,"[4] even he does not think that he has apprehended it, but "forgetting the things that are behind," he reaches out "to those which are before,"[5] and he groans, being burdened,[6] and his "soul thirsts after the living God," "even as the hart after the fountains of waters" and he says, "When shall I come to it?"[7] "Desiring to be clothed upon with his habitation which is from heaven,"[8] he calls to the lower deep, and says: "Do not be conformed to

this world, but be reformed in the newness of your mind."[9] And again: "Do not become children in mind, but in malice be children, that you may be perfect in mind."[10] And again: "O foolish Galatians, who has bewitched you?"[11]

But now it is not in his own voice but in yours, who sent your Spirit from on high[12] through him who ascended on high[13] and opened up the floodgates[14] of his gifts, so that the streams of the river might make your city joyful.[15] For him does this "friend of the bridegroom"[16] sigh, already having "the first fruits of the Spirit" laid up by union with Christ, but still does he groan within himself, "waiting for the adoption, . . . the redemption of his body."[17] For him does he sigh, a member of the bride,[18] and he is zealous for him, for he is a friend of the bridegroom; he is zealous for him, not for himself. For in the voice of your floodgates and not in his own voice, he calls to that other deep, of which, since he is zealous, he is fearful, "lest as the serpent deceived Eve by his guile,"[19] so also might their minds be corrupted from chastity, which is in our Spouse, your only Son. O, what is that light of beauty, when "we shall see him as he is,"[20] and there shall have passed away "the tears that have been my bread day and night, while it is said to me daily: Where is your God?"[21]

Chapter 14
Vessels of Honor

(15) And I say, "Where are you, O my God?" Behold, where you are! In you I take breath a little,[1] when I pour out my soul upon myself in the voice of joy and praise, the sound of him who celebrates a feast.[2] But it is still sad, because it slips back again, and it becomes a deep, or rather, it perceives itself still to be a deep. My faith, which you have enkindled before my feet in the night, says to it: "Why are you sad, O my soul, and why do you trouble me?[3] Hope in the Lord.[4] His word is a lamp unto your feet."[5] Hope and persevere, until the night, the mother of the wicked, passes, until the anger of the Lord passes[6]—of which we also were once children,[7] for we were heretofore darkness, the relics whereof we carry in our body, "dead because of sin"[8]—"until the day

breaks, and the shadows retire."[9] Hope in the Lord. "In the morning I will stand, and I will see."[10] I shall forever give praise to you. In the morning I will stand, and I will see the salvation of my countenance,[11] my God, who shall quicken also our mortal bodies, because of the Spirit who dwells in us,[12] because he was mercifully borne above our dark and fluid inner being. Whence on this pilgrimage we have received a pledge,[13] that now we may be light, while still we have been saved by hope,[14] and "are the children of light, and children of the day, not children of the night, nor of darkness,"[15] which heretofore we were. Between them and us, in this still uncertain state of man's knowledge, you alone distinguish, "who prove our hearts"[16] and "call the light day, and the darkness night."[17] For who discerns what we are but you? What have we that we have not received from you,[18] being made vessels unto honor from that same lump from which others also have been made unto dishonor?[19]

Chapter 15
A Firm Foundation

(16) Who except you, our God, has made for us a firmament of authority over us in the form of your divine Scriptures? For "the heavens shall be folded together like a book"[1] and now they are stretched over us like a skin.[2] For your divine Scripture is of a more sublime authority, now that those mortal men, through whom you dispensed it to us, have suffered this present death. You know, O Lord, you know, how you clothed men with skins, when by sin they became subject to death.[3] Hence you have stretched out the firmament of your book like a skin, that is, your discourses, truly in harmony, which you have placed over us by the ministry of mortal men. For by that death of theirs, the strong firmament of authority in the words you uttered through them is sublimely extended over all things that are beneath it, whereas while they lived here, it was not so sublimely extended. You had not as yet extended the heavens like a skin; not as yet had you spread abroad on every side the glory of their death.

(17) Lord, let us look upon the heavens, "the works of your

fingers."[4] Clear away from our eyes the cloud which you have drawn under them. There is your "testimony, giving wisdom to little ones."[5] Perfect, O my God, your praise "out of the mouth of babes and sucklings."[6] For we do not know any books which so destroy pride, which so destroy "the enemy and the defender,"[7] who resists your reconciliation by defending his own sins. I do not know, O Lord, I do not know any such pure words, which so persuade me to make confession and make my neck meek to your yoke, and invite me to serve you without complaint. Let me understand them, O good Father! Grant this to me who am placed under them, because you have established them for such as are placed under them.

(18) Other waters there are above this firmament, I believe, immortal and kept free from earthly corruption. Let them praise your name.[8] Let the supercelestial peoples, who are your angels, praise you, they who have no need to look up at this firmament, or by reading to know your Word. They always behold your face,[9] and, without any syllables of time, they read upon it what your eternal will decrees. They read your will; they choose it; and they love it. They read forever, and what they read never passes away. For, by choosing and loving, they read the actual immutability of your counsel. Their book is never closed, nor is their scroll folded up, because you yourself are this to them, and you are this for eternity. For you have set them in order above this firmament, which you have made firm above the infirmity of a lower race, where they might look upwards and know your mercy, telling in time of you who made all times.

"O Lord, your mercy is in heaven, and your truth reaches even to the clouds."[10] The clouds pass away, but the heavens remain. The preachers of your word pass out of this life and into another life; but your Scripture is extended over the nations even to the end of the world. "Heaven and earth will pass away," but your "words shall not pass away."[11] For the skin will be folded up, and the grass over which it was stretched shall with its glory pass away, but your word endures forever.[12] Now it appears to us under the dark figure of the clouds and in the mirror of the heavens,[13] not as it is. For even as to ourselves, although we are the well-beloved of your

Book 13. The Creation of the World

Son, "it has not yet appeared what we shall be."[14] He looked through the lattice of the flesh, and he spoke tenderly, and aroused our love, and we ran after his odor.[15] But "when he shall appear, we shall be like him, because we shall see him as he is."[16] As he is, O Lord, will be our vision of him, but as yet it is not given to us.

CHAPTER 16
Light and the Enlightened

(19) For even as you totally are, so do you alone totally know, for you immutably are, and you know immutably, and you will immutably. Your essence knows and wills immutably, and your knowledge is and wills immutably, and your will is and knows immutably. Nor does it seem just before you that in exactly the same way as Light unchangeable knows itself, so should it be known by the mutable being enlightened by it. Therefore, "my soul is like earth without water unto you."[1] Just as it cannot of itself enlighten itself, so it cannot of itself be sufficient to itself. Thus "with you is the fountain of life," even as "in your light we shall see light."[2]

CHAPTER 17
The Embittered and the Compassionate

(20) Who was it that gathered the embittered[1] into one society? For all of them, there is one same end of temporal and earthly happiness, because of which they do all their deeds, although they waver back and forth amid a countless variety of cares. Who, Lord, if not yourself, who said that the waters should be gathered together into one gathering[2] and that there should appear dry land, which thirsts after you, for the sea is yours, and you made it, and your hands formed the dry land.[3] For not the embittered wills, but the gathering together of the waters is called sea. You restrain the wicked lusts of souls, and fix limits for them, as to how far the waters may be permitted to go, so that their waves may break upon one another.[4] Thus do you make the sea by the order of your sway over all things.

(21) But by a sweet and hidden spring you water souls that thirst after you and appear before you, kept apart by a different boundary from the society of the sea, so that the earth too may bring forth her fruit. By command of you, its Lord God, our soul germinates works of mercy according to its kind. For that it loves its neighbor is shown in the relief of bodily necessities, and it has seed in itself according to its likeness.[5] For by reason of our own infirmity we have compassion on others, so that we relieve the needy and help them, even as we would wish to be helped, were we in the same kind of need. We do this not only in things easy, like a herb yielding seed, but also by giving the protection and assistance of a mighty oak, like the fruit-bearing tree, that is, such assistance as will rescue from the hand of the strong man one who suffers injury, and gives shelter and protection under that great oak tree which is just judgment.

Chapter 18
Signs and Times

(22) Thus, Lord, thus, I beseech you, let there spring up, as you cause to be done, as you give joy and power, let there spring up truth from the earth, and let justice look down from heaven,[1] and "let there be lights made in the firmament."[2] Let us break our bread with the hungry, and let us bring the needy who is without roof into our house. Let us clothe the naked, and let us not despise those of our own flesh.[3] When such fruits are born out of the earth, see, how good it is.[4] Let our light that lasts but for a time break forth.[5] And as we pass from this lower fruit of action to the delights of contemplation, and obtain the word of life on high, let us appear like lights in the world,[6] holding fast to the firmament of your Scripture.

In it you hold discussion with us, so that we may distinguish between intelligible and sensible things, as between day and night, or between certain souls dedicated to intelligible things and other souls given over to things of sense. This is to the end that now not only yourself in your hidden judgment, even as before the firmament was made, may distinguish between light and darkness, but also your spiritual children,

Book 13.   The Creation of the World   349

given place and distinguished from one another in that same firmament, may, with your grace made manifest throughout the world, shine upon the earth, and divide night and day, and mark off the seasons.[7] For "the old things have passed away, behold, they are made new,"[8] and "now our salvation is nearer than when we came to believe,"[9] and "the night is passed, but the day is at hand,"[10] and you "bless the crown of the year,"[11] sending "laborers into your harvest,"[12] at the sowing of which "others have labored,"[13] sending them also to another sowing, the harvest whereof is at the end. Thus do you answer the prayers of him who asks of you, and thus do you bless the years of the just man. "You are the Selfsame,"[14] and in your years, which do not fail, you prepare a garner for the years that pass. Truly, by an eternal counsel, you bestow in their proper seasons heavenly goods upon the earth.

(23) For "to one through the Spirit, is given the word of wisdom," "a greater light,"[15] as it were, for the sake of those who are delighted by the light of manifest truth, as "for the rule of the day;" "to another, the word of knowledge according to the same Spirit," "a lesser light," as it were; to another, faith; to another, the gift of healing; "to another, the working of miracles; to another, prophecy; to another, the discerning of spirits; to another, divers kinds of tongues."[16] All of them are like stars. For "all these things one and the same Spirit works, dividing to every one according as he wills," and making the stars to appear as a manifestation for profit.[17]

But the word of knowledge, wherein all mysteries are contained, which are varied in their seasons, like the moon, and those other descriptions of gifts, which have been narrated in order, like stars, in so far as they differ from the brightness of wisdom, in which the predicted day rejoices, are only to rule the night. They are necessary to those to whom your most prudent servant could not speak as to spiritual men, but only as to carnal,[18] even he who speaks "wisdom among the perfect."[19] But the natural man, like a babe in Christ, and a drinker of milk until he become strong enough for solid food, and can steady his eye so as to look at the sun, let him not hold his night to be bereft of all light, but let him be content with the light of the moon and the stars. These things you, our God, wisely discuss with us in your book, your firmament, so that we may discern all things in wondrous contemplation, although as yet in signs and in times, and in days and in years.[20]

Chapter 19
The Rich Young Man

(24) But first "wash yourselves, be clean, take away the evil" from your souls and from the sight of my eyes,[1] so that the dry land may appear. "Learn to do good, judge for the fatherless, defend the widow,"[2] so that the earth may bring forth the green herb and the tree yielding fruit.[3] Come, let us discuss it, says the Lord,[4] so that lights may be made in the firmament of the heaven to shine upon the earth.[5] That rich man asked of the good Master what he should do to attain eternal life. Let the good Master, whom he thought to be man and nothing more—but he is good because he is God—tell him that if he wishes to enter into life, he must keep the commandments; that he must put away the bitterness of malice and wickedness; that he must not kill, commit adultery, steal, or bear false witness, so that the dry land may appear, and bring forth honor of father and mother and love of neighbor. "All these have I done," he says. Whence then so many thorns, if the earth is fruitful? Go, root up the spreading thickets of covetousness, "sell what you have," and be filled with fruits by giving to the poor, and you shall have treasure in heaven. Follow the Lord, if you will be perfect, a comrade of those among whom he speaks wisdom, who knows what to distribute to the day and to the night, so that you also may know it and so that for you lights may be made in the firmament of heaven. But this will not be done unless your heart is in it, and again this latter will not be done, unless your treasure is there, as you have heard from the good Master. But that barren earth was sorrowful,[6] and "thorns choked the word."[7]

(25) But you, "a chosen generation,"[8] weak things of the world,[9] who have forsaken all things,[10] so that you may follow the Lord, go after him, and confound the strong;[11] go after him, you beautiful feet,[12] and shine in the firmament so that

the heavens may declare his glory,[13] making division between the light of the perfect, although they are not yet like the angels, and the darkness of the little ones, although they are not yet like those without hope. Shine over the whole earth, and let the day, brightened by the sun, utter unto day speech of wisdom, and let the night, shining with the moon, declare to the night the word of knowledge.

The moon and the stars shine for the night, and yet the night does not darken them, since they give it light in accordance with its measure. For behold, it is as if God says, "Let there be lights made in the firmament of heaven,"[14] and "suddenly there came a sound from heaven, as of a mighty wind coming, . . . and there appeared parted tongues as it were of fire, and it sat upon each one of them,"[15] and there were made lights in the firmament of heaven, holding the word of life.[16] Run into every place, O you holy fires, you beautiful fires! You are the light of the world, and you are not put under a measure.[17] He to whom you have held fast has been exalted, and he has exalted you. Run forth, and make it known to all nations.

Chapter 20
What the Sea Brings Forth

(26) Let the sea also conceive, and let it bring forth your works and "let the waters bring forth the creeping creatures having life."[1] For by separating the precious from the vile, you have been made the mouth of God,[2] through which he said: "Let the waters bring forth," not the living soul which the earth brings forth, but "creeping creatures having life, and the fowls that fly over the earth."[3] For your mysteries, O God, through the works of your saints, have crept amid the waves of the world's temptations, to imbue the nations with your name in your baptism. Among these deeds, great wonders were wrought, like great whales,[4] and the voices of your messengers, winged creatures above the earth, in the firmament of your book, which was set in authority over them and under which they were to fly, wheresoever they went. For "there are no speeches nor languages where their voices are not heard," since "their sound has gone forth into all the earth, and their

words to the end of the world."[5] For by your blessing O Lord, you multiplied them.

(27) Do I lie, or do I confuse things together and fail to distinguish between clear knowledge of these things in the firmament of heaven and corporeal works in the restless sea and beneath the firmament of heaven? Our knowledge of certain things is made solid and complete without increase in generations, such as are the lights of wisdom and knowledge. But in these same things there are many different corporeal operations, and with one growing out of another, they are multiplied under your blessing, O God. For you have consoled us for the weakness of our mortal senses, so that for the knowing mind a single thing may be pictured and expressed in many ways by bodily motions. "The waters have brought forth" these things, but it is in your Word. The needs of people alienated from your eternal truth have brought them forth, but in your gospel. For these waters have cast them forth, of which waters a bitter disease was the cause whereby these things came forth in your Word.[6]

(28) All things are beautiful because you made them, but you who made all things are inexpressibly more beautiful. If Adam had not fallen away from you, from his reins[7] there would not have flowed that salt sea water, the human race, so deeply active, so swelling in storms, and so restlessly flowing. Then there would have been no need for your dispensers to work corporeally and sensibly amid many waters, and thus produce mystical deeds and words. For now the creeping things and the flying animals seem to me to be such. Men subject to corporeal rites, and instructed and initiated by such signs, would not make further progress unless the soul began to live spiritually upon another plane, and after words of admission[8] would look forward to their consummation.

Chapter 21
The Living Soul

(29) Because of this, in your Word, it was not the depths of the sea, but the earth, separated from the bitterness of the waters, that brought forth not creeping creatures possessed of

Book 13. The Creation of the World 353

life and the fowls of the air, but "a living soul."[1] It does not now have need of baptism, as the heathen have need, and as it also once had need, when it was covered over with the waters—for there is no other entrance into the kingdom of heaven from the time that you decreed that such should be the entrance—nor does it seek after great and wonderful things whereby its faith would be established. It is not such that unless it sees signs and wonders, it does not believe,[2] for now the faithful earth is separated from the sea's waters, which were bitter with infidelity, and "tongues are as a sign, not to believers but to unbelievers."[3]

Nor does the earth, which you have established over the waters, need that kind of flying fowl which by your Word "the waters brought forth." Send your Word into it by your messengers. We narrate their works, but it is you who work in them,[4] and they labor and produce a living soul. The earth brings it forth, for the earth is the cause why they may work these things in it, just as the sea was the cause why they bring about "the creeping creatures having life, and the fowls that fly under the firmament of heaven."[5] Of these the earth now has no need, although it feeds upon the Fish,[6] raised out of the deep and put upon that table which you have prepared in the sight of believers.[7] He was taken out of the deep to the end that he might nourish the dry land. And the birds, offspring of the sea, are yet multiplied upon the earth. Man's infidelity shows itself to be the reason for the first words of the evangelists, but the faithful also are exhorted and blessed by them many times, day after day. But the living soul takes its beginning from the earth, for it profits no one except those faithful to keep continent from the love of this world, so that their soul may live to you, for it was dead while it lived in pleasures,[8] in pleasures that bring death, O Lord. For it is you who are the life-bringing pleasure of the pure of heart.

(30) Therefore, let your ministers now work upon the earth, not as upon the waters of infidelity by preaching and speaking through miracles and mysteries and mystic words, where ignorance, mother of wonder, is made attentive out of fear of these secret signs. Such is the entrance into faith for the sons of Adam, forgetful of you, while they hide themselves from

your face[9] and become a deep. But let them work as upon the dry land, separated from the whirlpools of the great deep. Let them be a pattern to the faithful[10] by living before them and by arousing them to imitation. For thus do men truly hear, not merely to hear, but also to do. "Seek God, and your soul shall live,"[11] so that "the earth may bring forth a living soul." "Do not be conformed to this world."[12] Keep yourselves from it. The soul lives by avoiding what it dies by desiring. Keep yourselves clean from the monstrous savagery of pride, from sluggish delights of sensuality, and from the false name of knowledge,[13] so that the wild beasts may be tamed, the cattle mastered, and the serpents rendered harmless. In allegory, the passions of the soul are such things, but haughty pride, lustful delight, and poisonous curiosity are motions of a dead soul. For the soul does not die in such wise as to lose all action, since it dies by forsaking the fountain of life,[14] and so is taken up by the passing world and is conformed to it.

(31) But your Word, O God, is the fountain of eternal life,[15] and it does not pass away. Therefore, this departure of the soul is restrained by your Word, when it is said to us, "Do not be conformed to this world," so that the earth may bring forth in the fountain of life a living soul, a soul continent in your Word through the evangelists, by imitating the imitators of your Christ.[16] For this is to be "according to its kind," since a man is emulated by his friend. He says, "Be you as I am, because I also am as you."[17] Thus there will be in the living soul, beasts good in meekness of conduct. For you have commanded them by saying: "Do your works in meekness, and you shall be beloved,"[18] by all men. There will be good cattle, which will neither have too much if they eat, nor if they do not eat, will they be in need.[19] The serpents, too, will be good, not pernicious, so as to do harm, but wise to take heed, searching only so far into temporal nature as suffices for eternity to be "clearly seen, being understood by the things that are made."[20] For these animals are obedient to reason, when they are restrained from a deadly course, and thus live and are good.

Chapter 22
In His Image

(32) For behold, O Lord our God, our creator, when our affections have been restrained from love of this world, in which affections we were dying by living evilly, and when by living well a living soul has begun to exist, and your Word, by which you spoke to us through your apostle, has been fulfilled in us, namely, "Do not be conformed to this world," there follows what you immediately adjoined, and said, "But be reformed in the newness of your mind."[1] No longer is this "after one's kind," as though imitating our neighbor who goes on before us, or living according to the example of some better man. You did not say, "Let man be made according to his kind," but "Let us make man to our image and likeness,"[2] so that we may prove what is your will.[3]

It was for this purpose that that dispenser of yours, who begot children through the Gospel, lest he always keep them as babes, whom he would have to nourish with milk and cherish as a nurse,[4] said, "Be reformed in the newness of your mind, that you may prove," for yourselves "what is the will of God, what is the good and the acceptable, and the perfect thing."[5] Therefore, you do not say, "Let man be made," but, "Let us make man," and you do not say, "according to his kind," but "to our image and likeness." For since he is renewed in mind and perceives your truth that he has understood, he does not need a man to point the way so that he may imitate his own kind. By your direction, he himself establishes what is your will, what is the good, and the acceptable, and the perfect thing. Since he is now capable of receiving it, you teach him to see the Trinity of unity and the unity of the Trinity. Therefore, to what was stated in the plural number, "Let us make man," there is added in the singular, "and God made man," and to what was said in the plural, "to our image," is added in the singular, "to the image of God." Thus man "is renewed unto knowledge of God, according to the image of him who created him,"[6] and being made spiritual, he "judges all things," that is, all things that are to be judged, but "he himself is judged by no man."[7]

Chapter 23
Two Kinds of Dominion

(33) It is said that he judges all things, that is, that he has dominion over the fishes of the sea, and over the fowls of the air, and all herds and wild beasts, and the whole earth, and all creeping things that creep upon the earth.[1] He does this by the mind's understanding, through which he "perceives the things that are of the Spirit of God."[2] Otherwise, "man when he was placed in honor did not understand; he has been compared to senseless beasts, and made like to them."[3] Therefore, our God, in your Church, according to your grace which you have given to it, "for we are your workmanship, created in good works"[4] not only those who preside spiritually, but also those who spiritually are subject to those in authority—for in this way you made man male and female in your spiritual grace, where as to bodily sex there is neither male nor female, because there is neither Jew nor Greek, neither slave nor freeman[5]—therefore spiritual people, whether those in authority or those who obey, judge spiritually. This is not with regard to the forms of spiritual knowledge, which shine in the firmament, for they ought not to judge so sublime an authority. Nor is it of your book itself, even though something does not shine forth clearly from it, for we submit our minds to it, and we hold it for certain that even things closed to our sight are rightly and truly spoken.

Thus man, although now spiritual and "renewed unto knowledge of God according to the image of him who created him,"[6] ought to be "a doer of the law"[7] and not a judge. Nor does he judge concerning that distinction, namely, of spiritual and carnal men, who are known to your eyes, O our God, but have not yet become apparent to us by their works, so that we might know them by their fruits.[8] But you, O Lord, already know them, and you have divided them apart, and you have called them in secret before the firmament was made. Nor does he, although a spiritual man, judge the restless peo-

Book 13. The Creation of the World

ple of this world. What has he "to do to judge those that are without,"[9] not knowing which shall come from that state into your sweet grace, and which shall remain in the everlasting bitterness of impiety?

(34) Therefore, man, whom you have made to your image, did not receive dominion over the lights of heaven, or over that hidden heaven itself, or over day and night, which you called before the foundation of heaven, or over the gathering of the waters, which is the sea, but he has received dominion over the fishes of the sea, and the fowls of the air, and all beasts, and the whole earth, and all creeping things that creep upon the earth.[10] For he judges and approves what he finds right, and he disapproves what he finds wrong, whether in that sacramental administration whereby those men are initiated whom your mercy searches out in many waters;[11] or in that wherein that Fish is set forth, which, having been taken out of the deep, the devout earth feeds upon;[12] or in the signs and utterance of words, made subject to the authority of your book, like birds flying under the firmament, by interpreting, expounding, discoursing, disputing, blessing, or praying to you, with the signs thereof bursting from the mouth and sounding forth, to the end that the people may answer, "Amen."

The cause of the physical utterance of these words is the abyss of this world and the blindness of our flesh. Because of them, thoughts cannot be seen, so that there is need for sounds to strike our ears. Thus, although these flying fowls are multiplied upon the earth, they take their rise from the waters. The spiritual man also judges by approving what is right and disapproving what he finds wrong in the deeds and habits of the faithful: in their almsgiving, like the earth bringing forth fruit. He passes judgment on the living soul, with its affections made meek in chastity, in fastings,[13] in holy meditations on things perceived by the bodily senses. He is now said to pass judgment upon these things, over which he also has power of correction.

Chapter 24
Increase and Multiply

(35) But what is this, and what sort of mystery is it? Behold, you bless men, O Lord, so that they may "increase and multiply, and fill the earth."[1] By this do you give us no indication whereby we may understand something further? Why do you not bless in this same manner the light, which you have called day, and the firmament of heaven, and the lights, and the stars, and the earth, and the sea? I might say that you, our God, who created us to your image, I might say that you had willed to bestow this gift solely upon man, if you had not in like manner blessed the fishes and the whales, so that they should increase and multiply and fill the waters of the sea, and the birds, so that they would be multiplied over the earth. Again, I might say that this blessing pertains to such kinds of things as are propagated by being begotten from themselves, if I had also found it given to trees, and plants, and beasts of the earth. But now neither to herbs nor to trees, nor to beasts and serpents, has it been said "Increase and multiply," although all these, like fishes, birds, and men, by generation increase and preserve their kind.

(36) What then shall I say, O Truth, my light? That it means nothing? That it was stated in this way for no purpose? Not so, O Father of mercy! Far be it from a servant of your Word to speak thus. If I do not understand what you mean by that passage, let my betters, that is, men more intelligent than I am, make better use of it, according as you have given to each of them to understand.[2] But let my confession likewise be pleasing in your eyes, for in it I confess to you that I believe, O Lord, that you have not spoken thus to me in vain. I will not keep silent as to what occasion to read this suggests to me. For the passage is true, and I do not see what should impede me from thus understanding the figurative statements in your books.

I have known a thing to be signified in many ways by the body that is understood in one way by the mind, and a thing to be understood in many ways by the mind that is signified

Book 13. The Creation of the World

in but one way by the body. Consider sincere love of God and neighbor, see how it is expressed corporeally in many holy rites, and in innumerable languages, and in each language by innumerable turns of speech. Thus do the offspring of the waters increase and multiply. Note this again, whoever you are who read these words. See what Scripture delivers and how the voice pronounces it in one way only, "In the beginning God created heaven and earth." Is not this statement understood in many ways, not by deceit of error, but by various kinds of true interpretations? Thus do man's offspring increase and multiply.

(37) Hence, if we think of the actual natures of things, not allegorically but properly, then the words, "Increase and multiply," hold for all things that are begotten from seed. But if we interpret these words as set down figuratively—and this I am inclined to think is intended by Scripture, for surely it did not needlessly ascribe this blessing only to the offspring of water animals and men—then we find multitudes among spiritual and among corporeal creatures, as in heaven and earth; and among both just and unjust souls, as in light and darkness; and among the holy authors, through whom the Law has been administered, as in the firmament which is established between water and water; and among the society of embittered people, as in the sea; and in the zeal of holy souls, as in the dry land; and in works of mercy belonging to the present life, as in herbs bearing seed and trees bearing fruit; and among spiritual gifts made manifest for our profit, as in the lights of heaven; and among affections formed to temperance, as in the living soul.

In all these instances we meet with multitudes, fertility, and increase. But as to what may in such wise increase and multiply that a single thing may be stated in many ways and a single statement may be understood in many ways, this we find only in signs corporeally expressed and in things intelligibly conceived. By signs corporeally expressed we understand the generations of the waters, on account of causes necessitated by fleshly depth; by things mentally conceived, human generations, on account of the fecundity of reason. Therefore, we have believed, O Lord, that the words "Increase and multiply" have been said to both these kinds. In this blessing I conclude that the power and the faculty have been granted to us to express in manifold ways what we understand in but one, and to understand in manifold ways what we read as obscurely uttered in but one way. Thus are the waters of the sea replenished, and they are moved only by various significations. Thus by human offspring is the earth also replenished, the dryness of which appears in its longing, for you, and over which reason rules.

Chapter 25
An Obligation Prefigured

(38) I also wish to state, O Lord my God, what the following passage in your Scripture brings to my mind. I will speak out, and I will have no fear. I will speak the truth under your inspiration as to what you will me to interpret out of those words. For under the inspiration of none but you do I trust myself to speak the truth, for you are the truth,[1] but "every man is a liar."[2] Hence, he who "speaks a lie speaks of his own."[3] Therefore, that I may speak the truth, I will speak out of your gift.

Behold, you have given to us for food "every herb bearing seed which is upon the whole earth, and every tree that has in itself fruit of its own seed,"[4] and not to us alone, but also to all the birds of the air, and to the beasts of the earth, and to the serpents, but you have not given them to the fishes and to the great whales. We were saying that by these fruits of the earth are signified and figured forth in an allegory the works of mercy, which are provided for the needs of this life out of the fruitful earth. The devout Onesiphorus was of such an earth, and to his house you granted mercy, because he often provided refreshment for your own Paul and was not ashamed of his chain.[5] The brethren also did this, and brought forth such fruit, for those who came from Macedonia supplied what was wanting to him.[6] But note how he grieves over certain trees that did not give him the fruit that was due to him, where he says: "At my first answer no man stood with me, but all forsook me: may it not be laid to their charge."[7] For these fruits are owed to those who minister rational doctrine by means of their understanding of divine mysteries, and so they are owed to them as men. They are owed to them as the living soul, for they show themselves for imitation in every form of continence. Again, they are owed to them as flying creatures, because of their blessings, which are multiplied upon the earth, since "their sound has gone forth into all the earth."[8]

Chapter 26
The Gift and the Fruit

(39) But they who find delight in such fruits are fed by them, but those whose God is their belly[1] do not find delight in them. For in those who offer such things, the fruit is not what they give but with what sort of mind they give it. Hence I see plainly why that man who served God and not his own belly rejoiced,[2] and I rejoice greatly with him. From the Philippians he had received what they had sent to him by Epaphroditus; yet I perceive why it was he rejoiced. He is nourished upon that in which he rejoices, for speaking in all truth, he says: "I rejoiced exceedingly in the Lord, that now at length your thought for me has flourished again, wherein you were thoughtful,"[3] but it had become tedious to you.

These men, therefore, had now grown weak from long weariness, and had withered away as it were with regard to bearing that fruit of good works, and he rejoices with them because they had flourished again, and not merely for himself because they supplied his wants. Hence he continues, and says: "I do not speak because anything was wanting; for I have learned in whatsoever state I am to be content. I know how to put up with less, and I know how to live in abundance; everywhere and in all things I am instructed both to be full and to be hungry, and to have abundance and to suffer want. I can do all things in him who strengthens me."[4]

(40) Whence, therefore, do you rejoice, O great Paul? Whence do you rejoice; whence are you fed, O man renewed "unto knowledge of God, according to the image of him who created you,"[5] O living soul of such great continence, O

tongue that is a flying fowl, speaking mysteries?[6] In truth it is to such living souls that this food is due. What is it that feeds you? Joy! Let me hear what follows: "Nevertheless you have done well," he says, "by sharing in my affliction."[7] From this comes his joy, from this his nourishment, that they have done well, not that his troubles have been eased. He says to you, "When I was in distress you have enlarged me,"[8] because he knows how to live in abundance and how to suffer want in you who comfort him. "For you know," he says, "you also know, O Philippians, that in the beginning of the gospel, when I departed from Macedonia, no church communicated with me as concerning giving and receiving but you only. For unto Thessalonica also you sent once and again something for my needs."[9] Now he rejoices that they have returned to these good works, and he is glad that they have flourished again, like a fertile field again producing life.

(41) Was it because of his own needs that he said, "You sent something for my needs?" Does he rejoice because of that? No, it is not for that. How do we know this? Because he continues and says, "Not that I seek the gift, but I seek the fruit."[10] From you, O my God, I have learned to distinguish between gift and fruit. The gift is the thing itself given by a man who bestows these necessities, such as, money, food, drink, clothing, lodging, and help. But the fruit is the good and right will of the giver. For the good Master not only said, "He who receives a prophet," but adds, "in the name of a prophet." He says not only, "He who receives a just man," but he adds, "in the name of a just man." So it is that one receives the reward of a prophet, and the other the reward of a just man. He says not only, "Whoever gives to one of my little ones a cup of cold water," but adds, but only "in the name of a disciple," and concludes thus, "Amen, I say to you, he shall not lose his reward." The gift is to receive the prophet, to receive the just man, to offer a cup of cold water to a disciple. The fruit is to do this in the name of a prophet, in the name of a just man, in the name of a disciple. Elias was fed on such fruit by the widow who knew that she fed a man of God, and fed him for that reason. By the raven he was fed with a gift: not the

inner Elias, but only the outer man was fed, although he might well have perished for want of such food.

CHAPTER 27
True Works of Mercy

(42) Therefore, I will speak what is true in your sight, O Lord. When unlearned men and infidels[1]—for to make a start with them and win them to the faith, there is need for the initiatory sacraments and great miracles, which we believe to be signified by the names of "fishes and whales"—when such men offer bodily refreshment to your servants or aid them in some way useful to this present life, since they are ignorant why this must be done and to what it pertains, they do not feed those servants nor are they fed by them. For the first do not perform the work out of a right and holy will, nor do the second rejoice at their gifts, wherein they do not yet see any fruit. The mind feeds on that in which it finds joy. Therefore, the fishes and whales do not feed upon food that the earth alone brings forth if it is separated and kept apart from the bitterness of the ocean waves.

CHAPTER 28
The Good and the Very Good

(43) And you, O God, saw all the things that you had made, and behold, "they were very good."[1] For we also see them, and behold, they are all very good. In each separate kind of your works, when you said that they should be made, and they were made, this one and that one, you saw that it is good. In seven places I have counted it written down that you saw that what you made is good. And this is the eighth, that you saw all the things that you made, and behold they are not only good, but even very good, as all existing together. For separately, they were only good, but all existing together they are all both good and very good. All beautiful bodies likewise say this, because a body that is made up of members, all of which are beautiful, is far, far more beautiful than the several

members themselves, by whose most orderly arrangement the entire being is made perfect, although each several member is likewise beautiful.

CHAPTER 29
Time and God's Vision

(44) I looked carefully so that I might discover whether it was seven or eight times that you saw that your works were good when they pleased you, and in your sight of them I did not find any time, whereby I might understand just how many times you saw the things you made. I said: "Lord, is not this your Scripture true, since you who are true and you, Truth itself,[1] have set it forth? Why then do you tell me that in your seeing there is no time, whereas this passage in your Scripture tells me that on different days you saw that the things you have made are good, and when I counted them, I discovered how often?"

To this you answer me that you are my God,[2] and with a mighty voice you speak to your servant in his interior ear, and break through my deafness, and cry out: "O man, true it is that what my Scripture says I myself say. Yet that Scripture speaks in time, but time does not affect my Word, because that Word exists along with me in equal eternity. So the things that you see through my Spirit I see, just as those things which you speak by my Spirit I say. So also it is that when you see those things in time, I do not see them in time, even as when you say those things in time, I do not say them in time."

CHAPTER 30
Manichean Dualism

(45) I listened, O Lord my God, and I drank in a drop of sweetness out of your Truth. I understood that there are certain men to whom your works are displeasing. They say that you were compelled by necessity to make many of those works, such as the fabric of the heavens and the arrangement of the stars, and that you did not make them out of your own

resources but they were already created elsewhere and from another source, and that you merely assembled them, fastened them together, and built them up, when out of your vanquished enemies you raised up the ramparts of the world, so that being bound down by that structure, they could not again rebel against you.[1] As to other things, such as all things of flesh, all very minute living beings, and whatsoever clings to earth by roots, they say that you did not really make them, did not even fit them together, but that a hostile intelligence and a different nature, not made by you and opposed to you, begets and forms these beings in the lower portions of the world. Madmen say these things, for they do not see your works by your Spirit and do not recognize you in them.

Chapter 31
Knowledge of the Good

(46) When men see these things through your Spirit, you see in them. Therefore, when they see that they are good, you see that they are good, and whatsoever things are pleasing because of you, in them you yourself are pleasing, and such things as are pleasing to us because of your Spirit are in us pleasing to you. "For what man knows the things of man, but the spirit of man that is in him? So the things also that are of God no one knows but the Spirit of God. Now we have received not the spirit of this world, but the Spirit that is of God, that we may know the things that are given us of God."[1] I am admonished to say: Truly, no one knows "the things that are of God but the Spirit of God." How then do we also know "what things are given us of God"? The answer is made to me that likewise the things that we know by his Spirit "no one knows, but the Spirit of God." Just as it was rightly said to those who would speak in the Spirit of God, "It is not you who speak,"[2] so it is rightly said to those who know in the Spirit of God, "It is not you who know." Therefore, no less rightly is it said to those who see in the Spirit of God, "It is not you who see," so that whatsoever in the Spirit of God they see to be good, it is not they but God who "sees that it is good."

It is one thing, therefore, for any man to think what is good to be evil, as the aforesaid men have said. It is another thing that a man should see that that which is good is good, just as your creation, because it is good, is pleasing to many men to whom, however, you are not pleasing in it. For this reason they desire to enjoy your creation rather than you. It is another thing still, that when a man sees a thing to be good, God may see in him that it is good, namely, to the end that he may be loved in that which he has made. For he cannot be loved except through the Spirit whom he has given. "Because the charity of God is poured forth in our hearts by the Holy Spirit who is given to us."[3] Through the Spirit we see that whatsoever exists in any way is good, for it is from him who does not exist merely in some certain way, but is what he is.[4]

Chapter 32

A Summation of Praise

(47) Thanks be to you, O Lord![1]

We see heaven and earth, whether the corporeal part, superior and inferior, or spiritual and corporeal creation. And in the adorning of these parts, whereof consists either the world's universal mass or absolutely all creation, we see light made and divided from darkness.

We see the firmament of heaven, whether the first body of the world, between the higher spiritual waters and the lower corporeal waters,[2] or this airy space, for it also is called heaven, through which wander the fowls of the sky, amid those waters which are borne as vapors above them, and, on calm nights, also drop down as dew, and those heavier waters which flow upon the earth.

We see the fair expanse of waters gathered together on the fields of the sea, and the dry land, whether bare or formed so as to be visible and put in order, the mother of herbs and trees.

We see the lights shining from above, the sun to suffice for the day, the moon and the stars to comfort the night, and that by all of them times should be marked and signified.

We see humid nature on every side, fruitful of fishes and beasts and birds, for the density of the air, which supports the flight of birds, increases from the exhalation of the waters.

We see the face of the earth, adorned with earthly creatures, and man, made to your image and likeness, and by this, your own image and likeness, that is, by the power of reason and intelligence, set over all non-rational animals. And even as in his soul there is one power which is master by virtue of counsel and another made its subject so as to obey, so also for man in the corporeal order there was made woman. Because of her reasonable and intelligent mind she would have equality of nature, but as to bodily sex she would be subject to the male sex, just as the active appetite is made subject, so as to conceive right and prudent conduct from the rational mind.

These things we see, and we see that each of them is good, and that all of them together are very good.

Chapter 33
Praise and Love

(48) Your works praise you,[1] to the end that we may love you, and we love you to the end that your works may praise you. Out of time, they have beginning and end, rising and setting, growth and decay, beauty and privation. Therefore, they have their sequence of morning and evening, hidden in part and in part manifest. Out of nothing have they been made by you, not out of yourself, not out of anything not your own, or which previously existed, but out of concreated matter, that is, out of matter simultaneously created by you, since without any intervening time you gave form to its formlessness. For since the matter of heaven and earth is one thing and the form of heaven and earth another, you made the matter entirely out of nothing, but the form of the world out of formless matter. Yet you made both of them together, so that form would not follow upon matter by interruption or delay.

Chapter 34
The Structure of the Church

(49) We have also examined those things in keeping with that mystical purpose whereby you willed them either to be

fashioned in such an order or to be described in such order. We have seen that things taken one by one are good, and that together they are very good, in your Word, in your Only-begotten, both heaven and earth, the head and the body of the Church, in your predestination before all times, without morning and evening. And you began to accomplish in time the things predestined, so that you might reveal hidden things and put in place our disordered parts—for our sins were upon us,[1] and we had departed from you into the darksome deep, and your good Spirit was borne over us to bring us help in due season—and you justified the ungodly[2] and divided them from the wicked, and made firm the authority of your book between those above who were docile to you, and between those below who were made subject to them, and you gathered together the society of unbelievers into one conspiracy, so that the zeal of the faithful might become apparent, and they might bring forth works of mercy, even distributing their earthly resources to the poor to the end of obtaining riches in heaven.

After this you enkindled certain lights in the firmament, your holy ones, possessing the word of life, and shining with the lofty and manifest authority of their spiritual gifts. Then, for the instruction of heathen nations you produced out of corporeal matter sacraments, and visible miracles, and voices and words in keeping with the firmament of your book, and in them the faithful would likewise find blessing. Next, you formed the living soul of the faithful through affections kept in order by a manly continence. Then, after your own image and likeness, you renewed the mind, made subject to you alone and needful to imitate no human authority. Its rational actions you made subject to the primatial intellect, as is woman to man. To all officers of your ministry, who are necessary for perfecting the faithful in this life, you willed that by those same faithful, works fruitful for the life to come should be offered for their temporal usage.

We see all these things, and we see that they are very good, because you see them in us, who have given to us your Spirit, by whom we might see them and in them love you.

Chapter 35
The Peace of God

(50) O Lord God, give us peace,[1] for you have given all things to us, the peace of rest, the peace of the sabbath, the peace without an evening. This entire most beautiful order of things that are very good, when their measures have been accomplished, is to pass away. For truly in them a morning has been made, and an evening also.

Chapter 36
The Everlasting Sabbath

(51) But the seventh day is without an evening, and it does not have a setting, because you have sanctified it to endure for all eternity, so that by the fact that you rested on the seventh day, having fulfilled all your works, which are very good, although you wrought them while still at rest, the voice of your book may proclaim to us beforehand that we also, after our works, which are very good because you have given them to us, may rest in you on the sabbath of eternal life.

Chapter 37
Eternal Act, Eternal Rest

(52) Then also you shall rest in us, even as now you work in us, and so will that rest of yours be in us, even as these your works are through us. But you, O Lord, are ever at work and ever at rest. You do not see for a time, nor are you moved for a time, nor do you rest for a time. Yet you make both that things be seen in time, and the times themselves, and the rest that comes after time.

Chapter 38
The Only Gateway

(53) Therefore, we see these things which you have made, because they exist, but they exist because you see them. We

see outside ourselves that they are, and within ourselves that they are good. But you saw them as already made, there where you saw them as to be made. At one time we have been moved to do good, after our heart conceived this out of your Spirit, whereas at a former time, having forsaken you, we were moved to do evil. But you, O one good God, have never ceased to do good. There are certain works of ours, done indeed out of your gift, but they are not eternal. After such things, we hope to find rest in your great sanctification. But you, the Good, needful of no good, are forever at rest, for your rest is yourself.

What man will give it to a man to understand this? What angel will give it to an angel? What angel to man? From you let it be asked. In you let it be sought. At your door let us knock for it. Thus, thus is it received, thus is it found, thus is it opened to us.[1]

NOTES TO INTRODUCTION

1. The name Aurelius Augustinus first appears in a work of his younger contemporary and friend, Paulus Orosius. Augustine himself is not known to have used this form.
2. The name is apparently Punic in origin. There does not seem to be sufficient reason to abandon the traditional English spelling, Monica.
3. Birth control is an instance.
4. Both works are now lost.
5. Cf. Plotinus, *The Enneads*, translated by Stephen MacKenna. Second edition revised by B. S. Page, with a foreword by Professor E. R. Dodds, and an introduction by Professor Paul Henry, S.J. (London: Faber and Faber Limited, n.d.) See also the editorial material *passim* in the original six-volume edition of MacKenna's translation (London: The Medici Society, 1917–1930).
6. The portrait is a fresco in the church of St. John Lateran in Rome, dating from the sixth or perhaps the fifth century.
7. The bibliography lists this and other Latin editions of the *Confessions*.
8. Cf. Ronald A. Knox, *On Englishing the Bible* (London, Burns, Oates, 1949), p. 12.

NOTES TO BOOK 1

CHAPTER 1
1. Cf. Ps. 144:3, and Ps. 146:5.
2. Cf. Jas. 4:6; I Pet. 5:5; Prov. 3:34.
3. "Our heart is restless until it rests in you" sums up Augustine's whole teaching on man's relation to God. It is perhaps the most quoted line in the *Confessions*.
4. Cf. Rom. 10:14.
5. Ps. 21:27.
6. Cf. Matt. 7:7.
7. The preacher was St. Ambrose (ca. 339–397), Bishop of Milan.

CHAPTER 2
1. Gen. 1:1. Augustine makes a long commentary on this text in Book 11.
2. Cf. Ps. 138:8: "If I ascend into heaven you are there; if I descend into hell, you are present." Cf. also Amos 9:2.
3. Cf. Rom. 11:36.
4. Jer. 23:24.

Notes to Book 1

CHAPTER 3
1. Cf. Acts 2:17 and Joel 2:28.
2. Cf. Ps. 145:8.

CHAPTER 4
1. Cf. Ps. 17:32.
2. Cf. Wisd. 7:27.
3. Cf. Job 9:5.

CHAPTER 5
1. Ps. 34:3.
2. Cf. Ps. 142:7; Exod. 33:20; Deut. 31:17.
3. Ps. 18:13–14.
4. Cf. Ps. 115:10.
5. Cf. Ps. 31:5.
6. Cf. Job 9:3.
7. Cf. Ps. 26:12.
8. Ps. 129:3.

CHAPTER 6
1. Cf. Gen. 18:27; Ecclus. 10:9.
2. Cf. Jer. 12:15.
3. Cf. Ps. 93:19; 68:17.
4. This sentence is subject to various interpretations.
5. Cf. Matt. 11:25.
6. Cf. Mal. 3:6.
7. Ps. 101:28.
8. Ibid.
9. Cf. Exod. 16:15; Ecclus. 39:26.

CHAPTER 7
1. Cf. Job 25:4.
2. Cf. Ps. 91:2.
3. God is referred to as the One and the supreme Form or Beauty in terms of Plotinian philosophy.
4. Cf. Ps. 50:7.

CHAPTER 9
1. Cf. Ps. 93:22.
2. Ps. 21:3.
3. This is one of the most involved sentences in the *Confessions*. Both form and thought reflect Augustine's horror at his early discipline in school.
4. This analogy between children's game and adult business was familiar to Augustine from Seneca.

CHAPTER 10
1. God is the creator of all things and the ruler of all things. Sin is not a thing, and God is not its creator. Yet God is the ruler

even of sins, since he forbids them, judges them, and punishes them.
2. Cf. Ps. 108:21, 22; 101:3.

CHAPTER 11
1. "I was signed with the sign of his cross, and seasoned with his salt. . . ." Although infant baptism was common in Augustine's time, he was not baptized at birth. The two rites that he mentions were among those administered to catechumens, that is, those preparing for baptism. Both are included in the Church's complete baptismal rite at the present time.
2. Cf. Gen. 28:15; Job 7:20.
3. Cf. Gal. 4:19.
4. When Augustine seemed to be in danger of death, his mother arranged for his baptism. Upon his recovery, the baptism was delayed on the ground that as he grew up he would surely fall into mortal sin and lose his baptismal innocence. Baptism, therefore, was to be delayed until he reached maturity and left behind his years of youthful vice.
5. Patricius was later baptized a Christian, shortly before his death.
6. That is, she wished that Augustine's probable sins would be committed in clay unhallowed by baptism, rather than by one in whom Christ's image had been fashioned by baptism. As a priest and bishop, Augustine wielded great influence in favor of infant baptism.

CHAPTER 12
1. Cf. Matt. 10:30.

CHAPTER 13
1. The "first teachers" taught the three R's; the *grammatici* were more than what we would call grammarians, and gave more advanced courses, such as composition, rhetoric, and literature.
2. Ps. 77:39.
3. As Dido was the legendary queen of Carthage, her story must have been a favorite in African schools.
4. Cf. Osee 9:1; 4:12.
5. Ps. 39:16.
6. Cf. Jas. 4:4.
7. Vergil, *Aeneid*, iv, 457.
8. Cf. Jer. 18:11.
9. Cf. *Aeneid*, ii, 772.

CHAPTER 14
1. Augustine's knowledge of Greek was probably much greater than is indicated by this passage. For this subject cf. J. M. Campbell and Martin R. P. McGuire, *The Confessions of St. Augustine* (New York: Prentice-Hall, 1931), p. 86.

Notes to Book 1

2. Augustine's native language was Punic, but he also learned Latin as a child.

CHAPTER 15
1. Cf. Ps. 60:2.
2. Cf. Ps. 17:30; I Cor. 1:8.
3. Ps. 5:3.

CHAPTER 16
1. Cicero, *Tusculan Disputations*, I, XXVI, 65.
2. Cf. Terence, *The Eunuch*, 585.
3. Ibid., 589 sq.

CHAPTER 17
1. Cf. *Aeneid*, i, 38. In the preceding chapter Augustine makes use of one of the adulteries of Jupiter, king of the pagan gods. In the present passage he refers to an account of the weakness of Juno, their queen. The immorality of the pagan divinities was a powerful apologetic weapon for the first Christians.
2. The fallen angels were identified with the pagan divinities.

CHAPTER 18
1. Cf. Ps. 102:8; 85:15; Isa. 42:14.
2. Cf. Ps. 85:13.
3. Cf. Ps. 26:8.
4. Cf. Luke 15:12–32.
5. The sin of dropping one's aitches. Augustine makes a powerful contrast between mere temporal conventions and eternal laws of morality coming from God and rooted in man's nature.
6. Cf. Tob. 4:16: "See that you never do to another what you would hate to have done to you by another." Cf. also Matt. 7:12: "All things therefore whatsoever you would that men should do to you, do you also to them," and Luke 6:31.
7. The passage is not entirely translatable. The orator is more afraid of incorrectly saying *inter 'omines* instead of the correct form *inter homines* (among men) than he is of unjustly causing a man to be condemned to death and thus to be taken *ex hominibus*, that is, from among men. Another reading has *inter hominibus* as the incorrect form, a grammatical error rather than one of pronunciation. That reading goes better with the *ex hominibus* (from among men) of the next sentence.

CHAPTER 19
1. Ps. 30:23.
2. Matt. 19:14.

NOTES TO BOOK 2

CHAPTER 1
1. The phrases "the one" and "the many" are from Neoplatonic philosophy. Cf. Plotinus, *The Enneads*. vi, 9, 1.
2. Cf. Dan. 10:8.

CHAPTER 2
1. Cf. Isa. 42:14.
2. Cf. Gen. 3:18; Matt. 22:30.
3. I Cor. 7:28.
4. I Cor. 7:1.
5. I Cor. 7:32, 33.
6. Cf. Matt. 19:12.
7. Cf. Ps. 93:20: ". . . who frame labor in commandment." The version given by Augustine is the result of an error in the translation he used.
8. Cf. Deut. 32:39.

CHAPTER 3
1. Madauros, or Madaura, the present-day Mdaourouch, was about twenty miles from Thagaste (Souk-Ahras). In Augustine's boyhood it was still largely pagan, and he must have been adversely affected by his surroundings and companions.
2. Patricius, Augustine's father, had the rights of a Roman citizen. He had some property, but apparently not too much. As a member of the municipal curia, he incurred expenses that must have been a serious burden to him.
3. Cf. Ps. 129:1.
4. Cf. Hab. 2:4; Rom. 1:17; Gal. 3:11; Heb. 10:38.
5. Cf. I Cor. 3:9.
6. Cf. Rom. 1:25.
7. Cf. Jer. 2:27.
8. Cf. I Thess. 4:8; II Sam. 12:9.
9. Ps. 115:16.
10. Cf. Cant. 4:14.
11. Cf. Jer. 50:8; 51:6. Babylon is here used as a synonym for a city of idolatry and vice.
12. Ps. 72:7.

CHAPTER 5
1. Cf. Ps. 63:11.
2. Augustine refers to Lucius Sergius Catiline (ca. 108–62 B.C.) against whom Cicero delivered four powerful orations.
3. Cf. Sallust, *De Catilina*, xvi.

CHAPTER 6
1. Cf. Rom. 12:19.
2. Cf. Job 7:2, as known to Augustine.

CHAPTER 7
1. Ps. 115:12.
2. Cf. Ps. 53:8.

CHAPTER 8
1. Cf. Rom. 6:21.
2. Cf. Ecclus. 2:10.

CHAPTER 9
1. Cf. Ps. 18:13.

CHAPTER 10
1. Cf. Matt. 25:21.
2. Cf. Luke 15:14.

NOTES TO BOOK 3

CHAPTER 1
1. In the Latin, *sartago*, here translated as caldron, repeats the sound of *Carthago*, as if we would say, e.g., "London, a dungeon." Carthage was notorious for vice.
2. Cf. Wisd. 14:11.
3. Cf. Job 2:7, 8.
4. Cf. Plato, *Gorgias*, 509, for this thought.

CHAPTER 2
1. Mercy, or compassion.
2. Cf. Isa. 34:9.
3. Cf. Dan. 3:52.
4. II Cor. 2:16.

CHAPTER 3
1. The Latin is *eversores*, i.e., overturners. Wreckers is Bigg's word.

CHAPTER 4
1. Cicero was, of course, a familiar author to Augustine. Apparently, he says, "a certain Cicero" to indicate detachment from a pagan author. The book was *Hortensius*, an exhortation to the philosophical life based on Aristotle's *Protrepticus*. Both works are lost.
2. Cf. Luke 15:18–20 for the parable of the prodigal son.
3. Cf. Job 12:13.

Notes to Book 3

4. Col. 2:8, 9.
5. Cf. Ps. 24:7.

CHAPTER 6
1. The Manicheans, or Manichees. Cf. *Introduction*, pp. 20–21.
2. Cf. I Tim. 3:7; 6:9; II Tim. 2:26.
3. Cf. John 14:16 and 26.
4. Cf. Plotinus, *The Enneads*, 6, 9, 4.
5. Jas. 1:17.
6. Cf. Luke 15:16.
7. Cf. Jer. 5:27.
8. The Manicheans listed five good elements, viz., pure air, living fire, fresh wind, pure water, and light. The demon has five evil elements: smoke, evil fire, evil wind, evil water, and darkness.
9. Cf. Prov. 9:13–18.

CHAPTER 7
1. Cf. Gen. 1:27.
2. Cf. I Cor. 4:3.

CHAPTER 8
1. Cf. Matt. 22:37–39.
2. Cf. Gen. 13:13; and chs. 18 and 19.
3. Cf. II John 2:16: ". . . the lust of the flesh, the lust of the eyes, and the pride of life."
4. Cf. Ps. 143:9.
5. Cf. Ps. 26:12.
6. Cf. Rom. 1:26.
7. Cf. Acts 9:5.
8. Cf. Jer. 2:13.
9. Augustine here makes use of Plotinian language to express Christian ideas.
10. Cf. Ps. 74:5, 6.

CHAPTER 10
1. Among the Manicheans, the saints or elect were supposed to follow a higher rule of life than the auditors or hearers, such as Augustine. Among their duties, the auditors were to serve the saints. The particles of light within the saints' food were held to be released by digestion, as Augustine scathingly describes in this passage.

CHAPTER 11
1. Ps. 143:7.
2. Cf. Ps. 85:13.
3. A wooden measuring rod, which was figuratively the rule of faith.
4. For Augustine's theory of questions as a form of teaching cf. his dialogue *On the Teacher*. Also John 21:5; Acts 1:11.

5. Cf. Ps. 10:17.
6. Ps. 68:3.
7. Cf. Ps. 87:3.

NOTES TO BOOK 4

CHAPTER 1
1. Augustine here says "we" since he is writing of himself and others who were both teachers by profession and Manichees in religion.
2. Cf. II Tim. 2:13. The *doctrinae liberales*, here translated as liberal arts, taught by Augustine included rhetoric and literature and also philosophy, mathematics, and music.
3. The Manichean religion had been proscribed both by pagan emperors in earlier times and later by the Church. In Augustine's day the Manichees still flourished.
4. The elect among the Manichees renounced marriage and abstained from meat and wine. The purification of which Augustine writes took place when this food was consumed and digested by the elect and they breathed forth "angels and gods," that is, particles of the principle of light.
5. Cf. John 6:27.
6. Cf. Ps. 73:21.

CHAPTER 2
1. Cf. Ps. 4:13.
2. Augustine lived with this unnamed woman for thirteen years, from 371 to 384. Their son Adeodatus was born in 372. That he was an unwanted child is apparent from this passage, as is also the fact that his parents came to love him dearly. A youth of great promise, he died in 388, aged seventeen. For evidence of his talents see St. Augustine's *On the Teacher*.
3. Cf. Osee 12:1.

CHAPTER 3
1. Ps. 40:5; cf. Ps. 91:2.
2. John 5:14.
3. Cf. Matt. 16:27; Rom. 2:6.
4. Cf. Ps. 50:19.
5. His name was Vindicianus. Cf. Book 7, ch. 6.
6. Cf. Prov. 3:34; I Pet. 5:5 and Jas. 4:6.
7. Hippocrates (ca. 460–ca. 377 B.C.), father of medicine. His reported writings were collected about two centuries after his death.
8. As the works of Vergil were often consulted in this way, the

Notes to Book 4

term *sortes Vergilianae* (Vergilian lots) was coined. The Bible and the *Imitation of Christ* have been similarly used.
9. Nebridius appears later in the *Confessions*. Certain letters of St. Augustine to him survive.

CHAPTER 4
1. Rom. 5:5.
2. Cf. Ps. 93:1.
3. Cf. Ps. 105:2.
4. Cf. Ps. 35:7; Rom. 11:33.
5. Cf. Lam. 5:17.
6. Cf. Ps. 41:6 and 12, and Ps. 42:5.
7. The conception of God held by Augustine as a Manichee was but a fantasy, without power to give him hope or comfort.

CHAPTER 6
1. Cf. Seneca, *Moral Epistles*, iv, i, 6.
2. Cf. Ps. 24:15.
3. Horace, *Odes* I, 3, 8.
4. Cf. Ovid, *Tristia*, 4, 4, 72.

CHAPTER 7
1. Cf. Ps. 241.
2. Cf. Horace, *Carmina* 2, 16, 19.
3. Augustine left Thagaste secretly, without telling anyone except his wealthy friend Romanianus, with whom he had been living after his break with Monica, his mother. The year was 376.

CHAPTER 8
1. Cf. II Tim. 4:3: "For there shall be a time when they will not endure sound doctrine; but, according to their own desires, they will heap to themselves teachers, having itching ears."

CHAPTER 9
1. Cf. Tob. 13:18.
2. Cf. Gen. 1:1; 2:1.
3. Cf. Jer. 23:24.
4. Ps. 118:142.
5. Cf. John 14:6.

CHAPTER 10
1. Ps. 79:4.
2. Cf. St. Ambrose's hymn, *Deus creator omnium*, quoted in Book 9, ch. 12.

CHAPTER 11
1. Cf. Matt. 4:23; Ps. 102:3.
2. Cf. I Pet. 1:23.

Chapter 12
1. Cf. Acts 17:24.
2. Isa. 46:8.
3. Cf. Wisd. 5:7.
4. Cf. John 6:33.
5. Ps. 18:6.
6. John 1:10.
7. I Tim. 1:15.
8. Cf. Ps. 40:5; 50:6.
9. Ps. 4:5.
10. Cf. Ps. 72:9.
11. Cf. Ps. 83:7.

Chapter 14
1. Cf. Matt. 10:30.
2. Eph. 4:14.

Chapter 15
1. Ps. 71:18; cf. Ps. 135:4.
2. Cf. Ps. 17:29.
3. Cf. John 1:16.
4. Cf. John 1:9.
5. Cf. Jas. 1:17.
6. Cf. John 8:52.
7. Cf. I Pet. 5:5; Jas. 4:6.
8. Cf. Ps. 77:39.
9. John 3:29.
10. Cf. Ps. 50:10.

Chapter 16
1. The *Categories* of Aristotle (384–322 B.C.) is one of the most influential books in the history of philosophy. It is the first of the six treatises on logic making up the collection known as the *Organum*, or instrument for philosophical investigation. The other treatises are *On Interpretation*, the *Prior Analytics*, the *Posterior Analytics*, the *Topics*, and the *Sophistical Arguments*.
2. Aristotle worked out his doctrine of categories or *predicamenta* (predicaments) with great care. Substance is what exists in itself and not in another as in a subject. It is the subject of which certain other things are predicated; it is not itself the predicate of some other subject. On the other hand accidents, in the ordinary course of nature, inhere in a substance and are affirmed of it.

Thus, in St. Augustine's illustration, a man is a substantial being, he is a substance. There are certain other realities that can be affirmed of him because he is the subject in which they are found. These are called the nine categories or classes of accidents. They may increase or decrease, or come and go, but as their subject, the man remains substantially the same. Thus Augustine himself through the course of his life grew in size: an instance of the category of quantity. He acquired certain vicious habits that were in time replaced by virtues. He acquired great skill as a writer and great learning: virtues, vices, skill, and the like come under the heading of quality, as do colors and certain other aspects of our being. Augustine was taught by other men (passion) and he in turn instructed students (action). He existed at different moments (time) and in many places (place). He had countless relations with others: men and other things. He was a son, a brother, a father, a disciple, a master, a priest, and a bishop (relation). He was clothed in various ways and equipped with tools or armor at different times (habit, in the sense of wearing a monk's habit or a soldier's uniform). He assumed various positions, such as kneeling in prayer (posture).

The distinction between the substantial or essential and the merely accidental is one of the most important and useful in human thought. Failure to know it and use it is often the cause of very gross errors.

3. Beauty, goodness, truth, unity do not exist in God as modifications of his being. God cannot become more or less good, true, or beautiful. He is absolutely good or goodness itself; he is truth itself, absolute truth, absolute beauty; absolute unity.
4. Cf. Gen. 3:18.
5. Cf. Ps. 58:10.
6. Cf. Luke 15:13.
7. Cf. Ps. 62:8; 16:8.
8. Isa. 46:4.

NOTES TO BOOK 5

CHAPTER 1
1. Cf. Ps. 6:3; Ps. 34:10.
2. Cf. Ps. 18:7.

CHAPTER 2
1. Cf. Ps. 138:7.
2. Cf. Wisd. 11:25.
3. Cf. Apoc. 7:17; 21:4.

CHAPTER 3
1. Faustus, the leading writer among the western Manichees, was born at Milevis in Numidia. Although ostensibly dedicated to a life of self-denial, he was noted for his love of luxury and de-

spised the poverty of his parents. He was exiled as a Manichee by civil authorities, although Christians interceded for him. St. Augustine wrote an important work, *Against Faustus the Manichee*.
2. Cf. I Tim. 3:7.
3. Cf. Wisd. 13:9.
4. Cf. Ps. 137:6.
5. Cf. Ps. 33:19.
6. Cf. Ps. 8:8–9. St. Augustine symbolizes pride by the birds flying aloft, vain curiosity by the fishes swimming in the depths of the sea, and luxury, or sins of the flesh, by the beasts of the field.
7. Cf. Deut. 4:24.
8. Cf. John 1:1–3.
9. Cf. Ps. 146:5.
10. I Cor. 1:30.
11. Cf. Matt. 22:21.
12. This quotation and the remainder of this paragraph are based upon Rom. 1:21–25.
13. Augustine calls him Manichaeus, the Latin form of the name of Mani, or Manes, the remote founder of Manicheism.

CHAPTER 4
1. Cf. Rom. 1:21.
2. Cf. II Cor. 6:10.
3. Wisd. 11:21.

CHAPTER 5
1. Cf. Job 28:28.
2. Cf. II Macc. 1:14.
3. Eph. 4:13, 14.
4. That is, Mani.

CHAPTER 6
1. Lucius Annaeus Seneca (ca. 4 B.C.–A.D. 65) statesman, at one time tutor of Nero, was one of the greatest of writers and thinkers among the pagan Romans. His writings on moral questions, found in his *Moral Letters* and *Moral Essays*, were held in high esteem by the Fathers of the Church and had very great influence in the Middle Ages. He also wrote several notable tragedies.
2. Cf. Ps. 49:26.

CHAPTER 7
1. Cf. Acts 8:21 and Ps. 77:37.
2. Cf. Joel 2:26.
3. Ps. 36:23.

CHAPTER 8
1. At Rome there were laws governing students.
2. Ps. 141:6.

Notes to Book 5

3. Cf. Ps. 39:3 and Prov. 20:24.
4. Cf. Phil. 3:19: ". . . who mind earthly things."
5. The reference is to the waters of baptism. Monica did not realize, nor did Augustine at the time, that the journey to Rome was a first necessary stage on his longer journey to Milan, where he would be baptized.
6. St. Cyprian, bishop and martyr. A convert, probably in his mature years, he was baptized c. 246 and about two years later became bishop of Carthage. He was martyred on August 14, 258, during the Decian persecution. A shrine marked the scene of his martyrdom and a basilica was built over his tomb. The memorial chapel or oratory to which Augustine refers was north of Carthage.
7. Cf. Gen. 3:16: "To the woman [Eve] also he said: I will multiply thy sorrows, and thy conceptions: in sorrow shalt thou bring forth children." Augustine pairs his mother's twofold travail, the first at his natural birth, the second at his rebirth by baptism.

CHAPTER 9
1. Cf. I Cor. 15:22: "And as in Adam all die, so also in Christ all shall be made alive."
2. Cf. Eph. 2:16: ". . . and might reconcile to God in one body by the cross, killing the enmities in himself."
3. As a Manichean, Augustine believed that what died upon the Cross was a phantom, an evil spirit pretending to be Christ. He asked, how could a believer in such a phantom believe that it atoned for his sins? As a Manichean his false beliefs and evil practices led him into sin, the death of his soul, and kept him there.
4. A twofold death: of both body and soul.
5. Cf. Gal. 4:19.
6. Cf. Phil. 2:1; Col. 3:12.
7. Cf. Ps. 50:19.
8. Cf. Ps. 118:1, and Ps. 137:8.
9. Cf. Matt. 18:32.

CHAPTER 10
1. Cf. Ps. 115:16.
2. Cf. Ps. 40:5.
3. Cf. Matt. 12:26: "And if Satan . . . is divided against himself: how then shall his kingdom stand?"
4. Ps. 140:3, 4.
5. The Third Academy, or third stage of Plato's school, flourished in the third and second centuries before Christ and was skeptical in character. Temporary addiction to this form of skepticism was another of Augustine's errors. He refutes it here and elsewhere, especially in his work *Against the Academics*.

CHAPTER 11
1. The Manicheans rejected the Old Testament and held that the Catholic version of the New Testament was corrupted in this manner.

CHAPTER 12
1. Ps. 138:22.
2. Cf. Ps. 72:27.

CHAPTER 13
1. At that time Milan was the usual seat of the emperors of the West.
2. Symmachus (ca. 340–ca. 402) was famous as the greatest orator of his time, and it was seemingly as such rather than as an official that he was asked to choose a professor of rhetoric for Milan. At the time he was the greatest supporter of paganism, especially while prefect of Rome. The fact that Augustine was not a Catholic, but a Manichean supported by Manicheans, may have had weight with him. In his anti-Christian activities he met defeat at the hands of St. Ambrose.
3. St. Ambrose (ca. 337–April 4, 397), came from one of the greatest of Roman families, the Aurelii. In 374 while he was still a catechumen, the people of Milan called him to be their bishop. He was great as a preacher, writer, administrator, and fearless defender of the faith. He is one of the four great Latin doctors of the Church. He presents a striking contrast to St. Augustine.
4. Cf. Ps. 80:17; Ps. 147:14.
5. Cf. Ps. 44:8; Ps. 4:8.
6. A quotation from St. Ambrose's hymn *Splendor Paternae Gloriae.* Cf. Eph. 5:18.
7. Cf. Deut. 33:1.
8. Ps. 118:155.

CHAPTER 14
1. Cf. II Cor. 3:6: "For the letter kills, but the spirit quickeneth." Augustine was killed, that is, brought into serious error and mortal sin, when he took in a literal sense passages that should have been interpreted in a figurative or spiritual sense.
2. Augustine considers himself to be a catechumen in view of his initial enrollment by his mother. (Cf. Book 1, ch. 11) which in spite of his Manicheism he had never entirely repudiated.

NOTES TO BOOK 6

CHAPTER 1
1. Ps. 70:5.
2. Cf. Ps. 10:1.
3. Cf. Job 35:10, 11.
4. Cf. Ps. 34:6; Isa. 50:10.
5. Cf. Ps. 72:26.
6. Cf. Ps. 67:23.
7. Cf. Acts 27:21–26.
8. Luke 7:14. Augustine has used the account of the restoration to life by Christ of the son of the widow of Naim.
9. Cf. Ps. 69:2.
10. Cf. Ps. 17:29.
11. John 4:14.
12. Cf. Gal. 4:14.

CHAPTER 2
1. The doorkeeper or porter was a cleric in the first one of the four minor orders. The others are lector or reader, exorcist, and acolyte.
2. Following St. Ambrose's example, Augustine later helped to stop the custom in Africa. The objections were twofold, as he indicates: there were associations with pagan customs and they were the occasion of drinking and revelry.
3. Cf. Acts 18:25; Rom. 12:11.
4. Cf. Prov. 6:23; 10:17; 15:10.

CHAPTER 3
1. It was the ancient custom to read out loud and in company with others. Augustine has already given an instance of this when he tells how he and Faustus read together. The present passage is reported to be one of the few descriptions of silent reading in ancient literature. The detail with which Augustine describes St. Ambrose's custom indicates how unusual silent reading must have been.
2. II Tim. 2:15.
3. Cf. Gen. 9:6.
4. Cf. I Cor. 13:12.
5. Cf. Gen. 1:26.

CHAPTER 4
1. Cf. Matt. 7:7: "Knock, and it shall be opened to you."
2. Augustine's Manichean errors.

386 Notes to Book 6

3. Cf. Col. 1:18–24.
4. II Cor. 3:6.
5. The Latin contains a very complex play upon words. After the custom of the skeptical philosophers, he held back from giving assent, lest he fall into error. He suspensed, i.e., hung up his judgment. But that very suspension, or hanging, caused his death, i.e., serious error.
6. Cf. Ps. 116:2.

CHAPTER 5
1. Cf. Ecclus. 19:4.
2. Augustine makes a contrast between the many and the few (cf. Matt. 7:13, 14 and 20:16), but it is to the effect that the simplicity of the Scriptures has an appeal to all men, while a smaller number are led on to a deeper study of them.
3. Cf. Matt. 7:13.

CHAPTER 6
1. Cf. Rom. 9:5.
2. The Emperor was apparently Valentinian II (372–392) at that time a mere boy who resided at Milan. He was murdered by Arbogast, a Frankish general in the Roman service.
3. Cf. Ps. 41:11; Isa. 38:13.

CHAPTER 7
1. As this chapter and other passages in the *Confessions* and elsewhere in Augustine's writings tell us, Alypius was born of a good family in Thagaste. Younger than Augustine, he was his student, and his victim in the Manichean sect. He was converted with Augustine and was with him at Cassiciacum. Made bishop of Thagaste in 394/5, he was associated with Augustine in his apostolic work and apparently outlived him.
2. Nebridius, also a Manichean, was converted shortly after Augustine. He returned to Africa and worked for the conversion of his whole household. In Book 9, ch. 3 of the *Confessions*, Augustine refers both to their correspondence and to the death of Nebridius.
3. Cf. Ps. 68:6.
4. Prov. 9:8.
5. Cf. Ps. 106:8.

CHAPTER 8
1. Cf. Jud. 5:15.
2. Cf. Isa. 57:13.

CHAPTER 9
1. For this chapter St. Augustine must be numbered among the pioneers of crime reporting.
2. Augustine's phrase *vico argentario* has been variously translated

Notes to Book 6

as "silversmiths' booths," "street of the silversmiths," "bankers' booths" and "street of the bankers."
3. The title of senator in the Roman provinces in the last century of the Roman Empire was little more than a social honor given to those who had considerable landed wealth or an official position or dignity.
4. As a bishop and diocesan official.

CHAPTER 10
1. Subject to the imperial treasurer were certain provincial treasurers, such as this official in Rome. As the treasurer was not necessarily a lawyer, he had a lawyer, like Alypius in this instance, as his counselor and assessor.
2. The Latin may mean either "he would have resigned" or "he would have voted against it."
3. The phrase "praetorian prices" has been interpreted variously. From the context it apparently means here "discount prices" that were a sort of perquisite of certain public officials. Alypius saw a moral problem in the ordinary, and presumably just, price that he would have to pay a copyist and this "discount price" that he could exact in view of his position.
4. Cf. Luke 16:10–12.
5. Ps. 144:15.

CHAPTER 11
1. Cf. Matt. 7:7.
2. A play upon words in the Latin is here repeated in "prepare" and "repair."
3. Cf. Ecclus. 5:8: "Delay not to be converted to the Lord, and defer it not from day to day."
4. That this is a dying life was a familiar thought among the ancients. "What else is this daily falling away of our corruptible being except a long-drawn-out death?" asked St. Gregory the Great. Here, however, Augustine contrasts the soul's life of grace in God, with its death by mortal sin, as he was then sinning and dying each day.
5. Cf. Wisd. 8:21: "And as I knew that I could not be otherwise continent, except God gave it, and this also was a point of wisdom, to know whose gift it was."

CHAPTER 12
1. Cf. Gen. 3:1.
2. Cf. Isa. 28:18.
3. Ecclus. 3:27.

CHAPTER 13
1. Augustine seems to have had little active part in arranging the proposed marriage. It was his mother's great aim to get him out of his life of sin and then into the Church.

2. The word *sapor* (savor, taste, relish, flavor) has an objective meaning. It was something Monica discerned in the content of the dreams and revelations, not a subjective taste or sense within her mind.
3. The legal age of consent to marriage was ten years.

CHAPTER 14
1. Romanianus was a very wealthy citizen of Thagaste, who took Augustine into his home after a break with Monica. Augustine won him to Manicheism and it is uncertain whether he was ever converted. His son Licentius was a member of Augustine's community at Cassiciacum and figures in some of Augustine's writings.
2. Cf. Matt. 7:13.
3. Cf. Prov. 19:21.
4. Cf. Ps. 144:15, 16.

CHAPTER 15
1. Augustine had lived in sin for about 12 or 13 years with this unnamed woman, the mother of his son Adeodatus. It is apparent that there was never any intention on his part of marrying her. However, they were obviously deeply attached to one another.
2. It is apparent that not even natural affection had a place in Augustine's sexual activities after the dismissal of his first companion. It was seemingly a cold-hearted lust and sensualism.

CHAPTER 16
1. Cf. Ps. 39:3.
2. Epicurus (341–270 B.C.), the founder of the Epicurean system, was born on the island of Samos and died at Athens, where he established his school in a garden outside the city walls. A voluminous writer, he developed an elaborate philosophy that was materialistic in its physics and metaphysics and hedonistic in ethics. Although he himself attempted to place the doctrine that pleasure is the only good and pain the only evil on a high plane, it inevitably found acceptance upon a very low level.
3. Cf. Isa. 3:9.
4. Cf. Ps. 31:8.
5. Cf. Isa. 46:4.

NOTES TO BOOK 7

CHAPTER 1
1. Augustine was now 31 years old. The words he uses to describe his age are *adulescentia*, here translated as "youth," and *iuven-*

Notes to Book 7

tus, translated as "early manhood." In classical usage adolescence was from 15 to 30 and *iuventus* from 20 to 40. When *iuventus* is used alone, as in this passage, it often meant simply manhood, or the period succeeding "adolescence."
2. That is "before I knew anything of philosophy."
3. Cf. John 17:3.
4. Phantasms, in Augustine's system, are sense-images fashioned by the mind itself. They are not fantasies, i.e., memory images of actual things once perceived. Thus a fantasy would be our memory image of the national capitol in Washington, whereas if we construct a sense-image of a non-existent Gothic skyscraper surmounted by a Renaissance dome it would be a phantasm.
5. Cf. Vergil, *Aeneid* iii, 233.
6. A reference to the traditional four elements, earth, water, air, and fire.
7. Cf. Matt. 13:15.
8. Cf. Ps. 17:29.

CHAPTER 2
1. Cf. II Tim. 3:13.

CHAPTER 3
1. That is, in attempting to solve the problem of evil, Augustine must not become evil by falling into sin and error.
2. That is, the Manicheans.
3. Cf. Rom. 1:29.
4. Cf. Heb. 12:15; Matt. 13:24–30.
5. Cf. Ps. 6:6.

CHAPTER 4
1. This passage may have been an occasion of St. Anselm's famous attempt to prove God's existence from the idea of the greatest of conceivable things. Cf. St. Anselm's *Proslogium* and *Monologium*. Also John K. Ryan, *Basic Principles and Problems of Philosophy* (Westminster, Md.: The Newman Press, 1954), pp. 124–30.

CHAPTER 5
1. This analogy apparently derives from Plotinus, *The Enneads*, IV, 3, 9.
2. Cf. II Pet. 2:20.

CHAPTER 6
1. For Vindicianus cf. Book 4, ch. 3.
2. Cf. Ps. 35:7.
3. Ecclus. 39:26.

CHAPTER 7
1. Cf. Ps. 17:13.
2. Ps. 37:9.

3. Cf. Ps. 39:9–11. God is the light of the soul. This light was first lost by Adam's sin. Augustine, being as yet unbaptized and perhaps still living a sinful life, did not have this inner light of God's grace. It is an inner light, whereas Augustine was not living within himself, but "outside himself," i.e., as he states, still concerned with bodily objects.
4. Cf. Job 15:26. Augustine made use of the text found in the Old Latin version.
5. Cf. Ps. 88:11.

CHAPTER 8
1. Cf. Ps. 32:11.
2. Cf. Ps. 84:6; 102:9.
3. Cf. Ecclus. 17:31.
4. Cf. Vergil, *Aeneid*, ii, 336; Acts 9:15.
5. The Latin is *ex occulta manu medicinae tuae*, "by the secret hand of your medicine." As *medicina* is often used by St. Augustine as a name for Christ, it is here translated as Physician.
6. Cf. Apoc. 3:18.

CHAPTER 9
1. In this marvelous chapter Augustine tells of his introduction to Neoplatonic philosophy, compares it with certain scriptural doctrines, and indicates why and where it may be used. Certain Neoplatonic doctrines parallel divine revelation with regard to the existence and nature of God, and some of them are relevant even to the doctrine of the Trinity. Recognition that God is light and that he enlightened men's minds is also found in part in the Neoplatonists. However, there are great contrasts: the Neoplatonists have no knowledge of the incarnation and the redemption, and there is the constant fact of idolatry among the pagans, even among their philosophers. Just as the Jews were permitted to take gold out of Egypt and to put it to God's use in the Promised Land, so Christians can and should take the gold, i.e., the truth that they find in pagan thought, and put it to the service of religion.
2. Cf. Prov. 3:34; Jas. 4:6; I Pet. 5:5.
3. John 1:14.
4. The man is unidentifiable.
5. Platonists, i.e., Neoplatonists, according to our usage. Among them was Plotinus, one of the greatest of Greek thinkers, Porphyry, his disciple, Iamblichus, and Proclus.
6. The translator was Victorinus Afer, whom Augustine discusses in Book 8, ch. 2.
7. John 1:1–5. The punctuation of Augustine's text, and consequently the meaning, of lines 3 and 4 differs somewhat from later versions.
8. Cf. John 1:8–12.

Notes to Book 7

9. John 1:13, 14.
10. Cf. Phil. 2:6–11.
11. John 1:16.
12. Wisd. 7:27.
13. Rom. 5:6; 8:32.
14. Cf. Matt. 11:25–29.
15. Cf. Ps. 24:9, 18.
16. Matt. 11:29.
17. Rom. 1:21, 22.
18. Cf. Acts 7:39; Exod. 32:1–6. "The Egyptian food" is lentils, the mess of potage for which Esau sold his birthright. Augustine is, of course, writing in allegory.
19. Ps. 105:20.
20. Cf. Gen. 30:23; 25:23; Rom. 9:12; Ps. 78:1.
21. Acts 17:28. The line quoted immediately afterwards by St. Paul, "For we are also his offspring," is from Aratus of Cilicia.
22. Rom. 1:25.

CHAPTER 10
1. Cf. Ps. 29:11.
2. Cf. Ps. 26:10.
3. Ps. 38:12.
4. Exod. 3:14.
5. Rom. 1:20.

CHAPTER 11
1. Ps. 72:28.
2. Cf. Wisd. 7:27.
3. Ps. 15:2.

CHAPTER 12
1. Cf. Gen. 1:3; Ecclus. 39:21.

CHAPTER 13
1. Cf. Ps. 148:7–12.
2. Cf. Ps. 148:1–5.

CHAPTER 14
1. Cf. Ps. 37:4.
2. Cf. Ps. 118:37.
3. Cf. Isa. 2:22.

CHAPTER 16
1. Cf. Ecclus. 10:10; 10:14, 15.

CHAPTER 17
1. Wisd. 9:15.
2. Rom. 1:20.
3. The thought and expression in this chapter are strongly Neoplatonic.

Chapter 18
1. Rom. 9:5; I Tim. 2:5.
2. John 14:6.
3. The divine nature.
4. John 1:14.
5. Cf. I Cor. 1:25.
6. Cf. Gen. 3:21.

Chapter 19
1. Augustine had been too weak and ignorant to accept the mystery of the incarnation, viz., the fact that the nature of God and the nature of man are united in the one person of Jesus Christ. Consequently he was affected by various Christological heresies.
2. John 1:14.
3. Augustine has repudiated the Manichean absurdity that Christ's body was merely a phantom. He recognized him now as a true man, one single unitary being made up of body and soul. As such, he has an intellect and will as well as a body.
4. Augustine does not as yet recognize that Christ is true God as well as true man: he is seen merely as a wonderfully great and good man. Augustine's phrase *persona veritatis*, literally "person of truth" has been given various interpretations. From the context, I believe that it should be translated as "person of Truth," that is, as "divine person."
5. Followers of Apollinaris (died ca. 292), bishop of Alexandria, taught variously that Christ had no human soul or no human intellect. Alypius foolishly attributed this heresy to orthodox believers.
6. Photinus, a 4th-century bishop of Sirmium, held that Christ was merely man, but divinely inspired.
7. By a strange perversion of logic Adolf Harnack, the 19th-century German historian of religion, thought that the errors of Augustine and Alypius as non-Catholics somehow represented absence of true doctrine within the Church.
8. Cf. Rom. 14:1 and II Tim. 1:10.

Chapter 20
1. Rom. 1:20.
2. Sins of pride bring with them their own punishment of spiritual blindness.
3. The fallacy which Augustine refers to appears not infrequently in our own time.

Chapter 21
1. Augustine had found difficulty with Rom. 1:3 and II Cor. 5:16 among other passages. Cf. *Contra Faustum Manichaeum*, XI.
2. Cf. Ps. 2:11.
3. Cf. I Cor. 4:7.

4. Ibid.
5. Cf. Ps. 101:24.
6. Cf. Rom. 7:22, 23.
7. Cf. Dan. 3:27–32.
8. Cf. Ps. 31:4.
9. Cf. Heb. 2:14; Dan. 3:52.
10. Cf. John 8:44.
11. Rom. 7:24, 25.
12. Cf. Prov. 8:22.
13. Cf. Luke 23:14, 15.
14. Cf. Col. 2:14.
15. Cf. Ps. 50:19.
16. Cf. Apoc. 21:2.
17. Cf. II Cor. 1:22.
18. Ps. 61:2, 3.
19. Matt. 11:28, 29.
20. Matt. 11:25.
21. Cf. Deut. 32:49.
22. Cf. Ps. 90:13.
23. Cf. I Cor. 15:9.
24. Cf. Hab. 1:2.

NOTES TO BOOK 8

CHAPTER 1
1. Ps. 34:10.
2. Ps. 115:16, 17.
3. Cf. Ps. 75:2.
4. I Cor. 13:12.
5. Cf. I Cor. 5:7.
6. Simplicianus succeeded St. Ambrose as Bishop of Milan in 397. Augustine dedicated his work *De divinis quaestionibus* to him. It is related that when St. Ambrose learned on his deathbed that his successor would likely be Simplicianus, he repeated three times in a strong voice, "Senex sed bonus": "An old man, but a good one."
7. Cf. Ps. 25:8.
8. Cf. I Cor. 7:27–35.
9. Matt. 19:12.
10. Wisd. 13:1.
11. Rom. 1:21.
12. Cf. Ps. 17:36.
13. Cf. Job 28:28.
14. Cf. Prov. 3:7.

15. Rom. 1:22.
16. Cf. Matt. 13:46.

CHAPTER 2
 1. Simplicianus was St. Ambrose's "spiritual father," i.e., he was very close to him, and may have instructed and baptized him.
 2. Gaius Marius Victorinus, the great 4th-century rhetorician, was of African origin. His translations of Plato, Aristotle, and certain Neoplatonists are lost, as is his commentary on Cicero's *Topica*. Certain other works survive, among them the *Ars grammatica* and various theological works written after his conversion, among them are commentaries on some of St. Paul's epistles, and a work on the Trinity directed against the Arian heresy. It has been conjectured that these theological works had considerable influence on Augustine.
 3. Cf. Col. 2:8.
 4. Matt. 11:25.
 5. Cf. Eph. 1:6.
 6. The manuscripts of the *Confessions* are unsatisfactory at this point and various emendations have been suggested. The most acceptable is that of Max Ihm, here translated as "with the cult of Osiris." It fits in with Augustine's meaning and with the quotation from Vergil.
 7. Cf. *Aeneid*, viii, 698–9.
 8. Cf. John 3:5.
 9. Cf. Gal. 5:11.
10. Cf. Ps. 143:5.
11. Babylon, i.e., pagan Rome.
12. Cf. Ps. 28:5.
13. Cf. Luke 12:9.
14. The word "sacraments" was used in a loose way. The sacraments of instruments, here referred to, were ceremonies connected with the beginning of the catechumenate, or period of instruction before baptism.
15. Cf. Ps. 111:10.
16. Cf. Ps. 39:5.
17. A public recitation of the Apostles' creed.

CHAPTER 3
 1. Cf. Luke 15:4–32.
 2. The angels.
 3. Cf. Matt. 24:31. Cf. also Cardinal Newman's five hymns in *The Dream of Gerontius*, each beginning

> Praise to the Holiest in the height,
> And in the depth be praise:
> In all His words most wonderful;
> Most sure in all His ways!

Notes to Book 8

CHAPTER 4
1. Cf. Cant. 1:3.
2. Cf. John 1:12.
3. As members of an audience stir up one another's enjoyment by their applause.
4. A modern instance is that of Newman during the Oxford movement.
5. Cf. Jas. 2:1–9.
6. Cf. I Cor. 1:27, 28.
7. Cf. I Cor. 15:9.
8. Cf. Acts 13:6–12.
9. Cf. Matt. 12:29.
10. Cf. II Tim. 2:21.

CHAPTER 5
1. Cf. Ps. 8:3; Wisd. 10:21; Matt. 21:16.
2. The enemy, viz., Satan.
3. Gal. 5:17.
4. Cf. II Tim. 2:4.
5. Eph. 5:14.
6. Cf. Rom. 7:22, 23.
7. Cf. Rom. 7:24, 25.

CHAPTER 6
1. Cf. Ps. 53:8.
2. Ps. 18:15.
3. Cf. Eph. 2:2.
4. Beyond what Augustine relates, nothing further is known about Ponticianus.
5. St. Anthony of Egypt (ca. 250–356) was the founder of Christian monachism. St. Athanasius (295–373) composed a biography of his fellow Egyptian about 357. About 370 it was paraphrased or translated by Evagrius into Latin, whose version was likely that read by Ponticianus. Athanasius himself lived at Trier on two occasions. Cf. St. Athanasius, *The Life of Saint Antony*. New translated and annotated edition by Robert T. Meyer (Westminster, Md.: The Newman Press, 1950).
6. Cf. Ps. 144:5.
7. Trier on the Mosel river in Germany was an important center of Roman authority, especially from the time of the Emperor Diocletian.
8. Matt. 5:3.
9. The "agentes in rebus" were an important class of public officials in the later empire. They acted as couriers, secret police, and in other ways.
10. "The friends of the Emperor" or Caesar were a group instituted by Augustus. As the title indicates, they were close to the em-

peror, acted as a sort of privy council, and had special honors and privileges.
11. Cf. Luke 14:28–30.

CHAPTER 7
1. Cf. Ps. 35:3.
2. Augustine says that the search for truth, which is less good than finding it, is better than wealth, power, and pleasure. A modern perversion of part of his thought is that the search for truth is better than its discovery.
3. Cf. Ecclus. 2:16.
4. Cf. Ecclus. 5:8.
5. Plato in *Phaedrus*, 249 states that the souls of philosophers receive wings for flight more easily than lesser men.

CHAPTER 8
1. Cf. Isa. 26:20; Matt. 6:6.
2. Cf. Matt. 11:12.
3. Cf. Ezech. 16:8.
4. Cf. Ps. 34:10.

CHAPTER 9
1. St. Augustine struggles in this chapter with most difficult psychological problems, involving the nature of the will and its acts. He interprets the will as an act rather than as a special power (or faculty, in the usual phrase) to act or to refrain from acting. Hence he distinguishes between complete and perfect acts of will and those which are incomplete and imperfect. It is in this sense that there are in man "two wills, one of which is not complete."

CHAPTER 10
1. Cf. Ps. 57:3.
2. Cf. Titus 1:10.
3. That is, the Manicheans, with their extreme dualism of two natures, one good, the other evil.
4. Eph. 5:8.
5. John 1:9.
6. Ps. 33:6.
7. Cf. Rom. 7:17.
8. Because of his greater gifts of nature and grace, the sin by which Adam fell was committed with more freedom than any of the sins committed by his descendants. Because of Adam's sin, in which the human race fell with him, his sons have a tendency to evil. Hence Augustine indicates that his own wrongdoing, voluntary as it is, issues from Adam's still "more voluntary sin" and is part of the punishment incurred by that sin.

Notes to Book 9

Chapter 11
1. This chapter is a marvelous display of Augustine's powers of psychological analysis and vivid description.
2. Cf. *Aeneid,* v, 457.
3. Cf. Eccles. 1:2.
4. Cf. Ps. 112:9.
5. Cf. Ps. 118:85.

Chapter 12
1. Cf. *Aeneid,* vii, 499.
2. Cf. Ps. 50:19.
3. Ps. 6:4.
4. Ps. 78:5.
5. Ps. 78:8.
6. Matt. 19:21.
7. A practice similar to the *sortes Vergilianae* (cf. *Confessions,* Book 4, ch. 3, and note) obtained among Christians, in which the Scriptures were used. Various councils of the Church condemned the practice.
8. Rom. 13:13, 14.
9. Rom. 14:1.
10. Cf. Eph. 3:20.
11. Cf. *Confessions,* Book 3, ch. 11.
12. Cf. Ps. 29:12.
13. Monica had made efforts to arrange a lawful marriage for her son. Cf. *Confessions,* Book 6, ch. 13.

NOTES TO BOOK 9

Chapter 1
1. Ps. 115:16, 17.
2. Ps. 34:10.
3. Ps. 34:3.
4. Cf. Matt. 11:30.
5. This is the only passage where Christ is addressed directly. Three times Augustine prays in the familiar formula "through Christ." Cf. Book 11, chs. 2 and 22.
6. Ps. 18:15.

Chapter 2
1. Cf. Ps. 118:70.
2. About the time of Augustine's conversion the Emperors Theodosius and Valentinian II decreed the times for court and perhaps for school vacations. The vintage vacation extended from August 22 to October 15. There were also Easter (two weeks)

and New Year (three days) vacation. In modern Italy the great vacation time (*ferragosto*) begins on August 15, the feast of the Assumption.
3. Cf. Ps. 83:7.
4. Pss. 119–133 are traditionally called "gradual psalms." In the Roman breviary the 15 psalms are arranged in three sets of five each, together with appropriate prayers. They were once of obligation on certain days for those held to recite the *Divine Office*. No satisfactory explanation of the title "gradual psalms" has been advanced.
5. Cf. Ps. 119:3, 4.
6. This passage is probably the immediate basis for Augustine's symbol in Christian art, a heart pierced by an arrow.
7. Rom. 14:16.
8. Cf. Ps. 45:11.

CHAPTER 3
1. The location of the villa at Cassiciacum has been a subject of much controversy. It was north of Milan and within sight of the Alps.
2. Cf. Matt. 9:2.
3. Cf. Ps. 67:16.
4. Cf. Luke 16:22.
5. Ps. 26:8.

CHAPTER 4
1. Augustine was accompanied to Cassiciacum by Monica and Adeodatus, Navigius, his brother, Rusticus and Lastidianus, his cousins, and Alypius, Trygetius, and Licentius, his students and fellow citizens. They remained for four months, from the end of October, 386 to early March, 387.
2. These are *Against the Academic Philosophers, On the Happy Life,* and *On Order*.
3. The *Soliloquies*.
4. Nine letters from Augustine to Nebridius and three from Nebridius to Augustine survive.
5. Cf. Isa. 40:4; Luke 3:4–6.
6. II Peter 3:18.
7. Alypius's attitude is evidently due to desire to make the writings purely philosophical. Augustine did not accept Alypius's position.
8. Cf. Ps. 28:5.
9. Ps. 18:7.
10. Cf. Ps. 4:2. A commentary on this psalm follows.
11. Cf. Ps. 30:7–8.
12. Ps. 4:3.
13. Cf. Ps. 4:4.
14. Cf. Eph. 1:20.

Notes to Book 9

15. Cf. John 14:16–17.
16. John 7:39.
17. Ps. 4:3–4.
18. Rom. 8:34.
19. Ps. 4:5.
20. Rom. 2:5.
21. Ps. 4:6.
22. Ps. 4:7.
23. John 1:8.
24. Cf. Eph. 5:8.
25. Ps. 4:7.
26. Ps. 4:8.
27. Ps. 4:9.
28. Cf. Ibid.
29. I Cor. 15:54.
30. Cf. Mal. 3:6.
31. Ps. 4:10.
32. Cf. Ps. 118:103–105.
33. Cf. Ps. 138:21.
34. Cf. John 20:28.
35. In his *Confessions of an English Opium Eater* Thomas De Quincey, whose addiction to opium was occasioned by severe toothache, remarks that if toothache were not so common an occurrence, it would be regarded as one of the worst of all pains. Augustine's pain was evidently so terrible that he looked upon both its coming and its cure as something mysterious.

CHAPTER 6
1. At the approach of Lent, catechumens who wished to be baptized gave in their names and were examined in the catechism. Ash Wednesday in 387 was on March 10.
2. While awaiting baptism in Milan, Augustine wrote several books, including *On the Immortality of the Soul*.
3. *On the Teacher*. This profound and beautiful dialogue, in which Augustine considers problems of semantics along with those of teaching and others, was written at Thagaste. There are at least two translations of *De Magistro* in English.
4. Adeodatus died at the age of 17.
5. During the night of April 24–25, A.D. 387.

CHAPTER 7
1. Augustine uses the term *rex* (king) for Valentinian as a synonym for *imperator* (emperor) and the adjective *regia* (royal) for Justina. They have been translated literally here, as it may be thought that Augustine uses them in a somewhat pejorative sense.
2. The Empress Justina Augusta was the wife of Valentinian I and mother of Valentinian Augustus II. Early in 385 she ordered

St. Ambrose to give over a church within the city to the Arians, but he refused. The struggle came to a climax in Holy Week 386 when she ordered him to leave Milan. He refused to do so and conducted services in the basilica as usual. In Easter Week Justina's troops besieged Ambrose in the basilica, but the movement collapsed when many of the soldiers joined him. Justina died a Catholic in 388 in Thessalonica.
3. Sts. Gervase and Protase, Milanese martyrs, probably of the second century. They are commemorated on June 19. Their remains, clothed in priestly vestments and with the palms of martyrdom in their hands, still rest under the altar of the Church of St. Ambrose in Milan.
4. Severus, a butcher by trade.
5. Cf. Ps. 115:15.
6. Luke 18:11.
7. Cf. Cant. 1:3.
8. Cf. Isa. 40:6.

CHAPTER 8
1. Cf. Ps. 67:7.
2. Evodius appears as interlocutor in Augustine's *On the Quantity of the Soul* and *On Free Will*. He was a member of Augustine's community in Thagaste and later became Bishop of Uzala in 396. Letters between him and Augustine survive.
3. Monica's desire to be buried with her husband very likely figured in this return to Africa.
4. The exact date of St. Monica's death is unknown. Apparently she died before November 387. Ostia is the part of Rome.
5. Ps. 5:8.
6. Ecclus. 19:1.
7. Cf. Jer. 31:28.

CHAPTER 9
1. Eph. 5:21.
2. Cf. I Pet. 3:1.
3. The first mention of his father's name. Augustine does not use his own name at all throughout the *Confessions*.
4. Ps. 58:18.
5. Cf. Gen. 9:25.
6. Cf. I Tim. 5:4, 9, 10.
7. Cf. Gal. 4:9.
8. Cf. John 11:13.

CHAPTER 10
1. Phil. 3:13.
2. II Pet. 1:12.
3. I Cor. 2:9.
4. Ps. 35:10.
5. Cf. Ezech. 34:14.

Notes to Book 9

6. Cf. Ps. 77:71.
7. Rom. 8:23.
8. Cf. Wisd. 7:27.
9. Ps. 99:3.
10. Cf. Ecclus. 18:1.
11. Cf. Gen. 22:11.
12. Ps. 76:18.
13. Cf. I Cor. 13:12; Num. 12:8.
14. Matt. 25:21.
15. I Cor. 15:51.

CHAPTER 11
1. Augustine apparently wants to give Monica's exact words, which we here translate literally. Instead of the imperative, she uses a colloquial form, the present indicative.
2. Cf. Col. 1:15.

CHAPTER 12
1. Augustine's *nec omnino moriebatur* may echo Horace's *non omnis moriar:* (I shall not wholly die).
2. I Tim. 1:5.
3. Ps. 100:1.
4. The Latin is *alio dolore dolebam dolorem*. Cf. Shakespeare's "with old woes new wail my dear time's waste." (Sonnet xxx).
5. Terence, *Andria*, 1, i, 90.
6. It was a custom in Italy for Mass to be offered for the dead person at the grave. In 1947 a marble slab was discovered in Ostia that was perhaps placed upon Monica's grave. Her body was removed in 1430 to the church of St. Augustine in Rome.

CHAPTER 13
1. Cf. I Cor. 15:22. "And as in Adam all die, so also in Christ shall all be made alive."
2. Matt. 5:22–23.
3. Cf. Ps. 129:3.
4. Cf. II Cor. 10:17.
5. Cf. Ps. 117:14.
6. Cf. Ps. 72:26.
7. Cf. Rom. 8:34.
8. Cf. Matt. 6:12.
9. Cf. Ps. 142:2.
10. Cf. Jas. 2:13.
11. Cf. Matt. 5:7.
12. Cf. Rom. 9:15; Exod. 33:19.
13. Ps. 118:108.
14. Cf. II Tim. 4:6.
15. Col. 2:14.
16. Cf. John 14:30.

17. Cf. Ps. 90:13.
18. Cf. Luke 8:15.
19. This is the only place in the *Confessions* in which Monica is named.
20. Cf. Heb. 11:10–16.

NOTES TO BOOK 10

CHAPTER 1
1. I Cor. 13:12.
2. Eph. 5:27.
3. Cf. Rom. 12:12.
4. Ps. 50:8.
5. John 3:21.

CHAPTER 2
1. Cf. Heb. 4:13.
2. Cf. Ps. 5:13.
3. Cf. Rom. 4:5.

CHAPTER 3
1. Ps. 102:3.
2. I Cor. 2:13.
3. I Cor. 13:7.
4. Cf. Ps. 31:1.
5. Cf. II Cor. 12:10.

CHAPTER 4
1. II Cor. 1:11.
2. Ps. 143:7, 8.
3. Cf. Apoc. 8:3.
4. Ps. 50:3.
5. Cf. Ps. 2:11.
6. Cf. John 13:1–17.
7. Ps. 16:8; 35:8.
8. I Cor. 4:3.

CHAPTER 5
1. I Cor. 2:11.
2. Cf. Job 42:6.
3. I Cor. 13:12.
4. Cf. II Cor. 5:6.
5. I Cor. 10:13.
6. Isa. 58:10.

Notes to Book 10

CHAPTER 6
1. Rom. 1:20.
2. Cf. Rom. 9:15; Exod. 33:19.
3. Anaximenes of Miletus, a Greek philosopher of the sixth century before Christ, who taught that air is the primordial material out of which all things are made.
4. Ps. 99:3.
5. Rom. 1:20.

CHAPTER 7
1. Ps. 31:9.
2. It is not so much the eye that sees, the ear that hears, etc., but rather I who see by means of one organ, hear by means of the other, etc. Augustine emphasizes man's organic unity.

CHAPTER 8
1. Must is new wine boiled down and strong in taste; also the bitter leavings from new-made cider which are fed to swine.
2. Augustine clearly has a very strong, vivid memory.

CHAPTER 10
1. Cf. Aristotle, *Posterior Analytics*, Book II, ch. 1: "The kinds of question we ask are as many as the kinds of things we know. They are in fact four: (1) Whether the connection of an attribute with a thing is a fact? (2) What is the reason for this connection? (3) Whether a thing exists? (4) What is the nature of the thing?"
2. St. Augustine here suggests something like the Platonic doctrine of reminiscence.

CHAPTER 12
1. The passage is difficult to translate because of St. Augustine's play upon the word "number." The eye, touch, and even other senses can perceive numbers as written or pictured, and so on. These are "the numbers that we enumerate" or name or count off. But the ideal numbers, "the numbers with which we enumerate," i.e., with which the mathematician works in his mind, are something different from and realer than the numbers that we hear in oral additions and the like.

CHAPTER 16
1. Cf. Gen. 3:17–23.

CHAPTER 17
1. Cf. Job 35:11.

CHAPTER 18
1. Cf. Luke 15:8.

Chapter 20
1. Isa. 55:3.
2. Adam, who committed the original sin. Cf. Genesis 3:1–19.
3. Cf. I Cor. 15:22.

Chapter 23
1. Gal. 5:17.
2. Cf. John 14:6.
3. Ps. 26:1.
4. Ps. 41:12.
5. Cf. John 12:35.
6. Terence, *Andria*, i, 1, 41.
7. Cf. John 8:40: "But now you seek to kill me, a man who have spoken the truth to you."
8. Cf. John 3:20: "For everyone that does evil hates the light, and does not come to the light, that his works may not be reproved."

Chapter 28
1. Cf. Ps. 30:10.
2. Job 7:1. The Vulgate has "Life is a warfare."

Chapter 29
1. Wisd. 8:21.
2. Both a Christian and a Plotinian thought.

Chapter 30
1. I John 2:16.
2. Christ forbids concubinage, sanctifies marriage, and counsels chastity.
3. Cf. I Cor. 4:1.
4. Cf. Ps. 102:3.
5. Cf. I Tim. 1:14.
6. Eph. 3:20.
7. Cf. Ps. 2:11.
8. I Cor. 15:54.

Chapter 31
1. Cf. Matt. 6:34.
2. Cf. I Cor. 6:13.
3. Cf. I Cor. 15:53.
4. II Cor. 6:5; I Cor. 9:27.
5. Luke 21:34.
6. Wisd. 8:21.
7. Ecclus. 18:30.
8. I Cor. 8:8.
9. Phil. 4:11–13.
10. Ps. 102:14.
11. Cf. Gen. 3:19.
12. Cf. Luke, 15:24–32.

Notes to Book 10

13. Phil. 4:11, 13.
14. I Cor. 1:31; Jer. 9:23, 24.
15. Ecclus. 23:6. The other man is Ecclesiasticus the Preacher.
16. Rom. 14:20; Titus 1:15.
17. I Tim. 4:4.
18. I Cor. 8:8.
19. Col. 2:16.
20. Rom. 14:3.
21. Cf. Gen. 9:2.
22. Cf. III Kings 17:6.
23. Cf. Matt. 3:4.
24. Cf. Gen. 25:34.
25. Cf. II Kings 23:15.
26. Cf. Matt. 4:3.
27. Cf. Num. 11:1.
28. Luke 5:8.
29. Cf. John 16:33.
30. Cf. Rom. 8:34.
31. Ps. 138:16.

CHAPTER 32
1. The dark, deep regions of the subconscious and the mind's powers of self-deception do not escape Augustine's sure analysis.
2. Cf. Job 7:1.

CHAPTER 33
1. In this chapter Augustine reveals his love of music, as he does elsewhere in his writings, and discusses the place of music in divine worship. He sees a twofold danger. First, a rigorous antiestheticism would reject music altogether, just as it would reject sculpture, painting, and good architecture. Upon the other hand, there is danger of the means, good sacred music, becoming an end in itself, turning into a distraction, and even displacing the worship that it should serve. By implication, Augustine also recognizes the familiar problem of Church music so bad it can only distract men from worship and even degrade it in their eyes.
2. The passage is obscure. It is here interpreted as meaning that those who are aroused to devotion and good works by music are asked to lament Augustine's failures in this regard. Those who are entirely unaffected will not be concerned with the problem.
3. Cf. Ps. 12:4; 6:3.

CHAPTER 34
1. Cf. II Cor. 6:16.
2. II Cor. 5:2.
3. Cf. Gen. 1:3.
4. Cf. Tob. 4:2–4.

5. Cf. Gen. 27:1-40.
6. Cf. Gen. 48:11-22.
7. A reference to St. Ambrose's evening hymn, the first two stanzas of which were quoted in Book 9, ch. 12. The meaning is that in the hymn worshipers make proper use of physical light as an occasion to praise God and are not disturbed by such light during hours of sleep.
8. Ps. 24:15.
9. Ps. 120:4.
10. Cf. Plotinus, *The Enneads*, 6, 9, 4.
11. Cf. Ps. 58:10.
12. Ps. 25:3.

CHAPTER 35
1. Literally, "the eyes are princes among the senses." Cf. Newman's description of sight in *The Dream of Gerontius* as "that princely sense."
2. Cf. I John 2:16.
3. Cf. Ps. 17:47.
4. A reference to his early passion for shows and interest in astrology.
5. Spiritism or necromancy never victimized Augustine.
6. Augustine was apparently subjected to severe temptations to seek some visible sign from God that he was assured of salvation.
7. Augustine's attitude may be contrasted with that of another philosopher. Spinoza is reported to have amused himself by arousing spiders to fight with one another.
8. This chapter would be misunderstood if it were thought that Augustine was opposed to valid and worth-while scientific knowledge. His intense interest in genuine knowledge and his consciousness of its value are everywhere apparent. He condemns superstition, frivolous waste of time, and idle curiosity.

CHAPTER 36
1. Cf. Ps. 102:3-5.
2. Cf. Matt. 11:30.
3. Cf. Isa. 37:20.
4. I Pet. 5:5; Jas. 4:6; Prov. 3:34.
5. Cf. Ps. 17:14 and 8.
6. Cf. Isa. 14:12-14: "How art thou fallen from heaven, O Lucifer, who didst rise in the morning? And thou saidst in thy heart: I will exalt my throne above the stars of God, I will sit . . . in the sides of the north. I will ascend above the height of the clouds, I will be like the most High."
7. Cf. Luke 12:32.
8. Ps. 9:24.

Notes to Book 10

CHAPTER 37
1. Cf. Prov. 27:21: "As silver is tried in the refining pot and gold in the furnace; so a man is tried by the mouth of him that praises."
2. Cf. Ps. 37:9.
3. Cf. Ps. 18:13.
4. Augustine offers some interesting applications of the inductive methods of agreement and difference.
5. Cf. Gal. 6:3.
6. Cf. I John 1:6.
7. Cf. Ps. 140:5.

CHAPTER 38
1. Ps. 69:6; cf. Ps. 108:22.
2. Cf.: "I thank my God for my humility." Shakespeare, *Richard III*, Act ii, scene 1, line 72.

CHAPTER 41
1. Cf. I John 2:16: "concupiscence of the flesh, concupiscence of the eyes, and the pride of life."
2. Ps. 30:23.

CHAPTER 42
1. A reference to the superstitious practices of some of the Neoplatonists.
2. Eph. 2:2.
3. II Cor. 11:14.
4. I Tim. 2:5.
5. Rom. 6:23.

CHAPTER 43
1. I Tim. 2:5.
2. Cf. Rom. 6:23 for the text Augustine makes the basis of his present phrase.
3. Cf. II Tim. 1:10; I Cor. 15:55.
4. Cf. John 1:1, 2.
5. Cf. Rom. 8:32.
6. Cf. Phil. 2:6–8.
7. Ps. 87:6.
8. Cf. John 10:17, 18.
9. Cf. Ps. 102:3.
10. Rom. 8:34.
11. John 1:14.
12. II Cor. 5:15.
13. Cf. I Pet. 5:7; cf. Ps. 54:23.
14. Ps. 118:18.
15. Cf. Ps. 68:6; 24:5; 6:2.
16. Col. 2:3.

17. Ps. 118:122.
18. A reference to the Holy Eucharist.
19. Ps. 21:27.

NOTES TO BOOK 11

CHAPTER 1
1. Ps. 95:4.
2. Matt. 6:8.
3. Cf. Matt. 5:3–9.
4. Cf. Ps. 117:1.

CHAPTER 2
1. Cf. Ps. 44:2: "My tongue is the pen of a scrivener who writes swiftly."
2. Augustine was ordained a priest in 391, and made a bishop late in 395 or early in 396.
3. As our phrase "the sands of time" is taken from the hourglass, Augustine's "drops of time" is from the water clock.
4. Ps. 60:2.
5. Cf. Ps. 10:17.
6. Ps. 85:1 and 5.
7. Cf. Ps. 129:1.
8. Ps. 73:16.
9. Cf. Matt. 7:7.
10. Cf. Ps. 28:9.
11. Cf. Ps. 118:72.
12. Ps. 25:7.
13. Ps. 118:18.
14. Cf. Ps. 26:7.
15. Matt. 6:33. Augustine lived a life of total poverty in his latter years.
16. Ps. 118:85.
17. Cf. Exod. 33:13.
18. Ps. 79:18.
19. Rom. 8:34.
20. Col. 2:3.
21. Cf. John 5:46: "For if you did believe Moses, you would perhaps believe me also; for he wrote of me." Cf. Gen. 3:15; 22:18; 49:10; Deut. 18:15.

CHAPTER 3
1. Gen. 1:1.
2. As the sinner cannot escape God but passes from God blessing him to God in wrath, (Cf. Book 4, ch. 9), so the good man

Notes to Book 11

passes from God blessing him in this world to God as his reward after death.
3. Job 14:16.

CHAPTER 4
1. Note how carefully Augustine writes. Things did not exist in such wise as to produce themselves. However, he leaves the way open for their existence as ideas in God's mind before they were made by him.
2. Augustine is here concerned with the fundamental philosophical problem of the analogous character of being and its transcendental attributes of unity, goodness, truth, and beauty.

CHAPTER 5
1. Cf. Ps. 22:9.

CHAPTER 6
1. Matt. 3:17.
2. Augustine apparently refers here to what we call sound waves. As he soon indicates, spoken words are not so much things as movements; they are becoming rather than being.
3. Cf. Isa. 40:8.
4. These words: "This is my beloved Son."

CHAPTER 7
1. Cf. John 1:1.
2. I Cor. 1:4.

CHAPTER 8
1. The Latin word in the Gospel is *principium,* which means both beginning and principle. Hence, according to Augustine, Christ, the Word of God, is not only in the beginning, but he is the beginning, a principle.
2. Christ is the sole master or teacher. Cf. St. Augustine's *On the Teacher.*
3. John 3:29.

CHAPTER 9
1. Cf. Ps. 30:11.
2. Cf. Ps. 102:3–5.
3. Cf. Rom. 8:24, 25.
4. Ps. 103:24.
5. Cf. Prov. 4:7.

CHAPTER 11
1. Cf. I Cor. 1:24.
2. Cf. Ps. 5:10.

Chapter 12

1. The Latin reads, *Ecce respondeo dicenti, "quid faciebat deus, antequam faceret caelum et terram."* The student of medieval philosophy will note the parallel to a formula used in the tripartite method of the schoolmen. After objections had been proposed, St. Thomas Aquinas would begin his answer with the words, *Respondeo dicendum.*
2. An application of the principle of non-contradiction, viz., that a thing cannot be and not be at the same time, in the same place, and under the same conditions. The objection in philosophical terms, involves an absurdity, or self-contradiction.

Chapter 13

1. Cf. Heb. 1:2.
2. Cf. Gen. 2:3.
3. Ps. 101:28.
4. Cf. II Pet. 3:8.
5. Ps. 2:7.
6. Before God created changing things, there was no time, no then, no succession of before and after among changing things. Augustine expresses his mind with great accuracy: God is eternal, he is before all temporal periods, and also there is never a time when there is no time. He could not correctly say there was a time when time was not.

Chapter 14

1. This is one of the most effective and well-known epigrams in philosophy. Augustine sums up here what Plotinus labors to express. Cf. *The Enneads*, III, 7, 1.

Chapter 15

1. Cf. Ps. 26:1; Mich. 7:8; I John 1:5.
2. That is, the explanation is absurd.

Chapter 17

1. Cf. Ps. 22:1; 27:9.
2. A reference both to Augustine's school days and to his work as a school teacher in Thagaste. Cf. Book 1, chs. 9, 12; Book 4, ch. 4; and Book 6, ch. 7.

Chapter 18

1. Ps. 70:5.
2. In this chapter Augustine gives both an a priori and an a posteriori theory of prediction.

Chapter 19

1. Cf. Ps. 138:6.
2. Cf. Ps. 37:11.

Notes to Book 11

CHAPTER 20
1. The terms "properly" and "improperly" must not be understood as meaning correctly and incorrectly, although when we use terms properly we will also use them correctly. In traditional philosophy, to use a term properly means to use it in the strict sense, whereas to apply it to something for which it holds only in an analogous or derivative way is to use it improperly, although not incorrectly. Only men smile in the proper sense of the word. However, nature also may be said to smile by an improper but still correct and readily understood use of the term.

CHAPTER 22
1. Matt. 7:11.
2. Ps. 72:16.
3. Ps. 115:1.
4. Ps. 26:4.
5. Ps. 38:6.

CHAPTER 23
1. The identification of time with the movement of the sun and other heavenly bodies is a naïve theory that Augustine demolishes without much difficulty.
2. The Latin is *communes notities*. It has been translated as "common notices," "common conceptions," and otherwise.
3. Gen. 1:14.
4. Because of their regularity, universality, and evidence, the movements of the sun and planets are used for ordinary measurements in time. Actually, any movement could be used, but to do so would be obviously impractical. Cf. John K. Ryan, *Basic Principles and Problems of Philosophy* (Westminster, Maryland: The Newman Press, 1954), pp. 53-57.
5. Cf. Jos. 10:12.

CHAPTER 24
1. An appeal to God as inner teacher.

CHAPTER 25
1. A reminiscence of the Socratic injunctions to know oneself and one's own ignorance.
2. Cf. Gal. 1:20.
3. Ps. 17:29.

CHAPTER 26
1. A cubit was 18 inches.
2. Augustine begins to formulate his definition of time. It is an activity of the mind, whereby the mind is not merely extended into the past, as in memory, or into the future, as in anticipation, but is distended, so as to hold things as present.

Chapter 27

1. Ps. 61:9.
2. Ps. 99:3.
3. Cf. *Aeneid*, iv, 586.
4. The opening words of St. Ambrose's hymn, quoted in Book 9, ch. 12.

Chapter 29

1. Ps. 62:4.
2. In this chapter Augustine makes use of his term for time (*distentio*) and related words for what may be called a moral purpose. *Distentio* can mean "distraction." Hence time and temporal things can lead us astray. We can be distended, that is, spread thin, over temporal good, instead of extended, that is, intent on God or eternity. We are then discontented, distracted and without purpose, instead of intent, purposive.
3. Ps. 17:36; 62:9.
4. Cf. Phil. 3:12–14.
5. Ps. 25:7.
6. Ps. 26:4.
7. Ps. 30:11.

Chapter 30

1. Cf. Ps. 143:8.
2. Phil. 3:13.
3. Augustine refers to the problem of whether time would begin with the creation of immaterial beings, namely, angels. In *The City of God* (Book 12, ch. 16) he says that they are subject to time. In scholastic terminology, the duration of angels is termed *aevum* or "eveternity."

Chapter 31

1. Gen. 1:1.
2. Cf. Isa. 57:15.
3. Ps. 145:8.

NOTES TO BOOK 12

Chapter 1

1. The phrase I have used here is found in Pascal, Schopenhauer, and Ernest Hello, among others.
2. Rom. 8:31.
3. John 16:24.
4. Matt. 7:7–9.

Notes to Book 12

CHAPTER 2
1. Cf. Ps. 11:9.
2. The body.
3. Augustine uses a Hebraicism found in Latin versions of Scripture, "the heaven of heaven," to name God's dwelling place in contrast to the term "heaven" as meaning the sky, which is, of course, as material as the earth.
4. Ps. 113:16.

CHAPTER 3
1. Gen. 1:2.
2. Cf. Ps. 70:17.
3. Cf. Wisd. 11:18: "For your almighty hand which made the world of matter without form." Augustine does not hold that matter existed eternally and independently of God, who formed things out of it. God created matter as well as the forms in which it is found. Cf. especially Augustine, *De Generi ad litteram*, 1, 15, 29.

CHAPTER 6
1. Questions have been raised as to what men are referred to here, and it has been suggested that they were uneducated Christians. It seems more likely that is a general reference to explanations of prime matter, or something analogous to it, offered by philosophers with whom he had discussed it.
2. True reason, or right reason, viz., the Aristotelian doctrine of prime matter, especially as found in Plotinus. Cf. Aristotle, *Metaphysics*, viii. 1. 1042^a 33–b7; *Physics* 1.6–7, 189^a 11–191^a 20. Plotinus, *The Enneads*, 2, 4, 1–2.

CHAPTER 7
1. Cf. Book 9, ch. 11.
2. Apoc. 4:8; cf. Isa. 6:3.
3. Cf. Book 11, ch. 10.

CHAPTER 8
1. Ps. 113:16.
2. Cf. Wisd. 11:18.
3. Cf. Gen. 1:6.
4. The Latin is *constat et non constat*. The passage can be given different interpretations. I believe that Augustine means that the world actually is and abides, but at the same time it is continually changing. It is (*constat*) and yet it is always becoming (*non constat*).

CHAPTER 9
1. Your servant, viz., Moses.

Notes to Book 12

CHAPTER 10
1. Cf. Ps. 118:176; Jonas 2:8.
2. Ezech. 3:12; Isa. 30:21. ³The Manichees are here described as enemies of peace or perhaps it may be a general reference to heretics who are by nature divisive. Cf. Ps. 119:7.

CHAPTER 11
1. Cf. I Tim. 6:16.
2. Ps. 113:16.
3. Cf. Ps. 24:4.
4. Ps. 41:3, 4, 11.
5. Cf. Ps. 26:4.
6. Cf. Ps. 101:28.

CHAPTER 12
1. Gen. 1:1.

CHAPTER 13
1. Cf. I Cor. 13:12.

CHAPTER 14
1. Cf. Ps. 149:6. The two-edged sword is interpreted elsewhere by Augustine as the Old and the New Testament.

CHAPTER 15
1. Cf. Ps. 47:15.
2. Ps. 148:6.
3. Ecclus. 1:4.
4. St. Paul, in II Cor. 5:21.
5. Cf. Gal. 4:26; II Cor. 5:1.
6. Cf. Ps. 148:4.
7. Cf. Ps. 25:8.
8. Ps. 118:176.
9. Cf. Luke 15:5.
10. Cf. Ps. 72:28.
11. Cf. Ps. 17:7.
12. Cf. Ps. 25:7.

CHAPTER 16
1. Ps. 27:1.
2. Cf. Matt. 6:6.
3. Cf. Rom. 8:26.
4. Cf. Gal. 4:26.
5. Cf. Rom. 8:23.

CHAPTER 17
1. The six days of creation described in Gen. 1:3–31.
2. Augustine has offered four opposing interpretations of Genesis 1:1. The fourth theory is introduced with words suggesting that it is a theory Augustine himself can conceive rather than one

Notes to Book 12   415

actually advanced by another thinker. The reader will note its striking anticipation of some modern evolutionary doctrines as to the origin and development of the universe.

CHAPTER 18
1. II Tim. 2:14.
2. I Tim. 1:8.
3. I Tim. 1:5.
4. Cf. Matt. 23:10. Master, or teacher.
5. Cf. Matt. 22:40.
6. Ps. 37:11.
7. By repetition of the word thought, Augustine emphasizes the subjective, yet true, character of different interpretations. Between the truth of divine revelation and that arrived at by human reason there will be no real conflict. The authors of inspired books, he indicates, may speak truer than they know, and readers may arrive at the additional truths that are in these books.

CHAPTER 19
1. Cf. Ps. 103:24.
2. Cf. I Cor. 8:6.

CHAPTER 20
1. Cf. John 14:17.

CHAPTER 22
1. Cf. Gen. 1:31.
2. Cf. Col. 1:16.

CHAPTER 24
1. Cf. Ps. 115:16.
2. Cf. Ps. 21:26.

CHAPTER 25
1. John 8:44.
2. Cf. Jer. 18:19.
3. Cf. I Tim. 1:8 and 5.
4. I Cor. 4:6.
5. Cf. Matt. 22:37–39.
6. Cf. Matt. 22:40.
7. Cf. I John 1:10; 5:10.

CHAPTER 26
1. Cf. Matt. 22:37–39.
2. Cf. Rom. 9:21. "Or has not the potter power over the clay, of the same lump, to make one vessel unto honor, and another unto dishonor."
3. Cf. Ps. 8:5.

Chapter 27
1. Cf. Ps. 50:3.
2. Cf. Job 39:15.
3. Cf. II Macc. 15:23.

Chapter 28
1. Cf. John 8:25.
2. A reference to an interpretation by St. Ambrose.
3. Another reference to an evolutionary hypothesis.

Chapter 29
1. The Latin is *non est absurdus:* he is not absurd. An absurdity in philosophy is a self-contradiction.
2. Or, material sound is prior to formal melody.
3. Augustine's analogy to illustrate the doctrine of matter and form is perhaps the best that has been offered.

Chapter 30
1. Ps. 66:1.
2. Cf. I Tim. 1:5, 8.
3. Cf. I John 4:11.

Chapter 31
1. Moses

Chapter 32
1. Cf. Ps. 142:10.

NOTES TO BOOK 13

Chapter 1
1. Cf. Ps. 58:18.
2. Augustine here makes use of the doctrine of prevenient grace. God's grace was necessary even for Augustine's recognition of sin and cry for pardon. As St. Paul says, God gives both "the purpose and the fulfillment."

Chapter 2
1. Augustine explicitly rejects the Plotinian doctrine that the universe is an emanation from the divine substance.
2. Cf. Ps. 103:24.
3. Cf. Ps. 72:28.
4. Cf. Eph. 5:8.
5. Cf. Ps. 35:7; II Cor. 5:21.

Notes to Book 13

CHAPTER 3
1. Gen. 1:3.

CHAPTER 4
1. Gen. 1:2.
2. Cf. Isa. 11:2.
3. Cf. Ps. 35:10.

CHAPTER 5
1. Cf. I Cor. 13:12.
2. Cf. Gen. 1:6.

CHAPTER 7
1. Rom. 5:5.
2. Cf. I Cor. 12:1.
3. I Cor. 12:31.
4. Cf. Eph. 3:14 and 19.
5. Cf. the words in the preface of the Mass.
6. Cf. Ps. 123:5: "a water unsupportable."

CHAPTER 8
1. Cf. Eph. 5:8.
2. Cf. Ps. 17:29.
3. Cf. Isa. 58:10.
4. Ps. 30:21.

CHAPTER 9
1. Cf. Acts 2:38.
2. Ps. 9:15.
3. Cf. Luke 2:14.
4. Cf. Ps. 83:6.
5. Cf. Book 9, ch. 2.
6. Cf. Ps. 121:6 and 1.
7. Cf. Ps. 60:8.

CHAPTER 10
1. Cf. Eph. 5:8.
2. Cf. John 1:9.

CHAPTER 11
1. The doctrine of the Holy Trinity is that there is but one God in three divine Persons, Father, Son, and Holy Spirit; the Father is God, the Son is God, and the Holy Spirit is God, yet there is but one God. Augustine offers an analogy based on a man's nature: there are in man three actualities: he is; he knows; and he wills. He is at once a really existent, a knowing, and a willing being. Is there a Trinity of Persons in God, because God is self-existent (the Father), self-knowing (the Son), self-willed (the Spirit)? Or is the Father self-existent, self-known, and self-willed, so also the Son, and so also the Holy Spirit? Or is each

Notes to Book 13

Person such, and at the same time the one God such? Since the Trinity is a mystery, the supreme mystery, Augustine indicates that it can neither be grasped by our minds nor expressed in words.

Chapter 12
1. Cf. Isa. 6:3.
2. Cf. I Cor. 1:15.
3. I have given a definition of the Church in terms of the four causes, material, formal, final, and efficient, as follows: Human beings can be taken as the material cause of the Church—"our earth", as Augustine says—the matter that is formed into the Church by Christ, its founder, through the doctrines he has given to us for the end of eternal salvation.
4. Ps. 38:12.
5. Ps. 35:7.
6. Cf. Matt. 3:2; 4:17; Ps. 41:7.
7. Cf. Ps. 41:5-7.
8. Eph. 5:8.

Chapter 13
1. Cf. II Cor. 5:7.
2. Rom. 8:24.
3. Cf. Ps. 41:8.
4. I Cor. 3:1.
5. Phil. 3:13.
6. Cf. II Cor. 5:4.
7. Cf. Ps. 41:2, 3.
8. II Cor. 5:2.
9. Rom. 12:2.
10. Cf. I Cor. 14:20.
11. Gal. 3:1.
12. Cf. Wisd. 9:17.
13. Cf. Ps. 67:19; Acts 2:2-4.
14. Cf. Gen. 7:11; Mal. 3:10.
15. Cf. Ps. 45:5.
16. John 3:29. The bridegroom is Christ. Here the term "friend" refers to St. Paul.
17. Rom. 8:23.
18. That is, a member of the Church, the bride of Christ.
19. II Cor. 11:3.
20. I John 3:2.
21. Ps. 41:4.

Chapter 14
1. Cf. Job 32:20.
2. Cf. Ps. 41:5.
3. Ps. 41:6.

Notes to Book 13

4. Ps. 42:6.
5. Ps. 118:105.
6. Cf. Isa. 26:20.
7. Cf. Eph. 2:3.
8. Rom. 8:10.
9. Cant. 2:17.
10. Ps. 5:5.
11. Cf. Ps. 42:5, 6.
12. Cf. Rom. 8:11.
13. Cf. II Cor. 1:22.
14. Cf. Rom. 8:24.
15. Cf. I Thess. 5:5.
16. I Thess. 2:4.
17. Gen. 1:5.
18. Cf. I Cor. 4:7.
19. Cf. Rom. 9:21.

CHAPTER 15
1. Isa. 34:4.
2. Cf. Ps. 103:2.
3. Cf. Gen. 3:21.
4. Ps. 8:4.
5. Ps. 18:8.
6. Ps. 8:3.
7. Cf. ibid.: "that you may destroy the enemy and the avenger."
8. Cf. Ps. 148:4, 5.
9. Cf. Matt. 18:10.
10. Ps. 35:6.
11. Matt. 24:35.
12. Cf. Isa. 40:6, 8: "All flesh is grass, and all the glory thereof as the flower of the field . . . but the word of our Lord endures forever."
13. Cf. I Cor. 13:12.
14. I John 3:2.
15. Cf. Cant. 1:3–9.
16. I John 3:2.

CHAPTER 16
1. Ps. 142:6.
2. Ps. 35:10.

CHAPTER 17
1. The embittered against God.
2. Cf. Gen. 1:9.
3. Cf. Ps. 94:5.
4. Cf. Job 38:10, 11.
5. Cf. Gen. 1:11, 12.

Chapter 18

1. Cf. Ps. 84:12.
2. Gen. 1:14.
3. Cf. Isa. 58:7.
4. Cf. Gen. 1:12.
5. Cf. Isa. 58:8.
6. Cf. Phil. 2:16.
7. Cf. Gen. 1:14.
8. II Cor. 5:17.
9. Rom. 13:11.
10. Rom. 13:12.
11. Ps. 64:12.
12. Matt. 9:38.
13. John 4:38.
14. Ps. 101:28.
15. Gen. 1:16.
16. Cf. I Cor. 12:7-11.
17. Cf. I Cor. 12:11 and 7.
18. Cf. I Cor. 3:1.
19. I Cor. 2:6.
20. Cf. Gen. 1:14.

Chapter 19

1. Isa. 1:16.
2. Isa. 1:17.
3. Cf. Gen. 1:12.
4. Cf. Isa. 1:18.
5. Cf. Gen. 1:14, 15.
6. The story of the rich young man is paraphrased here. Cf. Matt. 19:16-22; Mark 10:17-22; Luke 18:18-23.
7. Matt. 13:7.
8. I Pet. 2:9.
9. Cf. I Cor. 1:27.
10. Cf. Luke 18:28.
11. Cf. I Cor. 1:27.
12. Cf. Rom. 10:15; Isa. 52:7.
13. Cf. Ps. 18:2.
14. Gen. 1:14.
15. Acts 2:2.
16. Cf. Phil. 2:15, 16.
17. Cf. Matt. 5:14, 15.

Chapter 20

1. Gen. 1:20.
2. Cf. Jer. 15:19.
3. Gen. 1:20.
4. Cf. Gen. 1:21.
5. Ps. 18:4, 5.

Notes to Book 13

6. Cf. Matt. 16:4. "A wicked and adulterous generation seeks after a sign."
7. Augustine uses the word *uterus*, womb, of Adam, an example of catachresis. Adam contained within himself the whole human race. Some patristic commentators held that he was therefore bisexual. Cf. also Plato's *Symposium*, for an analogous idea.
8. Cf. Heb. 6:1.

Chapter 21

1. Gen. 1:24. The living soul is the baptized Christian, or group of such Christians, living the life of faith and grace.
2. Cf. John 4:48.
3. I Cor. 14:22.
4. Cf. Phil. 2:13.
5. Gen. 1:20.
6. The fish was a symbol of Christ. Here there is a further reference to the Holy Eucharist.
7. Cf. Ps. 22:5.
8. Cf. I Tim. 5:6.
9. Cf. Gen. 3:8.
10. Cf. I Thess. 1:7.
11. Ps. 68:33.
12. Rom. 12:2.
13. Cf. I Tim. 6:20.
14. Cf. Jer. 2:13.
15. Cf. Ps. 35:10.
16. Cf. I Cor. 11:1.
17. Gal. 4:12.
18. Ecclus. 3:19.
19. Cf. I Cor. 8:8.
20. Rom. 1:20.

Chapter 22

1. Rom. 12:2.
2. Gen. 1:26.
3. Cf. Rom. 12:2.
4. Cf. I Cor. 4:15; 3:2; I Thess. 2:7.
5. Cf. Rom. 12:2.
6. Col. 3:10.
7. I Cor. 2:15.

Chapter 23

1. Cf. Gen. 1:26.
2. I Cor. 2:14.
3. Ps. 48:21.
4. Eph. 2:10.
5. Cf. Gal. 3:28.
6. Col. 3:10.

7. Jas. 4:11.
8. Cf. Matt. 7:20.
9. I Cor. 5:12.
10. Cf. Gen. 1:26.
11. The sacrament of baptism.
12. The holy sacrifice of the Mass and holy communion.
13. Cf. II Cor. 6:5, 6.

CHAPTER 24
1. Gen. 1:28.
2. Cf. I Cor. 3:5.

CHAPTER 25
1. Cf. John 14:6.
2. Rom. 3:4; Ps. 115:11.
3. John 8:44. Christ in this passage refers to Satan, the father of lies. Satan, and hence any liar, speaks from his own nature.
4. Cf. Gen. 1:29.
5. Cf. II Tim. 1:16.
6. Cf. II Cor. 11:9.
7. II Tim. 4:16.
8. Ps. 18:5.

CHAPTER 26
1. Cf. Phil. 3:19.
2. Cf. Rom. 16:18.
3. Cf. Phil. 4:10.
4. Cf. Phil. 4:11–13.
5. Col. 3:10.
6. Cf. I Cor. 14:2.
7. Phil. 4:14.
8. Ps. 4:2.
9. Phil. 4:15–16.
10. Phil. 4:17.

CHAPTER 27
1. Cf. I Cor. 14:23.

CHAPTER 28
1. Gen. 1:31.

CHAPTER 29
1. Cf. John 3:33; 14:6.
2. Cf. Ps. 49:7.

CHAPTER 30
1. According to Manichean mythology, God built the captive powers of darkness into the structure of the universe. Abortive offspring of the captive powers fell to earth and produced the embodied forms of life named here.

Notes to Book 13

CHAPTER 31
1. I Cor. 2:11, 12.
2. Matt. 10:20.
3. Rom. 5:5.
4. Augustine makes use of the philosophical principle: "Every being is good in so far as it is a being." God, who is infinite being, is infinitely good, and conversely, being absolutely good is absolute being. In God essence and existence are identical. As he says in Exodus 3:14: "I am who am."

CHAPTER 32
1. Cf. Apoc. 11:17.
2. In *Retractationes*, 2, 6, 2, Augustine corrects this passage: ". . . this was not said with enough consideration, and the subject is in fact very abstruse."

CHAPTER 33
1. Cf. Ps. 144:10.

CHAPTER 34
1. Cf. Ezech. 33:10.
2. Cf. Rom. 4:5; Prov. 17:15.

CHAPTER 35
1. Cf. Num. 6:21; II Thess. 3:16.

CHAPTER 38
1. Cf. Matt. 7:7, 8.

BIBLIOGRAPHY

TEXTS

Confessiones, Argentorati, apud Ioannem Mantelin, c. 1469.
Confessiones, opera et studio Monachorum S. Benedicti a Congregatione S. Mauri, Paris, 1679. Reprinted in J.-P. Migne, *Patrologia Latina,* Vol. 32, cols. 659–868. Paris, 1845.
Confessionum Libri Tredecim, recensuit et commentario critico instruxit Pius Knöll. Vindobonae, F. Tempsky, 1896.
Confessionum Libri Tredecim, post P. Knöll iteratis curis edidit Martinus Skutella. Lipsiae in aedibus B. G. Teubneri, 1934.
The Confessions of Augustine. Latin text edited by J. Gibb and W. Montgomery, 2nd edition. Cambridge, at the University Press, 1927.
Confessions, texte établie et traduit par Pierre de Labriolle. 2 vols. 5th ed. Paris, Société d'édition "Les Belles Lettres," 1950.
Confessionum Libri XIII, curante P. A. C. Vega, O.S.A. Typis Augustinianis Regalis Escurialensis Monasterii, 1930.
Confessionum Libri XIII, introductione et notis aucti cura et studio J. Capello. Taurini-Romae, Domus Editorialis Marietti, 1948.
The Confessions of St. Augustine, Books I–IX (Selections), with Introduction, Notes, and Vocabulary by James Marshall Campbell and Martin R. P. McGuire. New York, Prentice-Hall, 1931.

STUDIES

Bardy, Gustave, *Saint Augustin, l'homme et l'oeuvre,* Paris, Desclée de Brouwer, 1940.
Bourke, Vernon J., *Augustine's Quest of Wisdom,* Milwaukee, The Bruce Publishing Company, 1944.
Boyer, Charles, *L'idée de vérité dans la philosophie de saint Augustin,* Paris, G. Beauchesne, 1920.
Burkitt, F. C., *The Religion of the Manichees,* Cambridge, at the University Press, 1925.
Copleston, Frederick, *History of Philosophy,* vol. 2, Westminster, Md., The Newman Press, 1950.
Courcelle, P., *Recherches sur les Confessions de saint Augustin,* Paris, E. de Boccard, 1950.
D'Arcy, M. C. and Others, *A Monument to St. Augustine,* New York, Sheed and Ward, 1930, Meridian Books, 1957.
Frend, W. H. C., *The Donatist Church,* Oxford, at the Clarendon Press, 1952.
Gilson, Etienne, *Introduction à l'étude de saint Augustin,* Paris, J. Vrin, 1943.
Grabowski, Stanley, *The Great God,* St. Louis, B. Herder, 1954.

International Augustinian Congress, Paris, September 21–24, 1954. *Augustinus Magister, Communications*, 2 vols., *Actes*, 1 vol. Paris, Etudes Augustiniennes, 1954.

Lesaar, Heinrich H., *St. Augustine*. Translated from the German by T. Pope Arkell, New York, Benziger, 1931.

Marrou, Henri, *Saint Augustine and His Influence through the Ages*. New York, Harper Torchbooks, 1957.

—— *Saint Augustin et la fin de la culture antique*, Paris, E. de Boccard, 1958.

O'Meara, John J., *The Young Augustine*, London, Longmans, Green, 1954.

Pope, Hugh, *St. Augustine of Hippo*, Westminster, Maryland, The Newman Press, 1949.

Portalié, E., "Augustin, saint," *Dictionnaire de théologie catholique*. Vol. I, part 2, cols. 2268–2472. Paris, 1900.

—— article, "Augustine, Saint," *Catholic Encyclopedia*, vol. 2, pp. 84–104.

Puech, H. C., *Le manichéisme, son fondateur, sa doctrine*, Paris, Civilisations du Sud, 1949.

Ryan, John K., Articles "Augustine, St.," and "Augustinianism," *Encyclopedia Americana*.

—— "Augustinian Doctrine of Peace and War," *American Ecclesiastical Review*, June 1947, 401–421.

Switalski, B., *Neoplatonism and the Ethics of St. Augustine*, New York, Polish Institute of Arts and Sciences in America, 1946.

Vega, A. C., *St. Augustine*, Philadelphia, Peter Reilly Co., 1931.

Weiskotten, Herbert T., *Sancti Augustini Vita Scripta a Possidio Episcopo*. Edited with Revised Text, Introduction, Notes, and an English Version, Princeton University Press, 1919.

INDEX

Abraham, 87, 208
Academics, 126, 131, 149, 383
Adam, 19, 124, 352, 390, 396, 404, 421
Adeodatus, son of Augustine, 20, 24, 34, 153–54, 214, 224, 225, 378, 388
Aeneas, 56
Alaric, 26
Alypius, 24, 30, 31, 142–48, 150–52, 154, 190, 202, 203, 209, 214, 386, 387
Ambrose, St., 24, 34, 130–34, 135, 183, 213, 226, 371, 379, 384, 385, 406, 416
Anaximenes, 234, 403
Anselm, St., 389
Anthony, St., 190, 202, 203, 395
Anubis, 183
Apollinaris, 178, 389
Arbogast, 386
Arians, 215
Aristotle, 18, 21, 23, 31, 110, 376, 380, 381, 403, 413
Athanasius, St., 261
Augustine, St.: birth and parentage, 18, 19; infancy and childhood, 19, 20, 46–63; adolescence and youth, 20–23, 55–92; education, 20, 23, 55–63; mistress of, 20, 94, 153, 154, 378, 388; death of friend, 97–100; at Carthage, 20–23, 30, 77–96, 114–21; at Rome, 23, 24, 122–29; at Milan, 23, 24, 129–42, 147, 213–15; as teacher, 21, 23, 94, 129, 130, 142, 143, 206; conversion of, 24, 193–203; as priest and bishop, 25; death of, 25; writings, 26–28; *Confessions* of: purpose and character of, 28–32; style of, 33; editions and translations of, 35–38
Aurelius Augustinus, 373

Baal Hammon, 19
Babylon, 69
Baptism, 19, 24, 39, 54, 97, 343, 373, 383, 399, 421, 422
Beauty, 70–72, 106, 108, 175
Berbers, 19, 20
Boniface, Count, 26

Caesar, 116, 395
Carthage, 21, 23, 30, 67, 77, 110, 114, 122, 128, 159, 245, 249
Cassiciacum, 209, 210, 386, 397
Catiline, 375
Christ, Jesus, 54, 81, 83, 124, 128, 132, 176, 177, 184, 189, 205, 210, 216, 226, 274, 279, 294, 343, 344, 349, 354, 389, 392, 397, 409
Church, Catholic, 18–20, 24–26, 32, 33, 92, 136–38, 157, 163, 167, 182, 191, 343, 356, 368, 418
Cicero, 21, 26, 81, 82, 120, 193, 375, 376
Cyprian, St., 123, 383

David, 85, 210, 260
Devil (Satan, the enemy), 82, 161, 188, 228, 265, 267, 273, 346, 422
De Quincey, Thomas, 399
Dido, 56, 373
Donatists, 25, 26
Drunkenness, 258–59

Index

Elpidius, 128
Epaphroditus, 361
Epicurus, 154, 388
Eternity, 168, 174, 199, 279–85, 302, 303, 330, 331, 369
Eve, 383
Evodius, 216, 225, 400
Evolution, 330, 416

Faustus, 34, 114, 119, 120, 149, 381, 382
Firminus, 164
Form. *See* Matter

Gervase, St., 215, 400
Gibb and Montgomery, 32
God, *Confessions* addressed to, 33. *See also* Christ, Jesus; Selfsame, *and* Trinity
Gods, pagan, 183
Gradual psalms, 206; text, 398
Greek, 55, 57, 241, 249, 250, 373
Gregory the Great, St., quoted, 387

Hebrew, 280
Hello, Ernest, 412
Hierius, 106
Hippo, 25, 27
Hippocrates, 96, 378
Homer, 57
Horace, 379, 401
Hortensius, 21, 81

Imitation of Christ, 379
Isaac, 85, 263

Jacob, 85, 263
Jerome, St., 26
Jerusalem, 228, 317, 341
John, St., the Baptist, 260
Joseph, 263

Julian, Emperor, 188
Justina, Empress, 215, 399, 400

Knox, Ronald A., 37, 371

Latin, 57, 241, 249, 250, 374

Madauros, 20, 21, 30, 94, 375
Mani, 20, 21, 117, 121, 382
Manicheans, 20–26, 82–85, 90–93, 108, 114–22, 126, 377, 378, 383, 384, 396, 414, 422
Manicheism. *See* Manicheans
Marriage, 66, 67, 94, 150–52, 387
Mary, Blessed Virgin, 128
Mass, 225, 401, 421
Matter, 162, 163, 306–17, 329–31, 336, 367
Matthew, Sir Tobie, 35
Medea, 84
Memory, 52, 63, 236–54, 291, 293, 301–3
Minerva, 183
Monica, (Monnica), 19, 90–92; death and burial, 152, 223–28; youth, 216–19; wife of Patricius, 218–21; vision at Ostia, 221–23; mother of Augustine, 388
Moses, 85, 87, 316, 318, 324–26, 327, 413
Music, 261, 262, 405

Navigius, brother of Augustine, 19
Nebridius, 26, 96, 148, 154, 159, 164, 190–91, 207, 208, 209, 386
Neoplatonism, 22, 23, 168, 178, 180, 183, 390, 407
Newman, Cardinal, quoted, 35, 36, 394, 395, 406

Index

Onesiphorus, 360
Orestes and Pylades, 99
Osiris, 183, 394
Ostia, 24, 221–26

Paraclete, 211
Pascal, 421
Patricius, 19, 67, 218–19, 375, 400
Paul, Apostle, 179, 190
Pelagians, 26
Perpetua, sister of Augustine, 19
Photinus, 178, 392
Plato, 17, 18, 23, 396, 404, 421
Platonists. *See* Neoplatonism
Plotinus, 18, 22, 371, 372, 375, 377, 389, 390, 404, 410, 416
Ponticianus, 190–94, 395
Protase, St., 215, 400
Punic, 374
Pusey, Edward Bouverie, 35, 36
Pylades, 99

Romanianus, 20, 388
Ryan, John K., 389, 411

Sacraments, 394
Scholastic method, 410
Schopenhauer, 412
Scripture, Sacred, 37, 38, 82, 168–70
Selfsame, 212, 221, 232, 287, 308, 312, 316, 342, 349
Seneca, 372, 379, 382
Severus, 400

Shakespeare, quoted, 401, 407
Simplicianus, 181–84, 393, 394
Socrates, 411
Solomon, 84
Spinoza, 406
Spirit, Holy, 97, 118, 316, 337–40, 344, 349, 364–66
Stoics, 23
Symmachus, 130, 384

Tanit, 19
Terence, 59, 401
Thagaste, 18, 21, 67, 100, 379
Theodosius, Emperor, 397
Time, 101, 174, 280–302, 369, 411, 412
Trier, 192, 395
Trinity, the, 308, 338, 342, 343, 355, 417
Truth, 83, 251–53, 280, 283, 318, 326, 395

Valentinian, Emperor, 215, 386, 397, 399
Valerius, Bishop, 25
Verecundus, 190, 207–8, 209
Vergil, 56, 57, 60, 370, 373, 374, 378, 390, 397
Victorinus, 183, 185, 187–88
Vindicianus, 34, 164, 378

Way, purgative, illuminative, unitive, 29–30
Will, 160, 175, 188–90, 196–99, 205, 396, 400

OTHER IMAGE BOOKS

OUR LADY OF FATIMA – William Thomas Walsh (D1) – $1.25

DAMIEN THE LEPER – John Farrow (D3) – $1.25

MR. BLUE – Myles Connolly. Modern classic about a contemporary St. Francis (D5) – 75¢

PEACE OF SOUL – Fulton J. Sheen (D8) – $1.25

THE IMITATION OF CHRIST – Thomas à Kempis. Edited with an Introduction by Harold C. Gardiner, S.J. (D17) – $1.45

ST. FRANCIS OF ASSISI – Johannes Jorgensen (D22) – $1.45

LIGHT ON THE MOUNTAIN: The Story of La Salette – John S. Kennedy (D33) – 95¢

THE STORY OF THE TRAPP FAMILY SINGERS – Maria Augusta Trapp (D46) – 95¢

ST. FRANCIS OF ASSISI – G. K. Chesterton (D50) – $1.25

VIPER'S TANGLE – François Mauriac. A novel of evil and redemption (D51) – 95¢

THE AUTOBIOGRAPHY OF ST. THÉRÈSE OF LISIEUX: The Story of a Soul – Translated by John Beevers. An Image Original (D56) – $1.25

THE CITY OF GOD – St. Augustine. Edited by Vernon J. Bourke. Introduction by Étienne Gilson. Specially abridged (D59) – $2.45

CANA IS FOREVER – Charles Hugo Doyle. Catholic guide to dating, courtship, and marriage (D62) – 95¢

ASCENT OF MT. CARMEL – St. John of the Cross. Trans. and ed. by E. Allison Peers (D63) – $1.95

RELIGION AND THE RISE OF WESTERN CULTURE – Christopher Dawson (D64) – $1.25

THE LITTLE FLOWERS OF ST. FRANCIS – Translated by Raphael Brown (D69) – $1.75

THE IDEA OF A UNIVERSITY – John Henry Cardinal Newman. Introduction by G. N. Shuster (D75) – $1.65

DARK NIGHT OF THE SOUL – St. John of the Cross. Edited and translated by E. Allison Peers (D78) – $1.25

THE PILLAR OF FIRE – Karl Stern. A psychiatrist's spiritual journey from Judaism to Catholicism (D83) – 95¢

ORTHODOXY – G. K. Chesterton (D84) – $1.25

A POPULAR HISTORY OF THE REFORMATION – Philip Hughes (D92) – $1.25

THE LIFE OF TERESA OF JESUS: The Autobiography of St. Teresa of Avila. Trans. and ed. by E. Allison Peers (D96) – $1.95

THE CONFESSIONS OF ST. AUGUSTINE – Translated with an Introduction by John K. Ryan (D101) – $1.75

A WOMAN CLOTHED WITH THE SUN – Edited by John J. Delaney (D118) – $1.45

OTHER IMAGE BOOKS

INTERIOR CASTLE – St. Teresa of Avila (Translated by E. Allison Peers) – (D120) – $1.45

THE GREATEST STORY EVER TOLD – Fulton Oursler (D121) – $1.45

LIVING FLAME OF LOVE – St. John of the Cross (Translated by E. Allison Peers) – (D129) – $1.45

A HISTORY OF PHILOSOPHY: VOLUME 1 – GREECE AND ROME (2 Parts) – Frederick Copleston, S.J. (D134a, D134b) – $1.75 ea.

A HISTORY OF PHILOSOPHY: VOLUME 2 – MEDIAEVAL PHILOSOPHY (2 Parts) – Frederick Copleston, S.J. Part I – Augustine to Bonaventure. Part II – Albert the Great to Duns Scotus (D135a, D135b) – $1.45 ea.

A HISTORY OF PHILOSOPHY: VOLUME 3 – LATE MEDIAEVAL AND RENAISSANCE PHILOSOPHY (2 Parts) – Frederick Copleston, S.J. Part I – Ockham to the Speculative Mystics. Part II – The Revival of Platonism to Suárez (D136a, D136b) – $1.45 ea.

A HISTORY OF PHILOSOPHY: VOLUME 4 – MODERN PHILOSOPHY: Descartes to Leibniz – Frederick Copleston, S.J. (D137) – $1.75

A HISTORY OF PHILOSOPHY: VOLUME 5 – MODERN PHILOSOPHY: The British Philosophers, Hobbes to Hume (2 Parts) – Frederick Copleston, S.J. Part I – Hobbes to Paley. Part II – Berkeley to Hume (D138a) – $1.45; (D138b) – $1.75

A HISTORY OF PHILOSOPHY: VOLUME 6 – MODERN PHILOSOPHY (2 Parts) – Frederick Copleston, S.J. Part I – The French Enlightenment to Kant (D139a) – $1.75; (D139b) – $1.45

A HISTORY OF PHILOSOPHY: VOLUME 7 – MODERN PHILOSOPHY (2 Parts) – Frederick Copleston, S.J. Part I – Fichte to Hegel. Part II – Schopenhauer to Nietzsche (D140a, D140b) – $1.75 ea.

A HISTORY OF PHILOSOPHY: VOLUME 8 – MODERN PHILOSOPHY: Bentham to Russell (2 Parts) – Frederick Copleston, S.J. Part I – British Empiricism and the Idealist Movement in Great Britain. Part II – Idealism in America, the Pragmatist Movement, the Revolt against Idealism (D141a, D141b) – $1.45 ea.

A DOCTOR AT CALVARY – Pierre Barbet, M.D. A moving account of the Passion of our Lord (D155) – 95¢

THE SPIRITUAL EXERCISES OF ST. IGNATIUS – Translated by Anthony Mottola, Ph.D. Introduction by Robert W. Gleason, S.J. (D170) – 95¢

THE WAY OF PERFECTION – St. Teresa of Avila. Trans. and ed. by E. Allison Peers (D176) – $1.45

OTHER IMAGE BOOKS

WE HOLD THESE TRUTHS: Catholic Reflections on the American Proposition – John Courtney Murray, S.J. (D181) – $1.25

LIFE AND HOLINESS – Thomas Merton. Exposition of the principles of the spiritual life (D183) – 85¢

MY LIFE WITH CHRIST – Anthony J. Paone, S.J. (D185) – $1.45

A FAMILY ON WHEELS: Further Adventures of the Trapp Family Singers – Maria Augusta Trapp with Ruth T. Murdoch (D187) – $1.25

AMERICAN CATHOLICISM – John Tracy Ellis. A comprehensive survey of the American Church (D190) – 95¢

THE COUNCIL, REFORM AND REUNION – with a new Introduction by Fr. Hans Kung (D198) – 95¢

WITH GOD IN RUSSIA – Walter J. Ciszek, S.J., with Daniel L. Flaherty, S.J. (D200) – $1.45

THE TWO-EDGED SWORD – John L. McKenzie, S.J. Outstanding interpretation of the Old Testament (D215) – $1.45

THE LILIES OF THE FIELD – William E. Barrett (D225) – $1.25

NO MAN IS AN ISLAND – Thomas Merton (D231) – $1.45

AND YOUNG MEN SHALL SEE VISIONS – Andrew M. Greeley. Letters to a young collegian on subjects of burning interest to young men today (D232) – 85¢

CONJECTURES OF A GUILTY BYSTANDER – Thomas Merton. A collection of notes, opinions, reflections (D234) – $1.45

THE POWER OF LOVE – Fulton J. Sheen (D235) – $1.25

THE STORY OF THOMAS MORE – John Farrow (D236) – 95¢

THE NOONDAY DEVIL: Spiritual Support in Middle Age – Bernard Basset, S.J. A funny-serious book of spiritual direction (D237) – $1.25

UNDERSTAND THE BIBLE – J. Holland Smith (D238) – $1.25

HEALTH OF MIND AND SOUL – Ignace Lepp (D239) – 95¢

RELIGION AND PERSONALITY – Adrian van Kaam, C.S.Sp. (D240) – $1.45

RELIGIONS OF THE WORLD (2 Volumes) – John A. Hardon, S.J. An account of the history, beliefs, and practices of the major religions of the world (D241a) – $1.75; (D241b) – $1.45

THE RELIGION OF TEILHARD DE CHARDIN – Henri de Lubac, S.J. (D242) – $1.65

MOMENTS OF TRUTH – Edited by Dan Herr and Joel Wells. An anthology portraying crises of the human spirit by 16 great authors (D243) – 95¢

CHRISTIAN RENEWAL IN A CHANGING WORLD – Bernard Häring, C.SS.R. (D244) – $1.45

A 73 – 3

OTHER IMAGE BOOKS

CHRISTIAN SACRAMENTS AND CHRISTIAN PERSONALITY – Bernard J. Cooke, S.J. (D246) – $1.25

THOUGHTS IN SOLITUDE – Thomas Merton (D247) – $1.25

WE NEUROTICS: A Handbook for the Half-Mad – Bernard Basset, S.J. (D248) – 95¢

NEW TESTAMENT ESSAYS – Raymond E. Brown, S.S. (D251) – $1.45

TEILHARD DE CHARDIN AND THE MYSTERY OF CHRIST – Christopher Mooney, S.J. (D252) – $1.45

THE NEW TESTAMENT OF THE JERUSALEM BIBLE: Reader's Edition – Alexander Jones, General Editor (D253) – $1.65

THE FOUR GOSPELS: AN INTRODUCTION (2 Volumes) – Bruce Vawter, C.M. (D255a, D255b) – $1.25 ea.

THE PROTESTANT CHURCHES OF AMERICA – Revised Edition – John A. Hardon (D259) – $1.95

EXISTENTIAL FOUNDATIONS OF PSYCHOLOGY – Adrian van Kaam (D260) – $1.75

THE CATHOLIC EXPERIENCE – An Interpretation of the History of American Catholicism – Andrew M. Greeley (D261) – $1.45

LOVE AND SEXUALITY: A CHRISTIAN APPROACH – Revised Edition – Mary Perkins Ryan and John Julian Ryan (D263) – 95¢

SHALOM: PEACE – The Sacrament of Reconciliation – Revised Edition – Bernard Häring, C.SS.R. (D264) – $1.35

MORALITY FOR OUR TIME – Marc Oraison (D266) – $1.25

THE WIT AND WISDOM OF BISHOP FULTON J. SHEEN – Edited by Bill Adler (D268) – $1.45

SUMMA THEOLOGIAE – Thomas Aquinas – Thomas Gilby, O.P., General Editor
  Volume 1: The Existence of God; Part One: Questions 1–13 (D270) – $1.45
  Volume 2: The Mind and Power of God; Part One: Questions 14–26 (D271) – $1.45

THE FREEDOM OF SEXUAL LOVE – Joseph and Lois Bird (D272) – $1.25

A FUTURE TO HOPE IN – Andrew M. Greeley (D273) – $1.25

THE MIDDLE AGES: A POPULAR HISTORY – Joseph Dahmus (D274) – $1.95

HISTORY OF ETHICS – Vernon J. Bourke (D275b) – $1.45

THE GOSPELS AND THE JESUS OF HISTORY – Xavier Léon-Dufour, S.J. (D276) – $1.75

WE AGNOSTICS: On the Tightrope to Eternity – Bernard Basset, S.J. (D277) – 95¢

A 73-4

OTHER IMAGE BOOKS

INTRODUCTION TO THE OLD TESTAMENT (2 Volumes) – André Robert and André Feuillet (D278a, D278b) – $1.95 ea.
A GOOD MAN IS HARD TO FIND – Flannery O'Connor (D279) – $1.25
THE HEAD OF THE FAMILY – Clayton C. Barbeau (D280) – 95¢
THE SEVEN STOREY MOUNTAIN – Thomas Merton (D281) – $1.95
GUIDE TO CONTENTMENT – Fulton J. Sheen (D282) – $1.45
THE PSALMS OF THE JERUSALEM BIBLE – Alexander Jones, General Editor (D283) – $1.45
THE PEOPLE ARE THE CHURCH – Eugene C. Kennedy (D284) – $1.25
CONTEMPLATIVE PRAYER – Thomas Merton (D285) – 95¢
THE CHALLENGES OF LIFE – Ignace Lepp (D286) – $1.25
THE ROMAN CATHOLIC CHURCH – John L. McKenzie (D287) – $1.75
LIFE FOR A WANDERER – Andrew M. Greeley (D288) – $1.25
BEING TOGETHER: OUR RELATIONSHIPS WITH OTHER PEOPLE – Marc Oraison (D289) – $1.25
PROJECTIONS: SHAPING AN AMERICAN THEOLOGY FOR THE FUTURE – Thomas F. O'Meara and Donald M. Weisser (D290) – $1.25
MARRIAGE IS FOR GROWNUPS – Joseph and Lois Bird (D291) – $1.45
THE FRIENDSHIP GAME – Andrew M. Greeley (D292) – $1.25
HOW TO BE REALLY WITH IT – Bernard Basset, S.J. (D293) – $1.25
THE ABORTION DECISION – Revised Edition – David Granfield (D294) – $1.45
MEETING GOD IN MAN – Ladislaus Boros, S.J. (D295) – $1.25
AUTHORITY IN THE CHURCH – John L. McKenzie (D296) – $1.25
A TIME FOR LOVE – Eugene C. Kennedy (D297) – $1.25
CHRIST IS ALIVE! – Michel Quoist (D298) – $1.25
THE MAN IN THE SYCAMORE TREE: The Good Times and Hard Life of Thomas Merton – Edward Rice (D299) – $1.95
THE NEW TESTAMENT OF THE NEW AMERICAN BIBLE (D300) – $1.75
INTRODUCTION TO THE DEVOUT LIFE – Revised Edition – St. Francis de Sales – Translated by Msgr. John K. Ryan (D301) – $1.75
TOWARD A NEW CATHOLIC MORALITY – John Giles Milhaven (D302) – $1.45
THE POWER AND THE WISDOM – John L. McKenzie (D303) – $1.75
INFALLIBLE? AN INQUIRY – Hans Küng (D304) – $1.45

OTHER IMAGE BOOKS

THE DECLINE AND FALL OF RADICAL CATHOLICISM – James Hitchcock (D305) – $1.25

IN THE SPIRIT, IN THE FLESH – Eugene C. Kennedy (D306) – $1.25

THE THIRD PEACOCK – Robert Farrar Capon (D307) – $1.25

THE GOD OF SPACE AND TIME – Bernard J. Cooke (D308) – $1.45

AN AQUINAS READER (Image Original) – Edited with an Intro. by Mary T. Clark (D309) – $2.45

CHRISTIANITY IN THE TWENTIETH CENTURY – John A. Hardon (D310) – $2.45

THE OLD TESTAMENT OF THE JERUSALEM BIBLE – Reader's Edition – Alexander Jones, General Editor
  Volume 1: Genesis – Ruth (D311) – $1.95
  Volume 2: 1 Samuel – 2 Maccabees (D312) – $1.95
  Volume 3: Job – Ecclesiasticus (D313) – $1.95
  Volume 4: The Prophets – Malachi (D314) – $1.95

CHRISTIAN COMMUNITY: Response to Reality – Bernard J. Cooke (D315) – $1.45

THE JESUS MYTH – Andrew M. Greeley (D316) – $1.25

THE SURVIVAL OF DOGMA – Avery Dulles, S.J. (D317) – $1.45

LIVING IN HOPE – Ladislaus Boros, S.J. (D318) – $1.25

LOVE IS ALL – Joseph and Lois Bird (D319) – $1.25

THE SOUL AFIRE: Revelations of the Mystics – Ed. by H. A. Reinhold (D320) – $1.95

CONTEMPLATION IN A WORLD OF ACTION – Thomas Merton (D321) – $1.95